Rebellious Hearts

British Women Writers
and the French Revolution

EDITED BY

Adriana Craciun and Kari E. Lokke

STATE UNIVERSITY OF NEW YORK PRESS

Published by
State University of New York Press, Albany

For information, address State University of New York Press,
90 State Street, Suite 700, Albany, NY 12207

Production by Diane Ganeles
Marketing by Patrick Durocher

Library of Congress Cataloging-in-Publication Data

Rebellious hearts : British women writers and the French Revolution /
edited by Adriana Craciun and Kari E. Lokke.
    p. cm. — (SUNY series in feminist criticism and theory)
    Includes index.
    ISBN 0-7914-4969-6 (alk. paper) — ISBN 0-7014-4970-X (pbk. : alk. paper)
    1. English literature—French influences.   2. France—History—Revolution, 1789–1799—Literature and the revolution.   3. Women and literature—Great Britain—History—18th century.   4. Women and literature—Great Britain—History—19th century.   5. English literature—Women authors—History and criticism.   6. English literature—18th century—History and criticism.   7. English literature—19th century—History and criticism.   8. Revolutionary literature, English—History and criticism.   9. France—History—Revolution, 1789–1799—Influence. 10. Feminism and literature—Great Britain.   11. Romanticism—Great Britain.   12. France—In literature.   I. Craciun, Adriana, 1967–
II. Lokke, Kari.   III. Series.

PR129.F8 R39 2001
821'.7099287—dc21

                                                        00-044069

For John Logan and Paul Wurst

Contents

List of Illustrations ix

Acknowledgments xi

Introduction

British Women Writers and the French Revolution, 1789–1815   3
Adriana Craciun and Kari E. Lokke

Revolution and Nationalism

Blurring the Borders of Nation and Gender:
Mary Wollstonecraft's Character (R)evolution   33
Jan Wellington

Challenging Englishness: Frances Burney's *The Wanderer*   63
Maria Jerinic

"The Mild Dominion of the Moon": Charlotte Smith and
the Politics of Transcendence   85
Kari E. Lokke

Revolution and Religion

The Anxiety of (Feminine) Influence: Hannah More and
Counterrevolution   109
Angela Keane

The French, the "Long-wished-for Revolution," and
the Just War in Joanna Southcott   135
Kevin Binfield

Napoleon, Nationalism, and the Politics of Religion in
Mariana Starke's *Letters from Italy*   161
Jeanne Moskal

Revolutionary Subjects

The New Cordays: Helen Craik and British Representations
of Charlotte Corday, 1793–1800   193
Adriana Craciun

Mary Hays's "Female Philosopher":
Constructing Revolutionary Subjects   233
Miriam L. Wallace

Indirect Dissent: "Landscaping" Female Agency in
Amelia Alderson Opie's Poems of the 1790s   261
Ann Frank Wake

Revolutionary Representation

Elizabeth Inchbald, Joanna Baillie, and Revolutionary
Representation in the "Romantic" Period   293
Terence Allan Hoagwood

Benevolent Historian: Helen Maria Williams and
Her British Readers   317
Deborah Kennedy

The Politics of Truth and Deception: Charlotte Smith and
the French Revolution   337
Judith Davis Miller

Afterword   365
Madelyn Gutwirth

List of Contributors   375

Index   379

Illustrations

Cover: Georgiana, Duchess of Devonshire by Maria Cosway, 1782. Devonshire Collection, Chatsworth. Reproduced by permission of the Duke of Devonshire and the Chatsworth Settlement Trustees. Photograph: Photographic Survey, Courtauld Institute of Art.

Figure 1.1
"The Contrast" by Thomas Rowlandson, 1793.
© Copyright The British Museum

Figure 1.2
"A French Gentleman of the Court of Louis XVIth; A French Gentleman of the Court of Egalité, 1799" Caricature by James Gillray, 1799.
© Copyright The British Museum

Acknowledgments

For the cover of *Rebellious Hearts,* we have chosen Maria Cosway's painting of Georgiana, Duchess of Devonshire (1782) for a number of reasons, which together illustrate the intricate connections among women, creativity, and public statement during the revolutionary period. Maria Cosway, married to society painter and famed miniaturist Richard Cosway, and mistress of Thomas Jefferson, reproduced in folio etchings a series of historical paintings assembled by Napoleon for the *Gallery of the Louvre* in 1802. In this pre-revolutionary painting, Cosway depicts the Duchess as a sublime Diana, goddess of the moon, an allegorical image that resonates throughout Charlotte Smith's sonnets, as Kari Lokke's essay elaborates. Cosway had also illustrated Mary Robinson's poem about social injustice, "The Wintry Day," in a series of striking images that are reproduced from engravings in Judith Pascoe's recent edition of Robinson's *Selected Poems* (Broadview, 2000). Robinson, who wrote repeatedly on the Revolution but who is unfortunately not represented here by an entire essay, was also known to the Duchess of Devonshire, whose patronage was instrumental to Robinson's early success, particularly when Robinson spent time in debtor's prison because of her husband's financial irresponsibility. Georgiana provided patronage for other women writers as well, among them Charlotte Smith and Joanna Baillie, for whom she wrote an epilogue to her play *De Monfort.* The Duchess herself was involved in political controversies that reveal the contradictory nature of women's ideological investments during this era. A close friend of Marie Antoinette from 1775 to her execution in 1793, the Duchess also publicly campaigned (as did Robinson) for the Whig Charles Fox in the 1784 Westminster election. Her foray into politics provoked much opposition, speculation, and sexual innuendo (not to mention merciless misogynist cartoons), and thus places her in the company of the writers in *Rebellious Hearts.*

We are fortunate to have found many colleagues and friends whose enthusiasm about women writers and the French Revolution nurtured this project through its development. The book began as a panel organized by Adriana Craciun at the 1996 MLA conference in Washington D.C., and we are grateful to the original participants— Kevin Binfield, Terence Hoagwood, and Ann Frank Wake—for forming the initial core of the book and sticking with it through completion. Thanks to the patience and diligence of all of the contributors, the editorial process ran smoothly and we never lost steam. James Peltz, our editor at SUNY, remained enthusiastic and helpful throughout the production process. Diane Ganeles and Patrick Durocher did an excellent job in the final editing and marketing of the volume. We are particularly fortunate to have among our contributors Madelyn Gutwirth, whose exemplary scholarship on women and the French Revolution in *The Twilight of the Goddesses* is one of the key texts that inspired our own exploration of this new field.

We benefited significantly from the advice and support of colleagues at both our institutions, and beyond. For ongoing expert advice we thank Stephen Behrendt, Dana Frank, Nancy Kushigian, Harriet Kramer Linkin, Anne Mellor, Seth Schein, and Nan Sweet.

Adriana Craciun completed her essay and much of her editorial work while at Loyola University, Chicago, where she benefited from the research support of the department, colleagues, and the university. She completed the research for her essay with the aid of a grant from the National Endowment for the Humanities. Graduate students and co-editors of Mary Robinson, Anne Irmen Close, Megan Musgrave, and Orianne Smith, took up the cause of Romantic women writers, and in so doing, remind us of the purpose of our endeavor. Steve Jones remains a fount of editorial expertise and enthusiasm for new approaches to the Romantic period, and his ongoing help and friendship are deeply appreciated. Jerome McGann's scholarship and support continue to inspire. Family, both in name and in spirit, and friends provided much needed stability (and often a place to stay) over the last few years of seemingly ceaseless change. John Logan made the cause of women writers and the French Revolution his own, tolerating much in the process, and never failing to "exude confidence and enthusiasm." Adriana Craciun dedicates *Rebellious Hearts* to him.

Kari Lokke is grateful to the University of California, Davis, for a Faculty Research Grant that facilitated the research and writing of her essay on Charlotte Smith. Elizabeth Langland, Dean of Humanities, Arts, and Cultural Studies, and Kevin Smith, Vice Chancellor for Research, generously provided funds for publication expenses. She thanks the staff of the English Department, Vita Simonsen and Terry Antonelli, in particular, for their expert administration of this grant and many others over the past ten years. Carol Beck, Ron Ottman, and Jeremy Smith provided much-needed computer and word processing support. Her greatest debt is to her graduate students in English and Comparative Literature at UC Davis. In 1988, Jane King's discovery of the women poets housed in the UC Davis Kohler Collection, and her brilliant presentation of their work in a seminar on "Women Writers of Romanticism," was a revelation. Christine Colón's research assistance and her expert, precise editing have been invaluable. Her interest in the religious discourse of nineteenth-century British women has informed the shaping of this volume. Wendy Nielsen's work on French, British, and German revolutionary drama makes clear the need for future comparatist dialogue on the inevitably gendered question of revolutionary performance and representation. And the dedication of Patrick Vincent and Mary Waters to women writers of the Romantic era as serious artists and professionals is a source of encouragement and hope. Kari Lokke is also forever grateful to Russell Block who, many years ago, opened her up to the permanent revolution. Finally, it was Paul Wurst who suggested Charlotte Smith's "rebellious heart[s]" as the title for this volume. In gratitude for fifteen years of unfailing compassion, love and friendship, Kari Lokke dedicates this book to him.

Introduction

British Women Writers and the French Revolution, 1789–1815

∾

Adriana Craciun and Kari E. Lokke

On 18 November, 1792, radical British expatriates in Paris met at White's Hotel to celebrate the new Republic and its military victory over the Austrians. Members of the "Friends of the Rights of Man associated at Paris," known as the British Club, this remarkable group of Irish, Scottish, and English citizens maintained their support for the French Revolution even after the recent September Massacres had alienated the majority of British at home. On this particular day, the British Club met to issue an address to the National Convention, a gesture of republican solidarity popular with such radical British associations.[1] The President of the British Club at this time was John Hurford Stone, who would soon become Helen Maria Williams's lover, and among those present were Thomas Paine, the poet Robert Merry ("Della Crusca"), John Oswald, and Helen Maria Williams.

Of the thirteen toasts which the British Club drank that evening, two specifically acknowledged the contributions of women, British and French, to the French Revolution and to liberty:

> (11) [to] the Women of Great Britain, particularly those who have distinguished themselves by their writings in favor of the French revolution, Mrs. (Charlotte) Smith and Miss H. M. Williams;

> (12) [to] the Women of France, especially those who have had the courage to take up arms to defend the cause of liberty, *citoyennes* Fernig, Anselm, &c.[2]

3

This clear connection between women's writing and the French Revolution drawn at such a significant historical moment speaks eloquently to the central purpose of this volume: the exploration of the remarkable diversity of British women's writings on the French Revolution.

As the second toast indicates, British women's interest in the French Revolution and the political debates it generated in Britain is not unrelated to French women's participation, both as agents and victims, in revolutionary events. Both toasts—celebrating women's contributions to the Revolution through their writings and through their public activism—must have seemed to those present to hail a new era in which women's public roles—political, intellectual, and even military[3]—were expanding, for the benefit of all.

Nearly one hundred were present for this occasion at the British Club, including Helen Maria Williams, who sang a song as part of the festivities. Williams, the second writer honored by the British Club, is increasingly recognized as an important, perhaps the most important, British interpreter of the French Revolution. Between the years 1790 and 1796, Williams published eight volumes of letters and essays on events in France, and these political writings, as well as her poetry, have steadily attracted increasing scholarly attention during the recent renewal of interest in Romantic-period women's writings. Charlotte Smith, too, has begun to regain the critical stature she enjoyed during her lifetime, yet studies of her poetry and novels have not done justice to her ongoing engagement with French Revolutionary politics. Recent criticism of her poetry, for example, has tended to privilege the *Elegiac Sonnets* and *Beachy Head* over the explicitly political *The Emigrants*. Author of three novels and one long poem that deal directly with the French Revolution—*Desmond, The Young Philosopher, The Banished Man,* and *The Emigrants*—Smith, in addition to being one of the most technically accomplished and influential of the Romantic poets, was also undeniably one of the most political, and politically radical.

Smith was in England when the British Club toasted her writings, immersing herself in radical politics; we imagine that she would have been honored by the British Club's praise of her writings, for a few days earlier she had commended a similar address to the National Convention, presented to the Convention on the same day as the British Club's. In her November 3 letter to the American radical Joel Barlow, Smith affirms her own republican beliefs, a dangerous creed in Britain after the September massacres and the abolition of the monarchy:

> I am extremely flatterd [sic] Dear Sir by your early and very
> obliging attention to my Letter—& indeed have great reason
> to quarrel with D[octor] Warner for neglecting an appoint-
> ment which would have been the means of introducing me
> to your acquaintance—I read with great satisfaction the
> "Address to the Privileged Orders"; and have been, as well as
> some of my most judicious and reasoning friends here, very
> highly gratified by the lesson had—Your Letter to the National
> Convention—Which cannot I think fail of having great effect
> not only where it is address'd; but on those who at present
> consider themselves as less immediately interested in the
> questions it discusses—[4]

Charlotte Smith was even more deeply involved with republicanism
and French politics than hitherto acknowledged,[5] given the radical
republicans to which this letter refers. Joel Barlow was granted
French citizenship as well as membership in the National Convention
in 1793; the letter he presented to the National Convention on behalf
of the London Society for Constitutional Information expressed the
radical hope, as did the British Club's toasts, that soon there would be
a National Convention of England. His *Address to the Privileged
Orders,* which Smith praises, was presented to the National Convention by Paine on November 7. The Doctor Warner whom Smith
mentions was nominated for French citizenship in September 1792
by Brissot because of "his energetic speeches, in which he deploys his
love of liberty and hatred for kings."[6] As she explained later in her
letter to Barlow, Smith was at work on her important poem *The
Emigrants,* a work in which her humanitarianism and republicanism
coexist comfortably:

> it seems to me wrong for the Nation entirely to exile and
> abandon these unhappy Men.—How truly great would it be,
> could the Convention bring about a reconciliation—. They
> should suffer the loss of a very great part of their property; &
> all their power—But they should still be considerd [sic] as
> Men & Frenchmen.

It is thus not surprising that Smith, author of the controversial
republican novel *Desmond,* merited a toast in the British Club alongside toasts celebrating the French Republic and "the coming Convention of England and Ireland." Indeed, while the British Club was
toasting her, Smith was writing to "Citoyen" Barlow, as she addresses

him, on November 18 from Brighton, denouncing "les formules de l'ancien esclavage," and requesting assistance with her plans to visit Revolutionary Paris the following March or April, a plan, she writes, "on which my *rebellious* heart is set."[7]

In Smith's little-known correspondence with Godwin, she articulated the (proto)feminism that subtly informs all of her writing. Comparing the loss of her favorite daughter, Augusta, in 1795 to Wollstonecraft's death in 1797, Smith suggests that her own private suffering is part of a larger system of injustice in Britain:

> And yet I have tears left for the event I shall always deplore as a friend; that of the 10th, of Sept. 1797—Is this world indeed govern'd by a benignant an omnipotent being—?—Why are we here—?—There is a sentence I shall never forget in the last work I have ever seen of Mary Woolstonecraft [sic]. "What is existence but a painful consciousness of wretchedness ?"—I have no other consciousness of my identity I think than that I am the same unhappy person who was at barely fifteen, sold to an idiot—& from the Sussex hills, condemn'd to be shut up in a wretched Street in the City.[8]

In this remarkable letter, Smith's inclusive gaze moves with ease from her personal loss, to the death of the era's most famous feminist, to her own unhappy fate as a woman "sold to an idiot." In an earlier letter to Godwin she notes that she "is reading (ought I to own for the first time?) Political Justice," and the reformist tone rings clear throughout: she writes seeking Godwin's assistance on behalf of her French future son-in-law, "a disciple of a better system & indeed there are few better Citoyens."[9] In contrast, her own son in the military is a "poor victim of our accursed systems." As Judith Miller elaborates in her essay, and as these letters bear witness, Godwin's (and Wollstonecraft's) influence on Smith was more pronounced than is generally known, helping to shape her evolving political, philosophical, and authorial perspective.

Charlotte Smith's intimate knowledge of this radical circle of British revolutionaries, and their recognition of her role in furthering their shared cause, attests to the complex interconnections between the world of women's writing in the 1790s and the politics of the public sphere. In exploring this rich field of inquiry one must first unlearn unhelpful assumptions about women's presumed relegation to the private sphere, even as one rediscovers these forgotten writers, texts, and questions. This volume thus shares with all recent work on women writers of the Romantic period the task of re-establishing the

public presence and influence of these writers, something their contemporaries never doubted, as the British Club reminds us.

Not all British women writers who responded to the Revolution
were republicans or even sympathetic to republicanism, of course,
and this volume seeks to help redress the tendency of scholars to see
women writers as a homogeneous group with identical economic
and political interests. Conservative writers such as the formidable
Hannah More, Elizabeth Hamilton (author of *The Memoirs of Modern
Philosophers*), and Laetitia Matilda Hawkins (author of a two-volume
critique of Helen Maria Williams's early *Letters from France*), wrote
confidently in defense of British nationalism and bourgeois propriety,
and their contributions to political dialogues on revolutionary politics
enjoy ample presence in this collection.[10]

Hawkins, the least well known of the three in modern criticism,
offers a helpful glimpse into the thorny intersection of gender, nationalism, and class that any writer discussing the French Revolution in
1793 had to negotiate. Hawkins's *Letters on the Female Mind,*
addressed to Helen Maria Williams, verbalizes the restrictions under
which we know women writers of the 1790s labored, but which we
should not imagine they fell silent beneath. She reproves Williams for
violating feminine propriety (and natural intellectual limitations) by
venturing into politics and the public sphere, and thus aspiring to
masculine regimes of power and knowledge. Hawkins writes in her
public letter to Williams that women's natural vulnerability and their
need for men's protection, is actually their strength, sheltering them
from moments of political crisis such as the French Revolution:

> from all ten thousand miseries of power, we happy women,
> and double happy as Englishwomen, are providentially exempt.
> Protected by laws, by custom, and the general sentiment of
> our country, we may, if we chuse it, live undisturbed in the
> possession of every earthly good. Public calamity must become
> personal suffering, it must pervade the recesses of our dwell-
> ings, before we, housed and sheltered as we are, in the hearts
> of our generous protectors, are exposed to it. The whole world
> might be at war, and yet not the rumor of it reach the ear of
> an Englishwoman—empires might be lost, and states over-
> thrown, and still she might pursue the peaceful occupations
> of her home. . . .[11]

Rather than making "inroads into the hostile lands of public feuds
and political contest" like Williams, Hawkins suggests, English women

must "render ourselves as amiable as possible—we will not throw by the cestus to put on the helmet" (2: 195, 126). Of course, it is highly unlikely that many Englishwomen would agree with Hawkins that "[t]he whole world might be at war, and yet not the rumor of it reach the ear of an Englishwoman." Written before war with France began in 1793, Hawkins's vision of Englishwomen existing in a sheltered domestic sphere is, of course, undermined by the public and overtly political nature of her own response.

On the eve of the declaration of war and just following the execution of Louis XVI, Hawkins does in fact "put on the helmet" by issuing a call to arms in her Postscript, effectively becoming one of "the odious . . . ministers of vengeance" (2: 126) she had accused Williams of being:

> For the sake of justice, for the sake of innocence, for the sake of all mankind, may the European powers rise and crush these execrable wretches; but should the Almighty defeat our designs, still punishment, the most dreadful of all punishments, impends over guilty France. (2: 210)

Hawkins published two volumes of political and public argument urging women to refrain from such intellectual speculation and to limit themselves to the domestic emotions of love and nurturance, even while she issued the above call to international warfare. Similar contradictions characterize much of women's writing from the Romantic period, writing that ostensibly argues for traditionally feminine values such as domesticity and the separate spheres, as in the polemics of Hannah More and the poetry of Felicia Hemans. In writings on the French Revolution such as Laetitia Hawkins's, these familiar contradictions are even more acute given the undeniably political subject matter and the traditionally "unfeminine" genres involved—polemic and political essay.

Conservative women writers like Hawkins and More are invaluable to our understanding and appreciation of the French Revolution's impact on Britain because they demonstrate that all women writers of the Romantic period, even those who published the most feminine domestic poetry, introduced with meek and self-effacing apologies to their readers, took part in a public sphere from the moment they read and responded to literature until they circulated and published their own work. Women writers who participated in the French Revolution debates assumed bolder public voices than did poets of domesticity because they had no choice, which is perhaps why, Laetitia Hawkins included, they were interested in these debates in the first place.

Despite the richness of women's writings on the Revolution and on the counterrevolutionary and Napoleonic wars that followed, no single study has yet attempted to account for the full spectrum of British women's participation in these political, social, economic, philosophical and poetic debates.[12] This collection thus restores an important part of British literary and political history: women's contribution to the public sphere, and to the most heated debates of their day. This important contribution was lost for nearly two hundred years, and remains obscured in current, prevailing models of women's writing from the Romantic period that focus on women's interest in and restriction to the private sphere and the realm of the heart. Already, new studies of women's writing from the Romantic period, such as the ground-breaking work of Marlon Ross, Anne Mellor, Stuart Curran, Margaret Homans, and others, have begun to impose gendered limits on our understandings of how women wrote and what they wrote about. These scholars emphasize how women writers were inhibited by the cultural identification of women with nature and with domesticity, and how they often chose to celebrate the domestic sphere and its associated feminine virtues of nurturance, cooperation, and empathy.[13] This collection, and the over one dozen women writers featured here, challenge these gendered, often complementary models of women's writing, and reveal the extent to which women writers of the Romantic period did indeed write on those most "masculine" of subjects: politics, revolution, and war.

In addition to our central goals of emphasizing the political range of women's responses, acknowledging their contribution to public sphere debates, and giving visibility to noncanonical writers, our volume also ranges far beyond the usual focus on novels and poetry by including plays, travel writings, letters, prophecies, and political essays. The French Revolution demanded a revolution in formal and generic conventions, and several of the writers discussed, i.e., Helen Maria Williams, Helen Craik, and Mariana Starke, wrote in ways that redrew generic lines. With these larger goals in sight, we have arranged the essays according to four subject groupings: Revolution and Nationalism, Revolution and Religion, Revolutionary Subjects, Revolutionary Representation. While all of the essays address questions of, for example, nationalism and representation, these groupings highlight four key recurring subjects—nationalism, religion, representation, and female subjectivity—that emerged as central to women's writings on the Revolution. This organizational device is meant to evoke questions crucial to all the essays collected here rather than to fix categories. Clearly, for example, though Ann Frank Wake's essay on Amelia Opie is grouped under the rubric of revolutionary subjectivity, it is also and fundamentally a discussion of religious and political dissent. And Judith Miller's analysis of Charlotte Smith's efforts to represent historical reality within the generic limitations of the courtship novel reveals Smith's astute understanding of the economic underpinnings of late eighteenth-century female identity and subjectivity.

The impact of the French Revolution on British literary history has been understood traditionally in terms of the apostasy of William Wordsworth, Samuel Taylor Coleridge, and Robert Southey, and the continued revolutionary enthusiasm, albeit tempered, of William Blake, William Hazlitt, and Percy Bysshe Shelley. Wordsworth's (reluctant) abandonment of his French lover, Annette Vallon, and their child in 1792, prefigures his abandonment of radical politics in France and in Britain;[14] likewise, his disillusionment and his yielding up of moral contraries in despair after his initial enthusiasm, as described in *The Prelude,* have been until recently regarded as the quintessential Romantic response to the painful realities of the Revolution.[15] This narrative of initial bliss and eventual betrayal has also been applied to Coleridge and Southey, both by the younger Romantics Byron and Percy Shelley, and by modern scholars, who have thoroughly documented the impact of the French Revolution on these canonical writers.[16] This is not a narrative, however, that satisfactorily explains British women's responses, because like their male counterparts, women did not form a homogeneous group with identical interests based on their gender, but instead were subject to a complex and often contradictory set of cultural and political forces. In fact, the surprising range, politically and generically, of British women's responses to the Revolution attests to the complex, and often contradictory, nature of British literary responses as a whole, beyond the range of responses traditionally ascribed to canonical writers.

The widely accepted account of the "general" British response to the Revolution unfolding in France is useful to keep in mind, however, in order to appreciate how individual women writers were and were not representative of their culture. With notable exceptions, such as Edmund Burke, the British generally welcomed the rise of the French constitutional monarchy from 1789 to 1792; with the September massacres of 1792, and the execution of the king in January 1793, however, British public opinion turned sharply against the Revolution, and the government ushered in a series of counterrevolutionary repressive measures that amounted essentially to a "state of emergency."[17] When we look at noncanonical women writers, however, we discover remarkable differences between their responses and the familiar narrative of bliss and betrayal that is generally applied to the "first generation" Romantics, differences which often reflect the impact of gender on class and nationalism, a factor unfortunately not always taken into account in the case of male writers. Thus, the revolutionary chronicler Helen Maria Williams emerges as the most staunch and outspoken British supporter of the Revolution in the Romantic period. As Deborah Kennedy demonstrates in her essay, Williams maintained her support for the Revolution even as her British reviewers and British popular opinion turned against the French, and against Williams herself, after the execution of the king and queen.

A wide range of political perspectives emerges once we depart from more familiar authors, such as Wordsworth and Coleridge, and even Wollstonecraft and Austen. Our section devoted to Revolution and Religion, for example, features writers who supported and even furthered the increasingly nationalistic counterrevolutionary British response to the Revolution. The laboring-class prophet Joanna Southcott is one such woman who, as Kevin Binfield demonstrates in his essay, spoke and wrote publicly in favor of the war against France. In her remarkable prophecies, often written in verse, Southcott called for a just war with France as a fulfillment of God's millennial plan for Britain. Modern readers may be surprised to read of this religious woman writing publicly in favor of war, but Southcott actually represents a larger trend that Linda Colley has described in *Britons,* one in which British women actively supported both the war effort and the climate of nationalism.[18] The Evangelical polemicist Hannah More, as Angela Keane shows, shared with Southcott a counterrevolutionary politics, in More's case centered on her vision of virtuous femininity and its central role in Britain's economy, in both the financial and moral senses of the word. Ironically, and as with Southcott, opposition to More's charitable and political efforts in the interests of British nationalism focused on her gender, demonstrating how More's counterrevolutionary politics found both their strength and ultimate opposition in women's uneasy relationship to the French Revolution.

The influential but neglected Mariana Starke offers another example of the volatile conflict between class and gender revealed by women writers' responses to the French Revolution. Jeanne Moskal demonstrates how, in her influential *Letters from Italy* (1800), the conservative and anti-Catholic Starke found surprising affinities with

Napoleon because of his defeat of papal power in the Italian campaigns. Moskal's account of Starke, expanding on Simon Bainbridge's reassessment of the emperor in *Napoleon and British Romanticism,*[19] challenges prevailing modern assumptions that writers of the Romantic period did not admire Napoleon, and instead demonstrates that British writers like Starke invested Napoleon with surprising religious and political significance, while maintaining their nationalism. Like Southcott, Starke grounds her nationalism in her Protestant identity; considered together, Starke's ambivalent praise of Napoleon's victories in Italy and Southcott's support of Britain's war against France serve as powerful reminders of the complexity of women writers' investment in and complicity with church and state.

In contrast, it is reconciliation across such religious and nationalistic lines that Fanny Burney urged in *The Wanderer* (1814). As Maria Jerinic argues, Fanny Burney's last novel suggested that her persecuted English heroine's unlikely ally was the unmarried Catholic clergy exiled by the Revolution, not the intolerant British gentlemen and ladies who persecuted her. Burney and More, along with Charlotte Smith and others, had written in support of the French emigrants, particularly the clergy, urging their fellow Britons to show mercy to these refugees of war despite the political and religious differences between Britain and France.[20] The pamphlets More and Burney published—*Remarks on the Speech of M. DuPont* and *Brief Reflections Relative to the Emigrant French Clergy: Earnestly Submitted to the Humane Consideration of the Ladies of Great Britain,* respectively—are part of a large-scale charitable response to the Revolution in which British women played a significant role. That both the fervently nationalist More and the distinctly antinationalist Smith and Burney could agree on the treatment of Catholic clergy reveals the significance of gender in the politics of nationalism, though gendered interests here cannot be defined in a politically consistent, feminist, sense. More was sympathetic to the French emigrant clergy because they were fellow Christians who shared her opposition to French atheism and political reform; Smith and Burney, on the other hand, saw in the exile and disenfranchisement of the clergy the political and economic disenfranchisement of larger groups—women and working people—and thus in *The Emigrants* and *The Wanderer,* women and clergy wander through the same treacherous British landscape, victims of a patriarchal ethos of economic and political violence. When we consider these authors together, we learn much about the untidy complexities of British responses to the Revolution, and how gender was a central force in shaping them.

Unlike Burney and More, Starke and Southcott are unfamiliar writers to most scholars of British literature, and for this reason these essays, in fact most of the essays in this collection, focus closely on the works and lives of a single, little-known writer. In addition to making a case for the significance of these noncanonical writers for a fuller understanding of the times and traditions in which they wrote and which they helped shape, these essays present detailed new research which we hope will serve as a starting point for new work. As Terence Hoagwood and Jeanne Moskal remind us in their essays, a prevailing trend in scholarship on women writers from the Romantic period is to project anachronistically onto these writers modern, liberal, and often feminist images of what a woman writer should write about, and what her values (feminist, liberal, antinationalistic, egalitarian) should be. Yet the essays on Revolution and Religion remind us that women writers held much more divisive, and often self-divided, views on the French Revolution, political reform, and nationalism, without ever undergoing the fall from bliss to disillusionment that canonical accounts emphasize. Furthermore, while writers such as More, Starke, and Southcott would not have confessed to any illusions about the Revolution they consistently opposed, they did encounter resistance to their public politics because of their gender. As religious outsiders, moreover, More and Southcott faced additional opposition and controversy, yet also articulated a conservative vision of British nationalism that is remarkably similar given their vast class and religious differences.

Nationalism naturally remains central to any study devoted to the French Revolution, and the writers featured in our section devoted to this subject—Mary Wollstonecraft, Charlotte Smith, and Fanny Burney—stand in significant contrast to Starke, Southcott, and More because of their shared opposition to nationalism. All three women were thoroughly professional writers who earned their living from their writings, part of the bourgeois cultural revolution and feminized print culture that Gary Kelly, among others, has written about at length.[21] Wollstonecraft's feminism, initial support of the French Revolution, and disparaging remarks regarding French women's perceived frivolity are widely known; what is not generally acknowledged is Wollstonecraft's subtle critique of nationalism and the ideology of national character. Jan Wellington illuminates these cosmopolitan qualities of Wollstonecraft's feminism, connecting Wollstonecraft's critique of gender as a natural category to her equally revolutionary critique of national character.

Charlotte Smith and Fanny Burney, highly regarded writers in their own day and increasingly so in ours, also critiqued nationalism and national character from their vantage points as women. Kari Lokke demonstrates how, in *The Emigrants* (1793) and in her popular sonnets, Smith employs the moon as an emblem of female transcendence, in an effort to represent a potentially emancipatory distance from and utopian resolution of what she perceives as the largely male-dominated political crises of 1792 and 1793. Smith's use of transcendence, then, differs significantly from William Wordsworth's, because it does not allow the poet to displace and escape from the political realities of the Revolution, but rather allows her a gendered vantage point from which to critique both French and British politics. In *The Wanderer* (1814), Burney also shows how women are outside of male political and economic institutions, but in Burney's case, women's exclusion from masculine political institutions is figured as a profound alienation and disenfranchisement. Maria Jerinic illuminates how Burney's last novel enacts a devastating critique of Britain's most cherished ideological constructs: companionate marriage, Protestantism, and British liberty. In Burney's bleak post-revolutionary England, and contrary to prevailing British nationalist self-images, women are helpless wanderers, preyed upon both economically and sexually, and excluded from the benefits of these central British institutions. As a privileged Englishwoman married to a French aristocrat, and exiled in France, Burney offered a controversial and unique perspective on nationalism and the war against France, one which emphasized their destructive consequences for women of different nations, classes, and races.

For Burney, whose southern English landscapes are ceaselessly crisscrossed by alienated figures, the act of wandering offers no liberation, no mystical transport, and no solace in nature, unlike the more familiar effects of wandering (and solitude) in the works of Wordsworth and Rousseau. In fact, Burney's *The Wanderer* appeared in the same year as Wordsworth's *The Excursion,* the poem for which he was best-known to his contemporaries. While in his poem the Solitary retreats from the grim realities of the French Revolution into the English pastoral landscape, Burney's novel suggests that no solace exists for solitary women Wanderers, either in the city, the country, or (especially) in fashionable society: her heroine "had severely experienced how little fitted to the female character, to female safety, and to female propriety, was this hazardous plan of lonely wandering."[22] Burney's novel provides one example among many in these collected essays of how women writers engage and revise canonical Romantic tropes and figures such as "transcendence," "the wanderer," "the sublime," and do so from their perspectives as women, and from overtly politicized perspectives as well. Such revision of canonical Romantic tropes, however, does not mean that these writers were not Romantic. While Burney and More certainly reject most qualities we associate with canonical Romanticism, and would in fact be more accurately described as anti-Romantic (in distinct ways), writers like Charlotte Smith, Mary Hays, and Amelia Opie are Romantic given their explorations of transcendence, passion, and the sublime, respectively. Thus Kari Lokke's essay on Smith, Miriam Wallace's essay on Hays, and Ann Frank Wake's essay on Opie, in addition to foregrounding these writers' engagement in revolutionary politics, also contribute significantly to current debates over women's relationships to Romanticism. When taken as a whole, this volume suggests that we must continue to widen our field of inquiry when we ask questions of women's relationships to Romanticism, since they continue to surprise us with their divergent political and poetic insights.

While scholarship on British women writers' involvement in French Revolutionary debates is in the initial stages of development, the last decade has seen much excellent work on French women and their significance in the Revolution. Joan Landes's *Women and the Public Sphere in the French Revolution,* Lynn Hunt's *The Family Romance and the French Revolution,* Madelyn Gutwirth's *The Twilight of the Goddesses: Women and Representation in the French Revolutionary Era,* and Sara Melzer and Leslie Rabine's *Rebel Daughters: Women and the French Revolution,* have focused the attention of French cultural historians on the significance of gender and sexual politics for the French public sphere.[23]

Rebellious Hearts: British Women Writers and the French Revolution engages in a dialogue with this influential work on the significance of gender in French Revolutionary culture at the same time that it complements that previous scholarship by offering a specific focus upon the discursive contributions of women to the French Revolutionary debates in late eighteenth-century Britain. Jürgen Habermas's original formulation of the notion of the public sphere in *The Structural Transformation of the Public Sphere* does indeed make room for women as readers essential to the literary public realm, but the essays gathered here suggest that British women played a crucial and active role in the creation of religious, philosophical, and political opinion and policy as well. Writers such as Helen Maria Williams, Charlotte Smith, Helen Craik, Elizabeth Inchbald, and Mary Wollstonecraft clearly saw themselves as vital participants in an international, cosmopolitan conversation about the moral and political fate of Europe.

Geoff Eley, scholar of eighteenth- and nineteenth-century British radicalism, and feminist critics Nancy Fraser and Joan Landes have all persuasively argued that Habermas's model of the eighteenth-century British public sphere as essentially limited to property-owning males does not do justice to the diversity of the participants in the crucial literary, philosophical, and political conversations of the era.[24] Building upon the concept of *Gegenöffentlichkeit* developed by Oskar Negt and Alexander Kluge, whose early revisions of Habermas were meant to acknowledge and to make room for contributions of the proletariat to public discourse, Fraser and Eley articulate concepts of "counter-public spheres" that emphasize the diverse and conflictual nature of the public sphere from the outset.[25] Fraser defines these counter-publics as "parallel discursive arenas where members of subordinated social groups invent and circulate counterdiscourses to formulate oppositional interpretations of their identities, interests, and needs" (123). The essays collected here provide valuable insights into and information about the precise nature and terms of women's participation in that ostensibly masculine arena, the public sphere, as well as offering a variety of responses to the question of whether women's writings on the French Revolution were indeed the product of an oppositional counter-public sphere as it is defined by Fraser and other feminist theorists such as Leonora Davidoff.[26]

That British women's voices did claim a powerful presence in the ideological debates surrounding the French Revolution and the Napoleonic wars does not, however, mean that British patriarchy sanctioned the breakdown of barriers between masculine and feminine roles, between public and domestic realms. Rather, the writings of the eighteenth-century authors represented here confirm Linda Colley's assertion that in the decades following the American Revolution, "separate spheres were being increasingly prescribed in theory, yet increasingly broken through in practice" (251). These writings clearly testify to the urgency with which women of a wide spectrum of political persuasions felt compelled to respond to the moral and political questions raised by the wars with Revolutionary and Napoleonic France, despite societal taboos against such intervention. Charlotte Smith's angry preface to her revolutionary novel *Desmond* (1792) gives eloquent expression to the conflicts engendered by such prescriptions:

Women it is said have no business with politics.—Why not?— Have they no interest in the scenes that are acting around them, in which they have fathers, brothers, husbands, sons, or friends engaged!—Even in the commonest course of female education, they are expected to acquire some knowledge of history; and yet, if they are to have no opinion of what is passing, it avails them little that they should be informed of what *has passed,* in a world where they are subject to such mental degradation; where they are censured as affecting masculine knowledge if they happen to have any understanding; or despised as insignificant triflers if they have none.[27]

Yet on the heels of this defiant logic, Smith still finds it necessary to reassure her public, though with sharp irony, that, in becoming a novelist she is earning the money necessary to support her family, and thus fulfilling, rather than neglecting, her domestic duties:

> Knowledge, which qualifies women to speak or to write on any other than the most common and trivial subjects, is supposed to be of so difficult attainment, that it cannot be acquired but by the sacrifice of domestic virtues, or the neglect of domestic duties.—I however, may safely say, that it was in the *observance,* not in the *breach* of duty, *I* became an Author. (6)

Such tactics of claiming to remain within the sphere of properly female behavior while in fact blurring the boundaries between public and private or even enacting a "masculine" role are common among the women writers represented in this volume. Indeed, these tactics are keys to understanding the formal and intellectual complexities as well as the ideological contradictions identified by several contributors to this collection as central to the texts under discussion. One such tactic common among these late eighteenth-century women writers is to assert the apolitical nature and thus the acceptable femininity of their writing by claiming its disinterestedness, impartiality and lack of partisanship.[28] Thus, as Maria Jerinic notes, Burney presents *The Wanderer* as a politically neutral novel, a picture of life and manners, devoid of "materials for political controversy," or "any species of personality, either in the form of foreign influence, or of national partiality" (*Wanderer,* 4). Similarly, Angela Keane shows More channeling her counterrevolutionary sentiments into humanitarian efforts on behalf of the emigrant French clergy, efforts that she explicitly asserts are of "no party." Judith Miller identifies a strategy of "open concealment" as a means by which Smith's novels assert a clear political philosophy while seeming to remain within the confines of the apolitical genre of romance and courtship. And Kari Lokke demonstrates that Smith in *The Emigrants* portrays "party rage perverse and blind" as the ultimate threat to a utopian ideal of universalist and disinterested compassion figured in the explicitly female "mild dominion of the moon." In asserting the universality of their positions under cover of a "feminine" refusal of politics, these writers are paradoxically asserting their right to public speech and political influence by challenging the false universalism of the bourgeois public sphere that excluded women, as Landes has argued, on the basis of their perceived association with "particularity, interest, and partiality" (144), and most specifically with "bodily and affective particularity" (144).

Many of the women writers represented in this collection chose the genre of the letter for their means of self-expression as a way of both camouflaging and legitimating their entry into public and political debates. The essays collected here on women writers of the Romantic era fully confirm Mary Favret's assertions in *Romantic Correspondence: Women, Politics and the Fiction of Letters* that during this period, "the letter—public and private—became the focus of ideological and political struggle."[29] Rather than simply reinforcing women's association with the sentimental and domestic, the epistolary genres examined here were powerful polemical tools that allowed women to redefine the terms of their political and intellectual engagement with the most pressing concerns of that historical moment.

Deborah Kennedy shows how the choice of the letter as the genre best-suited to the recording of Helen Maria Williams's immediate eyewitness responses to the Revolution, as well as to expressing her emotional commitment to its original ideals, allowed Williams to create a new and influential form of history. Similarly, as Jeanne Moskal argues, Mariana Starke's *Letters from Italy,* written while she was travelling there as nurse to an invalid relative, provide a venue for the assertion of her conservative, Anglican responses to the Napoleonic invasion of Italy at the same time that they enable her to challenge and redefine the Grand Tour as no longer an exclusively male and aristocratic tradition. As travel-writings, Starke's works formed the basis for a new genre of tourist travel literature, John Murray's popular and lucrative *Handbooks for Travellers,* begun in the 1830s.

The epistolary works of Mary Hays and Mary Wollstonecraft also offer innovative uses of the letter that combine forms of public and private address as well as reminding us of the importance of the non-rational in women's contributions to the public sphere. In *The Memoirs of Emma Courtney,* Miriam Wallace demonstrates that Mary Hays incorporates letters to her mentor William Godwin and to her beloved William Frend as a courageous means of seeking control over the raw material of emotion and of redefining true philosophy as encompassing sensibility and passion. In an inverse gesture, Mary Wollstonecraft presents her *Letters Written during a Short Residence in Sweden, Norway, and Denmark* (1796) not just as travel memoirs meant for publication, but also as love letters to an anonymous beloved, when in fact they represented an entirely different set of texts from those sent to her American lover Gilbert Imlay. In his *Memoirs of the Author of a "Vindication of the Rights of Woman,"* William Godwin may have read these *Letters* as "a book calculated to make a man in love with its author,"[30] but according to Jan Wellington, they represent a serious and radical effort to challenge stereotypic and fixed conceptions of character, both individual and national.

Finally, Charlotte Smith's most explicitly political novel *Desmond* takes an epistolary form that enables her to represent in detail a variety of positions in the revolutionary debates, and to claim, as Judith Miller argues, the objectivity of Desmond's explicitly stated radical politics. As Smith asserts with customary cleverness in her Preface, "I have given to my imaginary characters the arguments I have heard on both sides; and if those in favour of one party have evidently the advantage, it is not owing to my partial representation but to the predominant power of truth and reason, which can neither be altered nor concealed" (5–6). The framing correspondence between the older mentor, E. Bethel, and the younger Desmond clearly responds to Edmund Burke's epistolary framing of *Reflections on the Revolution in France* as a letter to Charles-François Dupont, a young gentleman in France. Thus not only does the letter as form challenge the distinction between public and private through its presence in such traditionally feminine forms as the memoir, the travel journal, and the epistolary novel. In the hands of these women writers, the letter also lends itself easily to a kind of generic hybridization that ultimately authorizes Revolutionary-era women to write philosophy, politics, and history.

Along with Mary Robinson, who set two of her novels, *The Natural Daughter* (1799) and *Hubert de Sevrac* (1796), in France and on the Continent during the turbulent early 1790s, Helen Craik and Charlotte Smith were among the earliest British writers to develop the historical novel as a genre. Traditionally traced to Sir Walter Scott's *Waverley* novels which began to appear after Napoleon's defeat, the origins of the historical novel and the new historical consciousness that made this genre possible are actually found in the French Revolution. Speaking of the European scale of the changes brought about by the French Revolution and its accompanying wars, Georg Lukács argued in his seminal study, *The Historical Novel,* that "the quick succession of these upheavals gives them a qualitatively distinct character, it makes their historical character far more visible than would be the case in isolated individual instances."[31] Yet contrary to Lukács' assumption that novels before Scott lacked "[the] derivation of the individuality of their characters from the historical particularity of their age" (19), historical villains and heroines walked the pages of Helen Craik's innovative novel *Adelaide de Narbonne, with Memoirs of Charlotte de Cordet* [sic] (1800). Marat and his assassin, Charlotte Corday, are central players in Craik's novel, who alongside fictional characters drawn from Walpole's *The Castle of Otranto* offer readers an illuminating historicization of the Gothic novel's central literary and gender conventions. As Adriana Craciun shows, Helen Craik used Corday's controversial example of public and violent agency to imagine new forms of female subjectivity, and by doing so, established a threshold between the Gothic and the historical novel. Craik's is not the only woman's novel inhabited by historical figures; Marat and Robespierre are the villains of Robinson's *The Natural Daughter* and, although he never appears in Burney's *The Wanderer,* Robespierre signifies the gravest threat to women in Burney's novel. In these pioneering works, as in Williams's *Letters from France,* the historical Marat and Robespierre emerge as the age's archetypal patriarchal villains, embodiments of the sexual and economic threats that British women, like their French counterparts, faced in this period of turbulent gender and political relations.

The generic innovations represented by many of the authors in this volume thus reaffirm Tilottama Rajan and Julia Wright's argument in *Romanticism, History, and the Possibilities of Genre* that we should reconceive genre as a "mobile category" which allowed authors to enact a process of cultural and political intervention. Rajan and Wright argue that writers such as William Godwin, in his historical fiction, and Lady Morgan, in her travel writings, "sought to change the very shape of history by drawing on new modes such as periodicals and travel writing to hybridize the more conventional genres of historiography and the historical novel."[32]

The focus on the letter and the novel should not, then, be allowed to obscure the striking variety of genres in which women writers of the Romantic period wrote about the Revolution. From Joanna Southcott's prophecies to Joanna Baillie's plays, from the influential travel writings of Mariana Starke to the *Cheap Repository* tracts of Hannah More, women's writings on the Revolution and the Napoleonic wars were as diverse generically as they were politically. Furthermore, the women writers represented here did indeed also appropriate more prestigious and conventional generic forms as well as exploit the freedoms allowed by the hybrid forms discussed above. Thus Charlotte Smith announces *The Emigrants* as a response to her friend William Cowper's long blank verse poem *The Task* and, with the epigraph from Virgil's *Georgics* that opens Book Two, implicitly asserts her identity as poet of the British nation, all the while advocating transcendence of party spirit and national prejudice. Ann Frank Wake argues that the conventional nature of traditionally masculine poetic forms—the ode, for example—and of the poetic tropes and stylized landscapes chosen by Amelia Opie clashes with received notions of female agency, in an aesthetic and ideological conflict that brings her to the brink of poetic exhaustion and artistic silence.

As previously noted, many of the women writers represented here took advantage of their culturally sanctioned roles as guardians of private and public morality to assert themselves in the name of both religious truth and religious tolerance. Habermas's concept of the public sphere, limited as it was to rational debate, must be broadened and substantially transformed to accommodate the religious prophecies of Joanna Southcott, products of clair-audience or direct revelations of the voice of God, and the enormously influential evangelicalism of Hannah More, founded not upon reason, as Angela Keane shows us, but upon absolute metaphysical faith. As David Zaret has emphasized, "Habermas's account glosses over the relevance of religion for the emergence of a public sphere in politics at a time when religious discourse was a, if not the, predominant means by which individuals defined and debated issues in this sphere."[33] This volume, then, reveals the central role played by British women in the formulation and the expression of religious opinion as it overlapped with positions taken on the counterrevolutionary and Napoleonic wars, thereby underlining the limitations of any purely secular understanding of the late eighteenth-century public sphere.

Yet women's relationship to public spiritual authority was profoundly conflicted, despite the powerful cultural influence of such figures as Southcott and More. Ann Frank Wake's essay on Amelia Opie, for example, reveals the gulf between the progressive demands for religious tolerance on the part of the Dissenting community in which she was raised and its rigidly patriarchal codes of proper female behavior that restricted women to private expressions of sensibility and shared (bodily) pain. Kevin Binfield shows that Southcott's efforts to sustain a public role as both woman and millenarian through the manipulation of mainstream nationalist and anti-French sentiments ultimately failed. Instead, the sixty-five year old prophet retreated into the refiguration of the virgin and post-menopausal births attributed to Mary and Sarah in the Bible by proclaiming herself pregnant with Shiloh, the future British redeemer. Similarly, Angela Keane depicts how, in response to the perceived Methodist and levelling tendencies of her Sunday school movement, Hannah More was vilified by members of the established church as a Pope Joan whose voracious sexuality drew members of the clergy and the peasantry into "the vortex of her petticoats." Thus the fate of each of these intensely spiritual women was marked by cultural efforts to limit woman to her own body and sexuality.

Given the double binds that ensnared women who sought to embody traditional feminine roles in public, it is wholly understandable that a number of the authors represented here sought to create new models for women as public subjects. As Adriana Craciun shows, Craik, in *Adelaide de Narbonne, with Memoirs of Charlotte de Cordet* [sic], imagines Charlotte Corday as a new Romantic heroine, a "free agent" who desires justice and who ultimately enacts it. Indeed, Craik's portrait of Corday as a revolutionary subject whose greatest desire is justice, not love, is her unique contribution to the newly forming tradition of revolutionary historical novels discussed above. Similarly, Miriam Wallace argues that Hays, in her novel *Emma Courtney,* envisages a model of active, public, and revolutionary subjectivity that privileges sensibility as well as reason and comes into being through rational reflection upon private emotion and sensation.

In her recent novel, *City of Darkness, City of Light* (1996), Marge Piercy asserts that she chose to write a novel about the French Revolution because, for her, modern politics—the modern left as well as the women's movement—began there.[34] The essays collected here do indeed emphasize the relevance of French Revolutionary debates for current political struggles, as well as suggesting links that may allow us to trace contemporary political movements back to that earlier historical era. The antinationalist, cosmopolitan stances of Burney, Smith and Wollstonecraft, for example, bear comparison with the pacifist strain of the international women's movement today. And, as Wallace shows, the tensions between the claims of sensibility and rationality, the personal and the abstract, individual identity and universality central to the works of Mary Hays prefigure debates about the role of the body and the specifically "feminine" in feminist theory today. And, according to Terence Hoagwood, Joanna Baillie's theory of drama, as expressed in the "Introductory Discourse"(1798) to her plays on the passions, with its emphasis upon the curiosity and pleasure induced by the spectacle of intense and violent emotion, initiates and celebrates a commodity culture still alive and well in Hollywood today.

In concluding our introductory essay by emphasizing contemporary political and cultural questions raised by these analyses of British women writers' constructions of the French Revolution, we wish to make clear that this collection represents only the first step in the exploration of a rich field of literary and historical scholarship. We have thus sought to raise questions and suggest new directions for research rather than to provide definitive answers. We also hope that future studies will examine, in depth, the writings of working-class British women on the Revolution, represented here by the sole example of Joanna Southcott. And Mary Robinson is an absolutely central figure in English radical culture whose political writings deserve serious study and generous commentary.[35] Women's responses to the Seven Years War, the American Revolution, and to Napoleon are also fascinating and largely unexplored fields of inquiry, as is the question of an identifiable and cosmopolitan response on the part of women throughout Europe to the cataclysmic political and cultural upheaval represented by the French Revolution. Lucia Maria Licher, for example, terms Karoline von Günderrode "the poet of revolution," and warns us to be wary of the conclusion drawn by Maria Mies in her contribution to Helga Brandes's collection on *Frauen und die Französische Revolution* (*Women and the French Revolution*) that, for women, the French Revolution did not take place.[36] In the spirit of the British women writers to whom this book is dedicated, we look forward to future dialogue on the significance of the French Revolution to women throughout Europe and beyond.

Notes

1. No fewer than eleven such addresses to the Convention were made by similar groups in Britain between November and December 1792. This particular address was read on November 28. See Albert Goodwin, *The Friends of Liberty: the English Democratic Movement in the Age of the French Revolution* (Cambridge: Harvard University Press, 1979), 508–09; see also David Erdman, *Commerce des Lumières: John Oswald and the British in Paris, 1790–93* (Columbia, Mo.: University of Missouri Press, 1986), 219.

2. The toasts and declaration to the National Convention are reprinted in David Erdman's excellent *Commerce des Lumières,* from which this quotation is taken (230), as well as in John Goldworth Alger's *Paris in 1789–94: Farewell Letters of Victims of the Guillotine* (New York: J. Pott & Co.; London, G. Allen, 1902); for a more concise account of the British Club, see Alger's essay "The British Colony in Paris, 1792–93" *English Historical Review* 13 (1898): 672–94 and chapter 8 in Erdman.

3. Women's armed militancy was on the rise in Paris in 1792 and 1793. The Citoyennes referred to in the toast had famously joined General Dumourier in battle, and were also praised by Mary Robinson in her 1799 *A Letter to the Women of England on the Injustice of Mental Subordination: A Romantic Circles Edition* <www.rc.umd.edu/editions/robinson/cover.htm>, ed. Adriana Craciun, Anne Irmen, Megan Musgrave, Orianne Smith (December 1998), 28. Theroigne de Méricourt gave a speech asking to form a battalion of armed women; on 31 July 1792, the women of the Hôtel de Ville Section petitioned the Convention for permission to bear arms and defend the city. See Section 3, "The Escalation of Women's Protest" in Darline Gay Levy, Harriet Branson Applewhite, and Mary Durham Johnson, *Women in Revolutionary Paris 1781–1795: Selected Documents Translated with Notes* (Chicago: University of Chicago Press, 1979). This collection of primary documents is invaluable for understanding women's perspectives on and involvement in the Revolution. See also Marilyn Yalom, *Blood Sisters: The French Revolution in Women's Memory* (New York: Basic Books, 1993), which tells in narrative form the stories of many leading female figures in the Revolution.

4. Smith, letter to Joel Barlow, 3 November 1792, Brighthelmstone (Huntington Library, MS BN404). This item is reproduced by permission of The Huntington Library, San Marino, California. Contrary to Erdman's speculation that Smith may have been present at the British Club toast, it seems impossible for her to have been in France then, given the dates of her letters from England in and around November 1792. According to Loraine Fletcher, Smith had been to Paris the previous year (*Charlotte Smith: A Critical Biography* [Houndsmills, Basingstoke: Macmillan, and New York: St Martin's, 1998], 142).

5. The extent of Smith's connections to radical politics has been questioned by some modern scholars; reviews of *Desmond,* however, alluded to these connections, which seem to have been public knowledge. For example, the *Monthly Review*'s positive review of Smith's novel noted that her depiction of radical politics was based in "conversations to which she had been a witness in England and in France, during the last twelve months." See *Monthly Review* 9 (December 1792): 406–12. The *Critical Review* 6 (September 1792): 99–105, wrote that Smith was "[c]onnected with the reformers, and the revolutionists," and that "she has borrowed her colouring from them, and represented their conduct in the most favourable light"; see also

her obituary, "Memoirs of Mrs. Charlotte Smith," in the *Monthly Magazine* 23 (April 1807): 244–48. Smith's sister, Catherine Dorset, in her well-known memoir, writes that during 1791 Smith moved from Chichester to Brighton, "where she formed acquaintances with some of the most violent advocates of the French Revolution, and unfortunately caught the contagion, though in direct opposition to the principles she had formerly professed, and to those of her family" (49). Dorset writes with regret of the negative reception Smith's politics received from critics, friends, and "literary ladies," and she would have little reason to exaggerate Smith's politics. *Prose Works of Sir Walter Scott,* Vol. 4: *Biographical Memoirs,* Vol. 2 (Edinburgh: Robert Cadell, 1834), 21–70.

6. Brissot, as quoted in Erdman, *Commerce des Lumières,* 189.

7. Charlotte Smith, *Letters,* ed. Judith Phillips Stanton (Bloomington: Indiana University Press, forthcoming), 86. Our thanks to Judith Stanton for making these letters available to Smith scholars and to Bill Brewer for sharing his copy of selections from the manuscript with us. There is no evidence that Smith actually made this 1793 trip.

8. Smith to William Godwin, December 7 [n.d., probably 1797], Bodleian Library (Abinger Deposit) Dep. C. 526, by kind permission of Lord Abinger, through the Bodleian Library. Smith (mis)quotes letter eight in Wollstonecraft's *A Short Residence in Sweden, Norway and Denmark,* ed. Richard Holmes (London: Penguin, 1987), 112.

9. Smith to William Godwin, September 1797, Bodleian Library (Abinger Deposit), Dep. b. 215/6, by kind permission of Lord Abinger, through the Bodleian Library. This earlier letter was probably sent during the week of Wollstonecraft's lying in and death, given that Smith asks for news of Wollstonecraft's health: "It will give me very sincere pleasure to hear a good account of Mrs. Godwin."

10. On women's investment in conservative patriarchal interests, see Elizabeth Kowaleski-Wallace, *Their Father's Daughters: Hannah More, Maria Edgeworth, and Patriarchal Complicity* (New York: Oxford University Press, 1991). M.O. Grenby includes Mary Robinson, Charlotte Smith, Fanny Burney, and Helen Craik in his list of anti-Jacobin conservative writers in "The Anti-Jacobin Novel: British Fiction, British Conservatism and the Revolution in France" (*History* 83 [1998]: 445–71). On the intersection of class and gender in eighteenth-century women's literature, see Donna Landry's excellent *The Muses of Resistance: Laboring Class Women's Poetry in Britain, 1739–1796* (Cambridge: Cambridge University Press, 1990).

11. Laetitia Matilda Hawkins, *Letters on the Female Mind, Its Powers and Pursuits; Addressed to Miss H. M. Williams, With Particular Reference to Her Letters from France,* 2nd ed. (London: J. and T. Carpenter, 1801) 2: 194; first published in 1793 by Hookham & Carpenter. On Hawkins and

Williams, see Steven Blakemore, "Revolution and the French Disease: Laetitia Matilda Hawkins's 'Letters' to Helen Maria Williams," *Studies in English Literature* 36.3 (1996): 673–91.

12. Several recent books focus on a select number of well-known British women writers: Steven Blakemore's *Crisis in Representation: Thomas Paine, Mary Wollstonecraft, Helen Maria Williams, and the Rewriting of the French Revolution* (Madison, N.J.: Fairleigh Dickinson University Press, 1997) and Gary Kelly's *Women, Writing, and Revolution, 1790–1827* (Oxford: Clarendon, 1993). The latter study discusses the work of Helen Maria Williams, Elizabeth Hamilton, and Mary Hays. In addition to these major studies, two earlier essays survey British women's responses to the French Revolution, the first limited to the writings of Mary Wollstonecraft, Helen Maria Williams, and Mary Shelley, the second discussing a much larger variety of writers, many of them noncanonical: Anne Mellor, "English Women Writers and the French Revolution," Sara Melzer and Leslie Rabine, eds., *Rebel Daughters: Women and the French Revolution* (Oxford: Oxford University Press, 1992), 255–72, and Margaret Doody, "English Women Writers and the French Revolution" in *La Femme en Angleterre et dans les Colonies Americaines aux XVIIe et XVIIIe Siècles: Actes du colloque tenu à Paris les 24 et 25 Octobre 1975* (Lille: L'Université de Lille III, 1975), 176–98. See also Eleanor Ty's *Unsex'd Revolutionaries: Five Women Novelists of the 1790s* (Toronto: Toronto University Press, 1993). More recently, Stephen Behrendt has discussed British women poets and radicalism: "British Women Poets and the Reverberations of Radicalism in the 1790s," in *Romanticism, Radicalism and the Press,* ed. Behrendt (Detroit: Wayne State University Press, 1997), 83–102. For essays on the French Revolution and individual writers mentioned in this introduction, e.g., Williams, Wollstonecraft, Smith, see the notes to the respective essays in *Rebellious Hearts.*

13. Margaret Homans, *Women Writers and Poetic Identity* (Princeton: Princeton University Press, 1980) and *Bearing the Word: Language and Female Experience in Nineteenth-Century Women's Writing* (Chicago: University of Chicago Press, 1986); Marlon Ross, *The Contours of Masculine Desire: Romanticism and the Rise of Women Poets* (Oxford: Oxford University Press, 1989); Anne Mellor *Romanticism and Gender* (New York: Routledge, 1993) and Anne Mellor, ed. *Romanticism and Feminism* (Bloomington: Indiana University Press, 1988).

14. Ronald Paulson writes: "The nodal point, the hidden center of Wordsworth's revolutionary experience, comes in book IX, and this is the experience of Annette Vallon," who hence becomes "interchangeable" with the Revolution for Wordsworth (*Representations of Revolution* [New Haven: Yale University Press, 1983], 265). Wordsworth's account of this romance with Vallon, fictionalized in the "Vaudracour and Julia" episode in *The Prelude,* was itself influenced by Helen Maria Williams's *Letters from France;* see Deborah Kennedy, "Revolutionary Tales: Helen Maria Williams's

Letters from France and William Wordsworth's 'Vaudracour and Julia'," *The Wordsworth Circle* 21 (1990): 109–14.

15. M.H. Abrams's characterization of "the spirit of the age" represents, and indeed, founded, this interpretive tradition: "The great Romantic poems were written not in the mood of revolutionary exaltation but in the later mood of revolutionary disillusionment or despair," (53) when "the militancy of overt political action" had evolved into "the paradox of spiritual quietism," (58). See "English Romanticism: The Spirit of the Age," *Romanticism Reconsidered,* ed. Northrop Frye (New York: Columbia University Press, 1963). Blake most obviously does not fit this model of quietism and despair, and neither do many of the women discussed in this volume. More recent work on canonical (male) writers has also begun to question the accuracy of this teleological model of Romantic disillusionment with the Revolution. Robert Maniquis, for example, argues that contrary to the assumption that writers such as Wordsworth, Coleridge, and Southey abandoned the Revolution after the Terror, they actually still spoke nostalgically of the Revolution, and for the most part blamed England for the Terror, because of its declaration of war ("Holy Savagery and Wild Justice: English Romanticism and the Terror" in *Studies in Romanticism* 28 [1989]: 365–96). See also *Revolution in Writing: British literary responses to the French Revolution,* ed. Kelvin Everest (Milton Keynes and Philadelphia: Open University Press, 1991), and *Revolution and English Romanticism: Politics and Rhetoric,* ed. Keith Hanley and Raman Selden (Hertfordshire: Harvester Wheatsheaf and St. Martin's, 1990). Both of these volumes approach the impact of the Revolution on (largely canonical) Romanticism by examining the impact of recent methodological shifts on the field as a whole, i.e., the emergence of new historicism and poststructuralism. Hanley and Selden conclude that "the familiar outlines of revolutionary and counter revolutionary positions in British culture of the Romantic period dissolve and form contradictory and ambiguous formations when we read texts with close attention to the interplay of their figurative and linguistic modes of interpretation" (xv–xvi).

16. For general accounts of the impact of the Revolution on British literary scenes, see: P.M.S. Dawson, "Poetry in an age of revolution," *The Cambridge Companion to British Romanticism,* ed. Stuart Curran (Cambridge: Cambridge University Press, 1993); *The French Revolution Debate in English Literature and Culture,* ed. Lisa Plummer Crafton (Westport, Conn.: Greenwood Press, 1997); David Bindman, ed., *In the Shadow of the Guillotine: Britain and the French Revolution* (London: British Museum, 1989); Ronald Paulson, *Representations of Revolution, 1789–1820;* Marilyn Butler, *Romantics, Rebels, and Reactionaries: English Literature and its Backgrounds 1760–1830* (Oxford: Oxford University Press, 1983); Marilyn Butler, ed., *Burke, Paine, Godwin, and the Revolution Controversy* (Cambridge: Cambridge University Press, 1984); Stephen Prickett, *England and the French Revolution* (Houndmills, Basingstoke: Macmillan, 1989). For

major studies on individual authors and the Revolution, see especially Nicholas Roe, *Wordsworth and Coleridge: The Radical Years* (Oxford: Oxford University Press, 1988); David Erdman, *Blake: Prophet Against Empire* (rev. ed.; Garden City: Anchor Books, 1969); David Duff, *Romance and Revolution: Shelley and the Politics of a Genre* (Cambridge: Cambridge University Press, 1994); Michael Scrivener, *Radical Shelley* (Princeton, N.J.: Princeton University Press, 1982).

17. The term is Ronald Paulson's, but the characterization is a common one (*Representations of Revolution,* 39). For cultural and political studies see: Ceri Crossley and Ian Small, eds., *The French Revolution and British Culture* (Oxford: Oxford University Press, 1989); H.T. Dickinson, ed., *Britain and the French Revolution, 1789–1815* (New York: St. Martin's Press, 1989).

18. Linda Colley, *Britons: Forging a Nation 1707–1837* (New Haven and London: Yale University Press, 1992).

19. Simon Bainbridge, *Napoleon and British Romanticism* (Cambridge: Cambridge University Press, 1995).

20. Seamus Deane identifies two distinct phases in British responses to the emigrants: "The first was marked by the view that the Revolution was a crusade against Christianity itself and that the émigrés, especially the clergy, were the direct victims of it. The second, less melodramatic, began to replace the first after the Peace of Amiens (1802); it was governed by the sensible conviction that the new Napoleonic France threatened the existence of England." In the second phase it was the constitutionalists, such as Staël, not the royalists, whom the British supported. Deane's cogent analysis does not consider the impact of gender on British nationalism, or on Staël's cosmopolitanism. See Seamus Deane, *The French Revolution and Enlightenment in England 1789–1832* (Cambridge: Harvard University Press, 1988), 23.

21. Gary Kelly, "Revolutionary and Romantic Feminism: Women, Writing, and Cultural Revolution," in *Revolution and English Romanticism,* ed. Keith Hanley and Raman Selden (Hemel Hempstead: Harvester Wheatsheaf, 1990), 107–30; *Revolutionary Feminism: The Mind and Career of Mary Wollstonecraft* (London, 1992).

22. Fanny Burney, *The Wanderer; or, Female Difficulties,* ed. Margaret Anne Doody, Robert Mack, and Peter Sabor (Oxford: Oxford University Press, 1991), 671.

23. Joan Landes, *Women and the Public Sphere in the French Revolution* (Ithaca: Cornell University Press, 1988); Lynn Hunt, *The Family Romance and the French Revolution* (Berkeley: University of California Press, 1992); Madelyn Gutwirth, *The Twilight of the Goddesses: Women and Representation in the French Revolutionary Era* (New Brunswick, N.J.: Rutgers University Press, 1992); Sara Meltzer and Leslie Rabine, eds. *Rebel Daughters: Women and the French Revolution.* Other major studies include

Dominique Godineau, *The Women of Paris and their French Revolution,* trans. Katherine Streip (Berkeley: University of California Press, 1998), Harriet Applewhite and Darlene Levy, eds. *Women and Politics in the Age of Democratic Revolution* (Ann Arbor: University of Michigan Press, 1990), and Shirley Elson Roessler, *Out of the Shadows: Women and Politics in the French Revolution, 1789–95* (New York: Peter Lang, 1996). On French women writers, see *Literate Women Writers and the French Revolution of 1789,* ed. Catherine Montfort (Birmingham, Alabama: Summa Publications, 1994).

24. Geoff Eley, "Nations, Publics, and Political Cultures; Placing Habermas in the Nineteenth Century, " and Nancy Fraser, "Rethinking the Public Sphere: A Contribution to the Critique of Actually Existing Democracy," in *Habermas and the Public Sphere,* ed. Craig Calhoun (Cambridge, Mass.: MIT Press, 1992), 289–349 and 109–42. See also Joan B. Landes, "The Public and the Private Sphere: A Feminist Reconsideration," *Feminism, the Public, and the Private,* ed. Joan B. Landes (Oxford and New York: Oxford University Press, 1998), 135–63.

25. Oskar Negt and Alexander Kluge, *Public Sphere and Experience: Toward an Analysis of the Bourgeois and Proletarian Public Sphere,* trans. Peter Labyani, James Oswen Daniel, and Assenka Oskiloff; foreword by Miriam Hansen (Minneapolis: University of Minnesota Press, 1993).

26. Leonore Davidoff, "Regarding Some 'Old Husbands' Tales: Public and Private in Feminist History," *Feminism, the Public and the Private,* ed. Joan B. Landes (Oxford: Oxford University Press, 1998), 164–94. Davidoff speaks of "multiple publics" rather than "counter-public" spheres.

27. Charlotte Smith, *Desmond,* ed. Antje Blank and Janet Todd (London: Pickering and Chatto, 1997), 6.

28. Having its roots in the outsider status of women in relation to bourgeois patriarchal institutions, this claim of non-partisanship bears comparison with the rejection of party politics attributed to the radical opposition of the 1790s and beyond by Kevin Gilmartin in *Print Politics: The Press and Radical Opposition in Early Nineteenth-Century England* (Cambridge: Cambridge University Press, 1992), 11–64. See also, Gilmartin, "Popular Radicalism and the Public Sphere," *Studies in Romanticism* 33.4 (Winter 1994): 549–58. This volume of *Studies in Romanticism* on "Romanticism and its Publics," contains excellent articles devoted to "publics and publicness" in Britain between 1780 and 1830. For a specific focus on British women poets and radical press politics, see Stephen C. Behrendt, "British Women Poets and the Reverberations of Radicalism in the 1790s," *Romanticism, Radicalism, and the Press.*

29. Mary Favret, *Romantic Correspondence: Women, Politics, and the Fiction of Letters* (Cambridge: Cambridge University Press, 1993), 18. See also Elizabeth Heckendorn Cook, *Epistolary Bodies: Gender and Genre in*

the *Eighteenth-Century Republic of Letters* (Stanford: Stanford University Press, 1996) and Deborah Heller, "Bluestocking Salons and the Public Sphere" *Eighteenth-Century Life* 22.2 (1998): 59–82.

30. William Godwin, *Memoirs of the Author of "A Vindication of The Rights of Woman"* ed. Richard Holmes (Harmondsworth: Penguin, 1987), 249.

31. Georg Lukács, *The Historical Novel,* trans. Hannah and Stanley Mitchell, intro. Frederic Jameson (Lincoln: University of Nebraska Press, 1983), 23.

32. Tilottama Rajan and Julia Wright, Introduction, *Romanticism, History, and the Possibilities of Genre,* ed. Rajan and Wright (Cambridge: Cambridge University Press, 1998), 10–11.

33. David Zaret, "Religion, Science, and Printing in the Public Spheres in Seventeenth-Century England," *Habermas and the Public Sphere,* 213.

34. Marge Piercy, *City of Darkness, City of Light* (New York: Fawcett Columbine, 1996), x.

35. On Robinson, see Sharon Setzer, "Romancing the Reign of Terror: Sexual Politics in Mary Robinson's *The Natural Daughter,*" *Criticism* 39.4 (Fall 1997): 531–55; Adriana Craciun, "Violence Against Difference: Mary Wollstonecraft and Mary Robinson," *Making History: Textuality and the Forms of Eighteenth-Century Culture,* ed. Greg Clingham (Bucknell: Bucknell University Press, 1998), 111–41; for new evidence regarding Robinson's radicalism see Craciun's essay on Charlotte Corday in *Rebellious Hearts.* An edition of *The Natural Daughter* edited by Setzer is forthcoming from Broadview Press.

36. Lucia Maria Licher, *Mein Leben in einer bleibenden Form aussprechen: Umrisse einer Ästhetik im Werk Karoline von Günderrodes (1780–1806)* (Heidelberg: Universitätsverlag C. Winter, 1995), 50. Maria Mies, "Die Französische Revolution findet für die Frauen nicht statt," *Frauen und die Französische Revolution,* ed. Helga Brandes (Wiesbaden, 1991). For a discussion of two novels about the French Revolution set in France and written by German women writers of the Romantic era, Therese Huber's *Die Familie Seldorf: Eine Erzählung aus der französischen Revolution* (1796) and Caroline de Fouqué's *Magie der Natur: Eine Revolutions-Geschichte* (1812), see Gerhart Hoffmeister "The French Revolution in the German Novel around 1800," *European Romantic Review* 2.2 (Winter 1992): 163–171.

Revolution and Nationalism

Blurring the Borders of Nation and Gender: Mary Wollstonecraft's Character (R)evolution

∽

Jan Wellington

> Real character is not one thing, but a thousand things; actual qualities do not conform to any factitious standard in the mind, but rest upon their own truth and nature.
>
> —William Hazlitt, "Of the Knowledge of Character"

> The clash of rival "characters" generates many narratives . . . .
>
> —David Oakleaf, "Marks, Stamps, and Representations"

"I went looking for my values the other day," intones a woman's voice, caring and sincere. Thus opens a public service spot airing on noncommercial television near the turn of the twenty-first century. The aim of this veritable ad campaign for virtue is to remind viewers that "character counts."[1] As this message reveals, what we tend to mean by *character* today is integrity or moral fibre, and the way we locate it is to look inside. Our understanding of what character is and where to find it may be traced to the eighteenth century, during which definitions proliferated and, according to recent commentators, conceptions of character underwent a shift from public to private. Originally conceived of as reputation or representation—what David Oakleaf terms a "publicly circulated sign" based on arbitrary factors such as birth or status—character increasingly came to denote identity or subjectivity.[2] As the epigraph above from William Hazlitt in 1822 suggests, the emphasis shifted from *what* one is said to be to *who* one really is. According to Oakleaf, this shift was the result of a discursive struggle for control of character that intensified in the century's second half; as he rightly observes, the struggle was political (298; 306–07).

This political struggle over character was played out on multiple levels and was part and parcel of the nation-building process in which England was engaged. Of particular interest to me is the discourse by which the English characterized themselves and their cross-channel rivals, the French, in the later eighteenth century, and especially during the French Revolution. During this half century, English patriots were involved in a struggle for national identity and integrity in which they pitted their nation's character against that of the French; one of the ways they conducted it was to devalue the French character by likening it to that of another group which public discourse on both sides of the Channel typically constructed as 'other' and, in the civic sense, lesser: women. As Linda Colley observes of the eighteenth century's last decades, "there was a sense at this time in which the British conceived of themselves as an essentially 'masculine' nation . . . caught up in an eternal rivalry with an essentially 'effeminate' France."[3]

One English citizen deeply concerned with representations of national and sexual identity was Mary Wollstonecraft, a woman whose ideas about character evolved and refined themselves in the crucible of the French Revolution. In this essay I explore the intersections between the two in several of her nonfiction works from the 1790s: *A Vindication of the Rights of Woman* (1792), "Letter Introductory to a Series of Letters on the Present Character of the French Nation" (1793), *An Historical and Moral View of the Origin and Progress of the French Revolution* (1794), and *Letters Written during a Short Residence in Sweden, Norway, and Denmark* (1796). Like her fellow English, Wollstonecraft often characterized the French, both implicitly and explicitly, as effeminate. I intend to show that, while the English, prior to and during the Revolution, often deployed gendered characterizations of the French in order to differentiate and disempower the national 'other,' Wollstonecraft, who seemed at times to engage in the same project, had something different in mind. Although she shared with her more nationalistic contemporaries a measure of the distaste they felt for a nation whose habits and manners were in many ways alien, her writing during the revolutionary years reveals an important difference. Swimming against the tide of nationalist propaganda, Wollstonecraft deployed unflattering characterizations as part of her attempt to recuperate character on multiple levels, in the process dismantling the barriers of nation and gender so many of her contemporaries labored to erect. Her arguments concerning nationality and gender feed and reinforce each other: France's struggle to throw off its effeminate character inspired her to urge women to do the same; her critique of sexual character shaped her opinions of the French, which her border-crossing experiences in Scandinavia forced her to revise. In each case her arguments hinge on a vision of character as a sociohistorical construct open to change.

Manly English, Effeminate French

The notion of character was crucial to the nation-building and consolidating process taking place in England in the eighteenth century's second half. Despite (or perhaps because of) their geographical, historical, and often literal kinship with the French, the English tended to define themselves in terms of opposition or counter-identity.[4] An outgrowth of intense economic competition and repeated military conflict, this propensity is especially pronounced in nationalist rhetoric from the mid-eighteenth century onward. Basically, this rhetoric depicted the English character as reserved (but impassioned), serious, deep, artless, original, and independent, in contrast with the French character which was seen as effusive, lighthearted, shallow, changeable, artful, and slavish.

These opposed clusters of national traits bear a striking resemblance to the prescriptive descriptions of male and female character used to construct and enforce gender roles at the time. Typically, men were characterized as rational, active, purposeful, and dominant, and women as emotional, trifling, passive, and submissive. English nationalist discourse in the century's last half makes a clear and persistent connection between Englishness and manliness, Frenchness and effeminacy, in effect allowing the discourses of nationalism and gender to "piggyback" and reinforce each other in a process of double-duty disempowerment. While there existed a long tradition of putting down the French, in its earlier years this discourse was not devoid of admiration; this is not surprising, considering the immense influence of French culture and manners on the upper orders and their imitators. By early 1793, however, public sentiment had taken a reactionary turn. As Revolution turned to Terror, the French were no longer perceived as models or imitators, but rather as murderous potential invaders. By 1797, France's absorption of its European neighbors and its threats to do the same to England had created an atmosphere of intense paranoia whose flames were fed by the government-backed press on both sides. In this atmosphere, public characterizations of the French were more than ever unflattering and clearly intended to erect firm psychic barriers between the threatened island nation and its enemies across the Channel. Indeed, a significant part of England's war against France was carried out on the front of character assassination. One way this was accomplished was to disallow the French the positive (masculine) characteristics of strength, bravery, honor, seriousness, and enterprise once allowed them by nationalist polemicists[5] and reserve them solely for the English. Stripped of these attributes, the French were likewise stripped of character.

Traveller William Hunter's observations typify late-century English representations of French character. In his *Travels through France, Turkey, and Hungary, to Vienna, in 1792,* Hunter, who visited France on the eve of the Terror, described the French character as "thoughtless, lively, and dissipated," notable for its wit, fickleness, and warm feeling: all qualities of superficial nature and in marked contrast to the soberness, prudence, and reflectiveness of the English.[6] The implicit gendering of these opposed sets of national traits is yet more marked in a statement that echoes the rhetoric of conservative gender polemicists, constructing males as rational and deep and females as emotional and shallow: the sociable French, observes Hunter, "are better calculated for the giddy flutter of the drawing-room, than the learned disquisitions of the closet" (I: 109). Although Hunter was far from flattering in his initial depiction of the French, in the 1798 second edition of *Travels* he felt the need to reassert the patriotism reactionary readers may have questioned. In its Preface he insists he is no friend of the alien, morally inferior French, whom he terms "enemies of the human race" (I: vii). Rallying readers around the English cause, he proclaims, "they cannot injure us, if we oppose them manfully" (I: x).

While the deployment of gendered national characterizations was only part of England's arsenal of representation, it was an important one. As theorist of nationalism Nira Yuval-Davis reminds us, "constructions of nationhood usually involve specific notions of both 'manhood' and 'womanhood.'"[7] Thus, there is a sense in which all demeaning representations of a national rival—especially when made by a nation that prides itself on its manliness and insistently equates patriotism with the need for a manly response to threat—can be conceived of as attempts to emasculate the national rival. Two English satiric prints or caricatures from the 1790s help illustrate the alienating agenda of English representations of the French, as well as the part gender potentially played in the process. The first, "The Contrast," by Thomas Rowlandson (Figure 1.1), dates from 1793 and contrasts English and French Liberty during the Terror.

Fig. 1.1. "The Contrast," by Thomas Rowlandson, 1793. © Copyright The British Museum.

In Rowlandson's caricature, we see a time-honored image of British liberty as a comely matron sitting by the shore of her prosperous island nation, adorned with the typical symbols of freedom and justice. In contrast, her French counterpart is depicted as a bloodthirsty, masculine gorgon trampling the bodies of Citizens s/he has slain. This image, a perversion of republican iconography undoubtedly influenced by Edmund Burke's unforgettable demonization of the Frenchwomen who participated in the Revolution's early stages, is meant to illustrate what happens when religion, law, and decency—not to mention gender roles—are abandoned to an ideal. And while it doesn't overtly depict the French character as effeminate, it suggests the evils that accrue to a nation whose women escape the domestic sphere—as many, under the promise of liberty and equality, did during the Revolution's early years—to meddle in affairs of state.[8]

James Gillray's caricature from 1799 (the year Napoleon ascended to first consul) presents yet another contrast, this one sarcastically depicting the outcome of the Revolution's remasculinization of French men (Figure 1.2). This image juxtaposes an effeminate *ancien régime* courtier, with his obsequious bow and "I am your humble servant," and a gentleman of the Republic. Outwardly manly with his republican dress and rather phallic staff, the latter invites his counterpart to "kiss my ass." Although these before-and-after images are at first glance diametric opposites, we must keep in mind an observation common among visitors to France during the 1790s: that, despite the massive alterations the Revolution had accomplished, the French character had *not* really changed, for while appearances may have altered, the French remained constant in their very fickleness. It is hard to ignore the homoerotic element in Gillray's print, which read as a whole suggests that the French, effeminate and virile alike, are homosexuals. To Gillray's English eyes, neither the simpering courtier nor his brutish republican counterpart is a "gentleman," and each is "equal" in representing a nation of questionable character—a perfect example of what has been called the "homogenizing rhetoric of anti-French propaganda."[9]

"A Strange Spirit of Contradiction"

Mary Wollstonecraft, who was born in 1761 and whose lifetime spanned the decades in which English nationalism came to fruition, made plentiful use of the gendered stereotypes and verbal caricatures that comprised its homogenizing rhetoric. She provides a striking

Fig. 1.2. "A French Gentleman of the Court of Louis XVIth; A French Gentleman of the Court of Egalité, 1799," James Gillray, 1799. © Copyright The British Museum.

equation of Frenchness, effeminacy, and lack of character when she writes that "a variety of causes have so effeminated reason, that the french may be considered as a nation of women."[10] She considers the French (in this case the Parisians, who played an instrumental role in the Revolution) as effeminate in the following ways: they are "[m]ore ingenious than profound in their researches; more tender than impassioned in their affections; prompt to act, yet soon weary; they seem to work only to escape from work, and to reflect merely how they shall avoid reflection" (*FR*, 121). Here again we see the self-negating weakness, shallowness, and lack of fortitude with which conservative polemicists of the day characterized women.

Wollstonecraft next accuses the French of evanescent, unenduring emotions: a "susceptibility of disposition" productive only of "transient gusts of feeling" that "prevent their forming those firm resolves of reason" (*FR*, 122) which, she consistently maintains, are the mark of strong character. As she notes sarcastically in the same work, the French, with their susceptibility to enervating gusts of emotion, are "an effeminate race of heroes" (*FR*, 213). Ironically disallowing the French real heroism, Wollstonecraft implies that an effeminate hero is *no* hero (or, just as bad in her book, a heroine). Like William Hunter, Wollstonecraft opposes effeminate French shallowness and manly English depth, observing that the French "have a singular fund of superficial knowledge, caught in the tumult of pleasure from the shallow stream of conversation . . . they never miss an opportunity of saying a pertinent thing, or tripping up, by a smart retort, the arguments with which they have not strength to fairly wrestle" (*FR*, 228). There are many other instances in the *French Revolution* in which Wollstonecraft derides the French for their effeminate lack of character, and reading the work in isolation, it is hard to escape the impression that she detests them. The truth, of course, is more complex: a compound of the disappointments made inevitable by both her idealism and her Englishness put into service of a rhetorical strategy common to her polemical works of the revolutionary decade.

It is important to recall that Wollstonecraft crossed the Channel favorably disposed towards the French. Her sympathy for and curiosity about the Revolution (in concert with the need to put her spurned love for painter Henry Fuseli behind her) spurred her in November 1792 to travel alone to France, where she resided throughout the Terror. This sympathy for the French, in fact, predated the Revolution. In March 1788, for instance, Wollstonecraft wrote to her sister Everina that she had long wanted to visit France.[11] In a February 1789 letter to friend George Blood she scolded a mutual acquaintance for criticizing the language "in which I am told the sweetest verses are written, and the people have still that simplicity of manners, I dote fondly on" (*CL,* 181). Yet upon her arrival in France, she found its reputed simplicity more complex than she had imagined and its sweetness not without taint.

From her early days in France, Wollstonecraft expressed equivocation about the French. Her letters reveal that, while impressed with their civility and cultivated manners, she was depressed by their preoccupation with surface—their propensity to "trifle their time away" like women did.[12] Although in this letter to her publisher Joseph Johnson, written little more than two months after her arrival, she could admire French gaiety and polish, in the long run they failed to compensate for the national lack of character that allowed the French to settle for selfish, sensual pursuits. Of such pursuits, she inquires, "what can render the heart so hard, or so effectually stifle every moral emotion, as the refinements of sensuality?" ("LI," 444). Paris, she writes, is the place where "the soul of Epicurus has long been at work to root out the simple emotions of the heart, which, being natural, are always moral. Rendered cold and artificial by the selfish enjoyments of the senses, which the government fostered, is it surprising that simplicity of manners, and singleness of heart, rarely appear, to recreate me with the wild odour of nature, so passing sweet?" ("LI," 445). It is hardly surprising that Paris lacked the "wild odour of nature" Wollstonecraft craved, but this is a point she either overlooked or chose, for the moment, to ignore.

In her correspondence she oftentimes associates France with all that is sweet, at the same time revealing how sweetness can be cloying to one not nurtured on it. To friend Ruth Barlow she wrote from Paris (also in February 1793), "I have a strange spirit of contradiction in me physically and morally, for though the air is pure I am not well, and the vivacity that should amuse me fatigue[s] me more than you can conceive. All the affection I have for the French is for the whole nation, and it seems to be a little honey spread over all the bread I eat in their land" (*CL,* 229–30). However, Wollstonecraft's affection for the nation in general is complicated by her particular experience. Missing her friends in England, unused to French manners and struggling to master the rapid-fire language, she is both pleased by and equivocal about French pleasantry. Her letter to Johnson likewise reveals this contradictory spirit: she refers to France as "a land flowing with milk and honey" ("LI," 444) but complains again about French vivacity, associating it with faulty morality, an ingredient that in effect soured the milk and made the French, despite their hospitableness and social ease, morally unpalatable. In addition to experiencing a moral distaste that verges on the aesthetic, Wollstonecraft was undoubtedly suffering from the shock of defamiliarization travellers inevitably experience on finding themselves in an alien place, especially one their native culture depicts as its antithesis. In short, she had imagined revolutionary France as a land of biblical promise, and her disappointment with the reality, intensified by culture shock, proved proportionate to her hopes.[13]

Tellingly, when Wollstonecraft left England to take a position as governess in the family of Irish aristocrats Lord and Lady Kingsborough in 1786, she had a similar reaction. Initially eager to visit Ireland and lavish in her praise of its national character, once separated from her intimates and exposed to the reality of the people and the place, she exchanged enthusiasm for dismay. In this instance, too, she fell ill shortly after her arrival, desperately missing her family and friends. To Everina she declared, "I am an exile—and in a new world"; of the "silly females" surrounding her (whom, like the French she would encounter later, she perceived as lacking sensibility), she wrote, "their boisterous spirits and unmeaning laughter exhausts [sic] me" (*CL,* 126). Perhaps, in fact, it was this set of chattering, shallow-minded female aristocrats with their trivial pursuits she recalled on encountering the French (and earlier envisioned when she drew her condemnatory sketch of the female character in *A Vindication of the Rights of Woman,* hopeful the Revolution would provide the much-needed seeds of improvement).

Although Wollstonecraft's "Letter Introductory" proved to be both introduction *and* conclusion to the series, her observations there served as a basis for those she would make and develop in later works. In this letter she observes that the French have been "emasculated by pleasure," writing to Johnson, "[e]ver on the wing, they are always sipping the sparkling joy on the brim of the cup, leaving satiety in the bottom for those who venture to drink deep. . . . They play before me like motes in a sunbeam, enjoying the passing ray; whilst an English head, searching for more solid happiness, loses, in the analysis of pleasure the volatile sweets of the moment" (443). Like so many English travellers upon first acquaintance with France, Wollstonecraft contrasts French superficiality and love of pleasure with English solidity and depth. And while her characterization exhibits grudging approval of the French ability to be happy (i.e., their sweetness), she equates them with morally undeveloped beings such as children or women. In fact, this passage hearkens back to her depiction (in the *Rights of Woman*) of the mass of women as flighty, childish and irrational. In particular, the image of the French as "motes in a sunbeam" is reminiscent of an earlier image of women as "ephemeron triflers"[14]—tiny, airborne insects that swarm for a day leaving no significant mark on their environment. In both instances the subject being addressed is the weak character of subjects of tyranny—their inability to develop either virtue or real happiness when kept in a state of ignorance disguised as innocence; in both she notes the "destructive fury" (*RW,* 49) that results. The connection is significant because it is the key to how Wollstonecraft's demeaning characterizations of the French depart from those of her English nationalist counterparts.

From Assassination to Resurrection

In the *Rights of Woman,* written before she travelled to France, Wollstonecraft is critical of both female and French character. In that work, of course, her argumentative strategy is to expose women's weakness in order to argue for their potential strength: to contrast their present situation with the future golden age for humanity that culminates her liberal teleology. This strategy is typical of the methodology of didactic literature and was not limited to advocates of women's rights: conservative writer Hannah More, in her 1799 *Strictures on the Modern System of Female Education,* also proceeds by exposing the defects of her sex. She explains that this "is not the office of an enemy. So to expose the weakness of the land as to suggest the necessity of internal improvement, and to point out the means of effectual defence, is not treachery, but patriotism."[15] Like Wollstonecraft, More exposes what the sex has become in order to reveal what it could be. The difference is that conservative writers in general emphasize the essential nature of sexual characteristics in order to justify women's subordinate position. Wollstonecraft, on the other hand, insists that women's weakness is a cultural construct, arguing that their feeble, vacillating characters—which she repeatedly describes as artificial or factitious—are a product of patriarchal institutions. She tells us, in the *Rights of Woman,* that, rather than attempting to extenuate women's faults, she intends "to prove them the natural consequences of their education and station in society. If so, it is reasonable to suppose that they will change their character, and correct their vices and follies, when they are allowed to be free in a physical, moral, and civil sense" (286). The constructed nature of character, with its concomitant potential for change, is a lynchpin of Wollstonecraft's political thought.

To make her point about women, she frequently embeds their situation within a larger sociopolitical context, comparing it alternately to that of French courtiers, soldiers, aristocrats in general—indeed, to all humans oppressed or limited by tyrannical systems. This embedding is clearly part of a democratizing project whose intent is to break down the barriers between classes and sexes by dismantling socially constructed forms of 'otherness' that impede civilization in its progress towards virtue. Wollstonecraft consistently and strenuously makes explicit the link between political and sexual oppression, repeatedly asserting that subjection to tyrants, be they husbands or monarchs, robs the oppressed of the education and independence essential to active virtue or manly morals—in other words, strength of character. She contests the "divine right of husbands and kings to oppress women" (*RW,* 78), maintaining that the "very constitution of civil governments" (*RW,* 96) creates in the sex an artificial, weak character, rendering them socially useless (*RW,* 53). As a result of this tyranny, she argues, women are either slaves or cunning petty despots who lack the mental development and independent spirit that create character.

A passage from the *French Revolution* concerning the Revolution's lapse into violence, which depicts the French in implicitly gendered terms, is worth quoting at length to show how Wollstonecraft's arguments about the constructedness of character and the evil that results from its lack work at the national level:

> The character of the french . . . had been so depraved by the inveterate despotism of ages, that even amidst the heroism which distinguished the taking of the Bastille, we are forced to see that suspicious temper, and that vain ambition of dazzling, which have generated all the succeeding follies and crimes. . . . This observation enforces the grand truth on mankind, that without morality there can be no great strength of understanding, or real dignity of conduct. The morals of the whole nation were destroyed by the manners formed by the government.—Pleasure had been pursued, to fill up the void of rational employment; and fraud combined with servility to debase the character;—so that, when they changed their system, liberty, as it was called, was only the acme of tyranny. (*FR,* 123)

Here, as in the *Rights of Woman,* Wollstonecraft expresses her conviction that humans kept in ignorance and deprived of the resources of reason will eventually react with excessive passion.

As for what has caused France's national effeminacy, and by implication, women's, no passage is so revealing as the one in which Wollstonecraft, pondering the causes and effects of French egotism, self-interest, and vanity, notes in them "that weak vacillation of opinion, which is incompatible with what we term character. Thus a frenchman, like most women, may be said to have no character distinguishable from that of the nation" (*FR*, 230). What she is getting at, of course, is that the French, in directing all their energies towards pleasing an absolute monarch, have no individuated identity; rather, their character is wholly subsumed in that of the King and the nation he embodies. Their situation as subjects in effect disallows them subjectivity.

Wollstonecraft is clearly thinking here of Alexander Pope's "Epistle to a Lady" (1735), in which he poetically illustrates the notion that "most women have no Characters at all." The gist of Pope's famous argument is that women's characteristics are so weakly marked and hopelessly shifty, they amount, in effect, to nonidentity. Wollstonecraft adverts to Pope's poem several times in the *Rights of Woman* and, like many of his female readers, recognizes his artistry while deeply wounded by the perceived injustice of his sentiments.[16] The reaction of another reader of Pope, twentieth century critic Ellen Pollack, sheds light on the nature of the injustice. She writes that

> Pope's text denies "character" to women in a more fundamental sense than even its own ironies would suggest. . . . [he] establishes an essentially unitary structure of sexual difference—an economy of gender in which woman is not other in an irreducible, but only in an appropriated sense. She is not a sign of a separate, autonomous otherness, is not a subject . . . but "his other," the *not man* that by opposition gives identity (gives "character") to man.[17]

Pollack notes of Pope's "Epistle" that even Martha Blount, the supposed exception to the "no character" rule, is defined by negation: her autonomous desire is effaced by the fact that "her pleasure has been elided with the imperatives of a masculine pleasure, because essentially her will is not her own" (469). This is the point Wollstonecraft makes in her statement that the French and most women have no character apart from that of the nation: as subjects lacking subjectivity, they are reduced to the trivial pursuit of pleasure incompatible with character.

In a section from the *Rights of Woman* addressing women's mis-
education, she argues a similar point. Making one of her frequent links
between women and the privileged, she remarks on the paucity of
greatness or achievement among the "superior ranks of life," attributing it to the "unnatural state" in which they are born (92): that is, a
state in which they are deprived of the stimuli that create character.
She continues:

> the human character has ever been formed by the employ-
> ments the individual, or class, pursues; and if the faculties
> are not sharpened by necessity, they must remain obtuse. The
> argument may fairly be extended to women; for, seldom occu-
> pied by serious business, the pursuit of pleasure gives that
> insignificancy to their character which renders the society of
> the *great* so insipid. The same want of firmness, produced by
> a similar cause, forces them both to fly from themselves to
> noisy pleasures, and artificial passions, till vanity takes place
> of every social affection, and the characteristics of humanity
> can scarcely be discerned. (*RW*, 92)

In each case, Wollstonecraft suggests, the socially determined lack of
opportunity to develop their intellects or their moral sentiments
makes women and the rich, paradoxically, both selfish and self*less*,
for in flying from themselves they fail to realize their human potential by acquiring "virtues which they may call their own" (*RW*, 92).
This is precisely the point she argues throughout the *French Revolution* with regard to the French, in effect patterning her argument
about the causes of the Revolution's excesses on the one she developed
in the *Rights of Woman*.

Wollstonecraft's several comments on Pope's "Epistle" in that
work support her central assumption that there is no innate character
difference between men and women, or no sex in souls. Both, she
believes, are capable of developing virtue, which comprises the positive or active qualities of reason, imagination, and fortitude rather
than the passive or negative qualities of "patience, docility, good-
humour, and flexibility" (*RW*, 101) traditionally allotted to women. She
is especially wounded by Pope's famous couplet characterizing women
as "matter too soft a lasting form to bear,/ And best distinguish'd by
black, brown, or fair" (*RW*, 279). Angry that Pope represents as essential and then mocks the nonentities he and male-dominated society
have created, she argues that, limited to mere physicality and deprived
of mental existence, women are necessarily, in character terms,

savages or ciphers. The sort of sexual distinctions perpetuated by the likes of Pope are, in short, "the foundation of the weakness of character ascribed to women" (*RW*, 100).

A passage that points towards Wollstonecraft's argument in the *French Revolution* about the destructive passion released by the Revolution demonstrates the absurdity of essentialist assumptions about sexual character:

> from the education, which they [women] receive from society, the love of pleasure may be said to govern them all; but does this prove that there is a sex in souls? It would be just as rational to declare that the courtiers in France, when a destructive system of despotism had formed their character, were not men, because liberty, virtue, and humanity were sacrificed to pleasure and vanity—fatal passions, which have ever domineered over the *whole* race. (*RW*, 104)

The mind-bending logic of this passage exemplifies the complex way Wollstonecraft deploys the language of gender in order to dismantle what Orrin Wang terms "the intrinsic identity of a gendered subject."[18] This aspect of her project has long been overshadowed by her emphasis on the term "manliness" and the rationality with which it is typically associated. Wollstonecraft herself made it clear that, when she urges women to become more manly (something she also requires of men), she is using the term in its inclusive sense, referring to "what is comprehensively termed mankind" (*RW*, 33). In the passage above, she forces the reader to perform a series of mental gender gyrations in order to arrive at her point: that the passions typically attributed to females (and thus "unsexing" when displayed by males) are characteristic of "the *whole* race," and that to sexualize such acculturated character traits is to deny their bearers the opportunity to become subjects in their own right, or fully human. Earlier in the same work she observed that women have been so artificially nurtured that "the characteristics of humanity can scarcely be discerned"; thus her insistence that "the sexual shall not destroy the human character" (*RW*, 92, 95). And what comprises the human character? Neither "masculine" reason nor "feminine" emotion, but both, accessible to each sex and necessary for the growth of virtue. As Susan Khin Zaw has persuasively argued, Wollstonecraft conceives of virtue as an outgrowth of the interplay between reason and feeling, neither of which is the innate property of a particular gender.[19] Wollstonecraft urged women to transcend the false, feminine character imposed on them by social institutions, calling on men, in turn, to abandon the licentious, unrestrained appetites of false masculinity. Clearly, her intention is to dismantle the barriers of constructed character in favor of the virtue (or character) that develops from within.

Whether the character in question belongs to man, woman, or nation, the dismantling process entails assassination for the sake of resurrection. Wollstonecraft's intensely negative sketch of the French character in the *French Revolution* is not only part of an intentional rhetorical strategy designed to show *why* the Revolution went wrong, it is also, despite her protestations of objectivity, a reflection of her intense disappointment at its failure, which she connects with the failure of the "liberated" French to attain the character that reason suggested their deliverance from tyranny would accomplish. And though the book deals only with the events that transpired during the Revolution's first six months, before she set foot in France, it is written through the lens of her later experience there: in particular, her failure to find that ideal amalgam of cultivation and naturalness, reason and virtuous passion, she epitomized as the acme of civilization. Like many first-hand observers, Wollstonecraft noted a disjunction between France's character and its political ideals, explaining that the French, because of the fickle, pleasure-loving character formed by *ancien régime* institutions, "were in some respects the most unqualified of any people in Europe to undertake the important work in which they are embarked" (*FR,* 230). In truth, as the passages I have quoted from her works written in France reveal, she found that the Revolution had *not* appreciably changed French manners or morals. The manliness the Revolution promised—and we must remember that for Wollstonecraft it entailed qualities both traditionally masculine and feminine—was yet to be realized. In her "Letter Introductory" to Johnson, written even before the height of the Terror, she admits, "everything whispers me that names, not principles, are changed," for "the turn of the tide has left the dregs of the old system to corrupt the new" (446). The "dregs" she speaks of are morals corrupted by voluptuousness and self-interest, now turned with a vengeance towards a selfish (and more pernicious because more widespread) passion for profit. Although she opines that "the good effects of the revolution will at last be felt" ("LI," 445), her pervasive tone is one of depression.

The *French Revolution* partakes of this critical view but ends on a hopeful note, Wollstonecraft reflecting that "[a] change of character cannot be so sudden as some sanguine calculators [and surely she was one of them] expect" (231). Recognizing that a sustained experience of liberty is needed to develop virtue, she predicts that when the changes the Revolution has brought about have had time to take effect, "the french will insensibly rise to a dignity of character far above that of the present race; and then the fruit of their liberty, ripening gradually, will have a relish not to be expected during it's crude and forced state" (*FR*, 231).[20] When Wollstonecraft crossed yet another national border in 1795, her own ideas about national character, and France's in particular, ripened.

"Snatching at Pleasure, and Throwing off Prejudices"

While living in France, Wollstonecraft became the lover of American adventurer Gilbert Imlay and bore his child. Eminently unsuited for domestic life, Imlay, in part to get the importunate Mary out of his hair, sent her to Scandinavia in 1795 to transact shipping business. Travelling with infant daughter Fanny and French nurse-maid Marguerite, she sent to Imlay the epistolary record of her travels that would be published the following year as *Letters Written during A Short Residence in Sweden, Norway, and Denmark*. Remarkable in many ways, these letters revealed to the public a side of Wollstonecraft they hadn't yet seen—vulnerable and full of sensibility—and were an instant hit.[21]

As Wollstonecraft travels through Sweden, Norway, and Denmark observing culture and manners, she naturally makes comparisons among the characters of the Scandinavians, the English, and the French, the upshot of which is a reevaluation (and revaluation) of the effeminate French character. What especially displeases Wollstonecraft about the Scandinavian middle classes is the same sort mindless prudence—that slavish observance of social forms—she found distasteful in Britain. She writes of the Swedes, "[s]o far indeed from entering immediately into your character, and making you feel instantly at your ease, like the well-bred french, their over-acted civility is a continual restraint on all your actions"; their politeness, "far from being the polish of a cultivated mind . . . consists merely of tiresome forms and ceremonies."[22] These are the same false, restrictive forms based on unthinking propriety that she consistently maintained were inconsistent with rational morality and especially restrictive to women. Now, however, in comparison with Scandinavian stiffness and decorum, the French ability to smooth social differences by "entering into" one's character begins to look more like the sensibility Wollstonecraft prizes: viewed in the light of mechanical Germanic decorum and materialistic pride, it begins to look something like the heart she denied the French in her letter to Johnson.

Further evidence of how Wollstonecraft's border-crossing experience in Scandinavia enabled her to revisit the French character occurs as she contrasts English and French observances of the Sabbath. She contends, "[t]he rest of labour ought to be gay; and the gladness I have felt in france on a sunday . . . which I caught from the faces around me, was a sentiment more truly religious than all the stupid stillness which the streets of London ever inspired where the sabbath is so decorously observed" (*LWS*, 287). While the adult Wollstonecraft never indulged in the brand of intense nationalism so many of her contemporaries did, her earlier letters reveal a fondness for England's charms—its domestic simplicity and common sense. "Exiled" to Ireland in the late 1780s, she constantly yearned for home. Always, though, her idealist's eyes remained open to her homeland's national flaws: in particular, that complacent devotion to decorum inconsistent with the rational, active pursuit of virtue.

Not only had Wollstonecraft's fondness for England cooled by the time she travelled beyond its borders, in her third year abroad she, in effect, rejected (at least for the moment) all identification with her homeland, referring to it in a private letter to Imlay shortly before her Scandinavian trip as "a country, that has not merely lost all charms for me, but for which I feel a repugnance that almost amounts to horror"; she is certainly thinking here of the cool reception she and her illegitimate daughter could expect on their return to a society that, she anticipated, would consider her its "prey" (*CL*, 280). In one of the few passages in the *French Revolution* sympathetic to the French, Wollstonecraft had observed that "in France, the women have not those factitious, supercilious manners, common to the english; and acting more freely, they have more decision of character, and even more generosity. . . . their coquetry is not only more agreeable, but more natural: and not left a prey to unsatisfied sensations, they were less romantic indeed than the english; yet many of them possessed delicacy of sentiment" (*FR*, 148). The suggestion is that not all French have been made hard-hearted (or weak of character) by their pursuit of pleasure and that "satisfied sensations" may, after all, be consistent with morality. This is a possibility she returns to in *Letters Written in Sweden*.

Significantly, it was in France that Wollstonecraft found satisfaction of her own sensations: her seduction (by an American) and the resultant burgeoning of her sexuality were surely assisted by the freer moral atmosphere there. In a sense, she was seduced by France: empowered by its moral liberty to plunge into a relationship in which physical passion, elevated above mere appetite by imagination, and sanctioned by reason, contributed to the synthesis of sentiment and principle she considered humanity's noblest expression. And though her sensations blinded her to the unworthiness of her partner, this passion-driven experience set the stage for a revaluation of the national character she had earlier disparaged.[23]

In the clarifying light of her own sexual experience (including the birth and nurturing of her daughter) and her observations in Sweden, Norway, and Denmark, Wollstonecraft is ready to rethink her alignment of the French character with all that is characterless in women. The hints at revaluation sprinkled throughout *Letters Written in Sweden* culminate, by her journey's end, in the admission that "I believe I should have been less severe in the remarks I have made on the vanity and depravity of the french, had I travelled towards the north before I visited France" (*LWS*, 326). The context of this passage is significant. Earlier in the same letter, Wollstonecraft described the freedom and intimacy allowed young Danish couples during the period of their engagement, which she refers to as "a kind of interregnum" between parental and spousal tyranny and "the only period of freedom and pleasure that the women enjoy" (326). Not only does she approve of the sexual intimacy these couples engage in, she sees it as conducive to character. Unlike the dull, mindless peccadilloes of their philandering elders, the innocent sensuality of the affianced, she suggests, is prompted by "an exuberance of life, which often fructifies the whole character when the vivacity of youthful spirits begins to subside into strength of mind" (326). Wollstonecraft makes a revealing mental transition when she moves from the virtuous sexual liberty of the Danish youth to the exuberance of the revolutionary French. She writes, "[w]e talk of the depravity of the french . . . yet where has more virtuous enthusiasm been displayed than during the last two years, by the common people of France, and in their armies? I am obliged sometimes to recollect the numberless instances which I have either witnessed, or heard well authenticated, to balance the account of horrours, alas! but too true" (326). What Wollstonecraft seems to have concluded since her 1793 "Letter Introductory" is that the voluptuousness she earlier portrayed as stifling the moral emotions is not necessarily one of the "gross vices" (*LWS*, 326) that contributed to the Revolution's horrors. Further, she has been forced to concede that the "simplicity of manners" she so values (and failed to find among the generality of French) is all too often allied with gross vice and ignorance (326). This recognition prompts her, in turn, to be more forgiving of effeminate French vanity and artifice.

The possibility that she had been overly severe in judging the French character occurred to Wollstonecraft in her letter to Johnson, but she did not pursue it ("LI," 445). Having become accustomed, however, to the national vivacity that initially exhausted her, and benefiting from a new, sexually mature perspective, she can now, in her Scandinavian letters, speak with wistful indulgence of nursemaid Marguerite's peculiarly French "arch, agreeable vanity," startlingly describing it as "happy thoughtlessness; aye, and enviable harmless vanity, which thus produced a *gaité du coeur* worth all my philosophy" (*LWS*, 334). In earlier letters Wollstonecraft clung with stubborn pride to her own melancholy character in the face of accusations that melancholy was unfeminine. Now, though, separated from the lover she knows she is losing, she revisions characteristic French sweetness—their determination to be happy in the face of adversity by indulging in impulsive freeplay, including the "depraved" sort—as strength that issues from the heart. The heightened appreciation for and understanding of happiness gained through her personal and political disappointments, filtered through her Scandinavian experience, would lead her to write to her new lover, William Godwin, in September 1796, "when I am happy myself, I am made up of milk and honey" (*CL*, 347). This suggests just how strongly she had come to identify with the French as a consequence of her physical and mental travels.

Wollstonecraft's experience in Scandinavia not only led her to revalue the French character, it also prompted her to analyze and critique the characterization process itself. Throughout *Letters Written in Sweden* we see her refining her ideas about how character is determined and represented, and how that representation can be used (or misused). An important part of her analysis involves the distinction she now makes between *types* of national character. Wollstonecraft observes that travel writers, "whose works have served as materials for the compilers of universal histories," are "eager to give a national character; which is rarely just, because they do not discriminate the natural from the acquired difference. The natural, I believe, on due consideration, will be found to consist merely in the degree of vivacity or thoughtfulness, pleasure, or pain, inspired by the climate" (*LWS*, 266). This difference in degree serves to explain the contrast between northern melancholy and southern lightheartedness observed by so many travellers and is no doubt what made Wollstonecraft, nurtured among the comparatively chilly, reserved English, fatigued by the vivacious French.[24] The notion that a nation's character is formed by physical causes such as climate and geography had become a commonplace by century's end despite the earlier objections of David Hume, who had attributed it to "moral" causes such as "the nature of government, the revolutions of public affairs, the plenty or penury in which the people live."[25] Wollstonecraft's take on the subject in *Letters Written in Sweden* departs from contemporary truisms about how national character is formed in that it accounts for both natural (physical) and moral (institutional) causes.

In contradistinction to natural character, she identifies acquired or institutional character, which accounts for the "varieties which the forms of government, including religion, produce"; this type of character, she observes, is responsible for differences which "are much more numerous and unstable" (*LWS*, 266) than those created by natural causes. This various, unstable difference is reminiscent of that Alexander Pope attributed to women in "Epistle to a Lady," provoking Wollstonecraft and a host of other women to complain that he had conflated the essential with the social in characterizing women as "chameleons" of "true No-meaning" (Lines 156, 114). These acquired traits are also the ones that Wollstonecraft, in her habitual analogizing process, earlier cited as the reason why the French, socialized into submission, had no character apart from that of the nation. In both cases she stresses the fact that such constructed characters are false or *un*natural. The distinction she now makes between natural and institutional characters is, perhaps, what has enabled her to overcome her distaste for French vivacity and levity and perceive the potential for character once obscured by irksome characteristics.

Continuing to make the distinctions that dismantle nationalism's homogenizing rhetoric (as well as her own), Wollstonecraft ponders the sort of sample population needed to come to a valid determination of national character. In her "Letter Introductory" she had unthinkingly represented the Parisians as exemplars of French character, much to the nation's detriment. By the time she travelled through Sweden in 1795, however, she had become "convinced, by repeated observation, that the manners of a people are best discriminated in the country. The inhabitants of the capital are all of the same genus; for the varieties in the species we must, therefore, search where the habitations of men are so separated as to allow the difference of climate to have its natural effect" (*LWS*, 259). Wollstonecraft suggests that the close cohabitation of people in cities is responsible for the misleading and unnatural sameness of manners that prompts observers to erroneously generalize about a nation's character rather than taking individuality and variety into account. Her language suggests not only that proximity creates unnatural sameness in populations, but that a certain separation of the objects of study is essential to accurate observation.

What is more, Wollstonecraft's next statement, which hearkens back to a point she made in "Letter Introductory," calls the accuracy of *any* observation of character into question. Of the difference among national characters she writes, "with this difference we are, perhaps, most forcibly struck at the first view, just as we form an estimate of the leading traits of a character at the first glance, of which intimacy afterwards makes us almost lose sight" (*LWS,* 259-60). Two years earlier she had written to Johnson, "[i]t is necessary perhaps for an observer of mankind, to guard as carefully the remembrance of the first impression made by a nation, as by a countenance; because we imperceptibly lose sight of the national character, when we become more intimate with individuals" ("LI," 443). At the same time she gives credence to the power of first impressions, Wollstonecraft's *perhapses* reveal reservations whose implications are radical. The revision of French character her Scandinavian experience has led her to make suggests what she suspected but neglected to mention early in 1793: that first impressions—particularly those that purport to encompass the character of an entire nation—can deceive.[26] They can do so not only because we may be looking in the wrong place, but because what we see when we look is necessarily tainted by preconceptions formed by our previous experience, including that of nationality. Further, her admission that intimacy with the individuals who comprise a nation in effect dissolves the character revealed at first glance calls the entire characterizing process into question by implying that, apart from degrees of superficial difference in manners, character does not exist in any absolute sense. To the extent it *can* be determined, it is merely a symptom of a nation's or group's position in history's continuum.

When Wollstonecraft complains in *Letters Written in Sweden* about Swedish boorishness, Danish sluggishness, Norwegian mercenariness, or the "English" stiffness their middle classes share, it may appear that she has simply exchanged one prejudice for others. But it is important to understand that her observations about character on all levels are couched in sociohistorical context, and that she views both individual and national character as dependent upon the state of a nation's institutions at a given historical moment and always on the verge of change. In early 1793 she made this point when she cautioned Joseph Johnson to keep in mind that, when she speaks harshly of France, that "land flowing with milk and honey . . . it is not the morals of a particular people that I would decry; for are we not all of the same stock? But I wish calmly to consider the stage of civilization in which I find the French, and, giving a sketch of their character, and unfolding the circumstances which have produced its identity, I shall endeavor to throw some light on the history of man" ("LI," 444). The point is that the "Present Character" Wollstonecraft sketches in this letter is only a relative one, for her idealist's vision is ever directed elsewhere: backward to that golden age of human perfection she knew was a myth, or forward to a time when the vulgar, apathetic, and materialistic may evolve into enlightened citizens such as those she had hoped to find in revolutionary France: humans who combine liberty and equality with cultivated, feeling manners. In the present of her travels, she continues to travel away from the monolithic conceptions of character that nationalist polemics demand and towards a future in which free, enlightened citizens transcend the limitations of gender and nationality to become citizens of the world.

Wollstonecraft sketches the mechanics of this ideal historical process when she speaks of the Norwegians, a people still in the early stages of enlightened civilization. She observes that "[t]hey love their country, but have not much public spirit. Their exertions are, generally speaking, only for their families; which I conceive will always be the case, till politics, becoming a subject of discussion, enlarges the heart by opening the understanding" (*LWS*, 274). In this quintessential illustration of her vision of the growth of virtue, Wollstonecraft depicts it as a process of enlargement in which the head and heart work in symbiosis, producing a sympathy that grows outward from family to nation. Her footnote to this passage makes it clear, though, that love for one's nation is but an intermediate step in humanity's progress toward a larger sympathy: an "enlarged humanity which extends to the whole human race" (*LWS*, 274). Tellingly, it is her observation of the Norwegians' support for the French Revolution that prompts these meditations. For Wollstonecraft, true public spirit is global, a product of the understanding we gain through science, art, and politics. As for what particular politics will create this sympathetic understanding, she writes, "[t]he french revolution will have this effect" (*LWS*, 274).

What is often obscured by the pronounced strain of disapproval in Wollstonecraft's characterizations is her hard-earned conviction that characterization can impede as well as promote sympathetic understanding. As if cognizant of her own tendency to make passionate generalizations, she recycles in *Letters Written in Sweden* her 1793 *caveat* to Johnson, reminding Imlay,

> Do not forget that, in my general observations, I do not
> pretend to sketch a national character; but merely to note the
> present state of morals and manners, as I trace the progress
> of the world's improvement. Because, during my residence in
> different countries, my principal object has been to take such
> a dispassionate view of men as will lead me to form a just idea
> of the nature of man. (*LWS*, 326)

Again, it is the essential unity of humanity she stresses—the notion
that "we are all of the same stock"—rather than the superficial differences which are merely symptoms of local conditions and ever prone
to change. The following passage, made possible by the enlarged
understanding her travels have afforded, is particularly revealing as
to why Wollstonecraft needs to have it both ways, sketching a character while insisting "this is not a character":

> Travellers who require that every nation should resemble
> their native country, had better stay home. It is, for example,
> absurd to blame a people for not having that degree of
> personal cleanliness and elegance of manners which only
> refinement of taste produces, and will produce every where in
> proportion as society attains a general polish. The most essen-
> tial service, I presume, that authors could render to society,
> would be to promote inquiry and discussion, instead of mak-
> ing those dogmatical assertions which only appear calculated
> to gird the human mind round with imaginary circles, like the
> paper globe which represents the one he inhabits. (*LWS*, 266)

Although prone to neglect her own tenets—either out of passion or
rhetorical necessity, or both—and make pronouncements that are
neither dispassionate nor objective, the Wollstonecraft who recollects
herself insists on situating character within a particular sociohistorical moment, emphasizing its fluid, unstable, and constructed nature.
Her striking simile in the passage above conveys her awareness that
the "dogmatical assertions" we make about character in our attempts
to understand the world we inhabit but never see whole are nothing
but constructs.

Just as the lines of latitude and longitude we draw help us
conceptualize our world and situate ourselves within it, she suggests,
they also circumscribe us. Furthermore, like these lines or the "paper
globe" itself, character is a sketch that dissolves on close inspection.
Wollstonecraft warns us that, like other constructs, hasty, irresponsible

characterization means limitation: that the substitution of restrictive, essentialist assumptions for the multiplicity of ideas which experience and inquiry produce makes us lazy and prejudiced. Read as a whole, her works suggest that the imaginary lines with which we inscribe our paper globe and the characters that inhabit it can become prison bars that control and oppress—that in effect "bastille" us. Whether it be the boundedness that oppresses women or the limitations that effeminize nations, she consistently fought the forces of laziness, complacency, and prejudice, advocating rigorous exercise of body, mind, and heart in her quest for the real-life experience that dissolves *characteristics,* replacing them with *character.*

Alan Liu has described the modern notion of nation as a "paradoxical-unity-in-difference": an apt description of a concept that derives its cohesive force by offering all citizens the illusion of inclusion while continuing to deprive its traditionally disenfranchised others of access to the political power that comprises civic existence, in effect "localizing" them in the same way Wollstonecraft believed tyrannical systems localize women and the rich.[27] Her solution was to imagine a community that recognizes, nurtures, and enfranchises the subjectivities of its historically effeminized citizens, allowing them the full range of experience their natural rights as humans entail. What is more, in the face of nationalism's imperative to localize on a grand scale, depriving neighbor nations of character, she clung to the Enlightenment universalism that helped her resurrect France's character potential and imagine a community not national, but global.[28] Sadly, two centuries later, despite our increasingly global economies and the high value our rhetoric places on character, we are still stymied by the psychic borders that Wollstonecraft labored, in her flawed, inconsistent, and very human manner, to dissolve.

Notes

1. Produced in 1996 for KNME TV, Albuquerque, on behalf of the Albuquerque Public Schools.

2. David Oakleaf, "Marks, Stamps, and Representations," *Studies in the Novel* 23.2 (1991): 299. Also see Deidre Lynch, who notes that, while earlier in the century character was envisioned as "a legible, consensual object," in the Romantic era it "became explicitly oriented to depth" (*The Economy of Character: Novels, Market Culture, and the Business of Inner Meaning* [Chicago: University of Chicago Press, 1998], 12). In the eighteenth century the term *character* was generally used with a qualifying phrase (for

example, "strength of character" or "dignity of character") to denote integrity or moral fibre.

3. Linda Colley, *Britons: Forging the Nation 1707–1837* (New Haven: Yale University Press, 1992), 252. During the Revolution, France's renovation of its political system included the attempt to renovate its national character. As J.P. Brissot, shaper and victim of the Revolution, put it in *New Travels in the United States, 1788* (trans. Mara Soceanu Vamos and Durand Echeverria, ed. Durand Echeverria [1791; Cambridge, Mass.: Belknap, 1961]), "the Revolution must change completely the character of the French and make them men in every sense of the word, or they will not long preserve their liberty" (22).

4. According to Gerald Newman in *The Rise of English Nationalism: A Cultural History, 1740–1830* (New York: St. Martin's, 1987), by the 1770s English nationalist writers shared "both a general state of consciousness and an increasingly comprehensive yet focused system of ideas" about English national identity (136). He maintains that, by the outbreak of the French Revolution, English nationality had become "an object of veneration and dogmatic assertion" (145). "It would perhaps be no exaggeration," he writes, "to say that a consciousness of France as England's military, commercial, and diplomatic enemy was one of the foundation stones of the national mind" (75). England's conception of France as its religious enemy was also an important factor.

5. For example, John Brown, in his 1758 *An Estimate of the Manners and Principles of the Times,* a treatise that is said to codify English nationalist sentiment at the time, writes that the paradoxical French are "effeminate, yet brave: insincere, yet honorable. . . . In Trifles serious, gay in Enterprize: Women at the Toilet, Heroes in the field" (cited in Newman, *Rise of English* 82–83).

6. William Hunter, *Travels through France, Turkey, and Hungary, to Vienna, in 1792 . . . in a Series of Letters to His Sister in England,* 3rd ed., vol 1 (London: J. White, 1803), 117, 109. In the Preface to the 1798 second edition of *Travels* (included in the third edition cited above), Hunter observes that "nationality [nationalism] may, in the phlegmatic notions of a frigid philosopher, be regarded as an imperfection"; nevertheless, he is convinced that a belief in the superiority of one's country is a source of "active virtue and manly exertion" (1: 110).

7. Nira Yuval-Davis, *Gender and Nation* (London: Sage, 1997), 1.

8. In *Reflections on the Revolution in France* (1790), Burke describes the Frenchwomen who escorted Louis XVI from Versailles to imprisonment in Paris as "furies of hell, in the abused shape of the vilest of women" (cited in Anne K. Mellor and Richard E. Matlak, *British Literature 1780–1830* [Ft. Worth: Harcourt Brace, 1996], 15). That these evils were not lost on French

Jacobins is made clear in a July 1793 article in the *Réportoire du tribunal révolutionnaire,* whose author wrote of Charlotte Corday, assassin of Jean-Paul Marat, "this woman absolutely threw herself out of her sex" by indulging in unnatural "pretensions to knowledge, wit, strength of character, the politics of nations" (cited in Madelyn Gutwirth, *Twilight of the Goddesses: Women and Representation in the French Revolutionary Era* [New Brunswick, N.J.: Rutgers University Press, 1992], 277).

9. Vivien Jones, "Women Writing Revolution: Narratives of History and Sexuality in Wollstonecraft and Williams," in *Beyond Romanticism: New Approaches to Texts and Contexts 1780–1832,* ed. Stephen Copley and John Whale (London: Routledge, 1992), 191.

10. Mary Wollstonecraft, *An Historical and Moral View of the Origin and Progress of the French Revolution,* in *The Works of Mary Wollstonecraft,* vol. 6, ed. Janet Todd and Marilyn Butler (London: William Pickering, 1989), 121; hereafter *FR.* See G.J. Barker-Benfield, "Mary Wollstonecraft: Eighteenth-Century Commonwealthwoman," in *Journal of the History of Ideas* 50.1 (1989): 95–115, for a discussion of how the Commonwealth philosophy of dissenting clergymen and political theorists James Burgh (1714–75) and Richard Price (1723–91) helped forge Wollstonecraft's linked rhetoric on gender and politics. See Claudia L. Johnson, *Equivocal Beings: Politics, Gender, and Sentimentality in the 1790's. Wollstonecraft, Radcliffe, Burney, Austen* (Chicago: University of Chicago Press, 1994) for Wollstonecraft's refinement of Commonwealth tradition for her feminist purposes.

11. Ralph M. Wardle, ed., *Collected Letters of Mary Wollstonecraft* (Ithaca, N.Y.: Cornell University Press, 1979), 172; hereafter *CL.*

12. Mary Wollstonecraft, "Letter Introductory to a Series of Letters on the Present Character of the French Nation," in Todd and Butler, ed., *Works of Mary Wollstonecraft* 6: 443; hereafter "LI."

13. In Exodus 3:8 Moses promises to deliver the Israelites from slavery and oppression "unto a land flowing with milk and honey." For Wollstonecraft, the Revolution promised the French a similar deliverance.

14. Mary Wollstonecraft, *A Vindication of the Rights of Woman,* ed. Charles W. Hagelman, Jr. (New York: Norton, 1967), 49; hereafter *RW.*

15. Hannah More, in Mellor and Matlak, *British Literature,* 220.

16. Alexander Pope, *Complete Poetical Works,* ed. Herbert Davis (Oxford: Oxford University Press, 1966). Pope, of course, considered inconsistency a hallmark of the human character but depicted women's characters as even more shifty and inconsistent than those of men. For women's attempts to "recharacterize" their sex in response to Pope, see poems by Anne Ingram and Anna Seward in Claudia Thomas, *Alexander Pope and His Eighteenth-Century Women Readers* (Carbondale: Southern Illinois University Press, 1994), 147, 218.

17. Ellen Pollack, "Pope and Sexual Difference: Women as Part and Counterpart in the 'Epistle to a Lady,'" *SEL* 24.3 (1984): 465.

18. Orrin N.C. Wang, "The Other Reasons: Female Alterity and Enlightenment Discourse in Mary Wollstonecraft's *A Vindication of the Rights of Woman*," *The Yale Journal of Criticism* 5.1 (1991): 134.

19. Susan Khin Zaw, "The Reasonable Heart: Mary Wollstonecraft's View of the Relation between Reason and Feeling in Morality, Moral Psychology, and Moral Development," *Hypatia* 13.1 (1998): 78–117. Both Zaw and Wang refute the critical tradition that depicts Wollstonecraft as imprisoned by Enlightenment dichotomies and the masculinist values they imply.

20. Earlier in the *French Revolution,* Wollstonecraft acknowledged the enormity of the change, writing that "every nation, deprived by the progress of its civilization of strength of character, in changing its government from absolute despotism to enlightened freedom, will, most probably, be plunged into anarchy, and have to struggle with various species of tyranny before it is able to consolidate it's liberty"; this, she believes, cannot be accomplished until a nation's manners and pastimes "are completely changed" (213).

21. Of this book Amelia Alderson (later Opie) wrote to Wollstonecraft, "[a]s soon as I read your Letters . . . the cold awe which the philosopher excited, was lost in the tender sympathy called forth by the woman. I saw nothing but the interesting creature of feeling and imagination" (cited in Claire Tomalin, *The Life and Death of Mary Wollstonecraft* [London: Weidenfield and Nicolson, 1974], 190). Wollstonecraft surely cultivated this persona as a woman of sensibility; it is important to clarify here that her Scandinavian letters were, from the beginning, intended for publication and that her actual personal correspondence with Imlay during the journey constituted a separate and distinct set of "private" texts. The quotation, "snatching at pleasure, and throwing off prejudices," that heads this section of my essay is from Wollstonecraft's private letter to Imlay of June 14, 1795. En route from France to Sweden, she revisited some of the scenes of her youth in England. In the passage quoted, she writes of how her intervening experience caused her to see the old in a new light (*CL,* 294).

22. Wollstonecraft, *Letters Written in Sweden,* in Todd and Butler, *Works* 6: 251; hereafter *LWS.*

23. Addressing the effect on Wollstonecraft of her politically and sexually progressive acquaintances in Paris, Claire Tomalin writes, "under the combined pressures of a different intellectual approach and the flagrant examples of so many of her friends, that severe and somewhat innocent lady was disappearing" (132). Wollstonecraft apparently began her affair with Imlay in the late summer of 1793; her subsequent letters to her lover suggest she has discovered (and revels in) the joys of the flesh, unlike the Wollstonecraft who was, to quote Claudia L. Johnson, "confessedly ill at ease

with the body" in the *Rights of Woman* (42). Discussing Wollstonecraft's novel *The Wrongs of Woman; or, Maria* (written in 1797), Johnson observes a new, positive attitude toward the female body and its capacity for sensuality (59). This new acceptance of voluptuousness, hinted at in the passage about French women and their "satisfied sensations" in the *French Revolution,* which was written during Wollstonecraft's pregnancy in 1794, becomes, as I will show, yet more apparent in *Letters Written in Sweden.* On September 13, 1796, Wollstonecraft would write to her new lover, William Godwin, "[w]hen the heart and reason accord there is no flying from voluptuous sensations, I find, do what a woman can—Can a philosopher do more?" (*CL,* 350).

24. Perhaps the best-known of these travellers was Germaine de Staël, who made the contrast between northern and southern characters a structural principle of works such as *On Literature* (1800) and *Corinne, or Italy* (1807). Like Wollstonecraft, de Staël believed a nation's institutions to be the key factor in forming its character.

25. David Hume, *Essays: Moral, Political, and Literary* (London: Oxford University Press, 1963), 203.

26. In a letter to her sister Everina not long after arriving in France, Wollstonecraft resisted making snap judgements about the French character, writing, "[o]f the french I will not speak till I know more of them" (*CL,* 226). Little more than a month later she contradicts herself in her letter to Johnson—a fact that suggests the inevitable constructedness of "first impressions," especially those intended for publication. One can't help suspecting that, after living among the French for a year and a half, Wollstonecraft had to "guard" her impressions especially well in order to fit them to her rhetorical purposes in the *French Revolution.*

27. Alan Liu, *Wordsworth: The Sense of History* (Stanford: Stanford University Press, 1989), 467. Also see Homi K. Bhabha's editor's introduction, "Narrating the Nation," in *Nation and Narration* ([London: Routledge, 1990] 1–7), in which he describes nationalism as "an idea whose cultural compulsion lies in the impossible unity of the nation as a symbolic force" (1). "The 'locality' of national culture," he writes, "is neither unified nor unitary in relation to itself, nor must it be seen simply as 'other' in relation to what is outside or beyond it" (4).

28. In *Imagined Communities: Reflections on the Origin and Spread of Nationalism* (London: Verso, 1991), Benedict Anderson defines the nation as "an imagined political community"; he notes that "communities are to be distinguished . . . by the style in which they are imagined" (6). Wollstonecraft's grand vision of a global community, which owes a debt to political mentor Richard Price and his vision of a "United States of the World" (Tomalin, *Life and Death,* 94), could likewise be considered an "impossible unity." It is, however, one that recognizes and resists the boundaries within and between nations that nationalism constructs.

Challenging Englishness:
Frances Burney's *The Wanderer*

∿

Maria Jerinic

> Such, therefore,—if any such there be,—who expect to find
> here materials for political controversy; or fresh food for
> national animosity; must turn elsewhere their disappointed
> eyes: for here, they will simply meet, what the Authour has
> thrice sought to present to them already, a composition upon
> general life, manners, and characters; without any species of
> personality, either in the form of foreign influence, or of
> national partiality.
>
> —Frances Burney, *The Wanderer* (4).

In the above quotation drawn from the prefatory address to
Doctor Burney, Frances Burney announces her intention to present
her fourth and last novel, *The Wanderer; Or, Female Difficulties,*
(1814)[1], as a politically neutral novel, one which refuses to participate in any of the self-congratulatory national sentiment of 1814,
the year of the first defeat of Napoleon. Such a project, however, was
not popular among the members of her contemporary audience.
After having experienced virtually twenty years of war with France,
Burney's English readers, as Rose Marie Cutting points out,
believed that a novel published at the end of this martial period
would and should "unmask the sins of French society."[2] Not only did
Burney disappoint these expectations by refusing to condemn the
French and to celebrate the English, her refusal actually contradicts her avowed desire to remain neutral and to separate herself
and her work from "political controversy." In *The Wanderer*, Burney
does not merely provide a study of "general life"; rather she delivers

63

a stinging critique of that component of English society which relies on a sense of "essential Englishness" in order to derive a sense of national superiority.

In this essay, I will look closely at the fabric of Burney's critique in order to demonstrate how she destabilizes the notion of an "essential Englishness" which is fundamentally different from an "essential Frenchness." Burney's attack on nationalist sentiment in *The Wanderer* has been well documented and examined by Margaret Doody, Karen R. Lawrence, and Claudia L. Johnson.[3] Building on this previous scholarship, I will here examine the way in which Burney treats three characteristics that many of the English at the end of the eighteenth century and the beginning of the nineteenth employed to define themselves in opposition to France: a respect for liberty, a belief in Protestant Christianity, and the practice of companionate marriage. While a celebration of these characteristics as essentially English was not confined to this historical period, the conviction of many of the English that they were unique in their possession of these characteristics helped to reassure them in the 1790s that a revolution would never erupt on their own soil, and it also helped them to understand why their nation, after years of war, was victorious in 1814.

The "construction of a French 'Other'" played a crucial role in forging English identity.[4] Consequently, "[e]ighteenth century Britons" as Linda Colley argues, "regularly defined themselves in opposition to what they saw as being French characteristics and manners" (250).[5] The French were seen as inferior, and the French government, be it a part of the ill-fated monarchy or the new Republic, was repeatedly represented in England as a despotic and tyrannical one. While the English considered themselves "naturally fitted to liberty," the "frivolity, instability, and immorality" of the French allowed them to be controlled and suppressed.[6] This stereotype permeates the "The Good Old Times" which appeared in the 13 June 1814, edition of *The Morning Chronicle*:

> 'Tis past—War drops his crimson lance;
>   The BOURBONS mount the Throne,
> And re-assume their Spain and France,
>   To rule by Love alone,
> Resolv'd to prove that France and Spain
>   Have better'd their condition,
> One bids the *Slave Trade* thrive again,
>   And one the *Inquisition*.[7]

Stella Cottrell argues that the English had for so long defined the French in terms of their "royal absolutism" that not even the downfall of the French monarchy could alter this English conception (265). While many of the English saw their own country as the land of liberty, France was depicted, as in the above poem, as no better than it ever was. France, whether under Napoleon or under the Bourbons, was seen as virtually the same tyrannical nation which perpetuated the same oppressive principles. According to this line of argument, France learned nothing from its trials.

Burney, in *The Wanderer,* challenges this sense of English national superiority by narrating the adventures of an English woman, Juliet, who journeys to England to escape the ravages of the French Revolution. Once in England, however, Juliet cannot attain liberty, her Protestantism does not afford her any special privileges, nor does she benefit from companionate marriage. Burney thus demonstrates that her heroine does not in any way benefit from her English identity or her existence on English soil. She is no better off in England than she was in France. For the most part, neither the English nor the French in the novel respect liberty, adhere to their faiths by offering Christian charity to the desolate, or enjoy companionate marriage. Consequently, within her novel, Burney collapses the national distinctions between the English and French, and in doing so, she disintegrates the very foundation of an English sense of distinctiveness and superiority.

By demonstrating that neither nation can lay sole claim to liberty, Christian charity, or companionate marriage, Burney's discourse encourages the inhabitants of both nations to develop the desire to attain them. Burney conveys the sense that the French are just as capable of respecting liberty as the English are, and while they may not choose to convert to Protestantism, Burney suggests that French Roman Catholicism may not be so very different from the "rational" Christianity which the English advocate. Finally, Burney demonstrates that citizens of both countries would benefit from companionate marriage, a type of marriage that, interestingly, no couple in her novel is quite capable of creating. Thus, instead of presenting a national novel which preserves an essential "Englishness" reigning over essential French inferiority, Burney offers her English audience a work which calls for an understanding of English and French identities as emerging from a common respect for liberty, a belief in Christian principles, and a desire for companionate marriage.

Burney began this novel in the late 1790s and then spent roughly the ten years of the war in France (1802–12) developing this work.[8]

Doody argues that if Burney had published this work "between 1798 and 1800," it would have found a better reception because "it would have fitted in with contemporary fictional debate" (*FB,* 332). *The Wanderer* is really a novel of the 1790s: "It belongs to a new genre of that decade, the English novel set during the French Revolution, in which characters are in various ways affected by historical events, trends, and ideas" (*FB,* 318).[9] But by the time *The Wanderer* was actually published, as stated above, the reading audience was more interested in celebrating the defeat of Napoleon and the inferiority of the French.[10] Consequently, Burney's transnational theme and ensuing critique of English society was not a popular message in 1814, and Burney's reading public let her know this. While the 28 March 1814, publication of this novel had been highly anticipated—for Burney had been a fantastically popular author in the late eighteenth century—interest in her novel dissipated once the initial copies sold out.[11] Furthermore, Burney and her work were violently attacked by reviewers such as John Wilson Croker and William Hazlitt. Croker, ostensibly, critiques the novel's lack of "vigour" and "originality" in his 1814 review, while Hazlitt, in 1815, observes that Burney, in this novel, did not use her sole skill as a novelist, her power of "immediate observation," to its fullest advantage.[12] These aesthetic comments, however, are only part of the critique.

As Doody points out, this novel "was more than unsatisfactory—it was an affront, especially to public guardians of the Right, like John Wilson Croker of the *Quarterly*" (*FB,* 333). Croker, in his review, articulates this conservative disgust, in part, by expressing his astonishment that Burney not only neglects to condemn Napoleon directly, but she actually speaks positively of the years she spent in France under Napoleon's rule. He dismisses these comments as evidence of Burney's self-serving attempts to ingratiate herself with the French authorities: "Madame D'Arblay might have been silent; but she ought not, as an Englishwoman, as a writer, to have debased herself to the little annotatory flatteries of the scourge of the human race" (130). For, in Croker's opinion, not only have Burney's years in France misplaced her allegiances, but they have "given Madame D'Arblay a very novel and surprising view of the state of religion, manners, and society in England" (128). Croker's argument reveals his opinion that, realistically, such female suffering could not happen on English land, an opinion apparently shared by the more politically liberal Hazlitt, who, in mocking the trials of *The Wanderer's* Juliet, claims that the "Female Difficulties" identified in the novel's subtitle "are difficulties created out of nothing" (337).

Yet a close reading of the novel contests this label of "nothing." *The Wanderer* opens with its English heroine Juliet Granville quite literally pleading for her liberty.[13] Disguised as a black Catholic maid, she begs for passage on a French ship carrying a group of English men and women who are fleeing to England to escape the wrath of the French Revolution.[14] While many of these English passengers view her plea for help as a dangerous imposition, an old Admiral sincerely offers her comfort and his promise of sanctuary in England: "An unprotected female, provided she's of a good behavior, has always a claim to a man's care, whether she be born amongst our friends or our foes. I should be ashamed to be an Englishman, if I held it my duty to think narrower than that" (22–23). Furthermore, he chastises his fellow English traveling companions who would leave her behind: "A woman, a child, and a fallen enemy, are three persons that every true Briton should scorn to misuse" (12). The behavior, however, that Juliet encounters on the ship and then upon her arrival in England, contradicts the Admiral's promises. With a few noble exceptions, she is insulted by all the "Briton[s]" she encounters. It is not clear whether she is freer in England than she would have been France. Her apparent racial identity, religious orientation, and class position earn her the scorn and derision of the remaining passengers. And although by the fourth chapter she sheds her disguise, revealing that she is not black, or Roman Catholic, or a maid, but a very educated Englishwoman, the English community within which Juliet attempts to subsist treats her with great suspicion and hostility. Yet this cruel treatment is particularly misplaced because Juliet is a patriot. She is proudly and gratefully English. Upon arriving in England, Juliet is "the first to touch the land, where, with a fervour that seemed resistless, she rapturously ejaculated, 'Heaven, Heaven be praised!'" (22). Even while she bemoans the fate of women and their lack of opportunities to support and protect themselves, she never condemns the English. Instead, in response to her own shock at the Admiral's generosity, she admonishes herself, "'Fie upon me! . . . to be in England and surprised at generosity'" (23).

The English, however, rarely live up to Juliet's good opinion. Despite the respect she holds for her country and its promise of freedom, Juliet suffers in her native land to such an extent that she eventually feels as if she is no better off than a "helpless foreigner" (214). This is largely because she is denied, in Lawrence's words, "access to the props of English patriarchal civilization while forced to live in its midst" (55–56).[15] Consequently, to claim her English identity is not enough for her countrymen and -women, who want to know her family name, her patriarchal connection. Yet she cannot reveal her family name, Granville, in part, because she is running from a cruel French husband, and because her English family resists acknowledging her existence, mistakenly believing that she is illegitimate. Consequently, Juliet is treated as an outcast, a corruptive influence, a most "eminent danger" of whom Lord Denmeath would like quickly to rid England so that her company does not taint Lady Aurora and Lord Melbury, flowers of the English nobility (209–10). Juliet only finds a semblance of peace when her English family finally accepts her and recognizes her as a Granville, thus reestablishing her connection to the English patriarchal system.

The England Juliet encounters, however, challenges the England imagined by popular nationalist sentiment. While England may not always have been blameless, it is the country, according to the *Edinburgh Review,* which "may claim the proud distinction of having kept alive the sacred flame of liberty and the spirit of national independence, when the chill of general apprehension, and the rushing whirlwind of conquest, had apparently extinguished them for ever, in the other nations of the earth."[16] England is the land of liberties, the guardian of "independence." Richard Price reinforces this notion in his speech "A Discourse on the Love of Our Country" (1789), which commemorated the English 1688 "Revolution."[17] He identifies liberty as one of the three "chief blessings of human nature," the others being Truth and Virtue (11). Price defines liberty as "inseparable from knowledge and virtue. . . . An enlightened and virtuous country must be a free country. It cannot suffer invasions of its rights, or bend to tyrants" (19). Similarly, Edmund Burke, in his *Reflections on the Revolution in France* (1789–90), claims that England, in particular, is the land of inherited liberties:[18] because of this tradition, "our liberty becomes a noble freedom. It carries an imposing and majestic aspect. It has a pedigree and illustrating ancestors" (30).

Many of Juliet's difficulties result from the fact that she has no access to this tradition. She left France running from the threat of actual imprisonment, yet she finds little succor in England. Endangered in France, abused in Britain, Juliet cannot find freedom or liberty in either country. Cutting argues that Juliet is in "economic" as well as "social bondage."[19] She is not able or allowed to support herself, she is unable to protect herself from a barrage of social stabs and indignities to which the English community—among whom she lives—subject her. Her subjection, her bondage is largely responsible for the fact that she "is deemed appropriate prey for any men—even those who are humane in all respects but sexual conquests" ("Defiant,"

529). Her body is never free from the potential of sexual assault as Juliet goes to great lengths to avoid the unwanted sexual advances of English men. She narrowly manages to avoid assault by two farm boys, and she is not even safe from the sexual interest of her half-brother, Lord Melbury, who propositions her while still unaware of her identity. The men of England, in this novel, are irresponsibly unaware of their own sexual misconduct. This lack of awareness is highlighted by the words of one of the novel's minor characters, Mr. Scope, who condemns the "morals" of Revolutionary France: "'A man's wife and daughters belong to any man who has a taste to them, as I am informed. Nothing is very strict. Mr. Robertspierre, as I am told, is not very exact in his dealings'" (79). Juliet's very experience challenges the sense of national superiority promoted by these sentiments. While it may be true that women in France are subject to unwanted sexual attention, certainly women in England suffer similarly. If Juliet is the "everywoman" that Cutting argues her to be, what possibility is there for the freedom of other women, in England or France ("Defiant," 528; "Wreath," 50)?[20]

Yet despite Burney's almost relentless cataloging of Juliet's sufferings, Hazlitt and Croker still feel that they are justified in their dismissal of her "difficulties." Colley provides a historical context which helps to explain why. British response to the French Revolution, particularly reactions to the fate of Marie Antoinette, focused, in part, on the dangers to which the Revolution exposed French women (256).[21] In response, the English could reassure themselves that they protected their women. In this light, it is conceivable why Burney's depiction of female suffering in England would have touched such a nerve; it eroded a conception of Englishness forged over years of war.

And why, according to the English, were French women subjected to such violence? Colley points out that many British "conservatives" saw the outbreak of revolution in France as "a grim demonstration of the dangers that ensued when women were allowed to stray outside their proper sphere:" "In Great Britain, woman was subordinate and confined. But at least she was also safe" (252, 256). This belief assured many of the English of their national superiority: "[t]he idealized position of women was a central theme in nationalistic claims to English superiority advanced by radicals and conservatives alike."[22] Ensconced in this "subordinate" protected position, English women provided a model of femininity for French women. According to one *Times* columnist, the latter group's failure to follow this model contributed to the violence which shrouded the events in

France: "[h]ad the Queen of France made the conduct of the Queen of England her model—the Revolution of France would have slept perhaps for another century."[23] Perhaps French women could not have prevented the Revolution. Their behavior, however, certainly hastened its arrival, and they suffered the consequences.

While strains of English nationalist sentiment positioned English women as models for the French, many Britons also feared that French women could influence English women. It was "common," according to Colley, "even before 1789" for the English "to invoke the supposed behavior of Frenchwomen as exemplifying what must at all costs be avoided in Britain" (250–51). Colley's argument identifies an anxiety surrounding the behavior of English women; English women could be too easily swayed to behave like the French, and perhaps enjoy "an unnatural prominence" as French women did, supposedly, before the Revolution.[24] The Reverend Richard Polwhele in his poem "The Unsex'd Females" (1798) links the corruption of English women to a sympathy with French ideals. Polwhele worries that English women, particularly those who advocate "Democracy," are becoming too much like French women: "The female advocates of Democracy in this country, though they have had no opportunity of imitating the French ladies, in their atrocious acts of cruelty; have yet assumed a stern serenity in the contemplation of those savage excesses."[25] French women are presented as more savage and immoral than English women, but Polwhele argues that the difference between the two is diminishing quickly. English women have simply not had "the opportunity" to behave in a similar fashion. The implication that follows suggests that if English women were to find the chance to abandon their proper English behavior, they too would be responsible for national chaos and disorder. Since, as Colley argues, Britons saw theirs as primarily a "'masculine' culture" (252), femininity, regardless of its nationality, was often linked, as in Polwhele's poem, to the chaos of rebellion. Thus the safety of both countries relied, in part, on the restrained behavior of their women.

Largely as a result of this thinking, English women found themselves in the interesting position of living in a country that celebrated freedom and liberty while denying them to its female inhabitants. Mary Astell addressed this hypocrisy almost a century before Price railed against tyrannical governments and celebrated English freedoms: "[i]f all men are born free, how is it that all women are born slaves?"[26] Burney poses a similar question in this novel. Her argument, as Doody points out, echoes familiar complaints of other women writers in the 1790s.[27] Mary Hays—in her *Appeal to the Men of Great*

Britain in Behalf of Women (1798)—addresses the tyranny in the home when the father and/or husband is the despot. Britain is "the favorite abode of liberty" and to be British is to crave liberty, but British women are not entitled to this privilege. According to Hays, British women are "chained and blindfolded . . . with respect to their own rights" (104). They are not allowed to vote; married women cannot hold their own property. Consequently, they are the "slaves of men," British men (127).[28] How then can Britain be the land of liberty?

A similar critique can be found in the pages of Ann Radcliffe's gothic romances.[29] Late twentieth century feminist criticism has demonstrated how Radcliffe's work provides a critique of the British domestic space.[30] Radcliffean Gothic, however, provides the heroine with a vehicle to attain her liberty: wandering. Kate Ellis identifies wandering as an act that allows Radcliffe's heroines to define themselves in opposition to debauched aristocratic male characters. By wandering, heroines, as well as positive male characters, may appreciate nature (a function of middle-class sensibility, which separates the heroines from villainous aristocrats).[31] Wandering also allows the Radcliffean heroine "to get away from what she does not want" (*CC,* 105); she can escape the tyrannical grasp of her insidious guardians or the suspect attentions of unwanted lovers. Wandering is also of particular importance because it signifies the heroine's desire to gain liberty, both physical freedom and the freedom to marry the man of her choice.

In Burney's novel, however, wandering does not provide Juliet with liberty;[32] instead, as Lawrence points out, "[f]emale wandering as represented by Burney is a narrow lot" (69).[33] While in Radcliffe's novels, wandering is integral to the power and success of her heroines, for Burney, Juliet's status as a "Wanderer" is a problem, as the novel's subtitle, *Female Difficulties,* suggests. In her quest to secure for herself some means of support and personal safety, Juliet must repeatedly "renew her melancholy wanderings" (527). However, while she runs from the ever-present threat of economic and sexual exploitation, her wanderings only intensify her vulnerability. While Juliet wanders through the English countryside, she has a difficult time finding shelter or food. Furthermore, she is constantly a target for unwanted male advances: ". . . she had severely experienced how little fitted to the female character, to female safety, and female propriety, was this hazardous plan of lonely wandering" (671). So pressing are these threats, that unlike Radcliffe's heroines, Juliet is unable to enjoy the beauties of nature which surround her: "The terrified

eagerness with which Juliet sought personal security, made her enter
the New Forest as unmoved by its beauties, as unobservant of its
prospects, as the 'Dull Incurious,' who pursue their course but to gain
the place of their destination" (674). The narrative voice in this
passage clearly privileges a Radcliffean appreciation of natural
beauty, but it also clarifies that Juliet, a woman forced to wander
through England, does not have the luxury to enjoy nature. At one
point in the novel, lulled by a false sense of security, she does stop for
just this purpose: "Here, for the first time, she ceased to sigh for social
intercourse: she had no void, no want; her mind was sufficient to
itself; Nature, Reflection, and Heaven seemed her own!" (676). But
her reverie is immediately interrupted by the attentions of two men
who mistake her for a woman with a "light" reputation (677). She is
again forced to fly, to wander to protect herself. These experiences
leave Juliet with the conviction that a woman is only safe in a domestic environment: "Alas! she cried, is it only under the domestic roof,—
that roof to me denied!—that woman can know safety, respect, and
honour?" (666). Yet, as the narrative of this novel demonstrates, she is
often not safe in this environment either.

Throughout her travels, the only man that Juliet can fully trust
is a Roman Catholic Bishop. His kindness presents him as a model of
male behavior. The Bishop's concern and affection for Juliet is disinterested on a personal and religious level. Having served as her
guardian while Juliet grew up in France, his attentions to her are
those of a kind father. Juliet, in turn, refers to him as her "first, best,
and nearly only friend" (615). The Bishop and Gabrielle, whom Juliet
met during her school years in a convent, are her closest and most
trustworthy companions. These two Roman Catholics love her and
protect her without violating her Protestant belief system or her
English identity. Neither the Bishop nor Gabrielle ever attempts to
convert her to Roman Catholicism. In fact, they both wish to help
Juliet re-discover her Englishness by reestablishing her ties with her
English family in England. Juliet returns this respect. At the end of
the novel, although remaining "firmly a Protestant," Juliet reminds
Lord Denmeath that Catholics are still Christians (615–16).

Burney's novel does not argue for the superiority of English
Protestantism over French Catholicism; instead, it presents the latter
group as comprised of the more sincere practitioners. Juliet is a devout
Protestant, and once in England, she attends church regularly. Her
prayers of thanksgiving for her escape from France, however, are
instantly perceived by the other English passengers as Roman
Catholic and thus detestable. But this apparent Roman Catholicism is

admired by the sympathetic Admiral who, while they all sail away safely from France, chastises his fellow English passengers: "To think that we should all get out of that loathsome captivity, with so little reverence, that not one amongst us should have fallen upon his knees, to give thanks, except just this poor outlandish gentlewoman; whose good example I recommend it to us all now to follow" (14). These admonishments fall on unsympathetic ears. Juliet's Protestant piety, which should identify her as an English subject, is misread, and thus Burney implies that the English cannot claim religious superiority over the French because they themselves have no convictions. They cannot even recognize practitioners of their own faith.

Yet a Protestant ideology had been a crucial component of England's process of self-definition since Henry VIII's break with Rome. While the rest of Europe was largely Roman Catholic, England officially was not, and its own state church became an important unifying element in Britain. Liah Greenfeld argues that Protestantism in England "facilitated and spurred" the "growth" of an "English national consciousness."[34] Colley points to the 1707 Act of Union, which joined Scotland to England and Wales, as the moment which defined Britain as one united kingdom "with one Protestant ruler, one legislature and one system of free trade" (11). Protestantism unified these three countries "[a]t odds in so much of their culture and secular history" (18).[35] Through Protestantism, Britain could distinguish itself from the rest of the world as a country with the king (or queen), and not the foreign Pope, at the head of the Church.[36] Consequently, an important and pervasive element of this English religious identity was an anti-Roman Catholic, or anti-papist sentiment that permeated England throughout the eighteenth century and well into the nineteenth (Colley, 22, 36).[37]

Juliet's relationship with the Bishop seems to be an extension of Burney's own feelings about the French Roman Catholic clergy. Burney, in her private correspondence as well as her public writings, reveals that she does not support an aggressive Protestant ideology or a sense of Protestant superiority. In a letter dated September 1792, Burney mocks the anti-Roman Catholicism of her neighbors, who hesitated in renting a house to newly arrived French émigrés because of "the Christian-like supposition that, being nothing but French papishes, they would never pay" (307).[38] While she does not condemn her own faith, she does not privilege it either. Rather, she suggests that to treat Roman Catholics with disdain is "unchristian," and thus an English man or woman must treat Roman Catholics with respect in order to serve his or her Protestant faith properly.

Her attitude might be better understood if one considers her 1793 pamphlet *Brief Reflexions Relative to the Emigrant French Clergy Earnestly Submitted to the Humane Consideration of the Ladies of Great Britain,* written in order to solicit charity for the sake of the French clergy exiled from France.[39] Many of these priests sought sanctuary in Britain, yet, unable to support themselves, they were reduced to poverty and succumbed to starvation. While in *Brief Reflexions,* Burney condemns the "lawless iniquity" and the "tyrannic sway" of "the sanguinary despots of the Convention" (4), she also suggests that the British, if they are not careful, may find that they are not so different. In admonishing her fellow Britons for not making more of an effort to help these refugees, Burney ask that her readers "anticipate the historians of times to come" who will ask what "land" allowed these priests to suffer and die on their shores: "'And what was this land? Some wild, uncultivated spot, where yet no arts had flourished, no civilization been spread, no benefits reciprocated? no religion known?'" (14–15). Instead, she argues, by helping these priests, the inhabitants of Great Britain will adhere to their national legacy, one informed by "indulgent benevolence" and a "munificence of liberality" (17).

In making her plea, Burney collapses the religious distinctions between Roman Catholics and Protestants by calling the Roman Catholic clergy "Priests of the Christian religion" (15). Burney condemns the British sense of national superiority—"We are too apt to consider ourselves rather as a distinct race of beings, than as merely the emulous inhabitants of rival states" (12)—which allows the English to condemn and dismiss the influence of "pious" men and then to let them starve. National and religious distinctions are merely arbitrary, for, as Burney argues, both the English and French are "all the creatures of one Creator" (12). With this ecumenical mindset, Burney then argues that the English may learn from the Roman Catholic Clergy: ". . . let us look at the Emigrant French Clergy, and ask where is the Englishman, where, indeed, the human being, in whom a sense of right can more disinterestedly have been demonstrated, or more nobly predominate?" (13).

While the French priests provide models of Christian charity for all English citizens, Burney, in this text, makes their plight the specific concern of British women whom she believes are too used to retirement from public affairs.[40] Burney's tract is a call to British women for public action; this season of "general calamity," this "astonishing period of political history," demands that British women push aside all expectations of female privacy and isolation from the public world, for in 1793, "public affairs assume the interest of private feelings" and "affect domestic peace" (1). In making this claim, Burney challenges popular English sentiment, discussed above, which positioned French women as models that English women should avoid at all costs. Instead, Burney asks that "the Ladies of Great Britain" follow the examples of French women who had for years supported the charitable endeavors of the Roman Catholic Church. Now, because these women have become victims themselves to the chaos induced by the Revolution, British women must step in to continue their work (7–8). What is, however, perhaps most shocking about this directive is that Burney ultimately argues that her countrywomen should model their behavior after a male French Roman Catholic saint, St. Vincent de Paule, known for his work in establishing French charitable institutions and for mobilizing affluent French women to perform charitable works (8, note).

Interestingly, in depicting the lack of compassion and generosity that the French clergy encountered in England, Burney prefigures the hostile reception that *The Wanderer's* Juliet encounters once she arrives in England.[41] In this way she cements the link between English women and French priests. By presenting celibate male Catholic clergy as the appropriate partners of and models for English women, Burney challenges an English sense of marriage. (It is not English husbands whom English women should work with and for, but French Roman Catholic Clergy.) Just as the English imagined themselves as the particular purveyors of liberty and as Protestant subjects, they also saw the nature of their marriage institution as different from not only the world, but from the rest of the Christian world. According to Alan Macfarlane, in England marriage was not primarily for procreation; rather it provided companionship and friendship to two independent adults.[42]

Furthermore, according to Felicity Nussbaum, many eighteenth-century British explorers focused, in their travel narratives, on the polygamous cultures they had encountered. While on the one hand polygamous arrangements were the practices of the "savage," polygamy held some attraction for British observers. Polygamy was seen to "[foster] female companionship" and it also provided a way for "an excess population of women to be protected through marriage."[43] The English also applied the term "polygamy" to describe some of their own cultural practices. It could describe the actions of a husband who married another wife after the death of his first one, or it could describe a man who was sexually involved with more than one woman (*TZ*, 76). The use of this term in this latter instance demonstrates that the English, despite their fascination with the practices in "savage" cultures, were very uncomfortable with any behavior that even slightly resembled polygamous practices. Consequently, monogamy became one way in which the English defined themselves in opposition to other cultures:

> England's toying with and ultimate rejection of polygamy near the end of the eighteenth century was part of a nation's defining itself both as distinct from and morally superior to the polygamous Other. Monogamy became instituted as part of England's national definition, and whatever practices its explorers might have found to tempt them in other worlds, England asserted its public stance that marriage meant one man, one wife, at least in law. (*TZ*, 83)

It is to this sense of a companionate English marriage which Mary Wollstonecraft appeals when she asks, in *A Vindication of the Rights of Woman,* that women be educated so that they can be "affectionate wives and rational mothers."[44] Mary Hays explains to English men that by providing English women with an education, they will increase their own domestic happiness: "the habits and pursuits of women of reading and reflection, are highly favorable, and assimilate, if I may so express myself, with every home enjoyment and social delight."[45] Both Wollstonecraft's and Hay's arguments suggest that by becoming the intellectual equals of men, English women would be better able to be the companions of English men, and thus form the English marriages to which the English aspire.

While the comments of Wollstonecraft and Hays suggest the possibility of such marriages, Jane Austen's novel *Persuasion* actually celebrates a companionate English marriage by placing it against a backdrop of patriotic triumph inspired by the Waterloo victory.[46] Within the context of this national celebration, Austen tells the story of a more personal victory[47]: Anne Elliot and Captain Wentworth are reunited after eight years of painful separation. Austen makes it clear that this marriage will be stronger, more equitable than if they had married earlier, in the first throes of their love. Wentworth, in particular, has come to understand that, previously, he did not fully appreciate Anne, her generous intentions and the "excellence" of her mind.[48] In fact, he admits that much of their mutual misery is his fault; his pride is his worst enemy (212, 221). With time, he has learned to respect her as a woman and a wife.

But while Austen celebrates an English marriage amidst a British triumph, Burney does not. *The Wanderer* depicts no such happy marriages.[49] This absence also forms a crucial component of Burney's critique of English national sentiment. The English are not presented as inherently capable of forming companionate marriages.[50] In this novel, the English marriages are as suspect as the French ones. Although Juliet is finally able to marry the man she loves, Mr. Harleigh, this marriage is rather incidental. As Doody points out, Harleigh is "weak," as are all the men who inhabit *The Wanderer*; they are "weak men with decided ideas as to their strengths in dealing with women, and all have some designs of their own for the women's roles" (320, 347). While Harleigh does attempt to help Juliet, his own desire for her physical person detracts from his ability to assist her. Furthermore, at the end of the novel, he abandons her at a critical moment by acknowledging the supremacy of her dastardly French husband who has tricked Juliet into marriage. It is only once the Granvilles acknowledge her relation to them, and Juliet falls back into her proper and accepted place within the English patriarchal family structure, that Juliet's marriage with Harleigh is possible. Consequently, marriage, British or French, in this novel, is primarily a way to become part of a man's family and thus gain protection. The French Gabriella is not subject to the indignities in England that Juliet suffers because she has a husband, a cold and unfeeling man, but a husband and thus a protector.

But while the practitioners of French Roman Catholicism are presented in this novel as models to the English, Burney does not celebrate the French marriage institution. Her narrative identifies the *ancien régime* as providing Gabriella with a "gloomy" history (622). Raised in a convent, married when she was "yet a child," Gabriella's married life is unhappy even before the Revolution because she was not even given a choice of partners. It is the "general custom of her country" to deny the female even a "negative" choice (622). That this lack of choice still existed within the Revolutionary society is evident in that Juliet runs from a French husband, an official of the Revolutionary government, who forced her to marry him so that he could obtain her English inheritance.

Burney's representations of marriage are quite interesting in light of her own marital situation. Literary history has popularized the happy relationship between Burney and her French husband, Alexandre d'Arblay, a man whom she called her "PARTNER IN ALL."[51] Burney, an English citizen, was advised by her intimates not to marry a penniless immigrant with no money or connections. Dr. Burney, in a letter dated May 1793, urged her "not to entangle yourself in a wild and romantic attachment," particularly one to a man from a "strange land, in which the generality of its inhabitants at present seem incapable of such virtues as friendship."[52] Burney, as we now know, did not listen, although she had assumed that she would never marry. In a letter dated October 1793 (found in her diary), Burney confides to a friend, "I had never made any vow against marriage, but I had long, long been firmly persuaded it was for me a state of too much hazard and too little promise to draw me from my individual plans and purposes" (*Diary,* 318–19). Burney, furthermore, was not only surprised by her decision to marry but also by her desire to marry a Frenchman:

> As my partner is a Frenchman, I conclude the wonder raised by the connection may spread beyond my own private circle; but no wonder on earth can ever arrive near my own in having found such a character from that nation. This is a prejudice certainly, impertinent, and very John Bullish, and very arrogant; but I only share it with all my countrymen, and therefore must needs forgive both them and myself.[53]

Burney's awareness of her own nationalist prejudices, as well as her ambivalent attitude towards marriage, helps to explain her representations of Juliet's struggles and the rather anti-climactic resolution of the marriage plot. She herself is guilty of feeling the very sentiments that she censures in *The Wanderer.* Yet while the majority of the English who inhabit her novel remain oblivious to the destructive nature of these opinions, in this 1793 passage Burney does reveal an emerging awareness of the prejudices she will eventually directly engage. Had she allowed herself to succumb wholly to these "John Bullish" opinions, as many of her characters do, she would have lost her chance for marital happiness.

Clearly, Burney values companionate marriage, and she is aware that this type of union is possible, while not common, with an Englishman as well as a Frenchman. However, English nationalist sentiment understood the English marriage institution as a product of a society that fostered a respect for personal liberty and a Protestant rationality. Were Burney to end her novel with a celebration of such a marriage, she would risk reinforcing the very notion of Englishness that she seeks to destabilize in *The Wanderer.* Instead, by dismissing the possibility for such a union, Burney's novel serves as a plea for the English to challenge their constructions of their own national character, suggesting that, in doing so, they may work at actually attaining those very qualities they already have claimed as their own.[54]

Notes

1. Frances Burney, *The Wanderer; Or, Female Difficulties,* eds. Margaret Anne Doody, Robert L. Mack and Peter Sabor with an introduction by Margaret Anne Doody (Oxford: Oxford University Press, 1991). Subsequent references to this text (*W*) will be provided in parentheses.

2. See page 47 in Rose Marie Cutting, "A Wreath for Fanny Burney's Last Novel: *The Wanderer's* Contribution to Women's Studies," *Illinois Quarterly* 37 (1975): 45–64. In addition, see Dale Spender, *Mothers of the Novel* (London: Pandora Press, 1986). Spender argues that Burney's readers were expecting *The Wanderer* to be "an exposé of French morals and manners," and the resulting lack of interest in the novel indicates that these expectations were not met (285).

3. See Margaret Anne Doody, *Frances Burney: The Life in the Works* (New Brunswick: Rutgers University Press, 1988), Karen R. Lawrence, *Penelope Voyages: Women and Travel in the British Literary Tradition* (Ithaca: Cornell University Press, 1994) and Claudia L. Johnson, *Equivocal Beings: Politics, Gender and Sentimentality in the 1790s: Wollstonecraft, Radcliffe, Burney and Austen* (Chicago: University Press, 1995). Doody identifies "[o]ne of the moral themes" of this novel as a "need for wider sympathies" particularly between the people of England and France (331). In addition, she points out that this novel "is scarcely patriotic at all" because "it says England ought to change" (332). Lawrence argues that in *The Wanderer* "exile is a metaphor for women's dispossession in English society" (73). Juliet, the female protagonist, is forced to wander through a society "in which she has no 'place'" (54.) Johnson's argument deviates somewhat from those of Doody and Lawrence in that she argues that, ultimately, *The Wanderer* does not provide a "direct criticism" of patriarchy "despite its ultimate responsibility for the Wanderer's trials as a woman without a father's name" (178). Since many of the English female characters are particularly cruel to Juliet, Johnson argues that the novel critiques the behavior of women: "because women have so much sway, the novel becomes a critique of their domination rather than their difficulties" (179).

4. Stella Cottrell, "The Devil on Two Sticks: Franco-phobia in 1803" in *Patriotism: The Making and Unmaking of British National Identity,* Volume 1, ed. Raphael Samuel (London: Routledge, 1989), 269.

5. Cottrell, 269. See also Linda Colley, *Britons: Forging the Nation: 1701–1837* (New Haven: Yale University Press, 1992), 250.

6. See Cottrell, 269, 266.

7. See *British War Poetry in the Age of Romanticism: 1793–1815,* ed. Betty T. Bennett (New York: Garland Publishing Inc., 1976), 475.

8. Burney attempted to support her family with her writings. Financial resources were tight, and in 1801, her husband, General D'Arblay, desperate to support his family, returned to France to resume his position in the French Army. He asked Burney and their son to join him, and they did in 1802 during a temporary peace between Britain and France. Once the peace ended, Frances Burney was unable to leave France for the next ten years. Also note that Margaret Doody, in *Frances Burney: The Life in the Works,* provides a summary of the manuscript's history which involved Burney efforts to avoid having her work confiscated by both French and British officials (315–7).

9. Rose Marie Cutting's 1977 essay cited below provides support for Doody's point. In response to those critics who would classify Burney as a conservative writer, Cutting argues that Burney "has ties with the women who applied the new ides of the Age of Revolution to their own sex," writers such as Mary Wollstonecraft, Charlotte Smith and Mary Hays (519).

10. Colley argues that following the British victory at Waterloo, the "chauvinistic euphoria that might have been expected . . . was for a long time strangely absent" (321). Britain was exhausted by the prolonged war effort, and simultaneously, peace did not help a British economy which "had been geared for so long to war" (321). Cottrell points out that the Peace of Amiens disintegrated and there was a surge in the publication of English propaganda attempting to convince an unwilling population to support the war with France (259–60).

11. In *The Life in the Works,* Margaret Doody tells us that the first edition of this novel "sold out at once"; 3,500 copies sold out immediately (332).

12. John Wilson Croker, review of *The Wanderer, or Female Difficulties, Quarterly Review* 11 (1814): 123–130 and William Hazlitt, review of *The Wanderer, or Female Difficulties, Edinburgh Review* 24 (1814-15): 320–38.

13. Lynch (cited below) points out that Juliet, upon her arrival in England, believes that she will "enjoy English 'liberty'": "The remainder of Burney's narrative confounds this schematic spatialization of political choices and, with it, the order of national differences" (60).

14. For a discussion of Juliet's "blackface," see 60–61 in Deidre Lynch, "Domesticating Fictions and Nationalizing Women: Edmund Burke, Property, and the Reproduction of Englishness," in *Romanticism, Race, and Imperial Culture: 1780–1834,* eds. Alan Richardson and Sonia Hofkosh (Bloomington: Indiana University Press, 1996), 40–71.

15. As Johnson points out, Juliet's "youth, beauty" and "seemingly endless array of female accomplishments" "avail her nothing in a world which regards her namelessness and lack of relation as grounds for suspicion rather than compassion" (1995, 167).

16. See "State and Prospects of Europe" in the *Edinburgh Review* 45, no. 23 (April 1814): 8.

17. See Richard Price, "A Discourse on the Love of Our Country, Delivered on November 4, 1789, at the Meetinghouse in the Old Jewry" (London: T. Cadell, 1789), 1–51.

18. Laura Doyle, in her essay "The Racial Sublime" (found in *Romanticism, Race, and Imperial Culture: 1780–1834*) highlights Edmund Burke's argument that if the French people had based their claims for liberty on their ancestral rights (as the English had) instead of presenting themselves as a "'gang of Maroon slaves', their Revolution would have been successful" (30).

19. See Cutting, "Defiant Women: the Growth of Feminism in Fanny Burney's Novels," *Studies in English Literature,* 17 (1977): 529. See also Cutting, "A Wreath for Fanny Burney's Last Novel," 50 and 54. Subsequent references to these texts ("Defiant" and "Wreath" respectively) will be provided in parentheses.

20. Burney forges an analogy between Juliet's condition and that of the protagonist in Defoe's *Robinson Crusoe,* according to Lawrence, in order to demonstrate "that a woman in the midst of English society is 'as unaided and unprotected as' a single, isolated man in the middle of the ocean" (53).

21. Johnson highlights Colley's presentation of British women's skepticism. Were they really that much safer than French women (*Equivocal Beings,* 99)? Certainly, Burney's novel can be seen as participating in this questioning.

22. See Leonore Davidoff and Catherine Hall, *Family Fortunes: Men and Women of the English Middle Class: 1780–1850* (Chicago: University of Chicago Press, 1987), 19.

23. *London Times* (23 July 1789): 2.

24. Colley also tells us that the post-1789 French Jacobins, like the "British moralists," would condemn the behavior and privileges of French women before the Revolution (251).

25. See note in Richard Polwhele, "The Unsex'd Females: A Poem," in *The Unsex'd Females: A Poem and The Female Advocate,* ed. Gina Luria (New York: Garland Publishing Company, Inc., 1974), 9–10.

26. See page 140, Mary Astell, "Some Reflections Upon Marriage" (1700), in *The Meridian Anthology of Early Women Writers: British Literary Women from Aphra Behn to Maria Edgeworth: 1660–1800,* eds. Katharine M. Rogers and William McCarthy (New York: Penguin Books, USA Inc., 1987), 128–41.

27. As Doody argues, "*The Wanderer* shows that Burney had at least been listening, seriously listening, to the feminists of the '90s, to writers like Mary Hays and Mary Wollstonecraft" (334).

28. See Mary Hays, *An Appeal to the Men of Great Britain in Behalf of Women,* ed. Gina Luria (New York: Garland Publishing Inc., 1974). According to Hays, to have liberty is also to have the vote. It should be "the lot of women" to be "allowed as men are, some vote, some right of judgment in a matter which concerns them so nearly, as that of the laws and opinions by which they are to be governed" (150).

29. Doody's argument encourages one to draw comparisons between Burney's work and Radcliffe's. Doody claims that "Ann Radcliffe is an obvious precursor of the Burney of *The Wanderer*" and that *The Wanderer* bears traces of Radcliffe's *Romance of the Forest* (424 n.59).

30. See Kate Ferguson Ellis, *The Contested Castle: Gothic Novels and the Subversion of Domestic Ideology* (Urbana: University of Illinois Press, 1989). Ellis argues that writing about Roman Catholic institutions, such as the monastery, allowed eighteenth century Gothic novelists to examine the "abusive power" found in the "private sphere" (146). Please note that subsequent references to this text (*CC*) will be provided in parentheses.

31. Ellis points out that Radcliffe's aristocrats "are too dissipated to appreciate nature as scenery" (116). Radcliffe's villains, for the most part members of the artistocracy, "never really wander in the positive sense of that word" (*CC,* 105).

32. In arguing that Burney's novel is positioned within the "Romantic mode," Doody compares the wandering Juliet to one of "Wordsworth's vagrants of a lower social class" (329–30).

33. Lawrence also argues that the narrative form of the novel, "with its deferrals and sudden aggressive outbursts, is a formal embodiment of Burney's feminism and directly linked to the trope of wandering" (67).

34. Liah Greenfeld, *Nationalism: Five Roads to Modernity* (Cambridge, Mass.: Harvard University Press, 1992), 51.

35. In considering the role of religion in English nationalist discourses it is interesting to keep in mind a point articulated by Dr. Carol Engelhardt in her paper "1874 and The Decline of Anti-Catholicism in Late-Victorian England," presented at the conference "The Formative Years: The Construction of Victorian Class and National Identities" held on 20 November 1998, at the College of Mount Saint Vincent in Riverdale, New York. Following the Henrician Schism, many Anglicans and Anglo-Catholics who were fervently anti-papist did not consider themselves to be Protestants.

36. Colley argues that Protestantism had such a large impact on British life that it "determined how most Britons viewed their politics" and how they "interpreted their material life" (18).

37. According to Kathleen Wilson, in 1780, Catholicism was considered by many British to be a "Continental religion of luxury, idolatry, and

superstition"; it "was seen as running counter to the spirit of improvement and the advance of knowledge in art, science and politics to which English citizens believed themselves to adhere." See *The Sense of the People: Politics, Culture, and Imperialism in England 1717–1785* (Cambridge: Cambridge University Press, 1995), 368. Catholics were not allowed to vote or run for Parliament "from the late seventeenth century until 1829" with the Catholic Emancipation Act (Colley 19). However Richard Altick, in *Victorian People and Ideas* (New York: W.W. Norton & Company, 1973), reminds us that Dissenters were also not allowed to participate in government until the Test and Corporation Acts were repealed in 1828 (85).

38. *The Diary of Fanny Burney,* Introduction by Lewis Gibbs (1940) (London: J.M. Dent and Sons Ltd, 1961), 307. Subsequent references to this text (*Diary*) will be provided in parentheses.

39. Frances Burney, "Brief Reflexions [*sic*] Relative to the Emigrant French Clergy: Earnestly Submitted to the Humane Consideration of the Ladies of Great Britain" (1793), *Considerations on Religion and Public Education and Brief Reflections Relative to the Emigrant French Clergy,* ed. Claudia L. Johnson (Los Angeles: William Andrews Clark Memorial Library, 1990).

40. Burney does clarify that by calling on the "ladies of Great Britain," she does not mean to imply that charity should not also be the province of her country*men*. However, the circumstances of those priests are so desperate that Burney asks that women spread this plan among their sex (7).

41. In her discussion of *Brief Reflections,* Johnson argues that Burney "feminizes the priests by identifying them with women" (1995, 174).

42. Alan Macfarlane, *Marriage and Love in England: 1300–1840* (Oxford: Blackwell Publishers, 1986), 125–26. Marriage in Britain was not taken for granted; in fact, it was often a deliberate choice among all classes. Marriage was seen as a sacrifice because it often involved "slipping down several rungs of that steep social ladder" (Macfarlane 10). Note that "[p]rior to 1753, a valid marriage required only a verbal exchange of vows in front of witnesses followed by consummation" (50). The establishment of the Hardwicke Act in 1753, however, required that a couple participate in a church wedding which would be "entered in a parish register and signed by both parties" following the reading of banns "on three consecutive Sundays in a parish where one of the parties lived" (50). The passing of this act was prompted by the kidnapping of heiresses who were then raped and married for their fortunes. According to Ellis, this act was passed more for the protection of their parents' property than for concern for the welfare of the daughters (50–1).

43. Felicity A. Nussbaum, *Torrid Zones: Maternity, Sexuality, and Empire in Eighteenth-Century English Narratives* (Baltimore: The John Hopkins University Press, 1995), 83. Subsequent references to this text (*TZ*)

will be provided in parentheses. Nussbaum points out that polygamy is not treated harshly in the African travel narratives that were written "before missionary zeal began to preach monogamy as a tenet of civilization" (76).

44. Mary Wollstonecraft, *A Vindication of the Rights of Woman,* 2nd ed. 1792 (New York: Norton, 1998), 7.

45. Mary Hays, *An Appeal to the Men of Great Britain in Behalf of Women,* 1798, ed. Gina Luria (New York: Garland Publishing Inc., 1974), 171.

46. Nicola J. Watson's argument, which emphasizes the fact that Austen placed Wentworth in the Navy and "[dated] . . . the inception of the novel as the summer of 1814 (just after the abdication of Napoleon) and its climax in late February 1815 (just before Napoleon's comeback from Elba that was finally crushed at Waterloo)," highlights the nationalist character of this novel and Anne Elliot's marriage. See Nicola J. Watson, *Revolution and the Form of the British Novel 1790–1825: Intercepted Letters, Interrupted Seductions* (Oxford: Clarendon Press, 1994), 108.

47. Watson argues that "it is both fitting and prophetic that the novel's final sentence should celebrate a new marriage of the personal and the public . . ." (108).

48. Jane Austen, *Persuasion,* 1818 (New York: Bantam Books, 1984), 216.

49. Doody comments on "[t]he conspicuous absence of marriage and of families" in this novel, and she argues that this "lack" indicates "a lack of future" in this English society (328).

50. Johnson suggests that *The Wanderer* is largely concerned with "the yearning" for "feminine sympathy" (178). The relationships between women are perhaps more important than those between men and women.

51. Quoted in Doody, 315. Doody points out that Burney and d'Arblay's relationship began as "an equal friendship . . . sweetened by mutual admiration" (200).

52. In May 1793, see *Diary,* 316–17.

53. In October 1793, see *Diary,* 320.

54. I would like to thank Patricia Comitini, Adriana Craciun, Kari Lokke, and Laura C. Valdez for their close, careful readings of this essay and their invaluable critical advice. Adrienne Munich deserves, as well, my heartfelt thanks for her feedback and advice.

"The Mild Dominion of the Moon":
Charlotte Smith and the
Politics of Transcendence

☙

Kari E. Lokke

Feminist theorists since Simone de Beauvoir have recognized Western culture's ancient and ever-present association of women with immanence and men with transcendence. Yet whereas de Beauvoir answers this tendency to see the "incarnation of transcendence in the phallus"[1] with a call admonishing women to "seek self-fulfillment in transcendence" (46), contemporary feminist theorists have questioned the very category of transcendence itself as a masculinist construct that creates and fosters an untenable and unhealthy division between spirit and body, mind and matter, male and female, subject and object, dominant and dominated. In this spirit, scholars as varied as Stuart Curran, Meena Alexander, Marlon Ross, Anne Mellor, and Nanora Sweet have all emphasized an investment, on the part of women writers of the Romantic era, in the beautiful, the quotidian and the domestic rather than in the sublimity, spiritual striving and visionary effort we traditionally associate with male Romantics such as Wordsworth and Shelley.[2] In emphasizing the manner in which these female poets reject the poetics of sublimity and transcendence, this strain of analysis serves an important function by calling attention to aesthetic modes that are traditionally undervalued because of their association with women. Yet this criticism also risks reinscribing women writers of Romanticism into the system of binaries it seeks to overcome, thereby imprisoning them in a present day version of the masculinist aesthetic created by Burke, Kant, and Schiller and the object of feminist attacks since Wollstonecraft.[3]

If one allows the rich body of women's Romantic poetry to speak for itself, an inevitably more complex picture appears, one in which women Romantic poets do indeed embody their struggles for the visionary and sublime in their writings, though the transcendence they envisage bears the stamp of their uniquely vulnerable and troubled sociopolitical position as women writers in a revolutionary and post-revolutionary age. I take as my example in this essay Charlotte Smith, the highly popular and influential author of the *Elegiac Sonnets* (1784), of whom Stuart Curran justly writes that she is "the first poet in England whom in retrospect we would call Romantic."[4] Well before the Alpine struggles of Wordsworth's *Prelude,* Byron's *Manfred,* and Shelley's "Mont Blanc," or the volcanic meditations of Chateaubriand's René and Gérard de Nerval's narrative persona, Charlotte Smith wrote to her Irish friend Joseph Cooper Walker in 1794: "I do not mind dying, but I want to see the Alps and Vesuvius first."[5] Significantly, unlike her Romantic descendants, Charlotte Smith, a woman who bore twelve children and was impoverished by her profligate husband, did not, in fact, see either the Alps or Vesuvius before she died.

My argument in this essay is that Smith employs images of transcendence and sublimity in an effort to achieve and to represent a potentially emancipatory distance and detachment from what she perceives as the largely male-dominated economic and political struggles of her time. Distance and detachment do not, however, represent escapism for the profoundly political consciousness of Smith; instead they make possible a clarity of vision that allows her to depict her own uniquely female perspective on her revolutionary and chaotic historical moment and to hold out hope, however attenuated, of the possibility of positive social change. Indeed it is precisely her gender that encourages Smith to represent her consciousness as transcendent, as "above the fray," in a sense, because she conceives of the political battles of her day as waged by and for male interests with women largely on the sidelines, looking on.

This position of "internal exclusion within Western culture" as feminist Foucauldian Biddy Martin argues, is "a particularly well-suited point from which to expose the workings of power"[6] in patriarchal society. In the late eighteenth and early nineteenth centuries, this position outside of powerful legal and governmental institutions gives women the potential to write from alternative points of view and perspectives of detachment unavailable to the men who inhabit these institutions or who can, at least, more easily imagine themselves doing so. Following Rita Felski in *Beyond Feminist Aesthetics*, I argue here that Charlotte Smith's writings partake of a feminist public sphere that "offers a critique of cultural values from the standpoint of women as a marginalized group within society. In this sense, it constitutes a partial or counter-public sphere; the experience of . . . oppression and cultural dislocation provides the impetus for the development of a self-consciously oppositional identity."[7] Yet whereas Felski suggests that this feminist counter-public sphere comes into being when the critical edge of the original bourgeois public sphere is blunted in the twentieth century by popular culture and mass media, the political writings of Charlotte Smith confirm Nancy Fraser's revisions of Felski in *Habermas and the Public Sphere* by affirming that this counter-public sphere is perhaps as old as women's contributions to print culture and to public discourse.[8]

My analysis of the function of images of transcendence in Smith's poetry is analogous to that of Wordsworth critics such as Jerome McGann, Marjorie Levinson, Alan Liu, David Simpson, and Marlon Ross[9] in so far as it suggests that a transcendentalizing impulse implies the poet's desire to detach him/herself from ever-present, intrusive, threatening and profoundly disenchanting historical realities. Yet whereas these Wordsworth critics argue, correctly I think, that Wordsworth in such poems as "Tintern Abbey" sought to displace sociopolitical struggles into an apolitical and ahistorical realm, Smith, on the other hand, seeks a transcendent perspective as a vehicle through which to represent with utmost clarity, detachment, and compassion the precise contours of her contemporary political landscape. Displacement has a clearly ideological and, I believe, predominantly progressive function in both authors,[10] but whereas in Wordsworth it represents a movement of rejection of the political sphere, an attempt at erasure of its corruptions and historical limitations, for Smith, metaphors of transcendence serve as a means of encoding her critique of British class prejudice, nationalism, and militarism into the poetry which she clearly presents as written from the perspective of a late eighteenth-century woman and member, though impoverished, of the landed gentry. Thus Smith's metaphors of transcendence and sublimity, in particular, are figures for the utopian function and oppositional nature of a late eighteenth-century (proto)-feminist counter-public sphere as Smith helps bring it into being.

Sonnet 59, entitled "Written September 1791, during a remarkable storm, in which the moon was perfectly clear, while the tempest gathered in various directions near the earth" is an exemplary instance of Smith's encoding of her political ethos in a vision of Romantic transcendence. The last sonnet in what came to be known as Volume I of the *Elegiac Sonnets* after the publication in 1797 of the second volume, this poem holds a privileged position in her sonnet collection. Published in 1792 along with a preface in which Smith attributes the uniformly melancholy and plaintive tone of her poetry to the legal battles over the settlement of her father-in-law's will that kept her and her children in dire financial straits,[11] this sonnet answers charges of the monotony of her melancholy or her affectation of grief with an image of the moon as an emblem of an emotionally detached, serene feminine consciousness. The specificity of its title suggests the crucial importance of the tumultuous historical moment in which it was written: "Written September 1791, during a remarkable thunder storm, in which the moon was perfectly clear, while the tempest gathered in various directions near the earth." I quote the sonnet here in full:

> What awful pageants crowd the evening sky!
> The low horizon gathering vapours shroud;
> Sudden, from many a deep-embattled cloud
> Terrific thunders burst, and lightenings fly—
> While in serenest azure, beaming high,
> Night's regent, of her calm pavilion proud,
> Gilds the dark shadows that beneath her lie,
> Unvex'd by all their conflicts fierce and loud.
> —So, in unsullied dignity elate,
> A spirit conscious of superior worth,
> In placid elevation firmly great,
> Scorns the vain cares that give Contention birth;
> And blest with peace above the shocks of Fate,
> Smiles at the tumult of the troubled earth. (52–3)

The moon, traditional symbol of the female psyche and its propensity for mutability and emotional flux, is here, in a significant reversal, an embodiment of sovereign calm and constancy. Indeed, throughout the *Elegiac Sonnets,* the prominent figure of the moon resonates in powerful tension with archetypal female symbolism. In Sonnet 4, "To the moon," for example, Diana "Queen of the silver bow!" reigns over a "benignant sphere" and "[s]heds a soft calm upon [the] troubled breast" of the sorrowing speaker. Sonnet 39, "To night" figures the faint and waning moon as an emblem of "deep depression" calmed by the darkness of night. In Sonnet 59, just as the moon, "unvexed by . . . conflicts fierce and loud" shines "in serenest azure" high above the dark shadows and thunder clouds below, so, Smith writes, a superior consciousness finds peace within itself, a peace that transcends conflict and vicissitude:

—So, in unsullied dignity elate,
A spirit conscious of superior worth,
In placid elevation firmly great,
Scorns the vain cares that give Contention birth[.] (53, 9–12)

Thus Smith concludes her volume with an implicit assertion of her own awareness of self-worth, mental superiority and spiritual elevation, a clear ideal of sublimity that enables the feminine consciousness to scorn the vanity stereotypically associated with women and most importantly to transcend "the shocks of Fate." Indeed Smith here anticipates Schiller's "On the Sublime," published a decade later in 1801, which defines sublimity as spiritual victory over "the treachery of fate"[12] and an assertion of mental freedom in the face of ineluctable destiny and the accidents of history.

This sonnet takes on even greater significance when one notes its remarkable similarity to that quintessential locus of Romantic transcendence, the Mount Snowdon passage at the conclusion of Wordsworth's *Prelude,* a passage very likely influenced by Smith.[13] Here the moon "in single glory" looks down upon a tumultuous sea of mist, vapors and clouds, appearing to the poet "The perfect image of a mighty mind / Of one that feeds upon infinity" (13. 69–70).[14] The passage concludes by evoking a state of mind precisely analogous to that depicted in Smith's sonnet: "the highest bliss / That can be known" (13. 107–08), "sovereignty within and peace at will" (13. 114).

Though both visions conclude with an invocation of transcendent spiritual freedom, "genuine liberty," as Wordsworth calls it (13. 122), the psychic process necessary to the achievement of this state of mind is significantly different in the two poems. Wordsworth depicts his poetic persona in ascent of Mount Snowdon "as if in opposition set / Against an enemy" (13. 30–31) when he is suddenly startled, by a flash of light into a revelatory vision:

I looked about, and lo,
The moon stood naked in the heavens at height
Immense above my head, and on the shore
I found myself of a huge sea of mist,
Which meek and silent rested at my feet. (13. 40–45)

Here the speaker is rewarded for his struggle with the mountain, or perhaps with nature itself, by an image of an immensely powerful and arguably feminized nature (moon and mist) unveiled, so that the poet now dominates the landscape resting "meek and silent" at his feet. This sea of mist, in turn, dominates the real sea below "that seemed / To dwindle and give up its majesty, / Usurped upon as far as sight could reach" (13. 49–51). The verb "usurp" and the phrase "give up its majesty" clearly suggest victory in a power struggle. The moon looking down upon this show "in single glory" becomes, famously, an emblem of the poetic imagination, "The perfect image of a mighty mind / Of one that feeds upon infinity" (13. 69–70). Like the moon that shines upon the chasm in the vapors through which roars the torrential voice of the waters, so the human mind finds sustenance in the "dark, deep thoroughfare" of the human unconscious, as we would call it today, "whatsoe'er is dim / Or vast in its own being" (13. 72–73).

The language of struggle and domination intensifies as Wordsworth describes the functioning of this sublime power of Nature as it is transmuted into the power of the poet, just as in the passage above, the moon, first compared to a naked woman, becomes "the perfect image of [the] mighty mind" of the poet:

> That domination which she oftentimes
> Exerts upon the outward face of things,
> So moulds them, and endues, abstracts, combines,
> Or by abrupt and unhabitual influence
> Doth make one object impress itself
> Upon all others, and pervades them so,
> That even the grossest minds must see and hear,
> And cannot chuse but feel. The power which these
> Acknowledge when thus moved, which Nature thus
> Thrusts forth upon the senses, is the express
> Resemblance—in the fullness of its strength
> Made visible—a genuine counterpart
> And brother of the glorious faculty
> Which higher minds bear with them as their own. (13. 77–90)

The power of the poet embodied in this vital, dynamic and aggressive landscape—now transformed from feminine Nature into a masculine brother—impresses itself upon others, thrusts itself upon their senses, and forces them to feel. We witness here an exemplary instance of the appropriation and displacement of the power of a feminized nature (and perhaps also of the artistic power of previous female poets like Smith) by an aggressive masculinist consciousness that Marlon Ross has so brilliantly shown to underlie much of male Romantic poetry.[15]

The "higher mind" in Smith's poem, on the other hand, eschews struggle; having achieved—perhaps as an act of self-protection—an almost absolute distance from the scene of conflict below her, she responds to it with scorn and amusement, as if it is unworthy of her. Written two years into the French Revolution, this sonnet is contemporary with Smith's strongly pro-revolutionary novel *Desmond* which shocked English conservatives when it was published in 1792.[16] Yet Sonnet 59 seems to express a desire for spiritual solace beyond the inevitably conflict-ridden realm of politics. Esther Schor, in *Bearing the Dead*, gives a plausible reading of this moon iconography based upon economies of emotional exchange, as an emblem of "sublime indifference" so that "the trappings of royalty—its exaltation, its pageants, and its pavilions—cast the moon as imperious and inclement, hoarding the blessings of peace."[17] Indeed the poem's first quatrain subtly evokes French Revolutionary struggles; the verb "shroud" and the phrase "deep-embattled" suggest a potential for deadly violence just as the opening reference to "awful pageants" hints at the cultural analogies Smith is drawing between this natural scene and the collective French political drama. I would argue, however, that this moon represents a necessary self-protection from and transcendence of violence more than it does a hoarding of peace. Smith's moon is ruler of another realm—spiritual, contemplative, transfigurative—beyond this earthly one;

> Night's regent, of her calm pavilion proud,
> Gilds the dark shadows that beneath her lie. (52, 6–7)

In contrast, the gilded pavilions of Versailles and of the French aristocracy were already bathed in blood. In the autumn of 1789, in the incident famously described by Burke, a Parisian mob of mostly women had invaded Versailles, threatened Marie Antoinette, and murdered the king's bodyguards.

These French Revolutionary struggles seem to have challenged and compelled Smith to envisage a female regent—significantly not a queen or a monarch—who transcends conflict and aggression. In addition to anticipating Wordsworth in this sonnet, Smith is also rewriting Milton's *Paradise Lost*, Book II, 427–33, where Satan asserts to the concourse of fallen angels that he will dare to leave Hell in search of a new realm of light:

> Satan, whom now transcendent glory raised
> Above his fellows, with monarchal pride
> Conscious of highest worth, unmoved thus spake:
> "O progeny of heav'n, empyreal Thrones!

> With reason hath deep silence and demur
> Seized us, though undismayed: long is the way
> And hard, that out of hell leads up to light.[18]

In Sonnet 59, Smith seems to have found her way to this realm of light and transcendence through a detachment from the implicitly political battles figured by both Milton and Wordsworth. At the same time, however, Smith's echoes of Milton suggest a Romantic satanism—a rebellion against the status quo—inflected in fascinating ways by her gender.

In order to clarify the political position Smith takes in Sonnet 59, and to hear even more clearly its feminist and pacifist undertones, beyond her claim to membership in a kind of spiritual elite or aristocracy, one must read it in the context of Smith's other poetry. Thus, for example, Sonnet 83, "The sea view," structured similarly to Sonnet 59, sets the serene joy of a shepherd, reclining on a mountaintop overlooking the "purple radiance" of an oceanic sunset in opposition to a fierce battle of British and French ships at sea and concludes:

> . . . the wide scene
> Magnificent, and tranquil, seems to spread
> Even o'er the Rustic's breast a joy serene,
> When, like dark plague-spots by the Demons shed,
> Charged deep with death, upon the waves, far seen,
> Move the war-freighted ships; and fierce and red,
> Flash their destructive fire[.]—The mangled dead
> And dying victims then pollute the flood.
> Ah! thus man spoils Heaven's glorious works with
>   blood! (72, 6–14)

In her last line Smith clearly exploits the implications of the tacit exclusion of women from the Enlightenment category of "man."

Smith's long blank verse poem of two books, *The Emigrants,* published in 1793 and written as a record of Smith's response to the plight of French émigrés in England, is undoubtedly her most powerful and significant anti-war poem. In *The Emigrants,* Smith seeks to evoke sympathy in her English readers for their French opponents and to create an internationalist consciousness of the need for reform of both English and French political systems, legal institutions and religious establishments.[19] Her critique of the social injustices that fed the French revolutionary effort turns insistently and ironically back on her British readers.

The poetic speaker of *The Emigrants* perceives her subject from a locus of detachment and potential transcendence in both books, on hills overlooking the beach and the sea. She has sought these scenes of peace and "tranquil seclusion" in a futile effort to escape the injustice of what she pointedly terms "legal crimes":

> How often, when my weary soul recoils
> From proud oppression, and from legal crimes
> (For such are in this Land where the vain boast
> Of equal Law is mockery, . . .
> How often do I half abjure Society,
> And sigh for some lone Cottage, deep embower'd
> In the green woods, that these steep chalky Hills
> Guard from the strong South West. (1. 35–44)

These radical lines, whose oxymoron "legal crimes" calls into question the rule of law, constitute a call for justice and are key to the understanding of Smith's sociopolitical positioning in relation to the French Revolution. It was Smith's marginalization and victimization as a woman by the patriarchal British legal system that awakened her acute political consciousness. The cadences of Smith's lines here are, of course, strikingly echoed in the opening of "Tintern Abbey." Instead of finding peace and protection in nature, however, as a Wordsworthian speaker might do, her poetic persona is approached by a group of French exiles driven from their homeland by "the name of Freedom misapplied" and "much abus'd / By lawless Anarchy" (1. 99–100). Her self-imposed isolation from and sense of victimization by the "legal crimes" of the British justice system opens her up to sympathy for these outcasts. Identifying with their plight, the speaker is compelled to a meditation on the political and spiritual lessons their fate teaches, lessons already expressed in cryptic fashion in Sonnet 59. And, analogous to the moon in that sonnet, freedom, in *The Emigrants,* is personified as a feminine consciousness transcendent of destructive emotion:

> And Liberty, with calm, unruffled brow
> Magnanimous, as conscious of her strength
> In Reason's panoply, scorns to distain
> Her righteous cause with carnage, and resigns
> To Fraud and Anarchy the infuriate crowd. (2. 57–61)

First and foremost, Smith attacks social hierarchy and economic inequality as the source of the violence of the French Revolution. In language reminiscent of Sonnet 59, she opposes the "pageant pomp of Courts" to the "genuine beauty of Nature" and paints Versailles, "rich with gold" as a "gay visionary pageant" of illusion and fancy that "gave charm to empire" and allowed aristocrats artificially to exalt themselves "o'er the race of common men" (1. 222–37). Like the moon in Sonnet 59 that stands above the "awful pageants" below and gilds that world with a light of her own emanating from "a spirit conscious of superior worth," so Smith accords the peasant, and not her addressee, the aristocrat, true worth and merit:

> —could *he* learn,
> That worth alone is true Nobility?
> And that *the peasant* who, "amid the sons
> Of Reason, Valour, Liberty, and Virtue,
> Displays distinguish'd merit, is a Noble
> Of Nature's own creation!" (1. 239–44)

Here Smith cleverly cloaks her egalitarian sentiments in a quote from James Thomson's adaptation of *Coriolanus,* but is unable to resist adding in a footnote that such sentiments "are now called (when used by living writers), not common-place declamation, but sentiments of dangerous tendency" (144). Once again Smith's observations here illuminate her differences with Wordsworth's ultimate conclusions about the Revolution. In a passage from Book Ten of *The Prelude* that strongly echoes both Sonnet 59 and *The Emigrants,* Wordsworth answers Smith's democratic instincts with a wish that the course of the Revolution might be set right by "one paramount mind" (10. 179) that would quell bloody conflict and clear "a passage for just government" (10. 185). In this masculinist counterpart to Smith's meditations on the moon, he imagines this "paramount mind" as an emblem of the collective divinity of humanity that is "Transcendent to all local patrimony, / One nature as there is one sun in heaven" (10. 139–140); "A spirit thoroughly faithful to itself, / Unquenchable, unsleeping, undismayed, . . ." (10. 147–48). This paramount spirit begins to look suspiciously like a Napoleon.[20]

Despite Smith's democratic ideals and impulses, there is, however, little idealization of English peasant life in this poem. In fact, Smith resists and exposes the falseness of the aristocratic, pastoral idyll and attacks economic and social injustice in France as a means of calling forth British self-critique. Rather than fomenting nationalism and war hysteria, she asks the British to take a hard look at themselves. The war against France, she asserts, is a scheme of "closet murderers, whom we style / Wise Politicians,"

> . . . to keep Europe's wavering balance even,
> Depopulate her kingdoms, and consign
> To tears and anguish half a bleeding world! (2. 320–24)

She furthermore sees the rural British landscape as "deformed" by figures of disease, poverty, and want awaiting from the Parish "the reluctant dole." Rather than propping up tyranny and oppression, as the counterrevolutionary forces sought to do, Smith urges her fellow Britons—pensioners and hirelings of the Court in particular—to "study a lesson that concerns ye much":

> And, trembling, learn, that if oppress'd too long,
> The raging multitude, to madness stung,
> Will turn on their oppressors; and, no more
> By sounding titles and parading forms
> Bound like tame victims, will redress themselves!
> Then swept away by the resistless torrent,
> Not only all your pomp may disappear,
> But, in the tempest lost, fair Order sink
> Her decent Head, and lawless Anarchy
> O'erturn celestial Freedom's radiant throne[.] (1. 333–42)

This address to pensioners and court hirelings is clearly an implicit warning to the counterrevolutionary Edmund Burke, whom Smith's hero in *Desmond* accuses of having prostituted himself to partisan interests and prejudices so that he has "become the champion of the placeman and the apologist of the pensioner":

> [W]hen he advances opinions, and maintains principles abso-
> lutely opposite to all the professions of his political life—when
> he dresses up contradictions with the gaudy flowers of his
> luxuriant imagination, in one place, and in another, know-
> ingly misrepresents facts, and swells the guilt of a *few*, into
> national crimes; to prove the delinquency of a whole people
> struggling for the dearest rights of humanity, Mr. Burke is
> become, in the opinion of these my courtier acquaintance, the
> most correct, as well as the most eloquent of men—for he is of
> their party. . . . (349)

Transcendence in this political context, then, means the capacity for self-awareness and self-critique born of a detachment from self-interest. In her effort to get British patriots like Burke to look at themselves, irony is her weapon of choice. Thus, in challenging the institution of hereditary nobility, and asserting that "worth alone is true Nobility" (1. 240), Smith queries, tongue-in-cheek:

> If even here,
> If in this land of highly vaunted Freedom,
> Even Britons controvert the unwelcome truth,
> Can it be relish'd by the sons of France? (1. 244–47)

And in a footnote to this section of the poem, Smith implies that the French upper classes are not necessarily more oppressive to the common people and are indeed "more mild and merciful" than the British in their treatment of Negro slaves. Considering Smith's frequent, insistent comparisons throughout her life of her own position as a woman in the British legal system to that of a slave or a piece of property, this seemingly off hand remark has a particular feminist bite.[21]

Finally, transcendence represents the overcoming of nationalism and what Smith terms "party rage" by the spirit of compassion and what she calls "acts of pure humanity" (1. 368). Once again it is the moon that embodies this form of transcendence in the climactic and concluding lines of Part I:

> These ill-starr'd Exiles, then . . .
> —well deserve
> To find that (every prejudice forgot,
> Which pride and ignorance teaches), we for them
> Feel as our brethren; and that English hearts,
> Of just compassion ever own the sway,
> As truly as our element, the deep,
> Obeys the mild dominion of the Moon[.] (1. 354–63)

The phrase "just compassion" is the key to understanding Smith's political position in this poem; she refuses to imagine compassion without justice. What Anne Mellor, following Carol Gilligan, has termed "an ethic of care," is for Smith inseparable from an "ethic of justice."[22] Indeed, the underlying emphasis on justice in *The Emigrants* links it to the radical stance of *Desmond* as forcefully asserted by its angelic heroine of sensibility, Geraldine, in her defense of the revolutionaries:

> While humanity drops her tears at the sad stories of those individuals who fell the victims of popular tumult so naturally

excited, pity cannot throw over these transactions a veil thick
enough to conceal the tremendous decree of justice, which,
like the 'hand writing upon the wall,' will be seen in colours of
blood, and however regretted, must still be acknowledged as
the hand of justice. (311)

Nevertheless, Smith's commitment to both compassion and
justice—to balancing an ethic of justice with an ethic of care—also
compels her to paint with great sympathy the suffering of her ideological enemies, the French aristocrats. "Whate'er your errors, I lament
your fate" (1. 107), she writes. As a woman, she depicts with especial
poignancy the suffering of women and children at the hands of the
French populace inspired "With savage thirst of kindred blood" by
figures like Marat, embodiment of "party Rage, perverse and blind"
(2. 118). Similarly, she expresses pity for Marie Antoinette, refusing to
idealize her as Edmund Burke had done or demonize her as republican sympathizers tended to do, instead providing an astute political
analysis of her fate as created by the institution of absolute monarchy:

> Ah! much I mourn thy sorrows, hapless Queen!
> And deem thy expiation made to Heaven
> For every fault, to which Prosperity
> Betray'd thee, when it plac'd thee on a throne
> Where boundless power was thine, and thou wert rais'd
> High (as it seem'd) above the envious reach
> Of destiny! Whate'er thy errors were,
> Be they no more remember'd; tho' the rage
> Of Party swell'd them to such crimes, as bade
> Compassion stifle every sigh that rose
> For thy disastrous lot. . . . (2. 154–64)

Furthermore, in expressing her empathy for Antoinette as a "wretched
Mother, petrified with grief," Smith is clearly writing as a mother
herself. We see here one of the many reasons why women readers in
particular responded so strongly to Smith, as is testified to by the
large number of poems dedicated to her throughout her career and
well beyond the date of her death. Smith's linking of compassion and
"pure humanity" with considerations of familial relations that cut
across nationalities and classes appeals directly to the sensibility
of her reader at the same time that it also clearly corroborates
Habermas's analysis of the private sphere in late eighteenth-century
Britain as the realm of "purely human" relationships glorified in the

sentimental novel.[23] Yet in setting these familial bonds against the backdrop of contemporary war and revolution, Smith politicizes her reader's vision of their ostensible purity and shows the private and the public realms to be inseparable.[24]

Compassion linked to a divine being worshipped "not in domes / Of human architecture, fill'd with crowds" (2. 390–91), but in the boundless beauty of nature, is also the source of the egalitarianism with which Smith concludes her poem. Transporting her reader to the perspective of an omnipotent power on high, as she had done in the final lines of Book One as well, Smith asks this power to view the earth with mercy, to "Restrain that rage for power, that bids a Man, / Himself a worm, desire unbounded rule / O'er beings like himself" (2. 423–26) and to teach "the hard hearts / Of rulers" that, seen from this god-like perspective, all humans are equal.

Charlotte Smith's poetry suggests the necessity of redefining our conceptions of Romantic transcendence to include visions of sublimity written from the sociocultural position of women. Born of her detachment from the locus of power in British legal and political systems, Smith's transcendence is a kind of self-doubling and self-awareness that allows one to see oneself from the outside, to appreciate one's worth as well as to practice self-criticism and to honor the common humanity even of one's ideological enemies. Indeed Smith opens her late masterpiece, *Beachy Head,* with a panoramic vision of a prehistorical moment when the Island of Britain and the European continent, and France, in particular, were one, thus challenging the very foundation of British national identity and patriotism in its opposition to France.[25]

In the final lines of *The Emigrants,* Smith also holds out freedom from any form of domination as the highest spiritual goal, one that Smith hopes will be the ultimate outcome of the tempestuous French Revolution. She concludes her poem not just with a call for empathy for the émigrés, but also with an appeal to "stern but equal justice" and to "public virtue," those watchwords of the French Revolution:

> May lovely Freedom, in her genuine charms,
> Aided by stern but equal Justice, drive
> From the ensanguin'd earth the hell-born fiends
> Of Pride, Oppression, Avarice, and Revenge,
> That ruin what thy mercy made so fair!
> Then shall these ill-starr'd wanderers, whose sad fate
> These desultory lines lament, regain
> Their native country; private vengeance then

To public virtue yield; and the fierce feuds,
That long have torn their desolated land,
May (even as storms, that agitate the air,
Drive noxious vapours from the blighted earth)
Serve, all tremendous as they are, to fix
The reign of Reason, Liberty, and Peace! (2. 431–44)

Thus, even as she expresses compassion for the French émigrés, Smith here also clearly asserts her allegiance to the ideals of the French Revolution, figured as an inevitable storm necessary to "Drive noxious vapours from the blighted earth," and significantly recasts "Liberty, Equality, and Fraternity" into "Reason, Liberty, and Peace." These concluding lines affirm, in my opinion, the strength and the courage of Smith's commitment to republican and emancipatory politics when one considers them in the light of the fact that they were written in April 1793, *after* the guillotining of Louis XVI and the declaration of war between England and France earlier that year.

Smith's politics of transcendence make her a pioneer in a powerful line of feminist and pacifist thought that took organizational form in the early twentieth century in the Women's International League for Peace and Freedom.[26] Virginia Woolf's masterpiece of pacifism and antifascism, *Three Guineas,* which was written in a similar spirit of detachment from and transcendence of the masculine public arena, as Woolf asserts from her "birds-eye view of the outside of things,"[27] is clearly a descendant of this line of feminist thought. Published in 1938, *Three Guineas* takes a courageously antinationalist stand reminiscent of Smith's unpopular critique of Britain's counterrevolutionary wars, a stance clearly rooted, as is that of Smith, in her identity as a woman, an outsider to patriarchal power. Woolf writes: "The outsider will find that she has no good reason to ask her brother to fight on her behalf to protect 'our' country. 'Our country,' she will say, 'throughout the greater part of its history has treated me as a slave; it has denied me education or any share in its possessions. . . . as a woman, I have no country. As a woman I want no country. As a woman my country is the whole world'" (197). Like Smith, Woolf still sees the history of women in British society as analogous to that of the slave.

Indeed Woolf, again like Charlotte Smith, employs the moon as an image of female power, now in the twentieth century a battle-scarred emblem of women's hard won potential for economic power after "the door of the private house was thrown open," (30) and the professions opened up to British women in 1919. Woolf imagines a woman who "issues from the shadow of the private house and stands on the bridge which lies between the old world and the new," twirling the "sacred coin" that she has recently earned. Looking up to the moon in the sky, as a votary of a modern-day Diana, she pledges uncompromising service to a religion of female freedom and independence. Once again, we see here the metaphor of slavery powerfully applied to woman's position, as it was so frequently by Charlotte Smith one hundred fifty years earlier.

> Through that light we may guess everything she saw looked different. . . . The moon even, scarred as it is in fact with forgotten craters, seemed to her a white sixpence, a chaste sixpence, an altar upon which she vowed never to side with the servile, the signers-on, since it was hers to do what she liked with—the sacred sixpence that she had earned with her own hands herself. And if checking imagination with prosaic good sense, you object that to depend upon a profession is only another form of slavery, you will admit from your own experience that to depend upon a profession is a less odious form of slavery than to depend upon a father. (30–1)

Furthermore, in a gesture that prefigures current analyses of situatedness and identity politics, Woolf defines her own perspective as aligned with that of other women of her class, "the daughters of educated men," as she terms it, and suggests that this perspective can never be the same as a man's perspective unless men and women are given what she cleverly terms "a memory transfusion"—a miracle notably still beyond the reach of modern science.

Three Guineas concludes, as does *The Emigrants,* with an activist, internationalist, and utopian vision of the potential that women's socially constructed differences can mean in their efforts to prevent war and protect liberty. Woolf proposes the formation of an "Outsiders' Society" consisting of "educated men's daughters working in their own class . . . and by their own methods for liberty, equality, and peace" (193).[28] Once again, the third term of the French Revolutionary triumvirate, "Fraternity," has been significantly changed to "Peace." Like Smith, though in a much more explicit and radical fashion, Woolf asserts that women can free themselves more easily than can men from the bonds of patriotism and nationalism because they have traditionally been dispossessed of their country's land, wealth, property, and legal protection. Yet Woolf does not naively idealize women or present them as ultimately outside of power, for she emphasizes that as women rise to power in legal, educational, and religious institutions, they face some of the same temptations as do men. Even more insistently than Smith, she calls for self-doubling, self-awareness, and self-critique in an effort to be ever vigilant against abuses of power. Thus she concludes *Three Guineas* with a picture of the German or Italian fascist dictator about whom she asserts, in Foucauldian fashion: ". . . we cannot dissociate ourselves from that figure but are ourselves that figure. . . . [W]e are not passive spectators doomed to unresisting obedience but by our thoughts and actions can ourselves change that figure" (259). The figure of fascism which for Woolf becomes a "picture of evil" is an evil that woman must combat in her own way as she explains to men seeking her political alliance and allegiance. Clearly, for Woolf, women's oppositional writings and political efforts constitute a public arena that is distinct from the masculine discursive sphere: "We are both determined to do what we can to destroy the evil which the picture represents, you by your methods, we by ours. And since we are different, our help must be different. We can best help you to prevent war not by joining your society but by remaining outside your society but in co-operation with its aim" (260).

Despite the tragedies of their personal lives, the legacy of international pacifism and utopian feminist spirit, linked originally to the cataclysmic upheaval of the French Revolution and embodied in the writings of Charlotte Smith and Virginia Woolf, lives on today and finds eloquent contemporary expression in the words of Burmese dissident and Nobel Peace Laureate Suu Kyi addressing the 1995 women's conference in Beijing, China: "It is not the prerogative of men alone to bring light into this world. Women, with their capacity for self-sacrifice, their courage and perseverance, have done much to dissipate the darkness of intolerance and hate."[29] [30]

Notes

1. Simone de Beauvoir, *The Second Sex*, trans. and ed. H. M. Parshley (New York: Knopf, 1952: Reprint, New York: Bantam, 1970), 43. All parenthetical references to *The Second Sex* are to this edition.

2. See Stuart Curran, "Romantic Poetry: The I Altered," *Romanticism and Feminism,* ed. Anne K. Mellor (Bloomington: Indiana University Press, 1988), Meena Alexander, *Women in Romanticism* (London: Macmillan, 1989), Marlon Ross, *The Contours of Masculine Desire: Romanticism and the Rise of Women's Poetry* (New York: Oxford University Press, 1989), Anne K. Mellor,

Romanticism and Gender (New York: Routledge, 1993), and Nanora Sweet, "History, Imperialism, and the Aesthetics of the Beautiful: Hemans and the Post-Napoleonic Moment," in *At the Limits of Romanticism: Essays in Cultural, Feminist, and Materialist Criticism,* eds. Mary A. Favret and Nicola Watson (Bloomington: Indiana University Press, 1994), 170–184 .

3. For examples of this feminist critique of the gendered opposition between the sublime and the beautiful, see Patricia Yaeger, "Toward a Female Sublime," *Gender and Theory,* ed. Linda Kauffman (Oxford: Basil Blackwell, 1989), 191–212, Paul Mattick, Jr., "Beautiful and Sublime: Gender Totemism in the Constitution of Art," *The Journal of Aesthetics and Art Criticism,* 48.4 (Fall 1990): 293–304, and Kari E. Lokke, "Schiller's *Maria Stuart:* The Historical Sublime and the Aesthetics of Gender", *Monatshefte* 82.2 (Summer 1990): 123–141.

4. Charlotte Smith, *The Poems of Charlotte Smith,* ed. Stuart Curran (New York and Oxford: Oxford University Press, 1993). See the introduction, xix. All parenthetical references to Smith's poetry and to the prefaces of the *Elegiac Sonnets* are to page and line numbers from this edition and, for *The Emigrants,* to book and line number.

5. Huntington Library Manuscript, HM 10812, Charlotte Smith letter to J. C. Walker, 25 March 1794. This item is reproduced by permission of the Huntington Library, San Marino, California. In *Charlotte Smith: A Critical Biography* (London: Macmillan, 1998), Loraine Fletcher describes Joseph Cooper Walker as a Dublin clergyman and antiquarian who "was interested in Irish history and Ireland's traditional music, poetry and dress. Like John O'Neill, who though a Protestant, supported Catholic emancipation and voted against the Riot Bill of 1787, he was involved in an early phase of Irish Revivalism and nationalism" (190). Walker arranged for an Irish edition of *The Old Manor House.*

6. Biddy Martin, "Feminism, Criticism, and Foucault," in *Feminism and Foucault: Reflections on Resistance,* eds. Irene Diamond and Lee Quinby (Boston: Northeastern University Press, 1988), 13.

7. Rita Felski, *Beyond Feminist Aesthetics: Feminist Literature and Social Change* (Cambridge: Harvard University Press, 1989), 167.

8. As Nancy Fraser writes in "Rethinking the Public Sphere: A Contribution to the Critique of Actually Existing Democracy," *Habermas and the Public Sphere,* ed. Craig Calhoun (Cambridge, Mass.: MIT Press, 1992), "[v]irtually from the beginning, counterpublics contested the exclusionary norms of the bourgeois public, elaborating alternative styles of political behavior and alternative norms of public speech" (116).

9. See Jerome McGann, *The Romantic Ideology* (Chicago: University of Chicago Press, 1983), Marjorie Levinson, *Wordsworth's Great Period Poems: Four Essays* (Cambridge: Cambridge University Press, 1986), Alan Liu,

Wordsworth: The Sense of History (Stanford: Stanford University Press, 1989), David Simpson, *Wordsworth's Historical Imagination: The Poetry of Displacement* (London and New York: Methuen, 1987), and Marlon Ross, "Naturalizing Gender: Woman's Place in Wordsworth's Ideological Landscape," *ELH* 53 (Summer 1986): 391–410.

10. I am, of course, indebted here to Jerome McGann, who argues in *The Romantic Ideology* that "Byron and Shelley are most deeply *engaged* (in a socialist-activist sense) when they have moved furthest along their paths of displacement and escape. This aspect of their work is what allies them to the 'Romanticism' of all the other Romantic poets" (124).

11. In this preface to the sixth edition, Smith protests against the "scorn and insult" directed at her by the lawyers charged with administering her children's estate, an inheritance from their paternal grandfather. She writes, "those gentlemen . . . , though they acknowledge that all impediments to a division of the estate they have undertaken to manage, are done away . . . neither tell me *when* they will proceed to divide it, or *whether they will ever do so at all*" (6). This preface constitutes an ironic meditation on the relation of private and public realms, for Smith claims to refuse to elaborate on her private sorrows in public, stating that they are of a "domestic and painful nature," and concludes with a bitter assertion that, despite the fact that she is "an Authoress," she is "well aware that for a woman—'The Post of Honor is a Private Station'" (6).

12. Friedrich Schiller, *Naive and Sentimental Poetry and On the Sublime* (New York: Frederick Ungar, 1966), 208.

13. One cannot rule out the role of direct influence here, since Wordsworth visited Smith in the months after she wrote Sonnet 59 on his way to France in November 1791 and might have seen an unpublished copy of it before he wrote the first version of the Mount Snowdon episode which appeared in *Descriptive Sketches,* written in 1792, one year after his walking tour in Wales. He certainly was likely to have read the published sonnet before composing the *Prelude* passage in February 1804.

14. Quotes are from the Norton Critical Edition of *The Prelude,* eds. Jonathan Wordsworth, M. H. Abrams, and Stephen Gill (New York: W.W. Norton, 1979). References are to book and line numbers.

15. See Marlon Ross, *The Contours of Masculine Desire* and "Romantic Quest and Conquest: Troping Masculine Power in the Crisis of Poetic Identity" *Romanticism and Feminism,* ed. Anne K. Mellor (Bloomington: Indiana University Press, 1988), 26–51.

16. Charlotte Smith, *Desmond,* ed. and intro. Antje Blank and Janet Todd (London: Pickering and Chatto, 1997). All references to *Desmond* are to this edition.

17. Esther Schor, *Bearing the Dead: The British Culture of Mourning From the Enlightenment to Victoria* (Princeton: Princeton University Press, 1994), 64.

18. John Milton, *Paradise Lost,* ed. Scott Elledge (New York: W.W. Norton, 1975), 44.

19. Curran's footnote to the poem's title renders evident the degree to which Smith's sociopolitical position as a woman makes possible her particular perspective on the émigrés and their wives, many of whom were widowed by their husbands' participation in futile counterrevolutionary violence: "The extent to which rules made by men at once keep women dependent and leave them no recourse when left alone links these distressed emigrants and the poet who observes them" (131).

20. I would like to thank Adriana Craciun for pointing out the echoes of Smith's imagery of transcendence in this passage from Wordsworth's meditations on the French Revolution in book 10 of *The Prelude.* I am also indebted to Adriana for noting the similarities between Sonnet 59 and *Paradise Lost,* II (427–30). Damian Walford Davies argues convincingly in "Hermits, Heroes, and History: Lamb's 'Many Friends'" *Charles Lamb Bulletin* 97 (1997): 9–29 that the "one paramount mind" to which Wordsworth refers here may be the Welshman David Williams, historian, religious thinker and radical political theorist.

21. The subject of slavery is a thorny one for Smith, because, as her biographer Loraine Fletcher points out, the inheritance that was the object of her interminable legal battles was based on a fortune from her father-in-law Richard Smith's Jamaican slave plantations. In attacking slavery, Smith attacks her own family and, in a sense, herself. This situation was set right by the next generation when Charlotte Smith's son Lionel became Governor of Jamaica as the slaves throughout the British Empire were freed. Fletcher writes, "[t]he planters tried to dodge the new law by charging rent for their ex-slaves' huts, ensuring that they still worked for nothing. Lionel's attitude to the West Indian oligarchy 'was not conciliatory,' the *DNB* entry notes. He had absorbed his mother's reformist politics at their brightest before he left home in 1794, and set about Emancipation energetically, gaining the respect of the black population and the loathing of the whites" (337).

22. See Anne Mellor, *Romanticism and Gender* (New York: Routledge, 1993), 3, 68, 71, 77, 105, 136, 209.

23. See Jürgen Habermas, *The Structural Transformation of the Public Sphere,* trans. Thomas Burger and Frederick Lawrence (Cambridge, Mass.: MIT Press, 1989), 48–50.

24. Relevant here in the discussion of Smith as mother is the fact that her favorite daughter, Anna Augusta, married a French émigré and aristocrat, Alexandre de Foville. Though contemporaries saw the political stance

of *The Emigrants* as attributable to this family connection and emphasize its departure from *Desmond,* Fletcher rightfully points out that Smith had expressed pity for the émigrés in a letter to Joel Barlow well before her daughter met de Foville. See Fletcher, 196–200.

25. Matthew Bray in "Removing the Anglo-Saxon Yoke: The Franco-centric Vision of Charlotte Smith's Later Works" in *The Wordsworth Circle,* 24 (Summer 1993), even asserts that in the last years of her life Smith viewed "English history as *French* history," articulating "an increasingly seditious vision of England's historical and political ties to France, a vision that went against the patriotic Anglo-Saxonism that consumed England during the early years of the war" (155). He suggests that, in *Beachy Head,* she implicitly welcomes Napoleon as a second [Norman] conqueror, a messiah who will unite France and England. That Smith would celebrate any such military conquest is highly debatable.

26. For an excellent history of this movement and the WILPF, see Leila J. Rupp, *Worlds of Women: The Making of an International Women's Movement* (Princeton, N.J.: Princeton University Press, 1998).

27. Virginia Woolf, *Three Guineas* (London: Hogarth Press, 1938), 41. All subsequent references to *Three Guineas* are to this edition.

28. Woolf considers it imperative for effective political discourse and action to acknowledge her own class background and to be honest about her distance from the working class. "If . . . the educated (as so often happens) renounce the very qualities which education should have bought—reason, tolerance, knowledge—and play at belonging to the working class and adopting its cause, they merely expose that cause to the ridicule of the educated class, and do nothing to improve their own. But the number of books written by the educated about the working class would seem to show that the glamour of the working class and the emotional relief afforded by adopting its cause, are today as irresistible to the middle class as the glamour of the aristocracy was twenty years ago (see *A La Recherche du Temps Perdu*). Meanwhile it would be interesting to know what the true-born working man or woman thinks of the playboys and playgirls of the educated class who adopt the working class cause without sacrificing middle-class capital, or sharing working class experience" (312).

29. Quoted in Rone Tempest and Maggie Farley, "Forum Tests China's Patience: Women Revel in Speaking Freely as Conference Opens," *The Sacramento Bee,* 1 September 1995: A1. Suu Kyi gave the keynote address by videotape; she did not attend the conference for fear that she would not be permitted to re-enter Burma.

30. An earlier version of this paper was presented at the UCLA Center for Modern and Contemporary Studies in a workshop on "Women and the Public Sphere in England, 1780-1840," organized by Anne K. Mellor. Kari

Lokke wishes to thank Anne Mellor and the participants—Isobel Armstrong, Ann Bermingham, Julie Carlson, Mitzi Myers—as well as the audience at this workshop, for their helpful responses to her work. Adriana Craciun's insights and suggestions for revision have also meant that this essay is much improved over earlier drafts.

Revolution and Religion

The Anxiety of (Feminine) Influence:
Hannah More and Counterrevolution

⌧

Angela Keane

Hannah More is an untidy figure for those who wish to draw up neat categories of British responses to the French Revolution, or of the broader ideological field of the 1790s. More's commitment to the campaign for the abolition of slavery, her material contribution to the reform and extension of the education franchise, her reevaluation of women's contribution to the national economy, and the "anti-establishment" character of her religious practices from the 1790s onwards would seem to be the essence of liberalism, if not radical populism. The more residing image of More is compiled from accounts of her fraught patronage of Ann Yearsley, her vociferous critique of the sexual character of her contemporary Mary Wollstonecraft, her self-confessed desire to use education to manage an increasingly self-conscious working-class mob, and the imperialist rhetoric of her anti-slavery poetry, all of which demonstrate the "disciplinary" dynamic which underpins her various public campaigns. More's explicit distrust of democracy, which culminated in her refusal to sign a petition for reform in 1832, for a long time sealed her fate in criticism as the reactionary to Mary Wollstonecraft's radical: a portrait which only relatively recent reappraisal of More's work has begun to contest.[1] Dispensing with the radical/reactionary binary, this essay will consider the revolutionary potential of More's counter-revolutionary polemics.

In the 1790s, much of Hannah More's considerable energy was devoted to keeping up with British "public opinion," which was constituted in and by the wide range of print media, corresponding societies, and ad hoc associations which often threatened to overwhelm the established channels of political opinion throughout the decade.

For many British commentators, fear of the speed with which changes in neighboring France had taken hold, and with which revolutionary events were being represented to a diverse and often disgruntled British readership, merged into an anxiety that a popular appetite for news and the spectacle of sensation, heroism, and tragedy in France would lead the public to play out such scenes in Britain. The crude response to this kind of revolutionary panic was censorship. Hannah More, however, had a more sophisticated grasp of the difference between medium and event, and saw the potential to mobilize the power of print for the counterrevolutionary cause and beyond. More was a canny manipulator not only of the press, but of social connection and of economic patronage. This political acumen meant that More could respond more rapidly, widely, and powerfully than many of her "counterrevolutionary" contemporaries (including Edmund Burke) to a public that was quickly redefining itself, its relationship with the British establishment, and with politics. More, as this essay will demonstrate, was willing to engage with the "popular imagination." If More's motivation was to harness and discipline the productive powers of that imagination, the discursive effects of her counterrevolutionary campaigns would have unforeseen consequences.

"A new Similitude Wherewith To Compare My Weakness"

> I have been an arrant stroller—amusing myself by sailing down the beautiful river Wye, looking at abbeys and castles, with Mr Gilpin in my hand to teach me to criticize, and talk of foregrounds, and distances, and perspectives, and prominences, with all the cant of connoisseurship, and then to *subdue* my imagination, which had not been a little disordered with this enchanting scenery, I have been living in sober magnificence with the Plantagenet Dowager Duchess at Stoke, where a little more discretion, and a little less fancy was proper and decorous.[2]

This wry correspondent, writing to Horace Walpole in 1789 to recount the overheated effects of a picturesque stroll, is neither the "great enchantress" Ann Radcliffe, nor the "solitary walker" Mary Wollstonecraft, who were both famed for their meditations on landscape, but the pious bluestocking Hannah More. This letter to Walpole is part of a correspondence that began in the 1780s and lasted until his death in 1796, and is the sign of a friendship which grew out of

More's involvement in London and Bristol literary circles. The pastiche
is significant not just as an illustration of the socialite side of "the
bishop in petticoats."[3] It also demonstrates her ability to mimic the
"popular," or here at least, the fashionable pursuits of her contemporaries while signaling her critical distance from them. The letter begins
in a similar vein, as she parodically anticipates Walpole's rebuke to her
for not writing sooner, and provokes him to find new terms in which
to describe her neglect:

> I have been so brutally negligent of your last favour, that you
> might *once* have taunted me with the proverbial reproach,
> that "ingratitude is worse than the sin of witchcraft"; but now
> that demonology, and miracles, and witchcraft are become
> fashionable and approved things, you must endeavour to find
> out a new similitude wherewith to compare my wickedness.
> (319)

This taunt at her friend's petulance (and at his taste for the Gothic)
also spells out More's sensitivity to the speed with which novelty
becomes orthodoxy, and the sacrilegious seems acceptable. She echoes,
of course, a charge which had become fairly commonplace in the field
of literary criticism, and which was frequently levelled at eighteenth-
century novelists who were simultaneously attacked for feeding, and
feeding on, the morally dubious public appetite for new matter, newly
told, and for failing to produce anything novel at all. More later
participated in this kind of critique when, in her *Strictures on Female
Education* of 1799, she described the means by which popular fiction
proliferates without the will of an author.[4] The "glutted imagination"
of the reader, she proclaims, "soon overflows with the redundance of
cheap sentiment and plentiful incident, and by a sort of arithmetical
proposition, is enabled by the perusal of any three novels, to produce
a fourth; till every fresh production, like the prolific progeny of
Banquo, is followed by Another, and another, and another!" (*M*, 8:
220). It was the public which read, and imitated, these fictions, and
which was voracious and restless in its taste, which alarmed counterrevolutionary political commentators in the 1790s. The fear of a newly
literate public was registered in Burke's *Reflections on the Revolution
in France,* "in a letter intended to have been sent to a young gentleman in Paris." Burke's "letter" is a querulous fantasy of political
discourse as an urbane exchange between men of a certain class, and
was a crucial discursive intervention at a moment when such upper-
class, masculine intimacy was under severe pressure from a new

constituency of politicians. In France, Burke claimed, such pressure had been exerted by the "men of letters" (he does not mention the women) that France had exploded into the chaos and anarchy of the revolution.

While More might have been reluctant to celebrate the fact, she understood that "public opinion" far outreached the 400,000 political citizens that Burke was ready to acknowledge in 1796, and that these unknown people had to be addressed.[5] Whereas Burke, at least superficially, eschewed the popular media which addressed this new public, More apparently immersed herself in it. For instance, while she was in Bath recovering from a chest complaint in February 1793, she wrote to Walpole and ironically figured herself as a pulp junkie, the boredom of her illness having produced an addiction to the quick fixes of expurgated texts :

> I wonder if I shall ever live to read a book again that shall cost a shilling. I have lived so long on halfpenny papers, penny cautions, twopenny warnings, and threepenny sermons, that I shall never be able to stretch my capacity even to a duodecimo! I shall try though, for I find my present studies very harassing to the nerves, and although like dram-drinking, they invigorate for a moment, yet like that too, they add to the depression afterwards. (*W,* 375–6)

The intoxicating power of these rapidly produced and disseminated texts is the theme of much of her correspondence with Walpole, and, in the privacy of their virtual literary salon, the two exchange jokes about the merits of the latest publications. Although More is addicted to pulp fiction, she determines not to keep up with some of the latest print fashions:

> I have been much pestered to read the *Rights of Women* [sic], but am invincibly resolved not to do it. Of all jargon, I hate metaphysical jargon; besides there is something fantastic and absurd in the very title. How many ways there are of being ridiculous! I am sure I have as much liberty as I can make a good use of, now I am an old maid, and when I was a young one, I had, I dare say, more than was good for me. (*W,* 370)

More's apparently complacent, post-feminist posture conceals a much sharper anxiety about the "ridiculous metaphysical jargon" of Wollstonecraft's *Vindication;* jargon which was saturating all kinds of discourse, and which, at least from some perspectives, had been wrenched from British political tradition, appropriated by the French and re-imported across the channel. Walpole joined More in exiling Wollstonecraft's tract, unread, from his library, preferring to give thanks for "the tranquillity and happiness we enjoy in this country":

> in spite of the philosophizing serpents we have in our bosom, the Paines, the Tookes, and the Woolstoncrafts [sic]; I am glad you have not read the tract of the last-mentioned writer: I would not look at it, though assured it contains neither meta-physics nor politics; but as she entered the lists in the latter, and borrowed her title from the demon's book, which aimed at spreading the *wrongs* of men, she is excommunicated from the pale of my library. We have had enough of new systems, and the world a great deal too much already. (*W*, 373)

The distaste for new systems which More shared with Walpole is expressed in her brand of "politics," and in her tendency to privilege the local and particular over the abstract cause.[6] Paradoxically, but not unusually in British political and philosophical traditions, her impatience with metaphysics stems from her own metaphysical logic and her faith in religion as the basis of all social action. More's is a "practical piety," however, and she is less given to speculative theology than to the performance of faith through humanitarian relief of suffering and Christian conversion of "the godless."

Practical Piety

More's attitude to the French Revolution, particularly as she expresses it in her correspondence with Walpole, demonstrates her apparent antipathy towards political abstraction. Like most liberal commentators, More welcomed the destruction of the Bastille. In a letter to Walpole she wrote that with the "extinction of the Inquisition" and the "redemption of Africa," the demise of the notorious prison amounted to the demolition of "three great engines of the Devil" (*W*, 321). However, More was quick to express her regret at the transfer of power in France, which she regarded as the triumph of "the lawless" and the godless: this was to be the tenor of the rest of her commentary on the revolution.

During July of 1790, while Paris was celebrating its new order with the Fête de la Fédération, More was taking refuge in Cowslip

Green, the house in the Mendips, which she shared with her sister Martha. The rural isolation of the house suited her antagonistic posture to the universalist sentiments issuing from France, and in a letter to Walpole, she dramatizes herself in geographical and historical exile. "I live here in so much quiet and ignorance," she writes, "that I know no more of what is passing among mankind, than of what is going on in the planet Saturn" (*W,* 340). Her Walpolean claim that she thinks of "anything but politics" does not bear scrutiny.[7] From her little corner of the world, she is quick to comment on the most current events, if only to dismiss their significance. Comparing the feast in the Champs de Mars, with which she supposes (sardonically paraphrasing Milton) "all Europe rings from side to side," with the Champs du drap d'or (the meeting near Calais between Francis I and Henry VIII in 1520) she finds in the latter "the remnants of chivalry, and old grandeur, of which modern festivity gives me no idea" (*W,* 340). Here, like Burke, she mocks the drabness of revolutionary spectacle and laments the passing of the age of chivalry. Three years later, commenting on the execution of the king, she again echoes Burke's *Reflections,* as she writes as the shocked surveyor of the incomprehensible scene: "the iniquity of today furnishes you with no data to conjecture of what sort will be the iniquity of tomorrow" (*W,* 376). Unwilling or unable to make sense of the disordered epic in France, she turns in her letters to singular episodes of her own charitable actions, relating them in all their in quotidian detail. When she *does* write of the revolution, she reserves her sympathy for the anthropomorphized country: "poor France," victim of the anarchic mob. She pities the monarchy too, as she colludes with Walpole in his portrait of wronged goodness, and depicts herself "weeping at the picture of the Queen carrying her little bundle into her narrow and squalid prison" (*W,* 388).

Walpole expresses ironic surprise at her reaction against the revolution, and claims it is at odds with her charitable bent and her penchant for a good cause. More's attention to suffering is frequently the subject of their letters, and Walpole regularly rails at the disproportionate relation between her concern for a passing charity case and her neglect of their friendship. When not berating More for ignoring him, Walpole sketches an astute, and more interesting, characterization of the paradoxical posture of retired sensibility that More adopts in her correspondence from Cowslip Green. When he writes in August 1792, with details of the Paris massacres, he demands a *political* response from More. That is, he pushes her to contemplate an epic scene in which a "whole nation," rather than an individual, is in need of salvation. "What must your tenderness not feel now," he asks "when a whole nation of monsters is burst forth?" Recounting details of the massacre, he taunts:

> why do I wound your thrilling nerves with the relation of such horrible scenes! Your *blackmanity* must allot some of its tears to these poor victims. For my part, I have an abhorrence of politics, if one can so term these tragedies, which make one harbour sentiments one naturally abhors; but can one refrain without difficulty from exclaiming, such a nation should be exterminated? (*W,* 372)

More was eventually to find less apocalyptic means of dealing with the August massacres by channelling her counterrevolutionary activism into a humanitarian cause: that of the French émigré priests who were exiled from France by the revolutionary government in August 1792. Their plight was brought to public attention by Edmund Burke, an acquaintance of More's on whose behalf she had campaigned in his election to Parliament as member for Bristol in 1774. Burke's plea for the recusants had led to a series of subscription appeals throughout Britain, and More was prompted by Charles Burney to invite some of the refugees into her home in Bath and to lend her services to a campaign addressed to the "Ladies of Great Britain." To this end, she wrote a tract, *Remarks on the Speech of M. Dupont,* which was published by Cadell, and donated the proceeds to the priests' relief fund.[8]

Here, as she was quick to point out, was a local cause, counterrevolutionary in a broad sense, but "of no party" (*R,* ix). Partyless politics was, of course, the hallmark of radical opposition, that multifaceted groundswell of opinion set against party political division and motivated by a desire to expose and overturn a corrupt political system.[9] More never turned her attention to the corruption within British party politics, willing as she was to accept the patronage of both Whig and Tory benefactors. Unlike William Cobbett, who saw the nation as a chain of dependence cultivated by an all-consuming center, she conceived of corruption as a kind of local weakness. One side-effect of More's diagnosis of corruption, and her prescriptions for its localized treatment, is the discursive production of female authority. This was an authority which radical opposition rarely imagined. More understood that the fate of national economy, patriotism, pedagogy, as well as the more conventionally feminine responsibility for moral and spiritual welfare lay in the hands of Britain's women, the *doyennes* of households and local community, and prophylactics against French corruption.

It is in the guise of "a private individual," then, that More banishes "lesser motives of delicacy," and makes a robust appeal to "the Ladies, etc. of Great Britain" for their charitable donations to the émigrés' relief fund. The subject of the pamphlet was another cause close to More's heart: national education. It was prompted by a speech made in the National Convention at Paris in December 1792 by Jacob Dupont, in a debate on the establishment of secular public schools in France. Dupont, a professed atheist, called for the overthrow of religious idolatry, the propagation of nature-worship, and the cultivation of reason in primary schools. The speech, which was published in the French paper *Le Moniteur,* was translated and reproduced in More's pamphlet. She did this in the face of criticism from "many good men" who believed that the speech "ought not to be made familiar to the minds of Englishmen; for there are crimes with which even the imagination should never come in contact" (*R,* 10). On the contrary, she argued, the speech was already so widely known in Britain that there was little point in shielding her readers from its pernicious policy. More chose rather to adopt the principles of "an ancient nation" which "intoxicated their slaves, and then exposed them before their children, in order to increase their horror of intemperance," in the belief that such impiety would strengthen rather than shake the faith of the Christian reader (*R,* 11). Further, she recorded the speech as a dramatic performance, as she included in the transcription references to the behavior of the Assembly during Dupont's address, and reproduced the scene as a combination of tragedy and blasphemous farce. So, as Dupont proclaims "Nature and Reason, these ought to be the gods of men! These are my gods!", More parenthetically describes the reaction in the Assembly: "(Here the Abbé Audrein cried out, "There is no bearing this"; and rushed out of the Assembly.—A great laugh)" (*R,* 9).

Having set and deflated the scene of Dupont's rhetorical impiety, More's commentary goes on to rail against the prospect of a system of secular education spreading to Britain. As she explained to Walpole, she was moved to comment on this speech and an attack on priests which had been addressed to the Jacobin club, in lieu of an intervention by the Anglican establishment. Their silence on the matter, she argued, would allow atheism to take hold of the British populace by virtue of its familiarity:

> Dupont's and Manuel's atheistical speeches have stuck in my throat all the winter, and I have been waiting for our bishops and our clergy to take some notice of them, but blasphemy and atheism have been allowed to become familiar to the

minds of our common people, without any attempt being made to counteract the poison. (*W*, 381)

More evidently had little faith in the revolutionary principles of rational education as the route to civil society. As she commented in her *Remarks,* her recommended pedagogical regimen is strictly metaphysical, based on absolute, not relative, truth:

> no degree of wit and learning; no progress in commerce; no advances in the knowledge of nature, or in the embellishments of art, can ever thoroughly tame that savage, the natural human heart, without RELIGION. The arts of social life may give a sweetness to the manners and language, and induce in some degree, a love of justice, truth, and humanity; but attainments derived from such inferior causes are no more than the semblance and shadow of the qualities derived from pure Christianity. (*R*, 33–4)

Given that More is writing this pamphlet on behalf of Catholic émigré priests, it seems that any Christian religion will do. She anticipates the hostility to her appeal on these grounds: "Christian charity is of no party. We plead not for their faith, but for their wants" (*R*, ix). This did not prevent the most immediate criticism of the *Remarks* turning on More not only to defend Dupont, but also to object to her support of "popery." Of three "answers" to her pamphlet, cited by More in a letter to Walpole, the only identifiable author is Michael Nash, who, she complains to Walpole, "declares, that I am a favourer of the old popish massacres" (*W*, 388–9). In *Gideon's Cake of Barley Meal: a Letter to the Rev. William Romaine . . . with Some Strictures on Mrs Hannah More's Remarks,* Nash moots the possibility that Hannah "may be a descendant of that bitter persecutor Sir Thomas More," and that "she would have made an excellent maid of honour to that bloody queen [Mary]" (quoted *W*, 388–89).

Edmund Burke, who initiated the campaign for the émigrés, came in for similar kinds of criticism from various quarters during his career, partly because of the Catholicism of his maternal family, the Nagles, and because of his advocacy of Catholic emancipation; like all counterrevolutionaries who based their opposition partly on religious grounds, Burke and More were bound to face ridicule from those who saw the irony of launching a defence of the British establishment through the cause of the Catholics of the French *ancien régime*. More than this, however, More's religious principles, though not Catholic, were not representative of the Anglican establishment. Indeed, as I shall suggest, the Evangelical circle in which More moved in the 1790s, the so-called Clapham Sect, which included William Wilberforce, the Tory Member of Parliament for Hull, and his cousin, the banker Henry Thornton, were more subversive than supportive of many facets of the established order in Britain.

The antiestablishment character of the Clapham Sect is apparent in a number of pamphlets written by More herself during the period she was involved with them, including *Thoughts on the Manners of the Great* of 1788 and *An Estimate of the Religion of the Fashionable World* of 1790. The *Remarks* too, while written to counteract the poison in the minds of the "common people," are addressed to their betters, with a mind to their reformation. More appealed to those in a position to afford the subscription to the priests' fund, and petitioned them to use their social authority in the vigilant watch against the invasion of French revolutionary doctrine. It is they, of course, who are most susceptible to infection. Addressing her *Remarks* in particular to women of "luxurious habits," who have little to spare, she pleads the case for sacrificing "one costly dish . . . , one expensive desert [sic] . . . , one evening's public amusement" to furnish "at least a week's subsistence to more than one person as liberally bred as herself" (4). She is careful, then, not to argue against luxurious habits but flatters her readers through appeals to their domestic acumen, and to their empathy for their social equals. The support of these priests, she argues, is not downward benevolence, but relief of those of similar social standing, victims of "the revolution of human affairs . . . thrown from equal heights of gaiety and prosperity" (*R,* 5). If one of the most resonant symbols of the cultural revolution in France was the women of the court donating their goods to the nation, then this welcoming gesture to the exiled clergy, "without a home—without a country!" has a powerful counterrevolutionary significance (*R,* 5).

More dwells less on the abstract power of empathy or on the political and symbolic value of the donations than on more immediate interests for the maternal and patriotic reader: that is, the promotion of domestic discipline and national wealth. She illustrates the bonus of "the lesson of economy" which the charitable mother can bestow on her daughter through her contribution. If the daughter as yet has no money of her own to bestow (which, More suggests, no daughter of a prudent mother would) she can learn to hold back on feathers, ribbons and "idle diversions": "if they are thus instructed, that there is no true charity without self-denial, they will gain more than they are called upon to give: For the suppression of one luxury for a charitable purpose, is the exercise of two virtues, and this without any pecuniary expense"

(R, 4). To those with less means, and to whom lessons in accumulation through restraint may be insufficient argument, More evokes the cause of national wealth. The small contribution of "the industrious tradesman" will bring relief with interest: "The money raised is neither carried out of our country, nor dissipated in luxuries, but returns again to the community; to our shops and to our markets, to procure the bare necessaries of life" (R, 5). More thus advocates a feminized, even maternal economy, in which resources are channelled into the sustenance of the home: a home which must be protected from the corrupting influence of parasitic neighbors.

Home Economics

More was to revive her arguments for national Christian peda-gogy and domestic economy a few years later in her *Strictures on Female Education*. The revolution having given way to war, More turned her attention to the education of female patriots, who would "come forward, without departing from the refinement of their char-acter, without derogating from the dignity of their rank . . . to raise the depressed tone of public morals, and to awaken the drowsy spirit of religious principle" (M, 7: 4–5). Her emphasis is now less on the sound management of expenditure, on the visible and local returns of money spent, than on the well-regulated household as the model and foundation of the British way of life:

> Oeconomy, such as a woman of fortune is called on to practise, is not merely the petty detail of small daily expenses, the shabby curtailments and stinted parsimony of a little mind, operating in little concerns; but it is the exercise of a sound judgement exerted in the comprehensive line of order, of arrangement, of distribution; of regulations by which alone well-governed societies, great and small, subsist. She who has the best regulated mind will, other things being equal, have the best regulated family. . . . A sound economy is a sound understanding brought into action; it is calculation realised; it is the doctrine of proportion reduced to practice; it is fore-seeing consequences, and guarding against them; it is expect-ing contingencies and being prepared for them. (M, 7: 6–7)

In this anti-speculative, and implicitly anti-Gallic vision, the economy of the household is not simply analogous to the economy of state. For

More, domestic and national economy exist on a continuum; moreover, the line from home to state begins with the well-regulated mind of the woman, which can bring "understanding" into "action," which can realize a calculation and reduce "doctrine" to "practice." The well-regulated woman of More's patriotic household carries on her tasks unseen; she exerts her influence without ostentation and with no expectation of reward. She is thus to be distinguished from the "narrow minded vulgar economist," to whom the details of the household are "continually present," and who is:

> overwhelmed by their weight, and is perpetually bespeaking your pity for her labours and your praise for her exertions; she is afraid you will not see how much she is harassed. She is not satisfied that the machine moves harmoniously, unless she is perpetually exposing every secret spring of observation. (*M*, 8: 7)

More's vilification of the woman who visibly labors under the burden of domesticity can be understood in the context of More's gendered intervention into a discourse of political economy which, she implies, has long assumed but not articulated or protected the role of the domestic economist. While, as Kathryn Sutherland has argued, Adam Smith had established the value of "a feminised space . . . as generative of long-term economic good," the worth of "the enclosed family groups" as "the nursery of some of the best characteristics of modern commercial man" and the significance of "the household's capacity for consumption" as a "vital stimulus to large-scale production," his economic vision of the wealth of nations paid scant attention to the actual running of households.[10] Smith was, in fact, largely responsible for severing the primary semantic link between the term "oeconomy" and the running of households, a move which gave rise to the qualifying term "home economics." More, on the other hand, not only followed Smith's contemporaries like James Steuart and Josiah Tucker in assuming the domestic referent, but she placed women at the centre of economic regulation, as the "invisible hand" of domestic and national organization. Following an earlier tradition of domestic manuals on household management, More sketched in her tracts and her *Strictures* models of domestic regulation for her female readers to emulate. Further, as Sutherland suggests, More stands along with Sarah Trimmer, Priscilla Wakefield, Jane Marcet, and Harriet Martineau within an "enlarged female tradition" which consciously feminizes "the public representation of the moral and political economy" and attributes a national importance to her models of household management (59).

More departed from Smith not only in the gendering of "oeconomy" but in her conception of the relationship between sound economy and virtuous community. Smith's models were based on secular fantasies of self-regulated exchange, and promulgated the idea of the marketplace as a series of sympathetic correspondences between people of common constitutions: a move which provided the possibility (if not the reality) that the sexes and the ranks could engage in mutual trade. More, again following Tucker, argues for a more providentially organized scheme of commerce, in which freedom of exchange is compatible with difference in rank and gender.[11] More's conception of a moral commercial society depends on the *acquisition* of sympathy rather than the reliance on the natural compassion of one being for another. She articulates this position in a discussion "On Sensibility" in her *Strictures,* where, typically, her economic model is embedded in a sketch of the woman of charity. The "tender-hearted woman," she writes, "whose hand . . . is 'Open as day to melting charity'; nevertheless may utterly fail in the . . . duty of christian love" (*M,* 8:118). As her feelings are "acted upon solely by local circumstance," her sympathies lack the principle to survive in "another scene, distant from the wants she has been relieving" (*M,* 8: 118). Proper sympathy must be *cultivated* if it is to resemble Christian compassion and not disappear at the first distraction. This apparent departure from More's own penchant for a local cause is, in fact, a critique of the logic of self-regulating relations of the Smithian market and its secular conception of sympathy. Only a systematized and regulated flow of sympathies, which does not disrupt the Providentially ordained distinction between ranks, will guarantee the efficient operation of the national body. The poor and women must be kept content but encouraged to keep their wants in check. An economy that encourages aspiration cannot guarantee the passive acquiescence of one part of its population to a lesser share of its resources. From More's perspective, there is no more chastening example of the effects of an unregulated economy than France, and no more dangerous economy than the unmonitored circulation of ideas.

Imaginative Labour

With the example of France before her, then, More outlines a scheme for the regulation of Britain's "sympathetic economy," which amounts to a program to ensure emotional and mental discipline for its citizens. In literary terms, the significance of More's disciplinary regime, at least as it is defined in the *Strictures,* is that it is based less on indoctrination in moral precept than on exposing would-be citizens to "works of the imagination." "When moderately used," More argues "works of the imagination" can "serve to stretch the faculties and expand the mind" (*M,* 7: 206). This "expansion of mind" comes to sound surprisingly like orientalist abandon, when More argues for the pedagogical merits of the "bold fictions of the east." More, of course, recommends oriental tales as mental discipline: as cultural histories, they afford "some tincture of real local information . . . which will not be without its uses in aiding the future associations of the mind in all that relates to eastern history and literature." When read alongside "accurate and simple facts" these "original and acknowledged fictions" can help to cultivate in the reader the distinction between "truth and fable" (*M,* 7: 206–7). The "true metaphors" of the literature of the East return unexpectedly in More's defence of the "hyperbolical style" of the Old Testament:

> The lofty style of the Eastern, and other rhetoric poetry, does not . . . mislead; for the metaphor, and the imagery is understood to be ornamental. The style of the Scriptures of the Old Testament is not, it is true, plain in opposition to figurative; nor simple in opposition to florid; but it is plain and simple in the best sense, as opposed to false principles and false taste; it raises no wrong ideas; it gives an exact impression of the thing it means to convey; and its very tropes and figures, though bold, are never unnatural and affected. (*M,* 7: 261–62)

This defence of rhetorical ornament, albeit a moral defence, does not sit easily with the prevailing image of More's literary opinions, informed largely by her dire warnings about the effects of pernicious reading matter on those morally susceptible orders: "the sex" and the lower ranks. This censoriousness is reserved largely, though not exclusively, for the publications associated with the French Enlightenment, which, as she suggests in her *Remarks,* puts More's faith in the freedom of the press under pressure:

> is the cheapness of poison, or the facility with which it may be obtained, to be reckoned among the real advantages of medicinal repositories? And can the easiness of access to seditious or atheistical writings, be numbered among the substantial

blessings of any country? Would France, at this day, have had much solid cause of regret, if many of the writings of Voltaire, Rousseau, and d'Alembert, (the prolific seed of their wide-spreading tree), had found more difficulty in getting into the world, or been less profusely circulated when in it? And might not England at this moment have been just as happy in her ignorance, if the famous orations of Citizen Dupont and Citizen Manuel had been confined to their own enlightened and philosophical countries? (*R*, 22–3)

While her liberal contemporaries put their hopes for progress in increased press freedom, easier access of information, ease of circulation, within and across national borders, More here called for the channels to be stemmed, or at least monitored. As in her attitude to national and domestic economy, More argues for controlled circulation of the press and print and has little faith either in the internally regulating force of market principle or freedom of information.

Perhaps unsurprisingly, while More gave to women a symbolic authority in the regulation of economic circulation, she characterized them as most vulnerable to the free circulation of Enlightenment and revolutionary thinkers and a host of other corrupting forces. She warned in the *Strictures,* that the "attacks of infidelity in Great Britain are at this moment principally directed against the female breast":

Conscious of the influence of women in civil society, conscious of the effect which female infidelity produced in France, they attribute the ill-success of their attempts in this country to their having been hitherto chiefly addressed to the male sex. They are now sedulously labouring to destroy the religious principles of women, and in too many instances have fatally succeeded. For this purpose, not only novels and romances have been made vehicles of vice and infidelity, but the same allurement has been held out to the women of our first country, which was employed by the first philosophist to the first sinner—Knowledge. (*M*, 7: 46)

Echoing Mary Wollstonecraft, More rails against a system of female education that has left women "susceptible," particularly the tendency to educate aristocratic and middle-class women in accomplishments that fit them for nothing but domestic decoration, and the sedentary occupations that render their minds and bodies delicate. While for the "perfectibilist" Wollstonecraft the prevailing mode of female education

violates women's natural capacity for reason, for More it exacerbates
their "corrupt nature and evil dispositions"; those very evils "which it
should be the main end and objective of Christian instruction to
remove" (*M*, 7: 67–8). This distinction is illustrated in their mutual
denigration of Rousseau as an author of female ills. Whereas Wollstonecraft condemns the legacy of Sophie, a woman educated to
please, More points to Julie, that "victim, not of temptation, but of
reason" (1, 34). More worries less about sexual promiscuity than the
plethora of distractions which erode women's "[p]atience, diligence,
quiet, and unfatigued perseverance, industry, regularity, and oeconomy of time" (*M*, 7: 182). It is not just the seductive fantasies of
Rousseauan fantasy that distract women's attention. In fact, a greater
threat lies in "that sober and unsuspected mass of mischief, which,
by assuming the plausible names of Science, of Philosophy, of Arts, of
Belles Lettres," have found their way into young ladies' dressing
rooms (*M*, 7: 33). These are subtle toxins, packaged as sober and
improving fare:

> Avowed attacks upon revelation are most easily resisted,
> because the malignity is advertised: but who suspects the
> destruction which lurks under the harmless or instructive
> names of General History, Natural History, Travels, Voyages,
> Lives, Encyclopedias, Criticism, and Romance? Who will deny
> that many of these works contain much admirable matter;
> brilliant passages, important facts, just descriptions, faithful
> pictures of nature, and valuable illustrations of science? But
> while "the dead fly lies at the bottom," the whole will exhale a
> corrupt and pestilential stench. (*M*, 7: 33)

The "corrupt and pestilential stench" of French Enlightenment,
banished once already in the century, More claims, by "the plain sense
and good principles of the far greater part of our countrymen" (*M*, 7:
43) is seeping back through the cracks and weak points in British
society. Britain's women are Eves and Julies, who succumb to the
philosophy of rights and reason and, through their power of "influence" drag their country down with them. Such women, More claims,
are seduced less by the heat of passion than by the "benumbing
touch," the "cool, calculating, intellectual wickedness" of this "most
destructive class in the whole range of modern corrupters" who:

> effect the most desperate work of the passions without so much
> as pretending to urge their violence in extenuation of the

guilt of indulging them. They solicit this very indulgence with a sort of cold blooded speculation, and invite the reader to the most unbounded gratifications, with all the saturnine coolness of a geometrical calculation. (*M*, 7: 51)

This philosophic vampirism is "the iniquity of phlegm rather than spirit" (*M*, 7: 51). The spirit is all More's as she concocts her antidote to the pernicious recipe of "English Sentiment, French Philosophy, Italian Love-Songs, and fantastic German imagery and magic wonders." Noting that the "corruption occasioned by these books has spread so wide, and descended so low, as to have become one of the most universal, as well as most pernicious, sources of corruption among us" she recommends a "preparatory course" of reading for middle-class girls and for "milliners and mantua-makers" (*M*, 7: 221–2). Her regimen is for "strong meat" to "act upon the constitution of the mind . . . and . . . help to brace the intellectual stamina": Watt's or Duncan's "little book of Logic, some parts of Mr Locke's Essay on Human Understanding, and Bishop Butler's Analogy" (*M*, 7: 214). It is a recipe for productivity as well as salvation, for in "trades where numbers work together, the labour of one girl is frequently sacrificed that she may be spared to read those mischievous books to the others" (*M*, 7: 221–2).

As I have suggested, her utilitarian and counterrevolutionary pronouncements on the benefits of literacy belie another kind of fascination with the power of imaginative arts and, indirectly, with the power of revolutionary thought (the recommendation of Locke as reading matter for milliners and mantua-makers exemplifies the ambivalence of More's conservatism). This power cannot be entirely accounted for in the disciplinary logic of More's imaginative economy, which is premised on the release of female productivity and the constraint of non-remunerative mental energy. This uncontainable imaginative power can be better understood in relation to More's pedagogical and religious practices. These not only had revolutionary potential but also provoked a public debate about the revolutionary character of her "missionary" activities in the rural communities of the south west in the 1790s. As I shall suggest, the so-called "Blagdon persecution" of 1800–1804, in which More was vilified for her suspected Methodism, brings to light the fear of the performance of new class and gender relations in the emerging Sunday School movement and its "religion of the heart," and exposes the transgressive nature of the social practices which were initiated by More's "regulative" régimes.

The Religion of the Heart

More was an Evangelical. Evangelicalism is a broad-ranging term used to describe a range of doctrinal positions embraced by members of the Anglican Church, but in its early years could be characterized as a movement designed to reinvigorate a lethargic established church. As I noted above, More was a member of the Clapham Sect, a group largely made up of business and professional men who doubled as crusaders for revitalized religion in England. The Clapham Sect was undoubtedly inspired by the zealous preachings of Wesley and the Methodists, who had led a new wave of religious enthusiasm among the lower classes, and which took hold strongly during the 1790s, partly because of the inadequacy of the established church to offer solace in the face of the radical social upheavals underway so close to home.[12] The utilitarianism of the orthodox church, it seems, was an inadequate source of consolation to a nation in need of conviction. Although the Church of England was equipped to denounce French infidelity, it could offer little in terms of belief or credible doctrine in the wake of a new modernity. As the social historian V. Kiernan argues, "dust lay on the Thirty-nine Articles. . . . what had seemed modern before 1789 was now antediluvian" (47). The broader character of "the public," too, called for a new public creed. "If high and low were to join in worship," Kiernan suggests, " it must be the worship of the poor" (47).

More, and other Evangelicals, espoused their unequivocal attachment to the Established Church and, as her first biographer Thompson suggests, a commitment to the promotion of "loyalty, good morals, and an attachment to Church and State."[13] It is apparent, however, that Evangelicalism was in many respects a "progressive" bearer of middle-class dissent, initiating demands for state reform based on a wide-reaching critique of aristocratic value. Under the respectable guise of the "Anglican saints," the Clapham Sect (who one of More's biographers Mary Alden Hopkins describes as leading "a sort of pruned and quieted Methodism within the Church of England"[14]), seized the opportunity which was given them by the French Revolution to undertake a radical critique of the British establishment. As demonstrated in More's *Remarks,* her first public commentary on the revolution, the Evangelical call for reformation was carried out in part on the back of anti-Gallic, and anti-aristocratic nationalism. Inevitably, Evangelical "patriots" were to find unlikely bedfellows not only in French Catholic priests but with English radicals. This was an association that brought More into conflict not only with the Established Church but with the conservative press with which she had allied herself at the beginning of the 1790s. The fact that More was a woman did not, of course, help to assuage doubts about her dangerous enthusiasms, as is evident in Polwhele's caricature of the bishop in petticoats, an image of female authority usurping the role of an established church. The conflict that haunted More during the early part of the 1800s was precipitated by the spectre of a woman engaging with the lower orders.

More had begun to court controversy with her social peers in 1793, when she addressed herself to a less than polite constituency of readers in her contribution to a series of tracts distributed by the Association for Preserving Liberty and Property against Republicans and Levellers: a counterrevolutionary pamphlet called "Village Politics."[15] She had been asked to write the pamphlet by the Bishop of London, Beilby Porteus. Porteus, who was afraid that the French Revolution was encouraging British factory and farm workers to consider the inequity of their own condition, asked More to write a simple tract to explain the terms "liberty" and "equality" to readers who might come across them in other contexts. More responded to the request with a departure from her usual polite idiom and produced "Village Politics." Written under the name of Will Chip, "a country carpenter," and "addressed to all the mechanics, journeymen, and labourers in Great Britain," it took the form of a dialogue between Jack Anvil the blacksmith and Tom Hod the mason (title page). As Olivia Smith suggests, More writes in "Village Politics" as though "righteously seducing people who have no control over their passions."[16] Tom has read *The Rights of Man* and has discovered that he is "very unhappy, and very miserable," which he would never have known "if I had not had the good luck to meet with this book" (*M*, 1: 346). It is up to Jack to disabuse him of his ideal miseries and to restore his faith in the blessings of the British constitution, the benefits of class organization, the dividends of high taxation and the merit of public credit. Jack's trump card is Tom's taste for ale:

> Tom, I don't care for drink myself, but thou dost, and I'll argue with thee, not in the way of principle, but in thy own way; when there's all equality there will be no superfluity: when there's no wages there'll be no drink: and levelling will rob thee of thy ale more than malt tax does. (*M*, 1: 366)

Two years after the publication of "Village Politics," More again seized on the methods of the Liberty and Property series and began to publish her monthly tracts, *The Cheap Repository*. These exemplary tales and parables for a virtuous and industrious life, aimed principally at a newly literate readership, circulated in large numbers in England and Ireland between March 1795 and November 1797.[17] Like Wordsworth in the Preface to the *Lyrical Ballads,* More sought not to woo a new class of readers, but to instruct a known constituency in a new aesthetic. Of course, Wordsworth's manifesto couched its social purpose (the production of a manly middle-class English readership to counteract the effects of an effete aristocracy) as a poetics (the cultivation of a taste for a native ballad tradition in the place of neoclassicism and sickly German sensation). More, on the other hand, advertized her tracts as a means to shape a public along particular national and class lines, explicitly contrary to the shape and direction of France. In 1818, when she reflected on her motivation for publishing the tracts in 1795 (a year of poor harvests and economic hardship in Britain), she claims she had judged it "expedient at this critical moment to supply such wholesome aliment as might give a new direction to the public taste" to counteract the "relish for those corrupt and impious publications which the consequences of the French Revolution had been fatally pouring in upon us" (*M,* 4: iii–iv).

The titles of the stories speak for themselves: the "histories" of "Mr. Fantom, the New-Fashioned Philosopher and Mr. Bragwell, or, the Two Wealthy Farmers"; of Betty Brown, with "some account of Mrs. Sponge the Money Lender," and Black Giles the Poacher, "containing some account of a family who had rather live by their wits than their work." As well as the moral fables, More included a number of ballads, renewing her early interest in a form with which she had experimented in the 1770s when she produced "The Ballad of Bleeding Rock" and "Sir Eldred and the Bower." These early ballads were part of a broader revival of interest in old English legends and a national ballad tradition which More shared with Percy, Beattie, and Chatterton, among others. More's return to the ballad in the 1790s, best exemplified in "The Riot: or Half a Loaf is Better than No Bread" of 1795, was less a "literary" than a political intervention, aimed not at redirecting tastes but deflecting the effects of hunger. Based on the unrest about scarcity in that year, More's "The Riot" used dialogue, rhyme, and the tune of "A Cobbler There Was" to convince "the people" that the famine conditions to which they were subject were not the effect of misgovernment. This was a common refrain in More's tracts. According to one of More's sympathetic biographers, it proved convincing, and More's jaunty ballad was reported to have stopped a food riot near Bath.[18]

As I have suggested, the apparent utilitarianism of the tracts, the allegorical method that subordinates medium to message, belies More's interest in the power of the imaginative arts. It is a fascination which, from a deconstructive point of view, is endemic to a utilitarian view of culture. Her view of the corruptibility of human nature, of life as a disciplinary struggle, and of an imaginative economy dedicated to curbing the expenditure of mind which exhausts rather than sustains the body, produces, of course, a textual preoccupation with excess, with luxury, and with decadence. In a more empirical sense, however, the ambivalence that More displays with respect to the powers of the imagination in particular is a legacy of her connections with London literary society.

More's interest in the literary was by the 1790s explicitly focused on its didactic potential. In her letters to Horace Walpole, More reflexively connects literary trends to social mores, and predominantly characterizes the imagination as an instrument, which simply molds material in response to local circumstance. This is, of course, a much more strategic, and empirical, understanding of the imagination than that which was being formulated by her Romantic contemporaries, for whom the work of Imagination would transcend the local and particular demands of mere social occasion.

More translates the empirical character of imagination into a utilitarian program for the use of imaginative "works," paying as much attention to the medium as the message of her reading regimen, in particular the figurative language of the Old Testament and the fancy of tales of the Orient. More's own didactic fictions do not display her interest in ornament. Her tracts "for the common people" are allegorical tales that leave little gap between figure and maxim, and no room for speculation. They are addressed to a readership who, More assumes, lack the mental discipline to tell the difference between East and West, fable and truth, theory and practice, and most crucially, between the English and French meanings of liberty. More orchestrates this discipline with the antirelativist confidence borne of metaphysical faith, and the utilitarian belief in her own control of her imaginative libido. Knowing her own poison, she dispenses it with evangelical abandon; not just in print, but in the pedagogical practice of her Sunday schools. Inevitably, the repressed returns, and More finds herself vilified for her own enthusiasms and the pernicious doctrine she preached in her classrooms and meeting houses.

Irregular Things

In 1789, More had the opportunity to put her pedagogical principles into practice outside the confines of the Bristol girls' school which she ran with her sisters, when she opened her first Sunday school in

Cheddar. When William Wilberforce "discovered" a community living in caves in the Cheddar gorge and was appalled at their poverty, illiteracy, and lack of religious conviction, he called on the Mores—Hannah and her sister Martha—to intervene. He had already made Hannah's acquaintance through antislavery campaigns and through their mutual involvement in the Society for the Reformation of Manners, a movement established in 1787 to curb the "excesses" of the poor. With the financial backing of Wilberforce (whom Elizabeth Montagu dubbed "The Red Cross Knight") and Thornton, the Mores went on in 1791 to open further schools in Conglesbury, Yatton, and Axbridge, and a year later in Nailsea.[19] The Mendips schools, undoubtedly part of a laudable humanitarian scheme in an area where local grandees had neglected and abused their "charges," were inevitably to be an extension of Wilberforce's "management project," with the emphasis on spiritual recovery before social reformation.

As in the rest of the Sunday School Movement in which the Mores played a founding role, the principles of industrial labor were inculcated in their schoolrooms.[20] Their pedagogical strategies were an extension of the maternal regulation of the household, instilling respect for hygiene and sexual decorum. The relationship between religious pedagogy and the industrial workplace was also literal, with the attachment of "schools of industry," offering rudimentary training in skills such as spinning to some of the Cheddar schools. Perhaps most surprisingly, given Hannah's antipathy to the autonomy of women and the lower classes, the Mores established a series of women's clubs modelled on men's friendly societies, to which members paid a subscription and could draw on the capital to support them through sickness, childbirth, or the cost of a funeral. The official logic of these clubs and schools was the maintenance of the status quo, the pacification of the lower orders, and the provision of training, particularly to women, in the regulation of households and moral management. However, it was not the regulative agenda but the seeds of female and working-class self-organization which drew most attention to the Mores' schools.

For about five years from 1799, two of More's Sunday schools became the focus of attack from conservative members of the Established church, who suspected them of spreading Methodist propaganda. The ostensible problem was the nature and location of the evening prayer meetings which the Mores held for the parents of children in the parish of Wedmore, and later in Blagdon: meetings which, their conservative antagonists suggested, contravened the 1664 Conventicle Act. This act decreed that religious meetings for more than five persons worshipping in any other than the established forms of the

Church of England would be punishable by imprisonment or transportation. The act was, of course, no longer enforceable but was still
invoked as a sign of the established church's intolerance of dissent. It
is less the origins of the controversy which interest me here than the
terms in which it was conducted in editorials and letters to magazines
and in twenty-three pamphlets which were published on the subject
in 1802.[21] Some of these were written in the Mores' defence, but most
were aggressive in their attack not only on the impropriety of the
prayer meetings, but on the sisters' "enthusiasm" and their suspected
Methodism. One of the best known of the pamphlets, *Truths,
Respecting Mrs. Hannah More's Meeting-Houses, and the Conduct of
her Followers; Addressed to the Curate of Blagdon,* written by Edward
Spencer, has for an epigraph a quotation from *Ward's Reformation,*
which crystallizes the fear of feminine influence that underpins much
of the criticism they received:

> O! Tom . . .
> Put not the Women into Pulpits,
> For they'll deride our Sex for Dull-pates;
> They'll murder with eternal din.[22]

Spencer's pamphlet continues to make this commonplace misogynist
connection between the elevation of female authority and the demise
of hegemonic masculinity. Addressed to the curate of Blagdon, who
had from Spencer's perspective been the victim of the Mores' "savage"
practices, it extends into a fantasy about men ensnared by the Mores'
uncontrollable sexuality. Thus, as evidence of Hannah's Methodism,
he depicts her "drawing within the vortex of her petticoats, numerous
bodies of the regular Clergy of the land, who are made subservient to
her views and accessory to her designs by the liberty of issuing her
bulls and promulgating her mandates" (*S,* 48). A dissimulating woman
who "indulges in fish with the Catholic, and in the company of a Jew
will not touch pork," this "Pope Joan" cast her wide spell over "simple
honest peasantry," dignitaries of the Established Church, and the
monarch (*S,* 50, 52; 64).[23] Spencer appropriates some of More's own
discourse when he calls for vigilance against the revolutionary potential of "puritanic fanaticism." To this, and "its concomitant levelling
principles" are to be attributed:

> most of the horrors of revolution, blood, and carnage, which
> mankind have so grievously mourned, since the unfortunate
> days of Charles I, and from which, to the discredit of our nation,

as can be regularly traced from that period to the present, in this country, all modern mischiefs took their origin; this has been the seed bed from which the whole have sprung. (*S,* 71)

For Spencer, then, More and her sectarian enthusiasts are a reanimated puritan faction. While Hannah preached against the influence of foreign infidels she was vilified as an orchestrator of native insurrection. Perhaps the greatest irony is that More was maligned in terms which were similar to those used by Edmund Burke a decade earlier to describe the monstrous women who took to the streets during the French Revolution, symbols both of a degraded femininity and the overturning of natural authority.

Perhaps unsurprisingly, Hannah More suffered what her biographers refer to euphemistically as "a great illness" in the years following the Blagdon controversy, although she continued to produce works of Christian dogma from her home, Barley Wood in Wrington, until several years before her death in 1833. More's loyalty to Church and State from the period when she became an active campaigner until her death never publicly swerved. The means that she chose to demonstrate that loyalty and to instill it in others produced more disruptive effects than she could have anticipated. Even though More's name would never appear on any petition in support of reform or the extension of the political franchise, her "influence" is evident both in a female literary tradition, nineteenth-century domestic realism, which stood against public corruption, and in the self-determination of a generation of newly literate political activists who would write their own petitions and organize their own fund raising campaigns.[24]

Notes

1. See Lucinda Cole, "(Anti)Feminist Sympathies: The Politics of Relationship in Smith, Wollstonecraft and More", *ELH* (1991): 58, 107–40; Donna Landry, *The Muses of Resistance: Laboring-Class Women's Poetry in Britain, 1739–1796* (Cambridge: Cambridge University Press, 1990), 254–73; Mitzi Myers, "Reform or Ruin: 'A Revolution in Female Manners,'" *Studies in Eighteenth-Century Culture* 11 (1982): 199–216.

2. *The Yale Edition of Horace Walpole's Correspondence,* ed., W.S. Lewis, Robert A.Smith and Charles H.Bennett. 48 vols. (New Haven: Yale University Press, 1961) 31: 320 (hereafter *W,* referring to vol. 31).

3. This is the caricature of More in Richard Polwhele's notorious misogynist poem *The Unsex'd Females* (1798), which included derogatory

sketches of, among others, More, Ann Yearsley, Charlotte Smith, Helen Maria Williams, Mary Hays, and Mary Wollstonecraft.

4. Hannah More, *Strictures on Female Education with a View of the Principles and Conduct Prevalent Among Women of Rank and Fortune* (1799), *The Works of Hannah More,* 18 vols. (London: Cadell, 1818), 7 and 8 (hereafter *M*).

5. For an analysis of Burke's fear of "the public," see Angela Keane, "Reflections and Correspondences: The Unfamiliarity of Burke's Unfamiliar Letter," *Edmund Burke's Reflections on the Revolution in France: New Interdisciplinary Essays,* ed. John Whale (Manchester: Manchester University Press, 2000).

6. See David Simpson, *Romanticism, Nationalism, and the Revolt Against Theory* (Chicago: University of Chicago Press, 1993) for an account of the broader antipathy towards philosophical abstraction in British philosophical and literary traditions in the eighteenth and early nineteenth centuries.

7. This, of course, was part of Walpole's prefatory description of his Gothic romance, *The Castle of Otranto,* defining his gothic aesthetic against public, classical discourse, and locating it in the wanton space of private fantasy.

8. Hannah More, *Considerations on Religion and Public Education, with Remarks on the Speech of M. Dupont, Delivered in the National Convention of France, Together with an Address to the Ladies, etc. of Great Britain and Ireland* (1794), ed. Claudia L. Johnson, The Augustan Reprint Society (University of Los Angeles: California, William Andrews Clark Memorial Library, 1990); hereafter R.

9. For an exploration of the "anti-party" rhetoric of early nineteenth-century radicalism see Kevin Gilmartin, *Print Politics: The Press and Radical Opposition in Early Nineteenth-Century England* (Cambridge: Cambridge University Press, 1996).

10. Kathryn Sutherland, "Hannah More's counter-revolutionary feminism," *Revolution in Writing: British Literary Responses to the French Revolution,* ed. Kelvin Everest (Buckingham: Open University Press, 1991), 27–61, 55. See also Sutherland's analysis of More in "Adam Smith's Master Narrative: Women and the Wealth of Nations," *Adam Smith's Wealth of Nations: New Interdisciplinary Essays,* ed. Stephen Copley and Kathryn Sutherland (Manchester: Manchester University Press, 1995), 97–121.

11. See Josiah Tucker, *A Brief Essay on the Advantages and Disadvantages which Respectively attend France and Great Britain, with regard to Trade. With some proposals for removing the Principal Disadvantages of Great Britain. In a New Method* (London, 1750).

12. For analyses of the subversive social register of the Evangelical movement in the 1790s see V. Kiernan, "Evangelicalism and the French Revolution," *Past and Present: A Journal of Scientific History* 1 (1952), 44–56 (hereafter cited by page number in text), and Gerald Newman, *The Rise of English Nationalism, A Cultural History 1740–1830* (London: Weidenfeld and Nicolson, 1987).

13. H. Thompson, *The Life of Hannah More* (London: Cadell, 1838), 222.

14. Mary Alden Hopkins, *Hannah More and Her Circle* (New York and Toronto: Longmans, 1947), 48.

15. First published in *Liberty and Property Preserved Against Republicans and Levellers; A Collection of Tracts* (London, 1795); hereafter "Village Politics" (M, 1).

16. Olivia Smith, *The Politics of Language 1791–1819* (Oxford: Clarendon Press, 1984), 94.

17. The order of the tracts was reorganized for the 1818 Cadell edition of More's *Works,* where they appear as *Stories for the Middle Ranks* (*M,* 4) and *Stories for the Common People* (*M,* 5).

18. Hopkins, *Hannah More and Her Circle,* 211.

19. See the Mores's account of this project in Martha More, *The Mendip Annals: Or, the Narrative of the Charitable Labors of Hannah and Martha More in Their Neighborhood. Being the Journal of Martha More,* ed. Arthur Roberts (London: James Nisbet, 1859).

20. For a full account of the status of the Sunday School movement in the broader context of education reform in this period, see Alan Richardson, *Literature, Education and Romanticism: Reading as Social Practice 1780–1832* (Cambridge: Cambridge University Press, 1994).

21. References to "the Blagdon Controversy" can be found, for instance, in *The British Critic,* Vols. 17–19 and the *Anti-Jacobin,* Vol. 5, Vol. 9, Vol. 11.

22. Edward Spencer, *Truths, Respecting Mrs. Hannah More's Meeting-Houses, and the Conduct of her Followers; Addressed to the Curate of Blagdon* (London: W. Meyler, 1802); hereafter S). I am grateful to the Folger Shakespeare Library in Washington, D.C., for allowing me to have access to this pamphlet.

23. Spencer is referring to More's association with the royal household and her advice on the education of Princess Charlotte, which was made public in 1805 in More's *Hints for Forming the Character of a Young Princess.*

24. See Barbara Taylor, *Eve and the New Jerusalem: Socialism and Feminism in the Nineteenth Century* (New York: Pantheon Books, 1983) for an important account of the emergence of the relationship between the British reform and women's movements.

The French, the "Long-wished-for Revolution," and the Just War in Joanna Southcott

∽

Kevin Binfield

> What if millenarianism meant not alienation from the spirit
> of the age but a total involvement with it?[1]

In discussing the role that the French Revolution and the Napoleonic wars played in the "widening" of the British consciousness beyond the parish, Linda Colley notes that "almost all section interest groups in Britain resorted to nationalist language and activism to advance their claims to wider civic participation."[2] In the recently expanded focus on British groups which were previously ignored (or written about rather than attended to), nationalism and anti-Gallic sentiments among members of those groups seem to have been discounted. Nevertheless, as Colley argues in her 1992 book, *Britons,* nationalism played an important role in enlarging the participation of British women in the public sphere at the time:

> Women's historians have largely ignored the wealth of evidence
> about female property and family politics contained in . . .
> patriotic subscription lists . . . perhaps because of the linger-
> ing belief that women are or should be more pacifist than
> men. . . . Instead, and exactly like many of their male country-
> men, some women found ways of combining support for the
> national interest with a measure of self-promotion . . . . Under
> cover of a patriotism that was often genuine and profound,
> they carved out for themselves a real if precarious place in
> the public sphere.[3]

According to Colley, women's places in the public sphere included participating in wartime subscriptions, doing local charity work, making flags and banners, collecting flannel garments, and urging the men to fight (*Britons,* 256–61). Jeanne Moskal follows Colley in recognizing that patriotism afforded women participatory roles in the public sphere but departs from Colley in assessing the relationship of those roles to the cultural mainstream. Moskal writes that "the role of patriot provided both protection from and subversion of conventional women's roles."[4] Given the parameters established by Moskal and Colley, one might expect the role of the woman patriot to be quite complicated. A gendered patriot matrix might be discernible, but other cultural elements, such as the role of millenarianism, need to be engaged.

Despite the new scrutiny of women patriots by Colley and others, the role of religious women writers in the English reaction to the French Revolutionary and Napoleonic threats has not been treated as a particularly complicated phenomenon.[5] In fact, few scholars have examined the strains of militancy and patriotism in the texts of religious women writers of the day. Many, not just the historians described by Colley, seem to assume that female religious thinkers and writers tend toward pacifism or, as in the case of Sarah Spence, quietist resignation. The treatment parallels Anne K. Mellor's identification of an "ethic of care" as one of the defining characteristics of much of the writing by women of the period.[6] Clarke Garrett's study of millenarian thought in France and England around the time of the Revolution typifies this attitude. In a chapter on the English millenarian prophet Joanna Southcott, Garrett emphasizes Southcott's pacifist messages and her counsels to her readers to wait patiently upon God's kingdom. Garrett consequently deemphasizes Southcott's more political, and militant, writings.[7] At other times, millenarianism is frequently tied to an emergent, sometimes insurrectionary, radicalism—a linkage posited by historians such as Roger Wells and J. F. C. Harrison.[8] And E. P. Thompson assumes that Southcottian millenarianism, as a reaction to the French Revolution, plays a role in the formation of English working-class consciousness.[9]

But what if William Lamont's observation, quoted at the beginning of this essay, holds as true for Southcott's early nineteenth-century millenarianism as for the seventeenth-century variety that Lamont was describing? What if, in her preaching and prophecies, Southcott engaged the mainstream public response to the Revolution in order to promote her public role or to counteract any hostility to her prophesying—hostility predictably founded on the conventional expectations of a woman's public role and Southcott's violation of those expectations? In this essay, I shall examine those of Southcott's writings that touch on the French Revolution and the Napoleonic wars in the course of arguing that, despite her primary concentration on spiritual matters and domestic affairs, and her secondary attacks on economic and social injustices in England, Southcott nevertheless advocates a theory of just war that locates her otherwise radical (or at least politically dissenting) discourses within the conventional, mainstream English reaction against the French. In this sense, Southcott's project may be thought to resemble "a millenialism of counter-revolution" described by W. H. Oliver.[10]

The reactions to the Revolution in English society at large varied widely: Radical organizations, such as the London Corresponding Society and similar provincial bodies, emerged alongside the volunteer corps and the Reeves Association. As Oliver and Robert Hole indicate, the reactions of religious thinkers were similarly various. For example, Mark Wilks, a Norfolk Baptist minister, welcomed the Revolution, arguing that "the French Revolution is of God"—a position that he continued to affirm even after the Terror, as the new French republic continued to be preserved against its enemies.[11] Hole also recounts the anti-Jacobinism of Anglican clergy, such as Suffolk curate William Jones. In a 20 October 1789 sermon, titled *Popular Commotions to Precede the End of the World,* Jones condemned the Revolution's removal of the restraints upon human nature that God had instituted in civil governments.[12] Not all texts by Anglican divines and other religious writers were millenarian, and, despite the title, Jones's 1789 sermon actually has less of eschatology in it than sermons written after the Terror. In his 1794 sermon titled *The Man of Sin,* Jones argues that the final days will be preceded by apostasy and the displacement of sovereign law by popular will.[13] In the age of Burke, Jones's sermons are unremarkable for their conservatism; however, their eschatological tenor is more noteworthy. Indeed, prophecy was one of the most significant forms of response to the Revolution. In *Prophets and Millennialists,* Oliver demonstrates the tremendous stimulating effect of the Revolution upon prophetical discourse in Britain—a discourse that, like nationalism, was readily available to all who chose to employ it.[14] Oliver argues that "Prophetic theology was normally neither revolutionary nor progressive; it was, for centuries, a normal exegetical activity, a concern of professional scholars, and a respectable way of saying things about God, man and their relationship in society and history" (*Prophets,* 13). By availing themselves of the morally significant (if not always predictively accurate) vision of a "fulfillment and vindication . . . *on earth*," prophets of the time "were attempting to say truthful and useful things about the society they lived in, about everything in its life from parental authority to international relations" (*Prophets*, 19, 14–15). Writers such as the Baptist radical James Bicheno were able to employ predictive rhetoric and modes of Biblical interpretation (similar to those used by Jones, his ideological opponent) in advancing the cause of radicalism and reform.[15] More importantly, Oliver says (despite his own concentration on well-educated prophetic writers) that "no social group and no intellectual level lacked access to these ideas, concepts and images, should any of its members want to use them" (*Prophets*, 17).

Foremost among the lower orders of English society that made use of prophetic modes was the Devonshire prophet, Joanna Southcott. Southcott was simultaneously the most influential and successful of the early nineteenth-century religious organizers and one of the most ridiculed public women of her day. Born in 1750 at Gittisham, near Exeter, Southcott worked on her father's farm as a dairy maid and in a managerial capacity until she left home to become an upholsterer and servant. Her career as a prophet began with visions and voices that she received in 1792, the critical year that saw the alliance of Britain with Catholic nations opposed to the French Republic.[16] Beset by dreams and instructed by the Spirit of the Lord to record and seal up the Spirit's explanations of dreams, events, Scripture, and other messages, Southcott refused offers of marriage and supported herself by upholstering and domestic service.[17]

Despite her perceived eccentricities, her gift for prophecy and accurate predictions regarding local affairs gave her some prestige in her Exeter neighborhood.[18] She continued to prophesy in Methodist and Anglican circles in Devonshire until the end of 1801. In December, while working as a servant in Exeter, she was visited and interviewed by several men, among them Anglican clergy and prominent merchants. Persuaded of the soundness of her faith and the accuracy of her prophecies, the men invited her to establish herself in London, where she arrived in May 1802.[19] Southcott's removal to London proved fruitful. She gathered around her a circle of energetic individuals: William Sharp, the radical engraver and former member of the London Corresponding; George Turner, a Yorkshire merchant who also prophesied; Reverend Stanhope Bruce, an Anglican minister; Jane Townley, a woman of independent means who provided lodgings and clerical assistance for Southcott in London and Blockley; and Elias Carpenter, a paper-mill owner who supported Southcott until their falling out in 1804. With the help of these people, Southcott was able to recruit followers across England, but especially in London and the North. Lists and contemporary estimates of the numbers of her followers range as high as 100,000 people, representing many segments of English society—especially artisans and "the poor," but also Church of England clergy, Methodists, and some propertied individuals.[20] Her later career was beset by scandal, as the British press denounced her for selling "seals" (papers signed by Southcott indicating their numbering among the faithful), for the involvement of some of her supporters in awkward financial dealings, and, finally, for announcing that she was pregnant with the Prince of Peace, Shiloh. Despite the ridicule and the allegations of scandals that pursued her until her death in 1814, the Southcottian church maintained some strength of numbers through the 1830s and continues to exist today.

I begin by assuming, with Colley, that the French Revolution may have expanded women's roles in the public sphere in general.[21] However, Southcott's project was not easily incorporated into the mainstream. Southcott was insightful enough not to hang her prophecies upon the Revolution, unlike Richard Brothers, the former military officer and prophet whose predictions of the fall of the British monarchy and the conversion of the Jews, viewed in retrospect, cleared a path for her.[22] Instead, she recognized a despairing yet patriotic ambivalence in England (E. P. Thompson's "chiliasm of despair" combined with Linda Colley's nation-forming), generated largely by domestic events in conjunction with the Revolution and the threat of invasion, and tapped that ambivalence rather than the more limited and clearly circumscribed despair resulting from the threats from France. Her early predictions of disasters that would precede the millennium dealt mostly with famine, but several dealt with the English political scene. The fact that she waited until 1801 to publish accounts of her visitations from and audiences with the Spirit of God, even though she actually had experienced clair-audience as early as 1792, marks her unwillingness to stake her prophecies upon political events. Once she did step upon a national stage, her books (numbering sixty-five published between 1801 and 1814) evidence a struggle as to how to cast the Revolution and the Napoleonic wars in her prophecies. The struggle is most evident in the books written between 1802 and 1807.

Typically, Southcott's early prophecies, cast in rhyming verse communicated to her by the Spirit of the Lord and framed by Southcott's own autobiographical and interpretive prose, counsel patient adherence to the belief that, even though the millennium is at hand, the reward for faith might not have a temporal dimension but would certainly consist of a place in heaven for her "Sealed People," those who received from her a seal indicative of their redemption and salvation. Her counsels usually accompany Biblical interpretation and analyses of economic and social problems within England. As Garrett has demonstrated, Southcott's millenarianism differs from earlier and competing versions in its patriotism.[23] For example, Southcott's interpretation of the vials described in the Revelation to John is not internationalist or transnationalist, as James Bicheno's, Robert Fleming's, and Richard Brothers's interpretations had been.[24] Consistently throughout the prophecies, Southcott combines Christianity and English nationalism in eulogies for England. In one early prophecy, she writes: "England, thou enlightened land, / That hath been guarded by the Gospel's pole, / You may rejoice and sing, while others fall."[25] But Southcott often tempers such eulogies with stern warnings of disasters to befall the nation if it fails to repent, and most of her warnings deal with domestic matters—domestic, in both the local-national and home-economical senses of the word:

> 'Tis on the SUN the Vial is poured out;
> And fervent heat it shall so strongly burn
> That all the earth shall feel it, and shall mourn;
> Because the Sun shall burn so very strong
> That All the Corn it surely will consume.[26]

A Warning to the World contains a great number of similar passages that treat famine and crop failure either as signs of God's displeasure with the nation or, in terms of their fluctuations and Southcott's predictions, as proofs of Southcott's special claim to divine favor. In one such passage, the Spirit tells Southcott that her flawed predictions of a crop failure in Devonshire were not actually flawed:

> But when they see their harvest clear,
> Their sun will cloud ere noon.
> Because the price will make men wise,
> Much dearer than the last;
> If not the wheat, they'll find it great
> In all things else is cast.[27]

Southcott elaborates on the Spirit's words in a lengthy discussion that taps the fears and suspicion of a *pacte de famine* held by many Britons in 1800:

Before one month was past in the harvest, the farmers began to change their words, and some said they had not two pecks an acre; and there was not corn enough in the land to last till Lady Day. . . . As soon as the harvest was over in 1800, the poor began to complain what martyrs they had been, and sold all they could part with to go through the dearth of 1799; but now they said there was another year come, in which they should be starved to death; and many, I was told, dropped down dead in the streets for want. (*Warning to the World,* 35)

Southcott is aware not only of deprivation but also of economic forces; nevertheless, she discusses them in terms of the state of the relationship between God and the English people.

Southcott joins to her domestic interests another great temporal concern—the correction of material and political inequities. Liberty, prosperity, and the elimination of poverty will mark the millennium:

When I my people do redeem
From every power of hell and sin,
Your houses I shall build anew,
And palaces to your view. . . . (*Word in Season,* 15)

Furthermore, the millennium will be decidedly English, not Hanoverian. In fact, the Hanoverian rule is most frequently cast in terms of usurpation and dispossession—almost a Georgian and millenarian version of the Norman yoke:

But now the heirs I mean to free,
And all these bondmen I'll cast out,
And the true heirs have nought to doubt;
For I'll cut off the bastard race,
And in their stead the true heirs place
For to possess that very land. . . . (*Word in Season,* 17)[28]

Despite her primarily domestic concerns, Southcott does address one of the most important international issues of her time—the role of her English believers in the wars with France. She eventually constructs her own 'just war' theory and engages a debate on the relation of the believer to the governments conducting war against the French. From the initial volumes of 1801, Southcott's prophecies (at least those regarding English domestic matters) tend much more than Brothers's toward peacefulness. Whereas Brothers's writings frequently had demanded English repentance for crimes against the poor and had predicted that England would be punished before it repents,[29] Southcott's early prophecies counsel peacefulness. The version of justice that she describes in *The Strange Effects of Faith* binds peacefulness and the enjoyment of prosperity to England's repentance:

> Then all your swords to plough shares you may turn,
> To plough with plenty your delightful trees.
> No thistles then shall hurt the reaper's hand;
> But peace and plenty flow throughout your land.
> No prickly thorns to hurt the binder's care;
> For God will bind in bundle ev'ry tare;
> And all the foxes he away will take,
> That doth so spoil and hurt the tender grape . . . .[30]

Later in *The Strange Effects of Faith,* the Spirit of the Lord tells Southcott to tell her readers, "But if your peace you'll keep at home, / My mind and will must be made known" (*Strange Effects, Third,* 109). The idea of keeping peace at home, thereby bringing to pass God's revelation of his "mind and will," is a consistent theme in Southcott's writings. Much of her early work prophesies peace—defined, that is, as freedom from invasion—as well as peacefulness, without a word about defense or resistance, except against Satan. It would appear that what the English need to do to remain safe is to attend to their own repentance—that is, the spiritual fight against Satan—in order to protect the shores of Britain:

> We have a peace; as I said, the year that begun [sic] in sorrow
> would end in joy. And how could it end in joy without a peace?
> I said we had nothing to fear from invasion by a foreign
> enemy. Then now take care one of another; as there is a peace,
> let it be a peace. But I may say, what peace, as long as Satan
> and his witchcrafts are so many to work in the hearts of men,
> to bring the day of vengeance on themselves.[31]

Freedom from invasion, however, was not unconditionally granted to England. The Spirit of the Lord perhaps recognized that his intention to encourage the English to desire their salvation might be rhetorically undermined by an absolute promise of safety. In a later communication, the Spirit does not entirely rescind his promise to protect the "enlightened land," but rather qualifies the promise by conditional markers ("if") and the threat of famine—a threat tied closely to Southcott's domestic and material concerns. Furthermore, the Spirit hints that only the "Sealed People . . . shall stand" and that "havoc great" may visit the rest of the land:

> If England will not turn to me,
> The famine they shall surely see;
> When I have stop'd the raging war,
> For short and sharp it shall now appear.
> The clouds will gather fast at first,
> That in your land they strong will burst;
> And if your foes I conquer here,
> It is for those that wish me here,
> Their King and Conqueror for to be,
> Then I must wound your enemy;
> If they invade this very land,
> My Sealed People they shall stand,
> I say to see their foes to fall;
> He cannot come to conquer all,
> Tho' havoc great I know he'll make,
> But, oh, my friends shall I forsake?
> No! - I will not leave them at that time.[32]

The early prophecies, simultaneously assuring peace and urging the repentance that will effect peace, suggest a sort of withdrawal from national and international political affairs. In fact, the prophecies dating from 1792 to 1801 indicate that Southcott treated the French Revolution and the early stages of war as a sign of the approaching final days and the need for spiritual renewal, not unlike the famines and crop failures that were, during these years, her primary focus.[33] Withdrawal continued for a time as a theme in Southcott's works. In an undated but early communication, Southcott records a remark made to her by the Spirit, who tells her that "the Sealed People do not trouble themselves about politics or parties and have no connection with desperate Men but it is their duty to avoid contention or strife."[34]

As late as 1804, in *The Trial of Joanna Southcott,* Southcott had recorded the Spirit's words of caution against finding "rebellion" in its words and also the Spirit's injunction "to be peaceable with all men."[35] Such admonishments against military involvement continued for a few years; nevertheless, it is possible to trace in the prophecies written between 1803 and 1807 a progression from peacefulness and non-involvement to a conventional affiliation with the English military resistance against the French, especially after the coronation of Napoleon, as the wars became less of a "sign" and more of a threat. The affiliation can be seen most clearly in *An Account of Trials on Bills of Exchange* (1807), where Southcott professes an almost Pauline or Augustinian loyalty to secular rulers. At one point, she even writes, "His majesty has no better subjects in his kingdom, or who wish more for the perfect happiness of the nation, than the true believers in my visitation" (*Bills of Exchange,* 54). Despite Southcott's eventual affiliation with the temporal aims of the English king, the war complicated her position enough that her work exhibits few attempts to square her acceptance of the military role of a legitimate prince with her opposition to the House of Hanover, whose legitimacy she had challenged in *Continuation of Prophecies.*

Southcott's shifting attitudes regarding the roles of her followers parallel her analysis of the war with France. That parallel places her "Sealed People" in positions of temporal significance, beyond simply being good subjects of his majesty. She argues that the war manifests a larger struggle between good and evil, which struggle also manifests itself in poverty and injustice in England. Her transcendentalizing of the struggle probably saves her the trouble of reconciling her later professions of loyalty with her opposition to the rule of George III. The higher, spiritual responsibilities recognized and fulfilled by Southcott and her followers seem to lift them above mere "rebellion," even as they make themselves exceptionally capable agents in the struggle against evil, one element of which is Buonaparte.

According to Hopkins, Southcottians claimed that only Southcott's Sealed People "knew how to deal with the principle of evil which animated her enemies and which earlier had overtaken the French Revolution."[36] That the Revolution had been "overtaken" is an important idea for Southcott, who initially had sympathized with its popular goals. The Spirit had told her that the Revolution had begun with God's sanction as a revolt against Roman Catholicism, a theme embraced by many millenarian writers, such as Richard Brothers and James Bicheno.[37] Indeed, according to some scholars, France seems to have been on a course toward tolerating Protestantism both before and after the Revolution. Alphonse Aulard has charted the movement toward tolerance in *Christianity and the French Revolution.* As Aulard points out, not only had the edict of November 1787 made it "allowable to call oneself a Protestant," but also Louis XVI had installed a Swiss Calvinist, Necker, as Prime Minister.[38] And after the Revolution, Article 13 of the Declaration of Rights had expanded toleration (Aulard, 79).

Charting Southcott's changing attitudes toward the Revolution involves attending to her later (after 1801) analysis of events. (It bears repeating that her Devonshire prophecies, prior to 1801, treated the Revolution and the wars of the 1790s as signs of the final days.) South-cott observes that, after the "principle of evil" overtook the Revolution, France gave into "the stronger party" or "the Beast," Napoleon, whose rise to power resulted from disloyalty and the absence of true religion among the French.[39] The rise of Napoleon was significant enough, even to God's own prophetess, that Southcott notes in her catalogue of portentous earthly events for 1804, "Buonaparte declared Emperor of France on the 20th of May."[40] In *The Long-wished-for Revolution,* Southcott answers a letter from Lewis Mayer, "from my own judg-ment of what had been revealed to me," pointing out that the Lord had "told me that [Buonaparte] was the Beast mentioned in the Revelation, and would have his power for a season; but that his destructive power should not be in this land, unless it was to his own destruction; for though, like Sennacherib, it was said he would conquer other nations, yet, like Sennacherib, it was said he would fall, if he ventured here."[41] And in 1807, Southcott predicts "That first a power to the Beast is given; / So will the heads of all these nations fall, / And then their leader I do tell you all / That I shall tread him down beneath my feet" (*Bills of Exchange,* 54). She explains,

> How perfectly true have the words followed! And where is the man who can . . . prove that the wars have not been fatal; and that Buonaparte's power hath not been great, like Senna-cherib's host, with the nations abroad, while he hath been kept from invading our land . . . which plainly told us the promise of protection . . . that no enemy should have the power to come into our land?[42]

Assurances combined with admonitions to suggest that England's safety was mostly, but not completely, settled. The problem that Southcott faced was to maintain the idea of England as an "enlight-ened land" while also encouraging vigorous repentance. Repentance had to be inward and oriented to a desire for a spiritual redemption, but spiritual repentance would not be sufficient to avoid a temporal struggle, even though it might protect the repentant Southcottian follower from the harm of war. Individual believers would not be harmed by war, even though they still would suffer from famine and other natural disasters also caused or permitted by God.[43] Neverthe-less, the *nation* as a whole was in danger from the war and famine.[44]

This is not the only difficulty to be found in Southcott's writings on the war. Her various pronouncements on the matter of the believer's role frequently appear to be contradictory—a point emphasized by comparison to the certainty and simplicity of other religious thinkers, such as Bristol's Reverend John Evans, discussed below.

As James Hopkins has demonstrated, a number of persons involved in the Southcottian movement observed in correspondences to both political and religious leaders that the war with France must be both temporal and spiritual. In other words, an Augustinian "fight," both internal and external, must take place, and, I would argue, the war with France seemed to be the locus of that dual struggle. The precise role of the individual believer, however, still needed to be resolved. Even in 1803, the year of the failure of the Treaty of Amiens, when invasion seemed imminent, Southcott urges in her *Communication on the Temporal and Spiritual Sword* that her followers "should have nothing to do with the contentions of the nations."[45] Pacifists within the Southcottian movement advanced this notion until 1807, despite some militarist pronouncements made by Southcott that same year. Southcott herself is uncertain and plays around the edges of the idea of "contentions of nations." The words of the Spirit of the Lord, recorded in Southcott's prophecies, had made clear that the Lord was an English nationalist, and, although he was not an ardent supporter of the House of Hanover, he recognized that a greater evil, Napoleon, threatened England. More importantly, Napoleon had been revealed to be "the Beast." Southcott struggles with the possibility that a spiritual battle against "the Beast" could perhaps take a temporal form, and any temporal form would have to be defined within nationalist and loyalist lines. Her followers have an obligation to fight for God during the last days, but she leaves unclear whether that obligation precludes or necessitates a temporal allegiance to the King. Southcott's uncertainty appears almost as pure sophistry in a private communication, also written in 1803, in which she argues that avoiding contention requires that the believers follow "their King and Country," despite her earlier warning to avoid "parties."[46]

The issue complicates her prophecies enough that she never addresses the question of whether the allegiance of believers to their King ought to be pure or incidental. Nevertheless, in texts written at the height of Southcott's public life between 1803 and 1807 (years that encompassed serious invasion threats), the Spirit, speaking to and through Southcott, resolves the apparently contradictory injunctions by outlining a just war theory quite similar to versions advocated earlier by Augustine, Aquinas, and Grotius.

Hopkins points out that Southcott's education was minimal. He notes that Southcott admitted having read very few books and he concludes that "there is little evidence that books, other than the Bible and her aunt's hymns, exerted any significant influence on her development" (*Woman to Deliver,* 10). Hopkins's conclusion that Southcott's reading went little beyond the Bible should perhaps be qualified. Other reading is evident in Southcott's prophecies, and that reading suggests some familiarity with contemporary pamphlets, political and religious tracts, and newspapers, as even a cursory glance at her titles indicates. It is very unlikely that she had any classical education that would have provided her with knowledge of Augustine or other early just war theorists; however, it would have been possible that Southcott gleaned an adequate understanding of just war theory at secondhand from the religious and political tracts of the day. Clergy whose educations might have included readings in Grotius and Augustine produced many sermons for and against the war, and many were published. Just war theories had been circulating in England at the time, justifying English Christians in taking up arms against the French, and the approach was common enough for a clever person such as Southcott to derive the basic outlines of the theory. In one such work, an 1804 sermon titled *War Not Inconsistent with Christianity* intended to encourage Bristol parishioners to take up arms in defense against the French, Reverend John Evans applies a thorough-going just war theory to the current situation facing England. Evans concludes that English Christian participation in and preparation for war is necessary and right.[47] His argument is largely based upon the work of Bishop Ezekial Hopkins and Hopkins's (entirely derivative) definition of just war: "Where the cause is just, the manner in which it is proposed warrantable, and the authority which engages, rightly constituted over us; it is fit and necessary we take up arms, and in war to right ourselves of injurious enemies."[48] Evans goes on to quote with approval a later passage from Hopkins which describes war as a method of settling disputes between nations: "[T]here being no common magistrate . . . , the injured may have recourse to war. For what law is to persons of the same nation, that war is to persons of a different nation."[49] Evans's concerns, like Southcott's, are domestic and economic, and his version of Christianity, patriotic. Describing "the distresses of a country vanquished," Evans writes, "See a country laid waste, its fruits, its produce, its verdure destroyed; and the before happy and peaceable Inhabitants taking up their wretched abode in woods and caverns" (*War,* 38).[50]

Even though Evans and Southcott have different visions of the social and economic circumstances in Britain prior to the war, both follow a fairly traditional just war model. Prior just war models contain at least three components. The first requirement of the just war is that it be conducted under the authority of a legitimate Christian ruler. Second, the war must be fought for a just cause. Typically, that just cause consists of either the defense of one's own country or the protection of an ally. Third, a just war must be conducted in pursuit of some identifiable good, either to punish evil or to preserve or reclaim some identifiable happiness. Additional components, often implied rather than expressly stated, are that the war must be conducted with mercy and that it must be conducted with the understanding that God will assure victory and will gain in glory.[51]

The earliest outline of Southcott's just war theory appears in *The Temporal and Spiritual Sword*. First, Southcott insists that her followers may participate in a war conducted with obedience to a legitimate prince: "Your King's command must be obeyed by them. / And so the armour I do bid them wear" (3). Oddly enough, her seemingly pacifist notion of avoiding contention is preserved even as it is turned into avoiding contention by obeying the temporal power. Southcott's own variation on this condition of the just war is evident in what she neglects to mention—that George is a Christian ruler (a neglect more pointed in light of her earlier condemnations of the House of Hanover). Second, the war must be fought for a just cause—in this case, defense: "Then if my sword doth in your land appear, / How can my followers it refuse to wear? / To draw the sword, yourselves for to defend."[52] The idea is entirely consistent with Southcott's thorough going English nationalism; furthermore, it is consistent with Southcott's identification of the location of "the Beast" in those nations which replace one ruler with another in a sequence that changes rulers but never eliminates "sin and sorrow."[53] Southcott's conditions, however, are important, if not manifestly clear: She limits her followers to military action only in the event that the French appear in England. She accomplishes this condition by referring to the appearance of God's sword in England. The Spirit had previously told Southcott that his sword would be engaged against the French; the only reason for its appearance in England would be a French invasion.

Third, a just war must be conducted in pursuit of some identifiable good, either to punish evil or to preserve or reclaim some identifiable happiness. In this case, Southcott insists upon "chastizing" French aggression and effecting Christ's return to England. It seems clear, however, that fighting against the French and bringing about

Christ's return are coincidental, unrelated to each other except perhaps through some other linking cause. That cause is the repentance and sealing of the English people. Finally, if their war is conducted with a holy intention, the believers cannot fail: "And now let them like valiant soldiers stand. / And every foe shall now before them fall: / This is thy Prophecies, I tell you all."[54]

The only Augustinian component of the just war that Southcott omits from *The Temporal and Spiritual Sword* is that war must be conducted with mercy. Earlier, however, in *The Strange Effects of Faith,* Southcott had examined the correlation of violence and mercy. However, Southcott adds some features of her own. Perhaps the most unique trait of Southcott's theory is that it is cast in terms of burdens imposed and relieved, evident in *An Account of Trials on Bills of Exchange:* "[T]hough we have a burden to keep off the enemy [France]; but the Lord has promised to remove that burden, if we turn unto him; but if the nation goes on to slight the mercies, and mock the threatenings to this nation—if they do not repent, then they will find the truth of the words in the Warning to the World, 2nd page—'Like a snare it shall come upon them, in a day they little think of, and in an hour unawares" (55).

Southcott's model of the just war is fraught with variations upon the traditional just war theory, even though the basic elements are clearly present in her writings. I would argue that the variations are not sloppy or naive renditions of the just war theory, but rather are, first, Southcott's attempts to use the war both to comfort and inspire her followers, and second, Southcott's clever qualifications upon the temporal engagements of her followers. In so far as she neglects to treat George III as a legitimate Christian prince, transcendentalizes Buonaparte as "the Beast," and conditions English victory upon the repentance of the nation, Southcott codes the "allegiance" with the English king as incidental rather than pure. Even within a discourse of loyalty, George becomes a tool for working out Southcott's prophecies of victory and domestic security.

Outlining a theory of just war for her followers would have secured Southcott an ancillary role in the public sphere, in support of the war against France. But this limited conception of the public sphere, however useful to describe the participation in manifest social life of many other Britons, women and men alike, is not adequate to describe Southcott's role. She claimed more for herself than participation in an externally focused program. Besides insisting that a fallen world could be redeemed only by the exaltation of a woman, to undo the effects of Eve, the woman who fell, Southcott was concerned with

the temporal as well as the spiritual welfare of her Sealed People.[55] It
is that concern that by 1806 seems to have led to her reconsideration
of just war theory and allegiance to state powers. She recognizes that
the temporal Revolution had failed, asking, "What happiness had it
caused to mankind. Only deluged Europe with blood. . . . No revolution against men can bring in this glorious and happy period."[56] But
the suffering that led to the Revolution and the rise of Napoleon on
the Continent had its double in Britain. In *The Long-Wished-For-
Revolution,* she denies that the happiness of humankind "alludes to
nations, king, or empires," denying, too, the value of the French Revolution even as she gathers all kings and monarchs under a single
expression of disapprobation (3). She acknowledges that loyalty to
self-interested temporal rulers had done just as little to bring on the
millennium:

> Behold! earth's monarchs now combine,
> With their proud nobles to decree;
> Pride, wealth, and pow'r together join,
> To quench the flame of liberty.[57]

The combination of "earth's monarchs" might also, at first glance,
appear to point out the irony of governmental combination in light of
the prohibitions on combinations among the working and artisan
classes from which she drew her largest following, but the passage
also might be read as a contemporary figuring of the joining of the
great powers in preparation for the final conflict foretold in the Revelation and in Daniel. In fact, in 1795, Nathaniel Halhed, a biblical
scholar and follower of Richard Brothers, had, with Brothers, concluded that the four beasts were "four kings *now*."[58]

By 1806, Southcott seems to have worked out the problem of the
millenarian roles of "earth's monarchs." Specifically, earth's monarchs
do not matter, she argues in *The Long-Wished-For Revolution,* as individual believers would be "unto our God kings and priests" (13). Only
after the spiritual, internal revolution had taken place could a war
against the opponents of God on earth proceed. Southcott's approving
citation of Zechariah suggests that the spiritual revolution might
merely re-orient, toward a religious end, the conduct of war on earth:
"Then shall the Lord go forth and fight against those nations, as when
he fought in the days of battle."[59]

By 1807, beset by a financial scandal, Southcott begins to turn
her attention to the English enemies of her mission. In fact, one possible explanation for Southcott's affiliation with temporal power in *An*

Account of Trials on Bills of Exchange may be perceived in the occasion of the work. Southcott's name had been introduced, although not as a party, in a suit involving several of her followers (Major Eyre, William Sharp, and John Wilson) and a moneylender named John King. King sought repayment of negotiable loans from Eyre, Sharp, and Wilson, and the three followers of Southcott charged King with improper moneylending practices. In *An Account of Trials on Bills of Exchange,* Southcott takes care to align herself with the side of the law and even notes that "the laws of God and man" agree in this instance" (2). Perhaps Southcott recognized that the occasion was not one for opposing the Crown or its agents. Nevertheless, she refrains from hinting that the Crown can be understood to be an agent for effecting divine ends, even though she acknowledges that "the ways of the Lord . . . demand justice between man and man" (*Bills of Exchange,* 15). The Spirit of the Lord remains interested in worldly affairs, but Southcott draws some interesting connections between the power of the Napoleonic "Beast" and the workings of Satan in England:

> Here stand the perfect likeness of the nation and my friends: the laws have defended my friends from falling a prey to the ruin their enemies designed; and yet they have sustained losses, by falling into their hands; in the perfect likeness stands this nation; for the Lord hath defended this land from the power of the enemy in coming to destroy it; and yet we have sustained losses, by defending ourselves from his power, and from what has fallen into his hands of our property; and yet when we see the destruction he has made in the nations abroad, we have every reason to bless the Lord for his defence against the enemy, to prevent his coming here. (*Bills of Exchange,* 57–58).

Through the idea of "perfect likeness," Southcott is able to demonstrate the actions of both God and Satan within Europe and within England. The "likeness" is consistent with her early prophecies, which see the workings of Satan in evil abroad and evil at home, both of which evils temporal power may be engaged, as tools, to suppress.

Southcott's notion of "perfect likeness" and the justness of war depended upon some simultaneity in spiritual and temporal movement and in progress against evils both abroad and at home. Such movement did not occur. In 1810, Bicheno directly challenged the justness of the war through its effects in Britain and abroad.[60] In subsequent years, after the failure of her hopes that earthly evils might be suppressed, Southcott follows a cultural trend of disillusionment and attends more and more to evils at home, as marked by the persistence of her hopes for the poor expressed in a Southcottian hymn:

> Christ's Second Coming is at hand,
> In Might and Pow'r 'twill be;
> For Christ will *Renovate* the land,
> And set the captive free.
> Then wars on earth shall be no more,
> All tears He'll wipe away:
> The *Lame,* the *Blind, Infirm,* and *Poor,*
> Will bless that happy day.[61]

This and other writings make clear that her fundamental concern remained the "renovation" of a Britain that continued to suffer.

Recognizing both the failure of geopolitical agendas and the complicity of rulers in suppressing liberty, and further recognizing that no war against Satan can be just when pursued by earthly rulers, Southcott eventually abandoned political analysis of worldly events and prophecies. She contracted her own sphere to the domestic realm, preaching throughout the West Riding (later the most violent center of the Luddite risings), concentrating on bread for body and soul before retiring for a time from public life.

Her return to public life was marked by old frustrations and a new attitude. *Prophecies Announcing the Birth of the Prince of Peace, Extracted from the Works of Joanna Southcott; to Which Are Added a Few Remarks thereon, Made by Herself,* dated 7 September 1814, shows her sense of the failure of attaching prophetic evangelism to worldly discourses. Napoleon had been exiled to Elba but had not yet returned. It might have seemed that the absence of the prime enemy of Britain and of Christianity would afford an opportunity for peace and spiritual transformation in Britain, but that appeared not to be the case— a sentiment reflected in the work of other writers, too. An anonymous "Squib" dated 2 July 1814 reveals a quashed optimism: "The gunpowder dealers began to complain / The war being over, their labour was vain, / But they soon were informed, no contracts would cease, / If not wanted for war, 'twould be wasted in peace."[62] In *Prophecies Announcing the Birth of the Prince of Peace,* Southcott reaffirms an earlier conviction that "this sword never shall depart from Man, till a Solomon doth appear, that will ask wisdom of God; then shall my throne be established, and the house shall be built in my name."[63] Aware of the need for a different kind of temporal ruler attached more to wisdom than to war (and perhaps hopeful that the establishment of the Regency in 1811 might set a precedent for the replacement of one ruler by another), she announced in 1814 that the birth of the second messiah, Shiloh, was imminent. The sixty-five year-old virgin Southcott would give birth to the heavenly savior, who would lead the Jews in a return to their homeland in Palestine, presumably converting them to Christianity. The two events had been held by English dissenters since Thomas Brightman to be necessarily precedent to the millennium, an idea held dear by Richard Brothers.[64] Unfortunately, she died before the miraculous birth could take place.

Perhaps it would not be unreasonable to assume that Southcott's announcement would be accompanied by an attitude of hope, but this is not the case. Southcott also is affected by the discourse of internal dissension, or dissension turned inward, that characterizes the "Squib" quoted above. In *Prophecies Announcing the Birth of the Prince of Peace*, Southcott writes,

> I am now compelled to flee, not only from the face of my enemies, but from my friends likewise, to conceal myself in a place of safety, where I am not known by any person; and my name I am obliged to conceal, to preserve my life from malicious and inveterate enemies, who threatened to set the house on fire where I lived, and to take my life if they by any means could get me in their power. (34–35)

Nevertheless, despite her fear of spies, false accusations, and persecution, she continues to assert her attachment to Britain, or perhaps more precisely, England; Shiloh is an English redeemer.[65]

To return to the quote from William Lamont with which I opened this essay, Southcott's engagement with the discourses of her time carries her from millenarian predictions interpreting the Revolution, through participation in the patriotic and Christian war against Napoleon, to a disillusionment with worldly affairs—attitudes also reflected in the mainstream of English culture. In the wake of the French Revolution and the Napoleonic wars, which early she had believed would concentrate Britons' spiritual efforts against Satan and his Corsican representative on earth, the seemingly desperate retreat from the public eye and into miracles, especially the refiguration of both the virgin and post-menopausal births described in the Mary and Sarah stories in the Bible, marks a resignation and recognition that the millennium would be less an earthly than a heavenly event. The meaningful conflicts were spiritual, and the allegiance with a temporal order suggested in her just war theory was merely incidental and ultimately fruitless when we consider them by the criteria used by Linda Colley, quoted early in this essay. Southcott's nationalistic discourse and her theory of just war, grounded though it was in the language of the times, failed to secure for her a sustainable public role as both woman and millenarian.

Notes

1. William Lamont, *Godly Rule: Politics and Religion, 1603–60* (London: Macmillan, 1969), 13.

2. Linda Colley, "Whose Nation? Class and National Consciousness in Britain 1750–1830," *Past and Present* 113 (1986), 116.

3. Linda Colley, *Britons: Forging the Nation, 1707–1837* (New Haven: Yale University Press, 1992), 262.

4. Jeanne Moskal, "Gender, Nationality, and Textual Authority in Lady Morgan's Travel Books," *Romantic Women Writers: Voices and Counter-voices,* ed. Paula Feldman and Theresa Kelley (Hanover: University Press of New England, 1995), 183–84.

5. There are a few exceptions. Gary Kelly does address Elizabeth Hamilton's use of Christian moral discourse in her "counter-revolutionary politics." Hamilton insists "that Christian faith is necessary to complete classical republican private and social virtue" (*Women, Writing, and Revolution, 1790–1827* (New York: Oxford University Press, 1993), 273).

6. Anne Mellor, *Romanticism and Gender* (London: Routledge, 1993), especially 3, 68, 77.

7. Clarke Garrett, *Respectable Folly: Millenarians and the French Revolution in France and England* (Baltimore: Johns Hopkins University Press, 1975), 223.

8. Roger Wells, *Insurrection: The British Experience 1795–1803* (Gloucester: Alan Sutton, 1983), 298n44; J.F.C. Harrison, *The Second Coming: Popular Millenarianism 1780–1850* (New Brunswick, N.J.: Rutgers University Press, 1979), 225.

9. E. P. Thompson, *The Making of the English Working Class* (New York: Vintage, 1968), 382–84. Thompson says that Southcott's "manner lacked the revolutionary specificity of [the earlier prophet Richard] Brothers; but her apocalypse was most certainly one in which the sheep were to be separated irrevocably from the goats" (384).

10. W. H. Oliver, *Prophets and Millennialists: The Uses of Biblical Prophecy in England from the 1790s to the 1840s* (Auckland: Auckland University Press, 1978), 16; cited as *Prophets.*

11. Robert Hole, "English Sermons and Tracts as Media of Debate," in *The French Revolution and British Popular Politics,* ed. Mark Philp (Cambridge: Cambridge University Press, 1991), 23–24.

12. Ibid., 19–20. Jones's sermons are quite remarkable for their marshaling of a variety of discourses against the Revolution and English Jacobinism. They are collected in Jones, *The Theological, Philosophical and Miscellaneous Works of the Rev. William Jones,* 12 vols. (London: F. and C. Rivington, 1801), especially the sixth volume.

13. Hole, "English Sermons," 28–29.

14. On the wide use of the discourse of nationalism, see Colley, "Whose Nation," 116.

15. On Bicheno, see Oliver, *Prophets,* 46–50 and Garrett, *Respectable Folly,* 140. Bicheno's most famous work, which had gone into at least six editions by 1799, is *The Signs of the Times; or, The Overthrow of the Papal Tyranny in France, the Prelude of Destruction to Popery and Despotism; but of Peace to Mankind* (London: 1793).

16. Southcott's personal history, told initially by herself in several of her prophetic volumes, is beyond the scope of this essay. Besides a brief summary in Garrett's *Respectable Folly,* it has been told well in G. R. Balleine's *Past Finding Out: The Tragic Story of Joanna Southcott and Her Successors* (New York: Macmillan, 1956), James K. Hopkins's *A Woman to Deliver Her People: Joanna Southcott and English Millenarianism in an Era of Revolution* (Austin: University of Texas Press, 1982); cited as *Past Finding Out* and *Woman to Deliver,* respectively.

17. In numerous texts, especially those written to her friend and housemate, Jane Townley, Southcott speaks of the Spirit's having chased off her many human suitors ("rivals"), saving her so that she could be Christ's bride upon his return. See Southcott, *Letters and Communications of Joanna Southcott. The Prophetess of Exeter: Lately Written to Jane Townley* (Stourbridge: 1804), 113.

18. Southcott, *The Trial of Joanna Southcott, during Seven Days, Which Commenced on the Fifth, and Ended on the Eleventh, of December, 1804* (London: 1804), 60; cited as *Trial of Joanna Southcott.*

19. Hopkins, *Woman to Deliver,* 73.

20. Hopkins, *Woman to Deliver,* 77–84.

21. See also Kelly, *Women, Writing, and Revolution,* 3.

22. Brothers's story is told in several historical works, but appears most concisely in Garrett's *Respectable Folly* (182–84), as well as in Harrison's *The Second Coming* (63–65). Born in Newfoundland on Christmas Day 1757, Brothers served as a lieutenant in the British Navy before his discharge at the conclusion of the American War at half pay. After having lived in London and refusing to take an oath of loyalty, Brothers was committed to a workhouse and shortly thereafter embarked upon a career of prophesying—a career that included a number of arrests. Brothers is most well-known for his "Israelism," the centering of his prophecies on a number of principles: the conversion of the Jews, the discovery that the English are tribes of Israel, Brothers's special role in leading the reconciliation and Christianization of the Jewish tribes, and his claims to the English Crown. Brothers's prophecies are fully engaged in interpreting the international events of the times as fulfilling the prophecies in Revelation and Daniel.

23. Garrett, *Respectable Folly,* 220–21, 227.

24. Brothers's internationalism is perhaps most evident in his announcement that he had been selected to discover the hidden Jews and return them to the Holy Land (Brothers, *Revealed Knowledge,* 2 vols. [London, 1795], 2: 82) and in his predictions of the deaths of monarchs (*Revealed Knowledge* 2: 7). See also Garrett's discussion (*Respectable Folly,* 187).

25. Southcott, *The Continuation of the Prophecies of Joanna Southcott. A Word in Season to a Sinking Kingdom* (London: 1803), 37; cited as *Word in Season.* Southcott cites these same assurances in a later work, *An Account of the Trials on Bills of Exchange* (London: 1807), 54; cited as *Bills of Exchange.* The practice of combining eulogy and censure in a single work was not uncommon during the first years of nineteenth century. See, for example, Brenda Banks's discussion of the combined purposes of William Wordsworth's sonnets in "Rhetorical Missiles and Double Talk: Napoleon, Wordsworth, and the Invasion Scare of 1804," *Romanticism, Radicalism, and the Press,* ed., Stephen Behrendt (Detroit: Wayne State University Press, 1997), 114.

26. Southcott, *The First Book of Sealed Prophecies* (London: Marchant and Galabin, 1803.), 81; cited as *First Sealed.*

27. Southcott, *A Warning to the World. Joanna Southcott's Prophecies* (London: S. Rousseau, 1804), 34. On the famines of 1799–1800, see Chapter Nine in Roger Wells's *Insurrection.*

28. Southcott's anti-Hanoverian attitude echoes Richard Brothers's early rebukes of, predictions about, and warnings to George III, whose crown Brothers had requested (see, for example, *Revealed Knowledge* 2: 73). By 1805, however, after a succession of military threats to Britain, even Brothers had changed his tune, professing "love most true" for the King (*Wisdom and Duty* (London: 1805), 22).

29. *Revealed Knowledge,* 2: 45.

30. Southcott, *The Strange Effects of Faith,* 2nd ed. (Exeter: 1801), 37; cited as *Strange Effects,* noted also by part (6 parts in total).

31. *Strange Effects, Fifth,* 235. The Spirit had apparently comforted Southcott and assured her of the safety of Britain when, in 1795, she awoke from a dream with a fear of French invasion (*Strange Effects, Second,* 87). The same assurance appears in *Strange Effects, Third,* 134.

32. Southcott, *Warning to the World,* 12. The threat, as revealed by the Spirit of the Lord, may have been more pronounced than Southcott was willing to admit to her readers. Earlier in 1804, in an unpublished communication, the Spirit warned that "Nine parts of the inhabitants of London would perish" (22 January 1804, MS 32633, f. 203, in the British Library).

33. See, for example, *The Second Book of Sealed Prophecies. An Address to the Public, Written in 1796* (London: S. Rousseau, 1805), 50–53.

34. Southcott, *Texas Collection,* 415, n. d., f. 44.

35. Southcott, *Trial of Joanna Southcott,* xiv; quoted in Hopkins, *Woman to Deliver,* 192. Southcott's "trials" are nonjuridical events during which men of some social standing, usually her most prominent followers and some Anglican clergy, examined her and judged the accuracy of her prophecies.

36. Hopkins, *Woman to Deliver,* 192. Hopkins's treatment of the question is especially important, despite his choice not to work out the rhetorical and philosophical difficulties in Southcott's work, because it contradicts and corrects some of the earlier scholarship on Southcott, scholarship that cast her as a pacifist.

37. *Strange Effects, Fourth Part,* 180.

38. Alphonse Aulard, *Christianity and the French Revolution* (New York: Howard Fertig, 1966), 24–25.

39. Southcott, *Communication by the Still Small Voice, on Monarchy in France* (London: 1846), 5–14. The date of composition is 21 December 1804.

40. Southcott, *The Full Assurance that the Kingdom of Christ Is at Hand, from the Signs of the Times* (London: 1806), 17.

41. Southcott, *Long-wished-for Revolution* (London: 1806), 16–17; see also *Word in Season,* 54.

42. *Bills of Exchange,* 54. Southcott was not the only writer of the period to refer to Sennacherib in the context of the French wars. Reverend Evans writes in a footnote commenting upon Isaiah 6: "The Rabbins refer this to the peaceable reign of Hezekiah, in opposition to the insolent, turbulent, and sanguinary conduct of Sennacherib" (Evans, *War Not Inconsistent with Christianity* [Bristol: C. and R. Baldwin, 1804], 6n; hereafter *War*).

43. See, for example, Southcott's promise that her sealed people would survive an Napoleonic invasion: "If they invade this very land, / My Sealed People they shall stand, / I say to see their foes to fall; / He cannot come to conquer all" (Southcott, *Warning to the World,* 12).

44. Southcott, *Second Book of Sealed Prophecies,* 2.

45. Southcott Collection, 74, *Communication on the Temporal and Spiritual Sword* (London, 1853), 2. Quoted by permission of the Harry Ransom Humanities Research Center at the University of Texas at Austin. Hopkins lists the manuscript date as 1803 (*Woman to Deliver,* 268 n47).

46. Southcott, *Temporal and Spiritual Sword,* 5; cited in Hopkins, *Woman to Deliver,* 195.

47. Evans, *War,* 37.

48. Evans, *War,* 34–35, citing Ezekial Hopkins, *The Works of the Right Reverend and Learned, Ezekiel Hopkins* (London: Jonathan Robinson, 1701), 195.

49. E. Hopkins, *Works,* 195; quoted in Evans, *War,* 5.

50. Church of England clergy generally supported the government's war efforts. Poems written by church divines in 1803 and 1804 take positions similar to Evans's sermon. For example, Reverend Richard Mant's "War Song, Written in May, 1803, on the Publication of the Negotiation Papers," concludes with an English rejoinder to Napoleon's threat to invade England: "Come, then, come thou Consul-King! / Launch thy navies, arm thine host, / And beneath night's favouring wing/ Thy banners plant on England's coast! / Come! but hope not to return—" (lines 37–42). The poem appears in Betty Bennett, ed., *British War Poetry in the Age of Romanticism: 1793–1815* (New York: Garland Publishing, 1976), 290. Bennett notes that the attitude reflected by persons such as Mant and Evans seems to have been typical among Church of England clergy (34).

51. For primary sources on the just war theory, see Augustine, *Letters,* trans. Wilfrid Parsons, 5 vols. (New York: Fathers of the Church, 1951–56), vols. 3 and 4, letters 138 and 189, and *Contra Faustum Manichaeum,* trans. Richard Stothert, in Philip Schaff, ed., *Nicene and Post-Nicene Fathers,* First Series (Grand Rapids: Eerdmans, 1974), vol. 4, sec. 22. Useful secondary sources include John Langan, "Elements of St. Augustine's Just War Theory," *The Ethics of St. Augustine* (Atlanta: Scholars Press, 1991), 174, and Joan Tooke, *The Just War in Aquinas and Grotius* (London: SPCK, 1965), 22.

52. Southcott, *Temporal and Spiritual Sword,* 3; cited in Hopkins, *Woman to Deliver,* 195.

53. Southcott, *Long-Wished-For Revolution,* 3.

54. Southcott, *Temporal and Spiritual Sword,* 3.

55. Southcott, *Word to the Wise,* 16, 27.

56. Southcott, *Long-Wished-For Revolution,* 9. In her remarks, South-cott seems to echo the 1795 objections of Amelia Opie, and to anticipate the use of similar images and language by Anne Grant (Stephen Behrendt, "British Women Poets and the Reverberations of Radicalism in the 1790s," *Romanticism, Radicalism, and the Press,* ed. Stephen Behrendt [Detroit: Wayne State University Press, 1997], 88, 92).

57. Philip Pullen (compiler), *Hymns, or Spiritual Songs, Composed from the Prophetic Writings of Joanna Southcott,* 4th Ed. (London: W. Tozzer, 1814), 201.

58. Nathaniel Halhed, *Testimony on the Authenticity of the Prophecies of Richard Brothers* (London: 1795), 22.

59. Zechariah 14: 3; Authorized (King James) Version.

60. Bicheno, *The Consequences of Unjust War: A Discourse Delivered at Newbury, Feb. 28, 1810* (London, 1810).

61. Pullen, *Hymns, or Spiritual Songs,* 194.

62. "Squib," *The Morning Chronicle,* 2 July 1814, in Betty Bennett, ed., *British War Poetry,* 475. See also another anonymous poem, "The Good Old Times," which points to a renewal of the slave trade and the Inquisition (*The Morning Chronicle,* 13 June 1814, in Bennett, *British War Poetry,* 475).

63. Southcott, *Prophecies Announcing the Birth of the Prince of Peace, Extracted from the Works of Joanna Southcott; To Which Are Added a Few Remarks Thereon, Made by Herself* (London: W. Marchant, 1814), 22.

64. Lamont, *Godly Rule,* 95–104.

65. Southcott, *Prophecies Announcing the Birth of the Prince of Peace,* 40.

Napoleon, Nationalism, and the Politics of Religion in Mariana Starke's *Letters from Italy*

∾

Jeanne Moskal

In 1914, scholar F. J. MacCunn formulated a schematic political map of British responses to Napoleon. The crucial question for Britons, MacCunn said, was this: was Napoleon the "champion, representative and child" of the French Revolution, "or was he its destroyer?"[1] MacCunn concluded that Tories, hating both Napoleon and the Revolution, identified the two and saw Napoleon as the "champion, representative and child" of this despicable development in history; Whigs admired the Revolution, hated Napoleon, and took him as its destroyer; and a third group of die-hard Radical admirers, such as John Cam Hobhouse and William Hazlitt, believed in Napoleon as the champion of the Revolution in its benevolent form, a champion whose fall was brought about by his own "monarchical, Revolution-destroying tendencies" (MacCunn, 32). Recently, however, Simon Bainbridge has provided a more nuanced map of British responses to Napoleon by showing that the first generation of male Romantic writers admired Napoleon exceedingly, especially during the earliest years of his public notoriety, 1798–1802, a period that spans Napoleon's stunningly successful campaign against the Austrians in Italy, his failed expedition to Egypt, his assumption of the Consulate, and his second Italian campaign.[2] But these writers retrospectively gave the impression that their disillusionment began years earlier. The literary corollary of this admiration was messianic imagery. S. T. Coleridge, for example, calls Napoleon "the Savior," registering "[t]he belief of many of the British Radicals and Whigs that this [the first Italian campaign] was a revolutionary campaign, fought to liberate the enslaved Italians from Austrian domination, rather than one of conquest fought on behalf of French ambition," a belief confirmed by the establishment of the Italian "sister republics" to France. Thus, our current view of early British Romantic-period responses to Napoleon takes into account the late nineties' admiration for "the hero of Italy" and attends to its millenarian imagery.

Here I use this corrected view to start a discussion of a travel memoir by Mariana Starke (?1762–1838), the playwright, translator, poet, and travel writer whose work formed the basis of publisher John Murray's lucrative *Handbooks for Travellers* series, which began in the 1830s. This travel memoir, *Letters from Italy* (1800), recounts Starke's travels in Italy as the nurse to an invalid relative while the French conquered Nice in 1792, Napoleon's "Army of Italy" campaigned in 1796–97, and the Papacy lost, for a few years, its temporal power.[3] Starke's memoir, like the material Bainbridge examines, attests to that *fin de siècle* admiration for the hero of Italy, clothed in millenarian imagery. However, Starke's Anglican conservatism is a far cry from the Radical and Whig belief that Italy needed liberation from the Austrians. In Starke's view, Roman Catholicism—what she calls "superstition"—not the Austrian empire, is the tyrant to be overthrown. With this religious motive paramount, she admires Napoleon's generalship and manliness, and, more importantly, she subordinates her disdain for Napoleon's atheism to her Protestant delight in Napoleon's defeat of the Papacy. Thus, the example of Starke shows that Napoleon was embraced and celebrated even by patriotic English writers, precisely because of their nationalism, as it shaded into anti-Catholicism. Adopting the position that Gary Kelly has designated "anti-Jacobin feminism," by which women writers of the late 1790s "rejected Revolutionary feminist civic 'woman' for a renewed model of 'domestic woman' as professionalized custodian of the 'national' conscience, culture, and destiny,"[4] Starke asserts her own capacity to speak for British Protestantism, which, Linda Colley has demonstrated, is fundamental to British national identity.[5]

The gendered politics of British nationalism were peculiarly contradictory at this historical moment. Women joined the public discourse of British patriotism and anti-French sentiment, despite the fact that their appearing in print as writers of *any* political persuasion allied them with the "French principles" associated with Mary Hays and Mary Wollstonecraft. The opprobrium for Wollstonecraft, sparked by William Godwin's *Memoirs* (1798), was consolidated by Richard Polwhele's *The Unsex'd Females* (1798), which condemns as licentious women's participation in political controversy.[6] Hannah More's *Strictures on the Modern System of Female Education* (1799) registers this ideological contradiction: on the one hand, More urges women to exert their patriotism publicly, by "com[ing] forward with a patriotism at once firm and feminine for the public good" to oppose "the most tremendous confederacies against religion and order, and governments, which the world ever saw." On the other hand, she maintains that she herself is "not sounding an alarm to female warriors, or exciting female politicians," thus distancing herself from Polwhele's charge.[7] Marlon Ross has articulated the historical dilemma More is negotiating:

> During the early Romantic period, women's political discourse—across the ideological spectrum—occupies a position of dissent. Simply to speak about politics is to place oneself *against* the political establishment, where women's role is normatively defined solely by silent obeisance. The woman who speaks out purposefully *not to dissent* but rather to reaffirm her total subordination to the political establishment inevitably finds herself in a problematic position of dissent (original emphasis).[8]

Starke, too, exemplifies the position Ross describes. Responding to More's call for female patriotism, Starke offers her firsthand account as evidence to modify More's characterization of the French as "the most tremendous confederac[y] against religion and order . . . which the world ever saw" by recounting the French conquest of the Papacy. At the same time, Starke's religious vocabulary protects her from the charge of impiety, saving her from the charge of "female warrior" despite her presence on the front lines of the war and from the charge of "[female] politician" despite her detailed opinions on the political errors of the Milanese, of Pope Pius, and of others. Religion thus has a dual function. It undergirds Starke's patriotism as a Briton and it also offers her, as a woman, a narrow means of acceptable entry into the field of political commentary.

The French Campaigns in Italy in the 1790s

Starke witnessed Napoleon's debut against the backdrop of a deeply divided Italy, which did not become a unified nation until the 1870s. In the 1790s, the Austrian Hapsburgs and the Spanish Bourbons split most of Italy between them, the Hapsburgs possessing the duchies of Milan (including Mantua) and Tuscany, and exerting control in Modena, Genoa, and parts of Piedmont. Daughters of the Austrian Empress Maria Theresa were married to the Spanish Bourbons who ruled Parma and Naples. The Spanish Bourbons also held Sicily. The third major player, the Papacy, controlled Rome and "the Legations," substantial dominions in central Italy. The nominally independent states included the republics of Genoa and Venice, the small states of Lucca and San Marino, and the Kingdom of Sardinia (comprised of the island of Sardinia, Piedmont, Savoy, and Nice), ruled by the House of Savoy. Based on this history of political disarray, Austrian Prime Minister Clemens Metternich maintained, as late as 1847, that Italy was "merely a geographical expression."[9]

Before Napoleon's advent, the French Constituent Assembly ordered its troops to invade this territory in 1792–93, beginning at Nice, as part of its aggressive plan to export its Revolutionary principles. General Montesquiou, leading a small French army, seized the Duchy of Savoy and the County of Nice in 1792, a move uncontested by their ruler, Victor Amadeus III of the House of Savoy, the King of Sardinia. In later developments, the French occupying army remained, poorly supplied, until 1794, when the fall of Maximillien Robespierre and the rise of the Directory led to a change in foreign policy from offense to defense. The French troops, accordingly, lay low until 1796, when the defeat of Kellerman and the Army of the Alps prompted Napoleon, then an assistant to General Schérer, to propose an aggressive course into Italy. The Directory accepted his plan, replacing Schérer with Napoleon as Commander in Chief. Napoleon began his first Italian campaign in April 1796, dividing Colli's army, which served Victor Amadeus, from his Austrian allies, taking Milan and driving the Austrians under General Beaulieu east and north, out of northern Italy and into the Alps (though a small garrison of Austrians held the fort of Mantua for much of the campaign). Impressive as his victories were in themselves, Napoleon shrewdly exaggerated the facts to his advantage (exaggerations which Starke, along with most of her contemporaries, accepts) to enhance his own reputation and that of his army.[10] The Austrians later resumed the campaign under Wurmser.

Politically, Napoleon's victories culminated in French domination of much of northern and central Italy, mostly in the form of several small "sister republics" to the French one, with constitutions modeled on the French, though Napoleon often chose the administrators directly. The most important was the Cisalpine Republic, founded in July 1797 at Milan. The Cispadane Republic ("south of the river Po") was established in October 1796, later merging (in July 1797) with the Cisalpine Republic. Genoa withdrew from the Cisalpine Republic to form the Ligurian Republic in June 1797. In less disguised versions of French domination, the Pope ceded most of the Legations to France at the Treaty of Tolentino in early 1797. The territories of the Republic of Venice were partitioned, under the terms of the Treaty of Campo Formio (October 1797) among France, the Hapsburgs, and the Cisalpine Republic. The French took Rome before Napoleon left for Egypt. In his capacity as the French envoy to the Vatican, Joseph Bonaparte encouraged Jacobin demonstrations there. At one, the French general Duphot was killed, and in retaliation, the Directory charged Berthier to march on Rome. The Roman democrats, seizing the initiative, proclaimed the Roman Republic in February 1798, and invited Berthier and his troops into the city. Pope Pius fled Rome for Siena, and later, the south of France, where he soon died. Encouraged by the presence of a British fleet under Admiral Nelson in the Mediterranean, Neapolitan troops tried to recapture Rome, but lost to the French under General Championnet, who chased them back into Naples and proclaimed the Parthenopean Republic in January 1799.

The Parthenopean Republic lasted only five months before the War of the Second Coalition reversed the tide, defeating French troops throughout Italy. The Austro-Russian army, led by General Surorov (famed from Byron's Siege of Ismail in *Don Juan*) spread across the Po region. Moreover, the religious army called the *sanfedisti,* led by Cardinal Ruffo, fought for the reconquest of Naples; and the army of Arezzo gave most potent expression to the general discontent with France that prompted guerilla warfare in much of Italy. The old order was, by and large, restored, except for Masséna keeping the sole French stronghold at Genoa. And a new pope, Pius VII, was elected in 1800, following the death of his predecessor.

Given the contrast between French victory in Italy under Napoleon and French defeat in Italy under the direct guidance of the Directory, the French government was completely discredited, laying the ground-work for the *coup d'état* of November (Brumaire) 1799. As First Consul, Napoleon attacked the Austrians (the Russians having with-drawn from the Coalition), waging and winning his second Italian campaign, culminating in his triumph at Marengo, Emperor Francis of Austria suing for peace. Concluded at the Treaty of Lunéville (February 1801), the peace left Italy much as it had been after Campo Formio. The temporal power of the Papacy was restored in a reduced fashion when Pius VII was allowed to rule the Papal States again by the terms of the Treaty of Lunéville. Well after the close of Starke's story, Napoleon, in his ongoing dispute with the Papacy, annexed

Rome and the patrimony of St. Peter in 1809, thus bringing about a second fall of the temporary power of the Papacy.

Starke as British Patriot at Nice

Given this exciting material, it is not surprising that *Letters from Italy* met with success, being translated into German and going into a second English edition with the new title *Travels in Italy,* but no other changes. It has a perfunctory epistolary form, written in twenty-five "letters" addressed to no named or described correspondent. The first seven letters are dated at intervals of about a year and narrate Starke's adventures in Italy, while the remaining letters are undated and present guidebook–style advice.

Part of the book's success can be attributed to Starke's seizing the role of British patriot and representative of the British nation. The memoir recounts how Starke's family found themselves tangled in the complex historical events noted above. They were visiting Nice when it fell to Montesquiou in 1792 (1: 25–47); the Florentines hustled Starke's family to safety in its suburbs when Napoleon entered Florence in June 1796 (1: 93). And they were on an extended visit to Rome from March 1797 to February 1798, from Napoleon's first threat to the papal government until the execution of that threat. Thus Starke's sojourn in Italy coincided not only with the remarkable military achievement of the French—what Starke calls "the most rapid and brilliant conquests ever gained in so short a period, either by ancient or modern Warriors" (1: 153). It also coincided with the rise of Napoleon's star; as David Chandler writes, "in March 1796, Napoleon Buonaparte was known only to comparatively restricted circles within France, but a year later his name had become a household word throughout Europe."[11] By the time Starke published *Letters from Italy* in 1800, her first-hand experience had multiplied in market value, due to the fear for British interests provoked by Napoleon's Egyptian campaign, and later to the *coup* of Brumaire 1799, when Napoleon came to dominate much of Europe.

Starke establishes her authority to comment on Napoleon by showing that her role as the representative of the British nation predates Napoleon's advent, beginning with the conquest of Nice. Her family's difficulties assume political importance as an instance of French harassment of Britons; the role of custodian of national conscience and identity is thrust upon her by circumstances and thus not by any unwomanly self-aggrandizement. She walks her reader through the hourly vicissitudes of the French attack on Nice in September 1792, foregrounding her own role in saving her family. The peril was grave, because, Starke contends, the leaders of Nice "resigned their city into the hands of the French, even before such a surrender had been demanded" (1: 35). The Nissards recede from the narrative, which focuses on the British visitors, who became vulnerable to escaped galley slaves as well as to the invading French army. Having been guaranteed safe passage out of Nice by the French commandant, Starke arranges for her family to leave by an English ship, only to be blocked by an embargo a few hours later. When the embargo is lifted, Starke escapes:

> We therefore prepared to embark, and being advised to make as little parade as possible on our way to the port, my Family went two and two by different paths, while I, being obliged to stay to the last, walked down, dressed as a Servant, passing all the French posts without the smallest molestation. . . . Others of the English, however, who went with more parade, did not escape insult, and even found some difficulty in getting on board. (1: 43–44)

Stressing her womanly dutifulness to her family, which "oblige[s her] to stay to the last," Starke implicitly takes up a nationalist duty as well in relation to "others of the English . . . who went with more parade." Starke's fellow Britons in Nice, either aristocrats or wealthy members of the middle class, insist, even in an emergency, on travelling with the accouterments appropriate to their status, on going "with more parade." In contrast, Starke herself exhibits a creative downward mobility, a psychological fluidity in dressing across class lines "as a Servant." Clever and resourceful on its surface, this action sounds an unsettling note of class mobility that Starke later uses in plotting her own upward mobility as a guarantor of the Grand Tour.

This strategy of "Starke representing Britain" continues when Starke recounts that her family has boarded the ship which is promptly boarded by French soldiers, enraged at the death of one of their company,

> now in an ill-humour with the British Nation, [they] jumped in considerable numbers upon our deck, which lay parallel with the shore, swearing we were Aristocrats, and threatening to rob and murder us; at length, however, their Officers

> appeased and removed them; but, nevertheless, we deemed it
> prudent to push off from shore . . . (1: 45).

The French soldiers direct their rage at both a nation, the British,
and at a class, the aristocracy. Starke hopes her readers will see her
under threat of death merely for being a Briton, thus securing her
status as a patriot. Starke's silence about class status strikes a
compromise. She could have deflected the soldiers' rage from herself
by identifying her own mercantile-class status, which we can infer
from her father's employment by the British East India Company in
Madras. But Starke often travelled with aristocrats, sycophantically
anxious to be associated with them. For example, on crossing the Col
de Tende, she writes: "The Dutchess Dowager of A***, (whose universal benevolence adds dignity to her high rank), knowing how great an
Invalid one of my Family is . . . permitt[ed] us to accompany her from
Turin to Geneva" in order to give the Starke family access to her
physician, who was English (1: 17). Thus Starke's recording, during
the capitulation of Nice, that the French perceived her family as aristocrats, may well have served the motive of class ambition we can
observe in her remarks on the Dutchess Dowager of A***. Recording
the French army's perception of her and her family as aristocrats
obliquely accords her some of the cultural cachet to which she aspires.
While Starke's conscious purpose in recounting the fall of Nice may
have been to demonstrate her acquaintance with pre-Napoleonic
Italy, the tale reveals as well the unconscious class dynamics that
later shape her response to Napoleon.

Protestantism and British National Identity

There is another way in which the account of the conquest of
Nice provides an essential component of Starke's authority to com-
ment on Napoleon. Her meditations on the religious dynamics of the
French Revolution establish her credentials as a spokesperson for
British Protestantism. "Atheist" France posed a problem for the
British nationalist habit of conflating Francophobia with anti-
Catholicism. The French Republic's official break with Catholicism
came when, in 1791, the Constituent Assembly dissolved the monas-
tic orders and required all clergy to swear allegiance to the Constitution. In response, Pope Pius VI condemned the principles of the
Revolution and declared the doctrine of the Church of Rome opposed
to the Declaration of the Rights of Man.[12] The Convention, under

Robespierre, promoted a Cult of Reason that affirmed the existence of the Supreme Being, the immortality of the soul, and the rewards of the afterlife (Lefebvre, 2: 115). This Deist spectacle looked "Atheist" to Starke and to Britons like her. Despite the efforts of the Convention, most of the French people remained loyal to Roman Catholicism and welcomed Napoleon's Concordat with the Papacy in July 1801, which restored the establishment, but not the wealth, of the Roman Catholic Church.

During the atheistic interval, Britons needed a new screen onto which to project their anti-Catholicism, and Italy fit the bill. Starke registers this shift of the religious and political world of the 1790s, as the binary structure—Catholic France versus Protestant England— triangulates into Atheist France, Catholic Italy, and Protestant England. As she recounts incidents in the French invasion, her two antipathies vie for preeminence: she can't decide whom she hates more. For example, in Letter III, Starke mocks the French clergy on the occasion of the execution of Louis XVI; the news must have been

> particularly afflictive to the crowd of Emigrant-Nobles and Ecclesiastics who saunter idly up and down the Pisa-Quay; for, had they remained in France and supported their unoffending monarch, it seems almost certain he would not have been led to the guillotine. I find, however, that the generality of Nobles and Prelates had long behaved so ill to Persons beneath them as to fear any revenge on the part of those they had injured; and this selfish fear induced them to desert their King, and leave France to the mercy of low men, who, like horses just escaped from their Drivers, set off full speed on the dangerous road to greatness, trampling Liberty, Justice, and Religion under-foot. (1: 49)

Here she initially denounces the "Ecclesiastics" of France on several counts: their long-term ill-behavior "to Persons beneath them"; their disloyalty to their King and their congregations; and their current wealth and indolence in "saunter[ing] idly up and down the Pisa-Quay." But in denouncing their sins, Starke finds herself cataloging the same grievances voiced by the atheist Revolutionaries, the "low men" "injured" by these clergy. In compensation for this apparent sympathy for their cause, she attacks the atheists in their turn as tramplers on liberty, justice, and religion.

In other passages Starke's ambivalence teeter-totters in a similar way as she recounts the "democratic Frenchmen," "missionaries" in

Pisa during 1793–94: "The absurdities of the Roman-catholic religion were painted [by the French democrats] in glowing colours; the licentiousness of it's Priests too justly reprobated, and it's tendency to thicken the veil of ignorance and strengthen the hands of arbitrary power, particularly enlarged upon and regretted" (1: 50). The despised French atheists, Starke has to admit, have a just grudge against the long–standing corruption of the Roman Catholic Church.

Monasticism, too, comes in for some heavy fire. Starke recounts the story of a captive nun freed during the siege of Mantua, an Austrian stronghold, by the French:

> While the French were besieging [Mantua], a Convent, which lay exposed to the cannon of the garrison, was evacuated by it's Nuns, and immediately occupied by the Besiegers; who, hearing groans issue from underneath the building, humanely followed the sound, and discovered, in a damp and gloomy dungeon, a Female seated on a crazy chair, and loaded with fetters, but whose countenance, though deeply furrowed by misery, looked youthful. On seeing the Soldiers, she earnestly petitioned for life and liberty; telling them, she had been four years confined in that cruel manner, for attempting to elope with a young Man who had long been Master of her heart: the Soldiers instantly struck off her fetters; upon which she besought them to lead her into the open air. They represented, that on quitting the shelter of the Convent she would be exposed to a shower of cannonballs. "Ah,!" replied the Nun, *"mourir, c'est rester ici!"* [It would be death to remain here]. (1: 81)

Here the young woman wants only "to elope with a young Man who had long been Master of her heart," but the institutions of Roman Catholicism seek to suffocate true affection by imprisoning the young woman in a Gothic "damp and gloomy dungeon." The French army responds "humanely" and frees her from both literal and spiritual slavery by "[striking] off her fetters." Starke's narrative here inserts a 1790s literary cliché of the nun prohibited by her vows from following the course of true love. It appears in a play, *Julia of Louvain, or Monkish Cruelty* (1797), by J. C. Cross.[13] And Radcliffe doubles the stakes in her novel, *A Sicilian Romance* (1792). There the true lovers Cornelia and Angelo take monastic vows because each believes the other is dead or unavailable. In addition to doubling the motif, Radcliffe adds some explicit anti-Catholic polemic. Her heroine Julia's view of the convent landscape conveys this larger, political meaning in the interplay of the shadows of "superstition" and the "sun of science":

> The dark clouds of prejudice break away before the sun of science, and gradually dissolving, leave the brightening hemisphere to the influence of his beams. But . . . [h]ere prejudice, not reason, suspended the influence of the passions; and scholastic learning, mysterious philosophy, and crafty sanctity, supplied the place of wisdom, simplicity, and pure devotion.[14]

Starke, capitalizing on the prerogative of the travel writer, incorporates the novelist's tools, when appropriate, in the service of a Protestant agenda. Curiously, Starke is implicitly pointing out one of the central ironies of Radcliffe's authorial career: that she never visited the locales so lavishly described in her novels, which were so stunningly successful throughout the nineties and beyond, but relied on the travel books of others. In a sense, then, Starke can be seen as re-appropriating the primacy of the travel writers and subordinating the novelistic plot to her use. Furthermore, Starke's anti-Catholicism is oddly linked with what she perceives to be loyalty to her own sex, by an opinion that marriage is a woman's only path to happiness, or at least what Jane Austen called the surest preservative against want.

Despite Starke's pervasive anti-Catholicism and her scorn for monks, nuns, and clergy in particular, she praises individuals, offering an admiring portrait of the Roman Catholic bishop of Nice. When the French took the city, Starke writes:

> So far the French acted liberally; but I must now mention a circumstance which disgraced them, while it gave pain to every lover of virtue. When Nice was to be taken possession of in the name of the [French] Republic, it was required that the keys should be given up in form, and as every Piedmontese and Nissard-Officer, both military and civil, had now disappeared, the BISHOP (who, in spite of repeated solicitations, refused to fly, declaring, he would remain to watch his Flock till forced from them), was now called upon to perform the above-named ceremony; he obeyed, taking with him two or three of his own Chaplains, one of whom addressed him as Monseigneur; upon hearing which, the French General proudly exclaimed, *"Il n'y a pas des Monseigneurs! Monsieur l'Abbé, s'il vous plait"* [sic] and then turning to the BISHOP,

whose cross hung suspended on his breast, he bade him throw away that bauble, and take the civic oath. The BISHOP indignantly refused; upon which he was desired to quit the City. On returning to his palace, he fainted; but, soon recovering himself, set out on foot, in a pelting rain, for Turin, where, however, he arrived in safety. (1: 40–41)

Starke does praise the bishop's fidelity. Yet one senses that the point of the story is to denounce the French Revolutionaries. And indeed, she soon calls them "people whose darling tenet is atheism, and their professed aim universal empire" (1: 46). The story thus illustrates the end result of the abolition of titles ("Il n'ya pas des Monseigneurs") not as equality but as universal French domination.

What are the stakes in Starke's anti-Catholicism? It is profoundly reactionary, despite its surface resemblance to support for the secularization and reform of the Roman Catholic Church, a resemblance (we saw) Starke immediately repudiated. Her suspicion of monasticism, for example, accords with a reactionary middle-class response to the French Revolution. As Joan Landes has observed, the effect of middle-class hegemony in the French Revolution was to privatize the role of women: "Women's duty consists of subordinating her independent aims and interests to a higher goal, the ethical life of the community. But unlike her male companion . . . woman is barred completely from active participation in the very sphere that gives purpose to all her actions . . . . As a result, woman's virtue acquires a spatial dimension. Her confinement to the private realm functions as a sign of her public virtue" (Landes, 69). Starke, along with novelist Radcliffe and playwright Cross, endorses the reinscription of women into marriage and private life under the aegis of true love by rejecting women's separateness in convents as unnatural and oppressive. Thus anti-Catholicism forms an almost unrelieved backdrop for Starke's response to the "Protestant hero" of Italy.

Napoleon the Protestant Hero

Starke's conflictedness about class status and about the relative evils of atheism and Catholicism, exhibited in her account of the conquest of Nice, are fully catalyzed by her portrayal of Napoleon. She endorses in him the virility traditionally associated with war, conquest, and the vocation of the soldier (Wollstonecraft's dissent from this link of virility with soldiers is a notable exception).[15]

Ambivalently, Starke presents Napoleon's virility as ruthless and domineering. But despite its regrettable excesses, it is fittingly imposed on a weak, silly, feminized Italy, a common British stereotype Starke exploits. Starke claims that the observant reader can see Napoleon's sinister intentions for Italy, even though most Italians missed them:

> Italy, too, was a mine replete with wealth; and while the major part of her Citizens, dazzled by specious promises, and fascinated by a phantom falsely called Liberty, were blind to the real intentions of their Conqueror, he, though naturally envelloped with reserve, was led by a pretty Woman to betray those intentions very plainly; for as he was dining at Milan with a large company of Italian Ladies, one of them ventured to ask, "What he designed doing with Italy?" He made no reply—again she asked the same question—he was still silent—but, on it's being repeated a third time, called for a lemon, cut it in two, squeezed all the juice out of one-half, threw it away; then squeezed the juice out of the other half, and threw that away likewise. Thus was the Lady answered; but this expressive hint did not open the eyes of the Cisalpini, though Milan had already been compelled to furnish the French Republic with twelve hundred thousand gold sequins, besides immense quantities of military stores. (1: 112–113)

Starke's politics of gender and class, diagrammed above, pervade this incident. Starke portrays Napoleon's masculine ruthlessness in remaining silent, in squeezing the lemon dry, and in exacting money and matériel from the Cisalpine Republic. Yet she obviously admires his virility and power, an admiration revealing itself in her scorn for Napoleon's pretty Italian interlocutor, "dazzled" and "blind" to his real intentions, gullible about "a phantom falsely called Liberty." It is significant that Starke chooses a woman of the aristocracy—"one of a large company of Italian Ladies"—who asserts what power she has indirectly, through manipulation and wheedling. As Landes has observed, the middle-class intellectuals of both France and Britain complained that women exerted too much power in the *ancien régime* and did so in devious ways, thus both feminizing the male monarch, who allows himself to be swayed, and also disenfranchising men of the middle class. Landes writes, "[t]he metaphor of 'the reign of women' signified the corruption of society at its heights. (By implication, only a corrupt and inadequately virile ruler would allow himself and his kingdom to be disarmed by the exercise of female power)" (Landes, 69).

Since Napoleon was First Consul by the time of Starke's publication, her reader is invited to ask: will he fall prey to the same corruptions of the women of the court as did his Bourbon predecessors? His virility differentiates him in an admirable way (to Starke's mind) from his effeminate Bourbon predecessors, while at the same time it is reprehensible that he deceives and robs the Italians. Starke implies that a properly virile British nation would not be so easily fooled as this silly Italian lady, in part because middle-class women would be subordinated in marriage and removed from such society, and in part because candid British men would have gotten the answer they desired. Moreover, as Gerald Newman has observed, the trope of effeminacy functioned as a class marker within British class dynamics; as middle-class writers forged a new sense of British national identity in the years preceding the French Revolution, the British aristocracy was tarred with the same brush as the French (as morally frivolous, dishonest, deceptive, and, the master trope of all, effeminate) while the middle classes, as John Andrews wrote in 1785, exhibited "the native manliness of the [British] disposition."[16]

Starke praises Napoleon's exhibition of such manly, soldierly virtues as courage, stoicism, and chivalric protection of women.[17] Starke mentions his grief at the death of two of his aides-de-camp at the Battle of Arcola, quoting his letter of condolence to the uncle of one of them: "where is the thinking man who, (vexed by the vicissitudes of human life,) would not gladly escape, by such a death, from a world frequently despicable?" (1: 126n). This letter demonstrates Napoleon's own personal courage, his generosity in praising the courage of others, and the stoicism in the face of death appropriate to a "thinking man." And Starke recounts his offer of "every consolation which his purse and interest could procure" to the pregnant widow of the other (1: 126n). Here we have Napoleon exhibiting those "chivalric," manly virtues, the loss of which Edmund Burke mourned in *Reflections on the Revolution in France* (1790) with the fall of the *ancien régime*. Starke embraces those Burkean values and, paradoxically, finds them reincarnated in the man some found the "child and champion" of the Revolution.

The conflicts concerning religion, outlined above, also crystallize in Starke's conclusion about the meaning of Napoleon's first Italian campaign:

> Thus was the ecclesiastical power completely annihilated, after continuing above twelve hundred years, and during great part [sic] of that period awing, if not governing, every monarchy in

Europe; while a poor epitome, a deceitful shadow of ancient Roman freedom rose upon it's ruins! To the short-sighted eye of Human Reason it appeared, that the Pope and the Cardinals, from the moment when BUONAPARTE first entered Italy, contributed to produce this change. . . . Such conduct was equally inexplicable to the Roman-Catholic and the Deist, but Protestants, enlightened by a firm confidence in Holy Writ, and not blinded by the veil of Monkish Superstition, saw, or at least thought they saw, throughout the whole of this extra-ordinary business, the immediate hand of Heaven, rendering the Pope himself the instrument of his own destruction, and thus wonderfully bringing on the accomplishment of the Prophecies. (1: 176–178)

Starke here stops short of declaring Napoleon the instrument of divine Providence in "bringing on the accomplishment of the Prophecies," by which she means the prophecies of the downfall of the Pope, loosely based on Scripture, that filled popular British almanacs during the eighteenth century (Colley, 20), and were thus widely available to British "Protestants [who are] enlightened by Holy Writ." Nonetheless, her account does attribute "the whole of this extraordinary business" to "the immediate hand of Heaven." And since the bulk of the travel book has been devoted to illustrating the extraordinariness of Napoleon's success in Italy, which she had called earlier "the most rapid and brilliant conquests ever gained in so short a period, either by ancient or modern Warriors" (1: 153), the reader may conclude that Starke finds Napoleon a place in this providential web. Thus while Napoleon is not given full credit, it is clear that "this extraordinary business" provided the occasion for divine intervention in history by giving Pope Pius VI the chance to make his self-destructive mistakes, for "the Pope and Cardinals . . . contributed to produce this change" "from the moment when BUONAPARTE first entered Italy."

Thus Starke's celebration of Napoleon's triumph grows from the nationalist roots of anti-Catholicism and its corollary, the conviction of the superiority of Britain and Protestantism. By calling the Roman Republic "a poor epitome, a deceitful shadow of ancient Roman freedom," she repudiates the spread of Jacobin ideals. And in writing that the Papacy spent over twelve hundred years "awing, if not governing, every monarchy in Europe," Starke implies that the English monarchy alone escaped such intimidation, beginning with the Reformation, confirmed by the Glorious Revolution of 1688 and the Hanoverian succession, which guaranteed that no Roman Catholic could ever rule

England. Starke exemplifies Colley's observation that Protestantism was deeply aligned with the British sense of their peculiar freedom (Colley, 48–49).

Supplying the Loss of Antiquarians:
Starke and the Disruption of the Grand Tour

In the title and the preface to *Letters from Italy,* Starke presents the vocation of antiquarian and art critic as central to her project, and, at each mention of this vocation, Napoleon's avocation as art collector (or plunderer) casts its long shadow. Her title, long in the style of eighteenth-century travel narrative, promises, in part, that the work will *"Likewise [point] out the matchless Works of Art which still embellish Pisa, Florence, Siena, Rome, Naples, Bologna, Venice, &c."*; the force of the word "still" registers Starke's mission to preserve what she can of the British Grand Tour after Napoleon's expropriations. In the preface, Starke elaborates:

> I shall likewise point out the Architecture, Paintings, and Sculpture, which still embellish Italy; lest Persons disposed to visit that Country should be led, by common report, to conclude that all her choicest works of genius are destroyed, or removed to Paris. . . . In my account of the Cities of Italy I have mentioned, in notes, those Statues, Paintings, &c., which I believe to have been either seized by the French, or sold by their lawful Possessors; and at the same time have given in the body of my Work, such a description of every remaining Object worthy of notice, as will, I hope, in some measure supply to Travellers the loss of those Antiquarians, whom war may have constrained to abandon their profession. (1: iii–iv, vii)

Starke, then, sets herself up as "supply[ing] to travellers the loss of . . . Antiquarians" who have been "constrained to abandon their profession" because of Napoleon's war. This statement foreshadows the travel book's pattern: Napoleon the art collector provides an ambivalent mirror to Starke the art critic and antiquarian. Both of them represent middle-class usurpers of the aristocratic privilege of possessing art works and of "appreciating" them in the context of the Grand Tour. This mirroring creates an ideological contradiction: on the one hand, Starke admires Napoleon for his *chutzpah* and actually depends on his military effort to create the vacuum of aristocrats and their assistants, a vacuum that she can then fill. On the other hand, she condemns him (the French *parvenu*) in order to construct herself as the British (*parvenue*) patriot she must be in order to negotiate the role of woman writer.

The Grand Tour was traditionally a two- to three-year journey made by a young British gentleman and his tutor, or "bearleader," to Paris and the four cities of Italy (Milan, Florence, Venice, and Rome). Rome, with its antiquities, functioned as the culmination of the Grand Tourist's journey and education, and the journeys were often timed so that the Holy Week ceremonies intensified the experience of arrival in Rome.[18] The explicit justification for such a massive expense was to give a man experience of the world, to improve his languages, and to seal his aesthetic and classical education in visiting works of art. However, the travel served the implicit function of providing leisure and sexual adventure to the student, and of allowing an able-bodied aristocratic father to continue his work unimpeded by a restless young son (Black, 122). The British Grand Tour had its counterpart in the *voyage de gentilhomme* which was practiced by young men of France, Germany, Russia, and other nations, and whose name reveals the gender and class prerogatives underlying the practice (Newman, 12). In its heyday in the eighteenth century, the Grand Tour functioned "to give a man 'parts'; to polish his conversation and manners, deepen his experience of the world, sharpen his judgment of art, habits and character, and, not least, provide him with an easy fluency in foreign languages, especially French . . . , which was in addition an essential prerequisite for careers in diplomacy" (Newman, 13). As Newman points out, it was only with the middle-class nationalist reaction late in the century that a contradiction at the heart of the Grand Tour was revealed, that the aristocrats who sought to become citizens of the world by their travel were, ironically, perceived by their fellow Britons not as cosmopolitan, but as "Frenchified." Starke registers this ambivalent moment in the history of the Grand Tour, in which the attitude towards the French serves as an index for class politics.

In terms of gender rather than class, the Grand Tour helped to construct British aristocratic masculinity by the presumed prerogative of men to travel and to have the sexual adventures associated with travel. Moreover, since it functioned as the capstone of a classical education, the Grand Tour was part of an educational structure routinely available to aristocratic and even middle-class men, while denied to almost all women. By the 1790s, the *role* of Grand Tourist remained deeply male-identified despite the actual demographics of

travel; British women began to take the Grand Tour, accompanied by
their families, in about 1750 (Black, 244). Ironically, Starke's posing
as the preserver of Grand Tourism disguises the fact that, as a woman
and a member of the mercantile class, she is one of its destroyers.

In general, Starke's ambivalence in her relation to the institution
of the Grand Tour is scored along nationalist lines. Like the traditional
aristocratic Grand Tourist, Starke presents a disdain for Italy, implicitly assuming British superiority. Traditionally, Grand Tourism's idea
of Italy pervasively bifurcates Italy's Roman past from its unworthy
Italian present, idealizing classical culture while ignoring contemporary Italians, or dismissing them as unscrupulous, stupid heirs.
The split may have been due, in part, to a worried identification with
the *Decline and Fall of the Roman Empire* (publication completed in
1788), chronicled by Edward Gibbon for a British public stunned by
the loss of its American colonies. Indeed, this Grand Touristic split of
classical Rome from contemporary Italy continues to inform the travel
books by Joseph Forsyth and John Chetwode Eustace, two of the most
widely read travel books on Italy of the first half of the nineteenth
century.[19] In order to participate in this powerful Grand Touristic
discourse, Starke replicates its rhetoric of splitting. In one example,
she writes from Lucca of a visit to the Armory. "Our Courier," Starke
writes, "who has great bodily strength, attempted to put one of the
smallest ancient helmets on his head, but found himself scarcely able
to lift it—so much are men degenerated!" (1: 243–244). It suits the
trope of splitting that this incident occurs at an armory and that the
artifact in question is an "ancient helmet." Thus Starke marks the
"degenera[tion]" of contemporary Italians, particularly in military
matters, a degeneration that has made them vulnerable to Napoleon's
advances. The device of feminizing contemporary Italians, which we
examined in the story of Napoleon squeezing the lemon dry, reinforces this split. In general, however, Starke's use of this split remains
tacit, residing most powerfully in the silent assumption that Britain
and France are vying for ownership of the cultural capital of the
Grand Tour, the French by taking art to Paris, the British by keeping
it in Italy, which serves as a kind of British national repository or
archive. The possibility that the Italians themselves might rightfully
possess this capital seldom occurs to her.

Starke also presents a break with the traditional Grand Tourist
in demonstrating a *parvenue*'s sense of resentment against the French,
who are clearly Britain's rivals for cultural as well as military hegemony in Europe, as Napoleon's ambitions for the Louvre made clear.
Her attitude towards France and the cultural mecca it represented as

part of the Grand Tour mystique is registered in her visit to Voltaire's villa at Ferney, near Geneva. Starke incidentally reveals her own *parvenu* status, as a woman and as a bourgeoise, to the tradition of the Grand Tour in Letter One. Starke recounts her family's visit to Ferney, ridiculing Voltaire and the house's current owners. She is confident that the Francophobia appropriate to a middle-class British woman will win over her audience. Since Voltaire's death in 1778, his house has had many masters, Starke writes, "but they all have deemed it sacrilege to alter anything, and, consequently, the rooms are furnished just the same as when he died" (1: 21). This spirit of preservation allows Starke to observe

> a large picture, *composed* by Voltaire himself, and executed by a wretched Artist whom he met with at Ferney: that Voltaire was vainest of Men I have always heard, but that any Man could have the overweening vanity to compose such a picture of himself is scarcely credible (Starke's emphasis; 1: 21).

She describes the picture, in which Voltaire presents his *Henriade* to Apollo, while all "the Authors and Authoresses who wrote against him are falling into the infernal regions" (1: 22). Moreover, Starke exploits the irony that the home's proprietors deem it "sacrilege" to make any changes unauthorized by the enemy of religion and the irony that Voltaire creates a pictorial and literary hell, in lieu of a religious hell, into which he can cast his personal enemies. The irony Starke does not perceive, of course, is that Voltaire's *Henriade* extols the virtues of Henry IV, author of the Edict of Nantes, which granted toleration to his Protestant subjects, the Huguenots (Newman, 9). She is thus unwittingly ridiculing the early advocates for Protestant religious freedom in France.

Starke's visit to Ferney situates her within aristocratic travel discourse, but her ridicule of Voltaire aligns her with the new British middle-class Protestant response to free-thinking France. As Newman argues, Voltaire was the lightning rod for Enlightenment, cosmopolitan values in Europe, and Ferney had been one of the required stops on the Grand Tour, where Voltaire had generously entertained about 150 British travelers, including Edward Gibbon and Adam Smith.[20] In fact, even when England and France were at war, Voltaire, who styled himself "the innkeeper of Europe," kept his salon open to young milords. Thus, for the generation of Britons who preceded Starke, Voltaire personified the Enlightenment, particularly its mistrust of national sentiments in favor of a cosmopolitan, European culture and its mistrust of Christianity in favor of reason and deism (Newman, 7). Though John Gay meant it as a compliment by writing of Voltaire, "where he was, there was Paris," by the time Starke visited Ferney, Voltaire's indissoluble connection with culture was seen as not cosmopolitan but partisan to the French, and the tide had turned. But unlike her aristocratic predecessors, Starke depicts Voltaire as personally vain and petty, condemning his literary rivals to hell, an accusation that exemplifies Newman's argument that "French vanity" was a staple in this cultural war, to set off claims of British frankness and sincerity (Newman,145–148). And, as Newman argues, middle-class Britons accused the British aristocracy of cultural treason in adopting "free-thinking" French manners and morals. While Starke does not explicitly say so, her discounting of the pretended cosmopolitanism of the travelers who preceded her suggests that the day of the middle-class British traveler has arrived.

Into this general set of new and inherited nationalist responses to the Grand Tour (old disdain for Italy, new disdain for France), Starke actively enlists Napoleon as the villainous art plunderer whose depredations create the loss she claims to supply. Napoleon's function in propping up Starke's discussions of classical antiquities is dramatically illustrated when she recounts Napoleon's victory at Lodi in 1795: "A victory so brilliant was naturally followed by the most important consequences; Pizzighitone, Cozmona, Pavia, and Milan, submitting to the Conqueror, who was hereby furnished with immense resources, vast magazines, and many valuable works of art" (1: 72–73). Starke's admiration for Napoleon's manliness (his "brilliant" victory at Lodi, famous because he himself led the Army of Italy across the bridge) is tempered by sarcasm in writing that such a victory was "naturally followed" by confiscation and plunder. Her outrage, in turn, is tempered by the scholarly tone of the appended note: "Among these were above thirty pictures; an Etruscan vase; a manuscript written on the papyrus, and above eleven hundred years old; a Virgil which belonged to Petrarch, containing notes in his own hand, and another curious manuscript relative to the history of the Popes" (1: 73n). Here the typographical dependence of the footnote on the main text suggests that Starke's ability to exhibit mastery of the classical material ("an Etruscan vase," an ancient papyrus, and a copy of Virgil) has a similar material dependence on the occasion of Napoleon's invasion, both in his stealing the art itself and also in frightening away the antiquarians who are its usual custodians.

In fact, Starke's admiration for Napoleon's skill as a collector (though she would never have used so benign a term) enables her to re-think the Grand Touristic disdain for the contemporary Italians, precisely because Napoleon has respect for them:

> Fifty pictures, among which was the celebrated St. Cecilia of Rafaelle, were now sent from Bologna to Paris, whither those taken from Parma, Milan, and Modena, had gone before. But, while, the republican General was thus robbing Italy of her most exquisite works of art, he took infinite pains to impress Artists and literary Characters in his favour, treating them with the utmost deference, respecting and even augmenting their property, declaring he considered Men of Science, whatsoever their Country, as Citizens of France, inviting those who were dissatisfied with their present situation to retire to Paris, promising them all possible encouragement in that City, and assuring them, that the French Nation would derive more pleasure from receiving and cherishing a distinguished Painter, a profound Mathematician, or any other Man eminent in arts and sciences, than from the most splendid territorial acquisitions; nay, he actually wrote a long letter, expressive of these sentiments, to Oriani, the great Astronomer at Milan, requesting him to circulate it's contents among the Literati; and thus while other Rulers were endeavouring to maintain the empire of force, he fought to establish one by far more powerful, namely, that of opinion. (1: 86–87)

The paragraph at first presents Napoleon's appeal to the Italian professionals and literati as a logical extension of his plunder: first, he sends "[f]ifty pictures, among which was the celebrated St. Cecilia of Rafaelle" down the same pipeline "whither those taken from Parma, Milan, and Modena, had gone before." But while he was (by force) "robbing Italy of her most exquisite works of art," he exerted "an [empire] far more powerful, that of opinion," in persuading the Italian literati, voluntarily, to follow that same pipeline to Paris. The real threat to Grand Tourism emerges in this shift of the center of gravity from Italy to Paris. Moreover, the fact that Napoleon wanted to attract "distinguished Painter[s]" of the present generation to Paris suggests a threat to the future of the Grand Tour, for if painters accept, the best paintings of the present generation will also have to be viewed in Paris: stolen, in a more profound way, before the fact of their composition, rather than, like Raphael's St. Cecilia, after the fact. Although Starke obviously mistrusts the promises Napoleon makes with such "infinite pains," as a middle-class writer and *parvenue* among aristocrats, she is also attracted to the meritocracy Napoleon proclaims, this "more powerful" empire "of opinion," in which they would receive "all possible encouragement," respect, and "augmented property" because "the French Nation would derive more pleasure from receiving and cherishing a distinguished Painter, a Profound Mathematician, or any other Man eminent in arts and sciences, than from the most splendid territorial acquisitions." Far from presenting Napoleon as a hypocrite (stealing art while persuading artists), her final comment that the empire of opinion is "more powerful" registers her own desire for this vision, her admiration for Napoleon, and perhaps unconsciously, her wish that *women* "eminent in arts and sciences" could also be citizens of such a city.

Moreover, along with this class-based chink in the monolith of inherited views of the Grand Tourist, Starke exhibits a softening of the traditional scorn of the contemporary Italians. Breaking ranks with the Grand Touristic convention, Starke reveals the richness of contemporary Italian "Artists and literary characters" and "Men of Science" who attract deference, respect, and subsidies from Napoleon. Starke obliquely hints at the power of Napoleon's "empire of opinion," namely that contemporary Italians might take ownership of their art if this happened: the Italians could join Napoleon's "empire of opinion," denying British Grand Tourists access to their works of art and shattering the illusory idea of Italy as a museum at Britons' disposal.

As a Francophobic reaction-formation against her admiration and envy for Napoleon, Starke stakes her claim, and her nation's, to be the continuing arbiters in the world of art associated with the Grand Tour in the denouement of her narration, Berthier's capture of Rome and his expulsion of the Pope in the winter of 1797–98. Starke portrays an even more serious loss to culture than that of the antiquarians. There is, in her account, a decay at the moral center, which she represents by proving both the Pope and the French unworthy to control the art of the Vatican, while she, the representative Briton, steps in. Starke recounts that her family went to Rome for the winter, and when the French army threatened, they tried to flee Rome. But as at Nice, most means of leaving were blocked: the Pope had decreed that no beasts of burden were allowed to leave Rome, so Starke finds herself trapped but, intrepidly, on the scene to expose the Pope's deceptions:

> Thus compelled to abide the threatening tempest, I directed my steps towards St. Peter's, wishing to see, perhaps for the last time, that beautiful and majestic edifice. On my way I overtook droves of mules and horses proceeding towards the

Castle of St. Angelo, at the gates of which fortress stood carriages guarded by cannon, and laden, as the Soldiers said, with the treasures of Loretto, which his Holiness was going to send to Terracina. (1: 137)

Here Starke the eyewitness exposes the deceptions and selfishness of Pope Pius. At St. Peter's, she witnesses "droves of mules and horses" on their way to the Pope's castle, having just heard from the British minister, Mr. Graves, that no beasts of burden could leave Rome. Evidently, the Pope would rather save his own belongings than save the lives of others—among them, her family's. Moreover, the information that the animals bear "the treasures of Loretto, which his Holiness was going to send to Terracina," directly refutes the Pope's claim to Napoleon that *"we have abstained from removing any thing out of Rome"* (Starke's emphasis; 1: 141). Here Starke implicitly stakes her claim, which to her mind is Britain's claim, to the art treasures in the Pope's possession, rivaling the claims of the Papacy itself and also those of France. She implies that the Pope has forfeited his right to them because of his duplicity with Napoleon and because he cared more about saving art works than about saving human life. The French have forfeited their right because their armies, led by Berthier, are invading Rome solely on an errand of personal vengeance over the accidental death of General Duphot in a scuffle.

Into this vacuum of rightful ownership steps Starke, the representative British patriot and devotee of art. Despite "the threatening tempest" of imminent battle, she braves the danger because of her love and appreciation for art and architecture, to view "perhaps for the last time," "the beautiful and majestic edifice" of St. Peter's. Her vocabulary stresses its status as an architectural masterpiece, an "edifice" not a "church" or "basilica," which is "beautiful and majestic" but not "awesome" or inspiring of any specifically religious sentiment. The Pope's imminent desertion of Rome accentuates the sense of a vacuum of rightful ownership—the reader is invited to think that the Pope should defend the architecture of Rome rather than just taking out the treasures that are portable—and makes it even more proper that Starke should "supply" such a "loss."

How Typical was Starke's Response to Napoleon?

The evidence suggests that Britons of both Tory and Whig persuasions were happy to give Napoleon the credit for defeating the

Papacy, this event occurring, of course, before the split in their opinion at the Peace of Amiens. Conservative spokesman Edmund Burke wrote in a vein similar to Starke's of the historical events in Italy in 1796–97: "It appears to me that the Protestant Directory of Paris as statesmen and the Protestant hero Bonaparte as a general have done more to destroy the said Pope and all his adherents in all their capacities than the Junta in Ireland has ever been able to affect."[21] Burke conflates two things that Starke holds distinct. By naming Napoleon "the Protestant hero," Burke could mean either that Napoleon himself was Protestant or that he was the hero of the Protestants and their cause. Yet Burke's parallel formulation about "the Protestant Directory of Paris," suggests that what Burke cares about is their complicity in the Protestant *desideratum* of collapsing the Papacy, not about the ostensible religious affiliation of the agents concerned, who were, by and large, either Roman Catholics of a modified, "civic" or constitutional sort, or else adherents of the "free-thinking" or "atheist" Cult of Reason instituted by Robespierre.

The archive also shows that Whig Dissenter Samuel Kenrick, like Starke, wrote about Napoleon in this millenarian way in 1799:

> What could possibly be more unexpectedly astonishing than the rapid downfall of civil and religious tyranny, wch [sic] we have been witness to? . . . The contest is between light & darkness—knowledge and ignorance—rational religion & superstition or if you will—virtue and vice. . . . light, knowledge & (I hope) religion & virtue have been gradually gaining ground for 3 centuries, in active exertions—while despotism & superstition are proportionally giving way—& as if by a sudden explosion have almost instantaneously vanished together at their two foundation heads in Europe—France & Rome. . . . What strikes me is, the visible hand of an over ruling Providence. . . .[22]

As Kelly writes about this passage, "Many in Britain saw Bonaparte as an instrument of this process and followed his rise with fearful fascination. The liberal-minded Kenrick saw him as the embodiment of the Revolution and the instrument of Providence in overthrowing 'Feudal tyranny & popish bigotry'" (166).

Against the backdrop of Burke and Kenrick, what does seem unusual, in my view, about Starke, is her granting primacy to religious affiliation. Starke would not endorse Burke in calling Napoleon "the Protestant hero." In fact, Napoleon's "free-thinking" comes in for ridicule despite his enormous service to the political goals of Protestantism:

> I cannot finish this sketch of the most rapid and brilliant conquests ever gained in so short a period, either by ancient or modern Warriors, without lamenting, that a Man whose great and amiable qualities at once excite our wonder and praise . . . should have been betrayed, by the false principles of a French education, to establish the dominion of Blasphemers, Regicides, and Robbers, dimming the lustre of his courage, by deriving it from ideas of predestination [Starke here refers to Napoleon's belief that no brave man would fall before his hour had come], and eclipsing the splendour of his victories by the wickedness of the cause they were gained to support. To that branch of French philosophy, however, termed FREE-THINKING, may we attribute the errors of Buonaparte, and the growth of those licentious maxims and manners, which have brought an unoffending Monarch to the guillotine, destroyed the peace of society, and deluged Europe with blood. (1: 153–154)

The religious cast of Starke's rhetoric is clear. Napoleon's valor was betrayed by the "False principles of a French education" and the errors of "French philosophy," "termed FREE–THINKING," to produce "the dominion of Blasphemers," thus "eclipsing the splendour of his victories by the wickedness of the cause they were gained to support." By religious language—falsity, error, blasphemy, wickedness—Starke resolves her ambivalence toward Napoleon as an admirable man serving a wicked cause. Religious language also underwrites her propriety despite her appearance in print. Explicitly, in denouncing the "licentious maxims and manners" of the French, she decries their immoral politics; implicitly perhaps, she distances herself, as a woman writer, from Wollstonecraft and the other "unsex'd females."[23]

Though neither MacCunn nor Bainbridge analyzes British *women's* responses to Napoleon, a few examples of the most politically forthright of them may serve to place Starke in the context of her sex. These examples suggest a peak of enthusiasm similar to the one Bainbridge describes with male writers at about 1798–1802. In 1801, Helen Maria Williams published *Sketches of the State of Manners and Opinions in the French Republic, Towards the Close of the Eighteenth Century,* which presents the *coup* of Brumaire 1799 as the action enabling Napoleon to carry out the remaining work of the Revolution.

She affirms that "the Revolution, that stupendous event which has awakened all the energies of the human mind," will defeat "the cheerless darkness of superstition, the iron-reign of despotism, and the debasing influence of error." She concludes, as Kelly writes, that "[t]he achievements of the feminized Revolution [are] now guaranteed by the manly hero Bonaparte,"[24] thus responding, as Starke does, in conventionally womanly ways to the cultural codes of virility associated with Napoleon. Later that year, Williams's loss of faith in Napoleon begins to show when she omits his name from her "Ode to Peace," celebrating the negotiation of the Peace of Amiens in October 1801, a loss that soured into active opposition as Williams's salon harbored Carnot, formerly of the Directory's Committee of Public Safety and an opposition leader during the Consulate and Empire, and as Napoleon suppressed Williams's translation of *Political and Confidential Correspondence of Lewis the Sixteenth* (1803). Like the Whig trajectory described by MacCunn, Williams sees Napoleon, in the long run, as the destroyer of the Revolution, despite the interval of hope she felt in 1801.

No such souring of enthusiasm plagued travel writer Anne Plumptre, author of *A Narrative of a Three Years' Residence in France.* Though it was based on her travels during 1802 to 1805—already quite late in the game for a Briton to write in support of Napoleon— Plumptre maintained her position unmodified when she published the work in 1810, closing it with several chapters defending Napoleon's character. Plumptre's final section on Napoleon makes her Radical alliances clear: to evaluate Napoleon properly "we must divest ourselves of prejudices which degrade us alike as a nation and as individuals, and be prevailed upon to contemplate things as they are, not as our deluders wish them to be."[25] Plumptre here counters the conservatism of Edmund Burke, which holds that "prejudices" are a valuable national inheritance, by characterizing them as "degrad[ing] to us alike as a nation and as individuals." Moreover, she explicitly aligns herself with the radical theories of Godwin and his project to see "things as they are," the title (later, the subtitle) of the 1794 novel better known as *Caleb Williams.* The substance of Plumptre's defense of Napoleon is that he restored the French nation's confidence in their government and provided civic order and stability. In addition, "among the crimes with which he is charged, there are scarcely any that do not strictly come within the inevitable consequences of war" (Plumptre, 3: 357). She defends even his murder of the Duc d'Enghien, regarded as inexcusable by most Napoleon watchers,[26] and calls the British hypocrites for criticizing Napoleon's expropriation of Italian art.

Plumptre, like Hobhouse and Hazlitt, shares the stubborn Radical position traced by MacCunn. Writing at that late date in the war, it is certainly likely that Plumptre's unpatriotic opinions were greeted with the same kind of scathing reviews that met Anna Barbauld's criticism of Britain in *Eighteen Hundred and Eleven* (1812) and forced her to retire from public view. The demand that women be patriotic thus had a steady grip on literary opinion from 1794 until 1815.

Starke, then, when placed within the context of Williams and Plumptre, ostensibly articulates the Tory party line, with its Francophobia and "Church and King" loyalties. The three writers, taken together, suggest a rough confirmation among women writers too of the pattern described in 1914 by MacCunn among men. The fact that women do not break ranks with their political affiliation and class should serve as a cautionary tale for those feminist scholars searching for a view of Napoleon among women writers that is shaped primarily by gender concerns. The example of Starke, in particular, suggests that gender concerns, particularly in conservative women writers, more often emerge in a quiet kind of guerrilla warfare, occasionally rearing quirky local contradictions in a general picture of conformity and alliances with other concerns than their sex. Her creativity in improvising ways for a woman writer to engage in this formation of public political discourse deserves our respect, if not our agreement. Starke and other writers like her challenge present-day literary scholars to confront the political conservatism of women writers of past eras, particularly their embrace of religious doctrine and metaphor, and to examine the extent of their apparent complicity in patriarchal systems.[27][28]

Notes

1. F. J. MacCunn, *The Contemporary View of Napoleon* (London: G. Bell and Sons, Ltd., 1914), 32.

2. Simon Bainbridge, *Napoleon and English Romanticism* (Cambridge: Cambridge University Press, 1995); the quotation below is from page 33.

3. Mariana Starke, *Letters from Italy between the years 1792 and 1798; containing a view of the revolutions in that country, from the capture of Nice by the French Republic to the expulsion of Pius VI from the ecclesiastical state* . . . , 2 vols. (London: R. Phillips, 1800); the second edition (1802) emends the title to *Travels in Italy* . . . but has no other verbal changes that I have discovered. I have cited the first edition here. For biographical information about Starke, see *DNB* s.v. "Starke," and Syvanus Urban, *The*

Gentleman's Magazine [London] (New Series) July to Dec. 1838, 10: 111. *Letters from Italy* was translated into German in 1802, according to J. D. Reuss, *Alphabetical Register of all the Authors actually living in Great Britain* . . . (Berlin: Frederic Nicolai, 1804), part 2, 350. For Starke's publication history in French, see J. M. Querard, *La France Littéraire,* 12 vols. (Paris: Maisonneuve and Larose, 1838), 9: 257. There are a few brief present-day discussions of Starke: Shirley Foster, *Across New Worlds: Nineteenth-Century Women Travellers and their Writings* (New York and London: Harvester/Wheatsheaf, 1990), chapter 2 *passim*; Francis Haskell, *Rediscoveries in Art* (Ithaca, N.Y.: Cornell University Press, 1976), 107–108; Jane Robinson, *Wayward Women: A guide to women travellers* (London: Oxford University Press, 1990), 194–195; and Claire Richter Sherman and Adele M. Holcomb, introduction to *Women as Interpreters of the Visual Arts, 1820–1979,* Contributions in Women's Studies, no. 18, eds. Sherman and Holcomb (Westport, CT: Greenwood Press, 1981), 10–17. For fuller discussion of Starke, see Jeanne Moskal, "Politics and the Occupation of a Nurse in Mariana Starke's *Letters from Italy,*" in *Romantic Geographies: Discourses of Travel 1775–1844.* ed. Amanda Gilroy (Manchester, England: Manchester University Press, 2000), 150–164; and Jeanne Moskal, "English National Identity in Mariana Starke's *The Sword of Peace*: India, Abolition, and the Rights of Women," in *Women in British Romantic Theatre: Drama, Performance, and Society 1790–1840,* ed. Catherine B. Burroughs (Cambridge, England: Cambridge University Press, 2000), 102–131.

4. Gary Kelly, *Women, Writing, and Revolution* (Oxford: Clarendon Press, 1993), 21.

5. Linda Colley, *Britons: Forging the Nation 1740–1830* (New Haven: Yale University Press, 1992).

6. The Rev'd Richard Polwhele, *The Unsex'd Females: A Poem* (London, 1798), 19n.

7. Hannah More, *Strictures on the Modern System of Female Education,* 2 vols. (London, 1799), 1: 6.

8. Marlon B. Ross, "Configurations of Feminine Reform: The Woman Writer and the Tradition of Dissent," in *Re-Visioning Romanticism: British Women Writers, 1776–1837,* eds. Carol Shiner Wilson and Joel Haefner (Philadelphia: University of Pennsylvania Press, 1994), 92.

9. Quoted in Harry Hearder, *Italy: A Short History* (Cambridge: Cambridge University Press, 1990), 164–165.

10. My account of Napoleon's first Italian campaign depends on: Elijah J. Adlow, *Napoleon in Italy* (Boston: William J. Rochfort, 1948); David G. Chandler, *The Campaigns of Napoleon* (New York: Macmillan, 1966); Georges Lefebvre, *The French Revolution, from 1793 to 1799,* trans. John Hall Stewart and James Friguglietti, from *The French Revolution,* vol. 2 (New

York: Columbia University Press, 1964), chapter 6; Giuliano Procacci, *History of the Italian People,* trans. Anthony Paul (New York: Harper and Row, 1971), chapter 9. For reservations about Napoleon's statistics, see Adlow, 50.

11. Chandler, 130. MacCunn locates the rise of Napoleon's notoriety somewhat later, with the Egyptian campaign (9).

12. Georges Lefebvre, *The French Revolution from its origins to 1793* from *The French Revolution,* vol. 1, trans. Elizabeth Moss Evanson (New York: Columbia University Press, 1962), 170.

13. Jeffrey N. Cox, "Ideology and Genre in the British Antirevolutionary Drama in the 1790's," in *British Romantic Drama: Historical and Critical Essays,* eds. Terence Allan Hoagwood and Daniel P. Watkins (Madison, N.J.: Fairleigh Dickinson University Press, 1998), 88.

14. Ann Ward Radcliffe, *A Sicilian Romance* (1792), ed. Jonathan Wordsworth (New York and Poole, England: Woodstock Books, 1995), 2: 28–29.

15. See *Vindication of the Rights of Woman* (1792), chapter 2, in *Works of Mary Wollstonecraft,* 7 vols., eds. Marilyn Butler and Janet Todd (London: Pickering, 1989), the analogy of soldiers to women occurs at 5: 92.

16. John Andrews, *Comparative View of the French and English Nations* (1785), quoted in Gerald Newman, *The Rise of English Nationalism: A Cultural History, 1740–1830* (New York: St. Martin's Press, 1987), 147. Newman's analysis is found on 145–156.

17. On chivalry in the period, see David Duff, *Romance and Revolution: Shelley and the Politics of a Genre* (Cambridge: Cambridge University Press, 1994); and Jeanne Moskal, "'To speak in Sanchean phrase': Cervantes and the Politics of Mary Shelley's *History of a Six Weeks' Tour,*" in *Mary Shelley in her Times,* eds. Stuart Curran and Betty T. Bennett (Baltimore: Johns Hopkins University Press, 2000), 18–37 and 234–239.

18. Jeremy Black, *The British and the Grand Tour* (Sydney: Croom Helm, 1985), 22.

19. Joseph Forsyth's *Remarks on Antiquities, Arts, and Letters during an Excursion of Italy in the Years 1802 and 1803* (1813) and John Chetwode Eustace's *Classical Tour of Italy,* first published in 1813 and going into numerous editions, were praised by P. B. Shelley as two of the three most useful books on Rome. Shelley writes: "I have said what I feel without entering into any critical discussions of the ruins of Rome, & the mere outside of this inexhaustible mine of thought and feeling.—Hobhouse, Eustace, & Forsyth will tell all the shew-knowledge about it—'the common stuff of the earth'—by the bye Forsyth is worth reading, as I judge from a chapter or two I have seen. I cannot get the book here." (*The Letters of P. B. Shelley,* ed. F. L. Jones, 2 vols. (London: Oxford University Press, 1964), 2: 495.

20. Black, 246; John Lough, *France on the Eve of the Revolution: British Travellers' Observations, 1763–1788* (Sydney: Croom Helm, 1987), 168. I also draw on Newman, 13, in this paragraph.

21. Edmund Burke, *Correspondence* [August 16, 1797]; 3: 271; quoted in MacCunn, 10.

22. Samuel Kenrick to John Woodrow, March 1799; quoted in Kelly, 166.

23. See Amy Rambow, "'Come Kick Me': Godwin's *Memoirs* and the Posthumous Infamy of Mary Wollstonecraft," *Keats-Shelley Review* 13 (1999): 24–57.

24. Kelly, 196–199; quotation from Kelly, 199; quotation from Williams is from *Sketches of the State of Manners and Opinions in the French Republic, Towards the Close of the Eighteenth Century*, 2 vols. (London: G. G. and J. Robinson, 1801), 2: 298–299.

25. Anne Plumptre, *A Narrative of a Three Years' Residence in France, principally in the Southern Departments, from the year 1802 to 1805: including some authentic particulars respecting the early life of the French Emperor, and a general inquiry into his character*, 3 vols. (London: J. Mawman and others, 1810), 3: 315–316.

26. For example, Mary Shelley calls this act one of Napoleon's "three crimes," along with the murders of Andreas Hofer and Toussaint L'Ouverture; Mary Shelley, *Rambles in Germany and Italy* (1844) in *Travel Writing*, ed. Jeanne Moskal, vol. 8 of *The Novels and Selected Works of Mary Shelley*, 8 vols., eds. Nora Crook and Pamela Clemit (London: Pickering, 1996), 8: 98.

27. See Beth Kowaleski-Wallace, *Their Fathers' Daughters: Hannah More, Maria Edgeworth, and Patriarchal Complicity* (London: Oxford University Press, 1991), as well as Ross's essay, cited above, note 8, as examples of scholarship that faces this problem.

28. The author thanks Terry Bowers, Adriana Craciun, Stuart Curran, Paola Frascari, Madelyn Gutwirth, Gary Handwerk, Radhika Jones, William Keach, Gary Kelly, Victoria Kirkham, Kari Lokke, Melissa Moorehead, Marjean Purinton, and Michele Strong-Irwin for their comments on earlier versions of this essay; and Tamara Chadaratana, Tamara Graham-Voelker, and Tim Sadenwasser for their research assistance.

Revolutionary Subjects

The New Cordays: Helen Craik and British Representations of Charlotte Corday, 1793–1800

∽

Adriana Craciun

> The women in the gallery I was in, most of them rising up, cried out: "The intriguer." "Down with the new Corday." "Get out, miserable woman, or we will tear you to pieces. [. . .]"
> Be assured, friends of liberty. I will hold firm in the face of this horde led only by passion.
>
> —Clare Lacombe, *Citoyenne Lacombe's Report to the Society of Revolutionary Republican Women* (1793)

Clare Lacombe, president of the Society of Revolutionary Republican Women, had good reason to fear being labeled "the new Corday" by her fellow Jacobin women, as my epigraph illustrates. Charlotte Corday's assassination of the Jacobin journalist Marat on July 13, 1793 (she had intended it to be on July 14, to commemorate the fall of the Bastille), exacerbated the schism already growing between men and women of the Jacobin party. The militant working-class Society was instrumental in helping the Montagnards oust the moderate Girondins in May 1793, and since Corday had publicly announced her loyalties to the Girondins before her execution, to be denounced a "new Corday" in the Jacobin club was particularly dangerous.[1] Yet militant Jacobin women such as Clare Lacombe and other members of the Society of Revolutionary Republican Women shared a similar fate with Corday: they too became the target of Jacobin misogyny, and were deemed dangerous examples of women's public political militancy. The Society was disbanded, along with all women's political clubs, by the Jacobins on October 30, 1793, and the Terror soon began in earnest. Lacombe and other Jacobin women lost their heads, as did

Marie Antoinette, the monarchist feminist Olympe de Gouges, and the Girondin Madame Roland—women of vast political and class differences, yet all "new Cordays" in the sense that their active and public political presence was no longer tolerated in the republic.

Charlotte Corday became a figure of contradictory political significance, a heroic republican in the eyes of some, a counterrevolutionary virago in the eyes of Jacobins, and an angelic royalist beauty in most British accounts. It is the first characterization—as heroic and republican—that is hard to come by in British accounts, which, as we shall see, tended to depoliticize her assassination and to transform her into an instrument of divine wrath against republicanism and atheism. But heroic and republican Cordays did emerge in British literature in the 1790s, and they are significant because they invite one to imagine a new type of heroine—one whose desire is justice, not love—and a new type of female subject—political, philosophical, and public. Like the 1790s feminism of Wollstonecraft, Robinson, Macaulay, Hays, et al, the promise of these new Cordays was short-lived, in part because Corday remained a dangerous example of women's violent activism.

Helen Maria Williams and Helen Craik, a little-known Scottish writer, both imagined Corday as a new kind of heroine in a distinctly Gothic revolutionary landscape: a beautiful and deadly *femme fatale,* and a new kind of (proto)feminist female subject, one who actively participates in the traditionally male realms of political debates and political assassination. Helen Craik's historical novel about Corday, lost to the world for two hundred years, is probably the sole British fictional account of Corday in the Romantic period, and offers a remarkable glimpse into the complex intersection of politics and gender embodied in the "new Corday."

Helen Craik's Revolution-Era Novels

Helen Craik (1750?–1825) published anonymously three novels that overtly engage with the French Revolution in 1793, all with William Lane's Minerva Press: *Julia de St. Pierre* (1796), *Adelaide de Narbonne, with Memoirs of Charlotte de Cordet* [sic] (1800), and *Stella of the North, or, The Foundling of the Ship* (1802).[2] These works are important contributions to the tradition of women's novels about the French Revolution that "produce the present . . . as history": thus does Margaret Anne Doody describe the important historical work of these women novelists.[3] While British Jacobin novelists such as William

Godwin, Robert Bage and Elizabeth Inchbald set their "revolutionary" novels in modern Britain, Charlotte Smith, Mary Robinson, and Helen Craik were the first in Britain to write novels set in revolutionary France: histories of the present. Only recently have these contributions to the historical novel, and to British responses to the French Revolution of 1789, been taken into critical consideration. Helen Craik's contributions to these traditions, in particular her attempt to forge a truly revolutionary heroine in her portrait of Charlotte Corday, are significant because of the subtlety of her attention to intersections of gender and political interests. Craik's portrait of Corday engages with contemporary debates over the Rights of Woman and the Rights of Man, and in its gendered critique of both revolutionary and counterrevolutionary politics, prefigures the conclusions of many modern feminist historians who have demonstrated how the French Revolution, in both theory and practice, was in many respects inimical to women and their diverse interests.

While the heroine of her first novel set during the French Revolution, *Julia de St. Pierre*,[4] was the quintessential figure of virtue in distress, in *Adelaide de Narbonne with Memoirs of Charlotte de Cordet* Craik creates a unique and truly revolutionary heroine in her Charlotte Corday. Craik's approach to revolutionary politics is overtly (proto)feminist: she insists throughout on the connections between paternal and political tyranny, and offers a compelling model of female action and solidarity that resists such masculine power in both private and public spheres. *Adelaide de Narbonne, with Memoirs of Charlotte de Cordet* is set in the isolated Castle of Narbonne in the Vendée, surrounded by impenetrable forests, sublime cataracts, mysterious towers, beetling cliffs, ruins, convents, republican and royalist banditti—all the requisite Gothic formal elements but in a modern (counter)revolutionary setting, populated with heroines, heroes, and villains of the Revolution. Craik was well-versed in Radcliffe, and transferred the sublime and beautiful Italian landscapes found in Radcliffe's novels to the war-torn Vendeé, and by doing so contributed to the Gothic's ongoing transformation, and its increasing tendency to address the present directly. Craik's novel also revisits Horace Walpole's Gothic ur-novel *The Castle of Otranto* (1764), borrowing the central plot and character names from Jephson's dramatic adaptation of Walpole's novel, *The Count of Narbonne* (first performed in 1781), with significant twists. As we shall see, at the center of her revisions of the Gothic's two most influential authors lies Craik's critique of women's legal and political disenfranchisement in modern Britain and France, a critique also present in Radcliffe's novels, but uniquely resonant in Craik's because of its immediate and overtly revolutionary context. Craik removes Walpole's Gothic plot of usurpation, enforced marriage, and heroines pursued by libertines, to the heart of counterrevolutionary France, and in doing so illustrates what readers then and now already intuited: that, in Sade's words, the Gothic was "the inevitable result of the revolutionary shocks which all of Europe has suffered."[5]

The Vendée was the scene of the bloodiest civil unrest during the Revolution, where counterrevolutionary forces, largely peasants, rose up against and were massacred by the National Army from March 1793 to May 1794. "If the war had been merciless on both sides" after the initial uprisings in March 1793, writes François Furet, "what began afterwards was of a different nature: it was mass repression organized from above, on the orders of the Convention, with intent to destroy not only the rebels but also the population, farms, crops, villages. . . . Starting from January, there came into action a decree . . . ordering the 'destruction of the Vendee'. . . , with the explicit mission of burning every dwelling and exterminating the population, including women and children."[6] Nearly one-quarter of a million, or one third of the total of the inhabitants (not including the republican soldiers) of the Vendée, Loire-Inférieure, and Maine-et-Loire were killed when the region was retaken by republican forces.[7]

The politics of the Vendéen civil war are as divisive and conflicted in Craik's novel as they remain in modern historiography; the complexity of these counterrevolutionary politics led the reactionary *Anti-Jacobin Review* to conclude, erroneously, that the author's politics remain "undiscoverable." The novel's aristocratic heroine, Adelaide de Narbonne, is a royalist, and most of the novel's sympathetic characters, including Corday, an avowed republican in Craik's novel, are opposed to the Convention and the recent execution (January 1793) of the king. The novel's chief villains are Marat and Robespierre, avatars of Walpole's Manfred whose inhuman sexual and political ferocity is directed primarily toward aristocratic women. Yet these royalist and anti-Jacobin politics are thoroughly and constantly in conflict with a simultaneous reliance on a discourse of natural rights and liberties that echoes Rousseau, Wollstonecraft, Godwin, Williams, and Robinson (the latter three whom Craik cites repeatedly throughout her revolution-era novels). Most significantly, Craik shows how both republican and royalist political interests, practices, and ideologies are inimical to women, their interests, and their safety. *Adelaide de Narbonne* enacts a (proto)feminist critique of both sides of the revolutionary debate, one that anticipates modern feminist revisionary accounts (by

Gutwirth, Landes, and Hunt) of the French Revolution's dangers to women.

Beginning with its first sentence and throughout all four volumes, *Adelaide de Narbonne* exacts an unrelenting attack on marriage as a form of political and economic tyranny: "Sacrificed in early youth to the avaricious disposition of a despotic and ambitious father, Adelaide de Narbonne had the supreme felicity of finding herself a widow almost from the hour she became a bride."[8] This critique of marriage echoes republican, anti-Burkean attacks on the "natural" authority of monarchs, husbands, and parents, particularly fathers, and is conducted on several different fronts: most obviously in her heroine Adelaide de Narbonne, whose melancholy existence almost wholly centers on her repeated attempts to avoid marriages forced upon her by powerful men: her father (who succeeds in marrying her to her cousin), and both royalist (unsuccessful) and republican (successful) libertines who attempt to marry her for her inheritance. Adelaide speaks out against marriage in the strongest possible terms: marriage means that she "should be the property" of her husband, that she would "be bartered for wealth," and forced "to prostitute my hand" (3: 118, 112, 123). This critique of marriage, prevalent in women's novels in the 1790s, is linked in Craik's novel, through allusions, rhetoric, and quotations, to French Revolutionary critiques of the *ancien régime*'s injustices. The vehemence of this critique, at times accompanied by highly emotional interjections from the otherwise nonintrusive narrator, seems to grow out of (in part because it refers to) the author's own experience, which I will discuss in the conclusion to this essay. In her dual focus on royalist and republican women, as her title's reference to both Adelaide and Corday suggests, Craik demonstrates what modern feminist historians of the French Revolution have shown: that, as Joan Landes has argued, the republic was constructed not just without women, but against them, and that, as Madelyn Gutwirth has shown, it institutionalized instead of challenged male sex right.

Adelaide de Narbonne is in many respects a traditional embattled heroine found in novels of sensibility and of the Gothic. She is a direct literary descendant of the ill-fated Matilda, Manfred's daughter in *The Castle of Otranto,* who in Jephson's stage adaptation of the novel had been named Adelaide de Narbonne.[9] In Walpole's novel and Jephson's play, Matilda/Adelaide is the sacrificial victim of paternal violence and power, and of maternal submission. Her heart-breaking plea to her mother to help her resist Manfred's decree that she marry the marquis against her will—"Ah! my mother ... stay and save me"—

meets with rejection from her mother, who reminds her that "Thy fate depends on thy father," and retreats to pray for her daughter.[10] The mother's resigned submission to masculine institutions, which leads to Matilda's death at her father's hands, is famously voiced in her disastrous advice to her daughter: "It is not ours to make election for ourselves; heaven, our fathers, and our husbands, must decide for us" (81). Craik revises this foundational Gothic plot by rejecting the mother's advice to her daughter, instead introducing a hero, Corday, who relies not on heaven, fathers, or husbands, but on her own action, and in so doing rescues Adelaide from these paternal institutions. Craik's plot is an elaborate one, and a generically innovative one, because it joins Gothic formal qualities to a contemporary historical setting and a political critique.

Onto Walpole's ur-plot Craik grafts Corday's story in such a way that the friendship between the two women emerges as the emotional center of the novel. Here she is also beholden to Radcliffe, who in *A Sicilian Romance* had made the daughter's search for and liberation of the mother the novel's central heroic quest. As in *A Sicilian Romance,* the Castle of Narbonne, where Adelaide lives in fear of Marat's plans to acquire her land and her body, is haunted by mysterious lights and sounds that are suggestive of the supernatural. Charlotte discovers the secret of these supernatural signs to be a woman, Victorine, the (mythical) heir to the French throne whom Adelaide is protecting from the Jacobins by hiding her in subterranean caverns. The republican Corday aids this would-be Queen of France, and Adelaide, in a chivalrous fashion; in fact, it is because she believes Marat murdered Adelaide that Corday assassinates him, a significant revision of the prevailing tendency at the time to make her actions those of a desperate woman who had lost her male lover. By overlaying the complex sexual politics of the French Revolution onto the sexual politics of Gothic, Craik produces a new kind of Gothic, and at its center, a new kind of heroic woman.

Craik's Adelaide, in contrast to the heroic Corday, remains the figure of virtue in distress and paragon of femininity made popular by Radcliffe. She strenuously upholds the virtues and privileges of aristocracy and is a staunch royalist who risks her life to hide Marie Antoinette's (fictional) niece, the possible heir to the throne, were the Vendéen counterrevolution successful in overthrowing the Convention. Yet Adelaide repeatedly equalizes both royalists and republicans in terms of gender, for both groups (of men) seek to use her economically, politically, and sexually. An aristocrat married (against her will) to a republican, she is "so unfortunately situated with both sides of the question," "reprobated by Royalists and Republicans, and trusted by neither" (2: 94). The bloody civil war in which the novel is set exposes other women who are "so unfortunately situated" between warring groups of men, such as nuns in a neighboring convent, to threats of rape and murder by both sides.

Most dramatically, the conclusion of Volume One rewrites the storming of Versailles, and Burke's famous account of Marie Antoinette's flight from the band of revolutionary brothers who would violate her, by showing the embattled Adelaide attacked by a mob of royalist soldiers.[11] Significantly, these royalist soldiers are often described in the same dehumanized and bestialized terms as their republican counterparts. Like Marie Antoinette, Adelaide narrowly escapes rape and death, guarded inside her room by a heroic Charlotte Corday, and outside by her faithful male protectors, who "by amazing efforts of valour, prevented the assailants from forcing their way to the apartments of Madame de Narbonne, though they had contrived to penetrate as far as the end of the gallery, where the guard was stationed for her protection" (1: 270). Denied the spoils of this attack, these "banditti of the Royal Army" unleash their "natural ferocity" on a nearby village, in one of the novel's most disturbing scenes of mob violence: "pillaging the inhabitants and setting fire to the villages through which they passed committing the most unheard-of barbarities on all who had the misfortune to fall in their way" (1: 283).[12] Thus, dehumanized depictions of republican mob violence, a traditional attribute of counterrevolutionary texts in the 1790s, are accompanied in Craik's novel by similar accounts of royalist violence, the similarity being the gender (and the class) of the "mob."

It was precisely such reports of the Vendéen insurgents as a mob of peasant "banditti" that *The Times* of London repeatedly tried to dispute in order to promote the Vendéens as bourgeois monarchists: "Their troops are not, as their enemies would have us believe, a set of robbers, or a parcel of unarmed, undisciplined peasants. Their victories . . . prove, on the contrary, how much they excel the regicides in valour and discipline."[13] Similarly, Craik's portrait of royalist soldiers as banditti has a class agenda: she attempts to distinguish the leaders of the royalist army, such as the historical Charette and the novel's main romantic hero, the aristocrat St. Julian, from the common soldiers who make up the "mob." Yet beyond her conservative characterization of rank and file soldiers (of both parties) as potentially dangerous banditti, Craik's main focus remains on the danger all classes of men pose to all classes of women, and on women's common efforts to resist these threats.

Craik further complicates her critique of Burkean chivalry and natural authority through a second rewriting of his account of Marie Antoinette; in addition to rewriting the storming of Versailles as a royalist attack on a vulnerable woman, she also introduces a new Marie Antoinette, her (fictional) niece Victorine,[14] the object of intense and secretive political maneuvering designed to place her on "the bloody throne." It is Charlotte Corday, however, who upon first setting eyes on Victorine's uncanny resemblance to the imprisoned Queen, responds chivalrously and heroically toward this would-be queen's "captivating loveliness" (4: 53):

> She [Victorine] then rose from her seat with the dignified air of a superior being, softened by an expression of the most fascinating sweetness; and advancing to meet them, received the offered hand of Charlotte, presented for her acceptance by the Countess [Adelaide], with an address so flattering, and a manner so irresistibly prepossessing, that Mademoiselle de Cordet secretly vowed from that instant to render her every possible service; and even determined to risk her own life in the defence of this amiable girl. (4: 50–51)

This chivalric defence of a would-be Marie Antoinette occurs entirely among women, and reads like a marriage ceremony. There is an echo here of *The Italian,* where Signora Bianchi, Ellena's guardian, placed Ellena's hand in Vivaldi's, and "from this moment he considered himself bound by ties not less sacred than those which the church confers, to defend her as his wife, and would do so to the latest moment of his existence."[15] Like Mary Robinson (in *Monody on the Death of the Late Queen of France*) and Helen Maria Williams (in her praise of French women throughout *Letters from France*), Craik celebrates both women's empire of beauty and sensibility, and simultaneously, women as rational, political, and intellectual agents, in effect insisting on women's access to both masculine and feminine regimes of power. Corday's heroic and romantic response to this excessively feminine figure is repeated throughout the novel, as Craik continually links these two disparate models of womanhood, showing the rational, heroic Corday coming to the rescue of the embattled heroine of sensibility.

Helen Craik's portrait of Corday is remarkable because so rare in British literature, and because Corday remained a dangerous subject on which to write, even in counterrevolutionary hands. Representations of Corday from 1793–1800 fell into two camps: misogynist Jacobin portraits of Corday as a monstrous woman, unsexed by her violent crime and intellect, and sentimental anti-Jacobin portraits of her as a counterrevolutionary angel of the apocalypse, typically thought to have committed the assassination as a crime of passion to avenge her murdered lover, or as a Christian avenger. Craik gives us neither of these traditional uses of Corday, but instead, follows and further develops Helen Maria Williams's characterization of Corday as a new kind of female political subject uniting both masculine and feminine qualities (mental, emotional, and physical). In order to appreciate the revolutionary subject Craik attempted to forge in Corday, we need to examine the politics of the new Cordays, British and French.

Representations of Charlotte Corday, 1793–1800

"Marat's barbarous assassin," wrote Sade in his elegiac tribute to Marat, "like those mixed beings to which one cannot assign a sex, vomited up from Hell to the despair of both sexes, directly belongs to neither."[16] Unsexed by her violent crime, Charlotte Corday epitomizes the anomalous status of violent women during the 1790s when middle-class political aspirations in Britain were firmly embodied in the domestic woman and the truth of her sex, to recall Foucault's helpful formulation.[17] Chantal Thomas summarizes the impossible position in which Corday was placed by writers like Sade, who were engaged in the ideological struggle over the term "woman" central to French revolutionary politics: "[t]he women of 1789 were set before a classic double bind: remain women, but deny themselves all exaltation and all heroic action, or else attain the sublime, but transgress the ideal reserved for their sex."[18] What we need to examine is precisely this "classic double bind," but as it is represented in the works of women. We know that "the militant participation of women provoked a violent and fearful response on the part of most men" (Landes 168), and Sade is but one example of many; but how did women, specifically women in Britain, respond to these images of women's public militancy and violence?

French and British accounts of the assassination alike tried to downplay Corday's individual agency, for different political ends yet with similar implications for women. Jacobin accounts, of which Sade's is representative, painted Corday as a monster unsexed by her violence and devoid of feminine sensibility. The Jacobins also immediately circulated another suspicion, which Corday vigorously denied throughout her trial, that she acted as agent of male Girondin conspirators and thus was not representative of the "general will," an explanation that resembles Wollstonecraft's belief that the working-class women who stormed Versailles were in fact motivated by the Duc d'Orleans. Jacobin attempts to deny Corday rational and political agency focused on uncovering the "truth" of her sexuality (which had to be either excessive or insufficient, given her violent action); the autopsy they performed revealed that she was a virgin at age 25 and therefore clearly lacking in natural feminine sensibility. The Jacobins' oft-quoted description of Corday traced her criminal act to an unnatural female body and sexuality: "This woman being called pretty was not pretty at all; she was a *virago,* chubby rather than fresh, slovenly, as female philosophers and sharp thinkers almost always are . . . Her head was stuffed with all sorts of books. . . . All these things mean that this woman had hurled herself completely outside of her sex."[19] Sade's elegy on Marat similarly insisted that Corday must not be represented as beautiful, and in fact must not be represented at all: "A funeral veil must envelop her memory forever; above all you must cease to present to us, as you dare to do, her effigy as the figure of enchanting beauty. Artists who are too credulous, break, reverse, disfigure the traits of this monster, or do not offer them to our indignant eyes, except in the guise of the Furies of Tartary" (121). Craik's historical novel about Corday did precisely what Sade and the Jacobins feared—it made visible her crime, and it made her beautiful. Corday's crime, because it was reasoned, political, and violent—in other words, "masculine"—threw into question her biological sex and the truth of that sex, and Sade's description of Corday as monstrous is typical, for such a woman exceeds all natural or social orders. The sexualization of Corday's political violence, as of Marie Antoinette's politics, is of course a misogynist response not unique to 1793 France, but it does crystallize the double bind in which women were placed in the emergent bourgeois public sphere, and reveals the violence, both physical and rhetorical, used to expel women from this sphere.

In contrast to these French depictions of Corday as "unsexed," British anti-Jacobin accounts of Corday were quick to characterize Corday as feminine, saintly in her martyrdom, motivated by romantic love for one of Marat's victims, and typically transformed into an "angel of the assassination," to use Lamartine's popular phrase, acting as an instrument of divine wrath against republicanism. *The Times* was quick to point out that "[s]he belonged to a noble family," never mentioning (like the *Anti-Jacobin*'s review of Craik) that she was a republican, and in its account of her trial praised her beauty with the assurance that "the idea of her as an assassin was removed from every mind."[20] *The London Chronicle* downplayed Corday's agency by devoting the majority of its article on Marat's assassination to the supposed (male) conspirators from Caen, quoting at length the official Jacobin theory that "[a] woman has been the first instrument of their crimes."[21] Yet in her famous letter to the Girondin Deputy Charles Barbaroux, published in part in translation in *The Times,* Corday herself had insisted that "I alone conceived the plan and executed it."[22] Corday, who declared at her trial that "I was a republican well before the Revolution,"[23] was in fact inspired by literature such as Rousseau's *Social Contract* and Plutarch's *Parallel Lives,* a text which no self-respecting Romantic hero failed to read (including that other notable female philosopher, Mary Hays's *Emma Courtney,* and that other monster, Frankenstein's creature); she wrote from prison that she hoped she would "enjoy the repose of the Elysian Fields with Brutus and the ancients" and predicted that "my memory will be more honoured in France than that of Judith in Bethulia."[24] James Gillray's print, "The heroic Charlotte la Cordé" (published 29 July 1793) uses this Biblical comparison for counterrevolutionary ends when he shows a rather matronly and aristocratic Corday delivering her speech before her bestialized accusers and Marat's corpse wracked with "Leprosy, with which Heaven had begun the punishment of his Crimes" of regicide and atheism.[25]

Even sympathetic accounts of Corday transformed her assassination into a crime of passion. Louis Du Broca's *Interesting anecdotes of the heroic conduct of women previous to and during the French Revolution*[26] (published in France, London, and in the U.S.) is one such example, which depicts women's political actions as motivated by private passions, in Corday's case, for a (fictional) lover whose death was brought about by Marat. Percy Bysshe Shelley's eroticized "Fragment Supposed to be an Epithalamion of Francis Ravaillac and Charlotte Corday" (1810) would take Corday's crime to a new level of apolitical and erotic explicitness. In contrast, poems such as Southey's "July Thirteenth. Charlotte Cordé Executed for Putting Marat to Death" (published 1798), and Miss Day's "Charlotte Corday" imagined a chaste "martyr'd Maid" (Southey) who "fulfilled/ The work that was decreed" (Day).[27]

Edmund John Eyre's decidedly counterrevolutionary play about Corday, *The Maid of Normandy and Death of the Queen of France,* illuminates the dangers posed by this revolutionary heroine regardless of the author's political intent. Eyre's play was suppressed by the examiner of plays, John Larpent, argues Jeffrey Cox, because the government feared that the play, "while trying to stage a conservative pageant, might ignite radical fireworks."[28] The government feared the recreation of revolutionary events and thus after 1793 "essentially eliminated history from the stage" (ibid, 605). Craik's recreation of revolutionary events in her novel is thus even more remarkable, given that stage representations of Corday were taboo, and even the English "Jacobin novelists" such as Godwin and Bage set their novels in modern Britain, not revolutionary France.

Beyond its general political narrative, Eyre's counterrevolutionary play was particularly dangerous because of its central theme of assassination, and the sex of its assassin. In 1804 Eyre retitled and revised his play as *The Death of the Queen of France,* a title that focuses exclusively on the more acceptable feminine victim of male republican violence, while obscuring the second theme of Corday the assassin; the most significant revisions are cuts of the 1794 play's more sexually explicit and sadistic lines in an apparent attempt to pass the censor's examination. As in other conservative British accounts (and unlike in Craik's and Williams's), in both versions of Eyre's play Corday is a royalist awakened to revenge when she sees "a King insulted & depos'd" ([1804] 1.ii), one who desires to kill Marat in the name of her lover, and actually murders him in self-defence when he tries to rape her. Despite his depoliticization (and repoliticization) of her crime, Eyre's representation of Corday nevertheless remains dangerous in its call to arms, which he added in his 1804 revision:

> Cordé: Oh that, ten thousand Charlottes in
> Our land may rise,
> Stung with resentment of their
> Country's wrongs,
> To stab each traitor.[29]

It is no surprise that this 1804 manuscript copy was rejected by Larpent as well, and doesn't even seem to have made it to print: a call to ten thousand Cordays avenging their country's wrongs with violence would open up dangerous possibilities indeed in Britain.

It is Mary Robinson who rises to the challenge: as "Tabitha Bramble," Robinson fired off an angry letter to the despotic Lord Advocate for Scotland, Robert Dundas, who had prosecuted the Edinburgh radical reformers (founders of the 1793 British Convention) for sedition, and upheld their sentences of transportation to Botany Bay. The Scottish radicals Muir, Skirving and Margarot were "contending for principles, & certain renovations which every body allows to be founded in Justice," insists Robinson. The government's persecution of the reformers, on the other hand, "will be found wanting in the Balance of Posterity." Raising the spectres of the Glorious Revolution and of the French Revolution in her letter, Robinson concludes with a startling warning that Dundas's "sanguinary harsh measures employed against the Reformers" deserves a new Corday: "Some Male, or rather more likely some Female Hand, will direct the Dagger that will do such an important Service and Britain shall not want a Female Patriot emulous of the fame of M. Cordet [sic]."[30] Corday embodied justice in the "Female Hand," and through her Robinson imagined avenging her "Country's wrongs." Such a "Female Patriot" was unthinkable to Jacobin and anti-Jacobin alike, and clearly not containable by royalist British interpretations of Corday. At the very least, this remarkable letter confirms Robinson's radical credentials, and Corday's radical potential.

Thus, while misogynist and sentimental views of Corday such as Sade's and Eyre's similarly rendered her violence apolitical, they also simultaneously made visible her crime, making possible further reinterpretations such as Robinson's. Corday herself knew full well the value of this visibility and of her example, and insisted on having her portrait painted in her cell before her execution to ensure that the funeral pall did not obscure her, as Sade and the Jacobins desired. Despite their intended effects, such portraits of the monstrous and the angelic Corday are important because they responded to (either by exaggerating or overcompensating for) the disturbing possibility that the natural limits of "woman" could be altered through violence. These portraits and their exaggerated treatment of Corday's femininity and masculinity indicate the urgency with which Corday's example had to be addressed.

Charlotte Corday and Helen Maria Williams

In her influential *Letters Containing a Sketch of the Politics of France* (1795), Helen Maria Williams gave an account of Corday's crime and trial that emphasized her sublimity and heroism while maintaining her beauty and sensibility. An important influence on Craik's *Adelaide de Narbonne, with Memoirs of Charlotte Cordet,* Williams's portrait of Corday attests to British women's interest in her as a model for active female subjects implicated in power, violence, and authority.

Williams's support for the Revolution throughout its violent stages shocked the English, and her writing of republican history amounted to "a triple violation—of sexual morality and generic decorum as well as national political loyalty."[31] Listed among Polwhele's "unsex'd females," she was described in one obituary as "preeminent among violent female devotees of the Revolution."[32] The *Gentleman's Magazine,* as Chris Jones has noted, "condemned her principally for not displaying the correct emotional responses of feminine sensibility" in "her famous expedition after the storming of the Tuileries," where, according to the *Gentleman's Magazine,* she had "walked, without horror, over the ground at the Thuilleries [sic], when it was strewn with the naked bodies of the faithful Swiss guards," and had shown no sympathy for the "ill-fated Queen."[33] Williams's radical politics were, like Wollstonecraft's and Corday's, publicly assailed on the grounds of their author's unnatural sensibility (either insufficient or excessive, often both) and their sexual impropriety (in Williams's case, her long-term relationship with the married dissenter and outspoken republican John Hurford Stone).

Charlotte Corday is one of Williams's most heroic figures in *Letters . . . of the Politics of France,* rivaled only by Madame Roland. Williams may have had a closer connection to Corday than has hitherto been recognized, and therefore her account of Corday takes on personal significance. *The Times'* (consistently counterrevolutionary) account of the trial reported that:

> This unhappy Lady [Corday] had two Counsellors, one of whom was MR. STONE, an Englishman, who during the last two hours of her trial incessantly felt her pulse, to distinguish if there was [sic] any symptoms of burning fever or timidity. . . . She did not manifest the least irresolution but in one interval, when Mr. Stone was so struck with her firmness and answers, that he was quite dismayed, and at that instant her undaunted courage fell, and tears of sweet sensibility declared her gratitude for his pleading for her. . . . She requested this Gentleman, as a last favour, which, said she, will make me die contented, to defray all the little debts she had contracted in the prison of the *Concergerie.* . . . Mr. Stone promised and executed her request.[34]

Mr. Stone must be none other than John Hurford Stone, Williams's lover, and a well-known figure among the Girondins. Williams's *Letters . . . of the Politics of France* confirm that "after conversing for a few minutes with her counsel and a friend of mine who had sat near her during the trial," Corday asked this friend "to discharge some trifling debts she had incurred in the prison" (1. 1: 133).[35] Corday's chosen counsel was Gustave Doulcet, but he refused to speak on her behalf and she was instead defended by Chauveau Lagarde. It seems *The Times* promoted Stone to Corday's counsellor in order to show an Englishman (a republican one at that, soon to be involved in a treason trial) inspiring "tears of sweet sensibility" in a woman whom the Jacobins described as possessing an unnatural *sang-froid*. It seems very likely that John Hurford Stone was present at the trial, and thus Williams's portrayal of Corday as both a heroic republican and a figure of sensibility gains even more significance, mediated as it would have been through her staunch republican witness Stone, the president of the remarkable "Friends of the Rights of Man associated at Paris," known as the "British Club."

The British Club had publicly called for France's invasion of England after France became a republic in 1792. In November 1792, after the September Massacres had alienated the vast majority of British from France's cause, the British Club, with Williams present, met to celebrate France's recent victory over the Austrians with a public address to the Convention, and thirteen toasts: one which toasted by name Helen Maria Williams and Charlotte Smith for writing in favor of the Revolution, and another which hailed "the Women of France, especially those who have had the courage to take up arms to defend the cause of liberty."[36] *The Times,* like most British accounts, had elided Corday's republicanism, and had ironically used the republican Stone to conveniently stand in for a chivalric England, a defender of sexual and political order which the English would have understood as true liberty—English bourgeois liberty. Yet Williams (and Stone) understood and represented liberty, and Corday's armed defence of it, in a different way than did the British press, despite their similar emphasis on sensibility—as Girondin republicans and English Dissenters they understood liberty as "the destruction of tyrants and tyranny" (as Corday herself did) and "the coming Convention of England and Ireland," a radical claim.[37]

Written in strong support of the recently ousted Girondins, Williams's account of Corday's trial consciously works against Jacobin accounts that portrayed her as a monstrous virago, describing "this extraordinary woman" in the words of one of Corday's greatest admirers, the journalist/novelist Jean-Baptiste Louvet de Couvray:

> She was tall and well-shaped, of the most graceful manners and modest demeanour: there was in her countenance, which was beautiful and engaging, and in all her movements, a

mixture of softness and dignity, which were evident indica-
tions of a heavenly mind. (2. 1: 129–30)[38]

Corday's trial and execution on 17 July 1793 illustrated Williams's
point that "the women have been peculiarly distinguished for their
admirable firmness in death" (2. 1: 213):

> She acknowledged the deed, and justified it by asserting that
> it was a duty she owed her country and mankind to rid the
> world of a monster . . . , and asserted her right to put Marat to
> death. . . . She trusted that her example would inspire the
> people with that energy which had been at all times the
> distinguished characteristic of republicans.[. . .] Her deport-
> ment during the trial was modest and dignified. There was so
> engaging a softness in her countenance, that it was difficult
> to conceive how she could have armed herself with sufficient
> intrepidy to execute the deed. Her answers to the interrogato-
> ries of the court were full of point and energy. She sometimes
> surprised the audience by her wit, and excited their admira-
> tion by her eloquence. Her face sometimes beamed with sub-
> limity, and was sometimes covered with smiles. (2. 1:131–2)

Significant in Williams's description is the repeated emphasis on
Corday's "energy," that most masculine of republican qualities which
Corday had proudly claimed during her trial: "I was a republican well
before the Revolution and I have never lacked energy" (*The Times*
did not include this or other republican statements by Corday). For
Williams, Corday's sublimity is always connected to her beauty, so
that her face is shown to shift from beaming to smiling, and Williams's
meditation on her "softness" follows the matter-of-fact description of
her stabbing of Marat ("she drew out a knife . . . and plunged it into
his breast").[39]

Corday embodies both sublimity and beauty, softness and firmness, much as the revolution itself did in Williams's eyes:

> The French revolution is not only sublime in a general view,
> but is often beautiful when considered in detail. . . . Posterity
> . . . will contemplate the revolution in the same manner as we
> gaze at a sublime landscape, of which the general effect is
> great and noble, and where some little points of asperity, some
> minute deformities, are lost in the overwhelming majesty of
> the whole. (1. 2: 22–23)

Whereas for Burke the "softer virtues" inspire love, for Williams these softer virtues are inextricably bound to the sublime qualities that inspire terror, and both are embodied in one political landscape, and in one woman. By embodying sublime and beautiful in one female subject, Williams redraws contemporary definitions of female subjectivity, and confronts the double bind which revolutionary era women faced by creating a heroine who possessed supposedly irreconcilable qualities.

Williams's vision of the Revolution, like Craik's, is decidedly Gothic:

> An historical sketch of this period is no common picture of human nature. . . . it is like the savage scenery of Salvator, where all is wildly horrible, and every figure on the canvas is a murderer. We are forced to wander through successive evils. (2. 3: 112)

The Gothic was, as Sade well knew, "the inevitable result of the revolutionary shocks which all of Europe has suffered," calling "upon the aid of hell itself"[40] to evoke the terror and uncertainty which the novel of sensibility could not. Williams's Gothic revolutionary history, like Wollstonecraft's *Maria, or the Wrongs of Woman,* grounds Gothic conventions in historical specificity, and endows this uncommon period and its agents with sublimity. This new, "wildly horrible" political landscape, where every figure is a murderer, women included, resembles the Gothic "perverse framework" of Shelley's *The Cenci,* in which, as Stuart Curran has argued, "to act is to commit evil," and even Shelley's innocent heroine Beatrice, like Corday, is implicated in violence.[41]

Charlotte Corday, *Femme Fatale*

The villains in Williams's Gothic revolutionary landscape are Marat and Robespierre, and the heroine is Liberty, "transformed into a Fury" by the Jacobins.[42] And it was Corday specifically who was transformed into a fury by the Jacobins, as Sade had insisted (i.e., "disfigure the traits of this monster, or do not offer them to our indignant eyes, except in the guise of the Furies"). Corday embodied both the beautiful and the terrible aspects of allegorical Liberty in Williams's account of the Revolution, and she thus emerges as a new type of Gothic heroine, and as an early version of the *femme fatale.*

Robespierre and Marat featured prominently as Gothic villains in novels and plays set during the French Revolution, such as Mary Robinson's *The Natural Daughter,* Eyre's *The Maid of Normandy,* and Sarah Pogson's play about Corday, *The Female Enthusiast;* yet Corday, rather than providing an occasion to use an already established type (i.e., the Gothic libertine villain, Manfred), provided writers with an occasion to imagine a new Romantic heroine, both feminine and fatal.

Robert Southey's poem on Corday, published in *The Morning Post* on 14 July 1798, bears witness to the influence of Williams's account, and serves as an important example of Corday's transformation into a new, and decidedly fatal, heroine. In his poem, Southey took on the role of Adam Lux, the young German deputy who, Williams says, fell in love with Corday and elevated her to a goddess of death:

> he talked of nothing . . . but Charlotte Corday and the guillotine; which, since she had perished, appeared to him transformed into an altar, on which he would consider it as a privilege to be sacrificed, and was only solicitous to receive the stroke of death from the identical instrument by which she had suffered. A few weeks after his imprisonment, he was executed as a counter-revolutionist. (*Letters from France* 2. 1: 135)

Southey's poem makes the same gesture of supplication to Corday on the altar:

> had I liv'd
> In these old days, methinks I could have knelt
> Before her altar, ev'n till I had known
> Imagination's realizing pow'r,
> And seen her present Deity. (74)

Southey is not saying he would sacrifice himself on her altar as Adam Lux had in Williams's account; rather, he longs for the "old days" when the "voluntary victim" (the self-sacrificing assassin) would be worshipped in a temple, like a goddess.[43] There, devotees such as Southey and Lux would receive divine inspiration, an "inebriate glow, the throb of that strange fear," which would lead them on to "per'lous deeds" of their own (Southey, 74).

The legend of Adam Lux persists in many modern accounts of Corday; Lux, a deputy from Mainz, was indeed executed because of his public celebration of Corday. He published a pamphlet, *Charlotte*

Corday (1793), in which he elevated "sublime Charlotte" to more than mortal status: "Charlotte, celestial soul! were you but a mere mortal? has history seen your likeness? France triumphs, Caen triumphs! for you have produced a heroine for the likes of which one must search Rome or Sparta in vain."[44] Lux's elevation of Corday to a goddess is complete: "I rejoice in your superiority; for is it not just that the adored object remain always elevated, and always above the adorer?" (6–7). Lux and Southey both pay homage to a sublime Corday in a gesture of masochistic self-sacrifice: their idealization of the sublime Corday and their desire to be similarly sacrificed enact a familiar Romantic fantasy of a beautiful and deadly woman, a *femme fatale*.

Helen Craik's Charlotte Corday longed to be both heroic and to inspire heroism in others, and as such shares an affinity with the Cordays imagined by Southey and Lux. For example, as she listened to an account of one woman's literal self-sacrifice in order to save the Princess Elisabeth, Corday dreamed of being deified on an altar:

> "This woman, when ancient Rome was at its highest summit of grandeur, would probably have been considered as a fit subject for deification after death, and been honoured with altars erected to her memory, while her worshippers represented her as an example worthy of imitation to the most distant ages."
>
> "And she well merited such a distinction," cried Charlotte, her fine eyes sparkling with the enthusiasm of animated emulation. (3: 223)

Like Southey and Lux, Craik, too, elevated Corday to a divine avenger, as in this scene where Corday believes that Marat has murdered her dearest friends:

> her eyes . . . struck fire, and a settled expression of some feeling, too big for utterance, which evidently nerved every fibre with additional energy, was strongly portrayed on her animated countenance, and gave a sublimity to her whole appearance that conveyed the idea of a being more than mortal. . . . (4: 276)

Corday's sublimity, strength, and energy are inextricable from her political violence, and in such portraits as Southey's and Craik's transform her into a new type of heroine, neither feminine nor masculine, but "more than mortal."

Charlotte Corday was an inspiration for the Romantic period *femme fatale,* especially in portraits such as Williams's which emphasized her beauty while maintaining her destructiveness, and in the eroticized republican portraits by Southey and Lux. Williams's portrait of Corday as a Gothic heroine indicates that, alongside men's fears, the *femme fatale* also embodied women's desires for alternative models of female subjectivity and physical agency. And Williams was not alone in her attempt to forge a new model of agency for women through the Gothic heroine.

Adelaide de Narbonne, with Memoirs of Charlotte de Cordet

Rather than merely using the Gothic as a metaphor for the revolution, as so many of her contemporaries did, Helen Craik sets her Gothic romance during the actual Terror, and casts Corday as an unique Gothic heroine. Craik's novel begins at the early stage of the Vendée uprising of 1793, and has Corday living in the region (the historical Corday lived in Normandy). Corday's status as a truly revolutionary Gothic heroine, implicit in Williams, is here explicit, and Craik acknowledges Williams's work as an inspiration. Craik borrows several long passages describing Corday's trial from Williams, and thus likewise succeeds in showing how Corday's heroic, firm, and sublime qualities converge with her feminine sympathy, beauty, and sensibility. Craik distinguishes this new fatal heroine from her predecessors by having her aid the Radcliffean sentimental and reclusive Gothic heroine Adelaide de Narbonne, much as a traditional male hero would.

Corday is introduced with a description lifted from Williams's account quoted earlier: "She was tall and well-shaped . . . there was in her countenance, and in all her movements, a mixture of softness and fortitude inexpressibly attractive" (1: 28–29). Whereas Sade had vilified Corday as a hermaphroditic "mixed being," Craik, like Williams, repeatedly points to Corday's "mixture" of masculine and feminine qualities, physical and mental, as positive, and rather than throwing her outside her sex, these mixed qualities are said to lift her above its limits:

> Alive to all the milder virtues of her sex, yet endowed with a degree of mental strength that raised her infinitely above the general character of those females who compose two-thirds of the universe, her black sparkling eyes turned their penetrating beams with contempt and indignation on the worthless individual who injured the cause of morality or justice. . . . (1: 29)

Corday befriends the melancholy Countess Adelaide de Narbonne who is haunted by the death of a beloved secret husband, and was forced into two marriages by patriarchal interests (once by her father, then by the Convention). Craik's consistent objects of attack in the novel are marriage and women's lack of property rights, injustices she correctly identifies as a central continuity between the *ancien régime* and the republic, much to women's great loss.

Craik's political critique goes beyond a critique of marriage, however, for she shows Corday engaged in public political discussions in which she ardently defends the republican cause. Moreover, in times of danger Corday remains unflinching and self-collected, since "to that miserable affectation of what is falsely called sensibility, and so conveniently displayed by the common run of those watery-eyed beings who are constantly weeping and sighing over every trifling occurrence, Charlotte was entirely a stranger" (1: 263). Corday's sympathy with women who choose domestic seclusion and self-effacement is repeatedly demonstrated, as she protests against injustices done to them. Yet her response to such women is never mere pity or sympathy, for she feels compelled to resist their oppression; responding to a nun whose thinks the safest place for women during the Revolution is a convent (an ill-fated choice, given the closing of the convents),[45] Corday argues against this gendering of public/private spheres: "In times of public danger she thought the moral duties of active life of much greater importance to her fellow-creatures, than dozing through existence within the gloomy walls of a convent" (1: 96). Rather than showing the disastrous effects of excluding women from the public sphere, as did, for example, Mary Shelley in *Frankenstein* and Mary Wollstonecraft in *Maria, or the Wrongs of Woman,* Craik offers a model for a public, political female subject, one who commits that most masculine of political actions, a rational, political assassination, and declares that her heart "feel[s] at times as if raised to the level of actions above the common reach of my sex" (1: 70).

In the only known review of the novel, the *Anti-Jacobin Review* commended the author on her ability to blend historical events within her fictional narrative, and on her denouncement of Marat and the Jacobins, but twice declared that "her sentiments on the form of government are undiscoverable" because "while she execrates the sanguinary horrors of a Revolution and all the miseries of a republican France . . . she describes [Charlotte Corday] as 'a republican but a *rational* one.'"[46] There is no implied contradiction between republicanism and reason in the novel, however, although irrational positions on all sides are offered in contrast to Corday's reasoned politics. The *Anti-Jacobin Review*'s recuperation of the republican Corday demonstrates how such a "paradox of gender," to use Landes's term, as a female assassin, or a female political subject, must be depoliticized in order to fit the increasingly masculinized political sphere. "By the way," added the reviewer, "those who seem to have known that heroine well, do not consider her to have been a republican." Craik, like Corday herself, repeatedly insisted that Corday was decidedly republican, and used the same feminist arguments for women's political activism and self-assertion, as had Williams and Robinson, both of whom she repeatedly quotes and cites.

Robinson's controversial novel *Walsingham* seems to have been one of Craik's favorites: to quote openly and approvingly from this novel (and three times, no less) in a work as deeply involved in French Revolutionary politics as is *Adelaide de Narbonne* took real courage on Craik's part. In combination with her ample quotes from Williams, and some from Hume and Voltaire, her admiration for Robinson removes much of the supposed "mystery" surrounding Craik's politics, and forestalls any reductive readings such as the *Anti-Jacobin's,* which collapse revolutionary politics into a simple Jacobin or anti-Jacobin equation. The passage from *Walsingham* quoted twice in *Adelaide de Narbonne* reads: "Nature will revolt, when persecution wrings the heart; and even a parent's rights lose their instinctive powers, when tyranny takes place of reason and affection."[47] In one of several enigmatic authorial interjections, Craik acknowledged that she too "is fatally authorised to say, that the ties of consanguinity and natural affection are inadequate to contend with determined prejudice, or the feelings of a selfish disposition!" (1: 216). The connection between parental and political tyranny[48] was a recurring theme in Craik's novels, and in Craik's life, as I shall show in the conclusion. *Walsingham* featured prominently in the famous cartoon "The New Morality" (published in the same issue of the *Anti-Jacobin Review* as the negative review of *Walsingham*)—beside Smith's *The Young Philosopher* and Wollstonecraft's *Wrongs of Woman*—as a product of an unnatural French republican cornucopia. That the *Anti-Jacobin* found Craik's feminist politics "undiscoverable" is evidence of the same dyssymmetry in British political and gender interests as in the French, for the sole political argument the *Anti-Jacobin* could discern was Craik's anti-Jacobin position. The historical Corday had faced this same problem when she was compared (by Sade, for example) to the royalist assassin of LePelletier, a comparison that as a republican she vehemently resisted.

Women writers such as Craik, Robinson, and Williams saw in Corday a rare opportunity to insist on the significance of women's participation in public politics, as well as in the politics of the domestic sphere. They understood the importance of Corday's partisan politics, given that British women, like their French counterparts, faced tremendous pressure to refrain from participating in the public political sphere in most respects. Yet Corday's politics, given the charges that they had unsexed her, also had to be balanced with appropriate, equal amounts of feminine sensibility: "the masculine fortitude of mind she possessed . . . [is] tempered by the softer characteristic virtues of her sex" (*Adelaide* 1: 76), most notably a sensitivity to Romantic poetry and sublime landscapes.[49]

The literary origins of Corday's republicanism, as well as her "fortitude of mind," are recurring themes in Craik's novel, and through them the author makes a case for the impact of women's reading not only on their private domestic characters but on their public actions. Although Craik was writing a novel published by the press largely responsible for the rise and success of the circulating library, the Minerva Press, the author repeatedly interrupts her narrative in order to disarm readers' romantic expectations for the heroine, Corday:

> "But is it possible that two characters . . . could spend so many hours together, in a cottage too, without falling desperately in love with each other?—What an unlikely story!" Exclaims a whole coterie of modern Novel readers.
>
> Yes, my good ladies!—yes, it is possible; . . . neither Charlotte nor her companions were learned in the rules of a circulating library! (1:129)

Craik is well-aware of her audience and their expectations of a heroine, and systematically undermines these by forging a new model for a Gothic heroine, based on a model of the hero whose central desire in life is justice, not love. Craik thus stands in significant contrast to other women writers of the Romantic period whose politics, as Anne Mellor has argued (drawing on Carol Gilligan), were grounded in an ethic of care, rather than an ethic of justice.[50]

"The Practical Part of Immutable Justice"

Craik's celebration of "the high-souled, lovely Charlotte de Cordet" (4: 282) includes a disclaimer inserted among the salutary passages borrowed from Williams's *Letters from France*:

> Charlotte remembered not that the executive part of justice is
> not permitted to the injured individual, whose fiat, in that case,
> would sometimes be apt to overlap the magnitude of the offence,
> and in the wild ebullition of passion, confound all sense of
> strict rectitude and impartial judgment in one self-impelled
> decision; while the consequences resulting from the sentence
> of such a tribunal would naturally prove destructive of personal
> safety, moral order, and all the forms necessary for the preser-
> vation of civil society throughout the universe. (4: 279)

According to Craik, nothing less than the stability of the world as we
know it is threatened when a woman actively takes up violence
rather than remaining passively good. Though Craik does not gender
the "individual" whose act would destroy all moral and civil order,
only a woman's act can be, as she later repeats, "subversive of all
order whatever in civilized society," because only a woman's violence
can violate the sexual order as well as the civil. Mary Robinson, whose
controversial novel *Walsingham* Craik quotes, and to whom Craik
may be alluding here, had similarly argued in her bold *Letter to the
Women of England, on the Injustice of Mental Subordination* (1799)
that if women, such as the admirable but "rash enthusiast, CORDAY,"
acted according to their own interests it would lead to "[t]he annihilation of all moral and religious order."[51] Craik and Robinson locate in
women's violent agency a dangerous potential that is neither inherently subversive nor normalizing. Such visions of women's violence
unleashed serve misogynistic ends in the work of contemporary male
writers such as Sade and the Jacobins, yet are also valuable because
they simultaneously question the accepted limits on women's political
and physical agency, and therefore exceed any misogynistic intentions.

Helen Craik's punning allegory of Corday as "executive" Justice
embodies the paradox that feminist historians of the Revolution have
discussed at length: the symbolic influence afforded women in such
allegorical representations (i.e., as Justice) in the public sphere was
disproportionate to their actual political power. For, while women's
images may represent abstract Justice, women acting as individual
dispensers of practical justice, even in Craik's sympathetic account,
are indeed subversive of all order. Craik warns that "the practical
part of immutable justice is not allowed to the arm of a single individual" (4: 303), because women are incompatible with the "practical
part" of political power, and women's bodies, though they may represent abstract Justice with sword in hand, are incompatible with the
"practical part" of violence.

Thus virtually all literary accounts of Corday sever her deadly arm or hand, and speak of her "arm of Death," as if the arm and the woman operate separately. Southey, for example, in his poem "July Thirteenth [sic]. Charlotte Cordé Executed for Putting Marat to Death," wrote that "She rais'd th' avenging arm, the arm of Death," and Miss Day likewise noted, "What though the fair smooth hand were slight!—/ It grasped the sharpened steel."[52] The weak body of woman and the virility supposed necessary for political assassination or violence are at odds in Corday, and the resulting contradiction distorts her proper female body by degenerating its feminine beauty and endowing her arm with a masculinized power of death. Corday herself, in her letter to Charles Barbaroux, wrote that her example would affirm that "[t]he valor of the inhabitants of Calvados cannot now be doubted, since even the women of that department possess firmness and fortitude."[53] Allegories of woman as Justice are thus double-edged, and cannot be dismissed only as a sign of women's exclusion from the "practical part" of justice, since Corday desired visibility so that she would serve as an allegory of Justice, and inspire others with her example.

Like her historical counterpart, Craik's Corday is a revolutionary heroine because her primary desire is justice, not love. Indeed, the author herself intervenes in her narrative at the close of Volume One, after her revisionary account of the storming of Versailles as a royalist attack on the Castle of Narbonne, with a passionate call for justice: "Immutable Justice! pure and unadulterated Spirit! may thy retributive hand lightly press the trembling heart of my relentless enemies, and illume the actions of my friends with thy brightest lustre!" (1: 286). The first-person slip to "my relentless enemies," which the author never explains further, suggests that Corday's dangerous role as agent of Immutable Justice, dutifully muted in the novel's closing pages, nevertheless acts on the behalf of more than the historical Corday's interests. Craik herself lived in exile in England from 1792 until her death in 1825, having fled Scotland probably because her lover had been murdered, and thus, as we shall see shortly, her concern with justice throughout her works grows in part from her own experiences. In Craik's dedication to her first novel, *Julia de St. Pierre*, about a French emigrée in 1792–3, she alludes to "peculiarly painful circumstances" in the life of the "once persecuted Author," and dedicates the novel to an unnamed female friend: "My principal view was rather an act of necessary justice, than the gratification of any other passion. Through the medium of Julia de St. Pierre . . . it has often shortened the solitary lapse of slow, receding time, or beguiled reflection of it's [sic] melancholy office."[54] Craik's consistent concern with "immutable justice" emerges in her novels in such authorial interventions, and in female heroines such as Corday in *Adelaide de Narbonne,* and Stella in *Stella of the North* (set near Dumfries, where Craik lived before her exile). Thus, despite her admonition against women taking up the practical part of immutable justice, Craik was interested in precisely this forbidden possibility, and in fact put it into practice with her writing.

Similarly, French women's putting into practice the female allegories of Liberty or Justice was precisely what the Jacobins feared. One month after executing Corday for her dangerous example, the Jacobins replaced Marianne as the symbol of the republic with the figure of Hercules, a symbolic shift which Lynn Hunt has shown indicated that "[i]n the eyes of the Jacobin leadership, women were threatening to take Marianne as a metaphor for their own active participation" (*Politics, Culture, and Class,* 104). Corday's assassination of Marat in July of 1793 was precisely the kind of identification with Marianne that male republicans began to repress in public women through executions and the outlawing of women's clubs. Madelyn Gutwirth, Lynn Hunt, and other feminist scholars have documented the profoundly destructive effects for women of such revolutionary allegories of woman as Liberty, Maenad, Republican Mother, or Medusa. Lynn Hunt has described the inverse relationship between women's symbolic importance and their actual political power, yet she also affirms that the use of female allegory created a dangerous potential: "Women were shown as actors, and even if these women in plaster and metal were not imagined as particular women, they were still women and hence potentially threatening" (*Family Romance,* 84). The practical part of justice embodied in a real woman, a "free agent," is precisely what Craik imagined through Corday, what the Jacobins feared, and what Robinson threatened to enact.

"The Romance of Helen Craik"

As the author of this remarkable heroine Corday, Helen Craik herself naturally invites interest. The details of Helen Craik's life have survived in the form of nothing less than a Gothic romance, complete with forbidden love, murder, exile, and, of course, ghosts. We know that she grew up on a large and prosperous estate, Arbigland,[55] near Dumfries, Scotland, and that she was friends with Robert Burns (who died in Dumfries in 1796), and Maria and Robert Riddell.[56] In an obscure essay titled "The Romance of Helen Craik of Arbigland,"[57] local historian Samuel Arnott elaborated on the dramatic details of Craik's mysterious departure from Arbigland in 1792. According to Arnott, Helen Craik had a relationship with a man employed by her father as a groom or horse-breaker, possibly named Dunn. One night in 1792 Dunn was found dead near the Arbigland estate with a bullet in his head. Shortly thereafter, Helen Craik left Scotland never to return, moving across the Solway Firth to a small town in Cumberland, England, where she lived with female relatives of her father's brother, and then independently and unmarried, until her death at age 74 in 1825. Dunn's death was officially considered a suicide, writes Arnott, but locals believed that he had been murdered by one of Craik's brothers, with her father's knowledge, because her father disapproved of the class disparity between the two lovers. Her father's position as Justice of the Peace and his considerable influence in the area are thought to have quashed any official investigation of foul play.

Arnott's account cites as evidence "local tradition" and oral history, to which we have no access today. He also cites Craik's poetry[58] (largely lost) as evidence, noting the "striking change in the tone of the poetry written by Miss Craik in later years as compared with her earlier verses. The latter were, as a rule, cheerful, almost sprightly, indeed, while those of her later years were of a melancholy kind, dealing largely with such subjects as murder and suicides" (77). "The Romance of Helen Craik" takes an even more Gothic turn after the mysterious death of Dunn, for according to "local tradition," his skeleton was disinterred and sent to Helen Craik in England. Predictably, the two lovers are thought to haunt Arbigland—either Dunn's ghost, or that of Craik herself as a "White Lady" (a ubiquitous type of Scottish phantom), is said to haunt the spot where he was murdered. This Gothic version is virtually all that has survived her death in obscurity, and can still be found in modern books of folklore and ghost stories from Dumfriesshire and Galloway.[59] "The Romance of Helen Craik" reads like a Minerva Press novel, and is currently impossible to prove or disprove, since her papers have disappeared, and I have not been able to find local sources to confirm the story.

But Craik's *Adelaide de Narbonne* does offer some intriguing parallels with Craik's own published account of her father, and with the biographical "Romance of Helen Craik," parallels which lend some veracity to the latter. Adelaide's lover (to whom she is already secretly married) is an unacceptable choice to her father because he is thought to be a commoner, and he is murdered. Her father then forces Adelaide to marry her cousin (whose name is not Narbonne, and who serves in the military—this is significant), so that the father can consolidate his property and power through a male heir, who, according to Adelaide, "since the period of my brother's death, was considered as the future male representative of the House of Narbonne; and on whom, at my father's decease, a . . . considerable portion of his wealth must necessarily devolve" (3:111).

We know from Helen Craik's own published account of her father in *The Farmer's Magazine* (1811) and from other sources that in 1792, the year she left for England, her father had "resigned all his property"[60] to her cousin Douglas Hamilton, then serving in the American army, since all of William Craik's legitimate sons were dead. Like her heroine Adelaide, Helen Craik lamented the death of her older brother, Adam Craik, and spoke bitterly of her cousin who inherited her ancestral home in her stead. Craik's pointed remarks about her father's insistence on a male heir, his authoritarian temperament, tendency toward drunken revelry, and unfavorable attitude toward women in general,[61] are consistent with the details of Adelaide de Narbonne's life. Adelaide's illicit relationship with an unacceptable suitor, her lover's subsequent murder, and her inconsolable depression are consistent with the "Romance of Helen Craik" (as well as with the plot of *Julia de St. Pierre*[62]). Adelaide's eventual retreat to "the peaceful and romantic county of Cumberland" (4: 153), where Craik herself retreated, concludes the novel and locates author and heroine in the same place of refuge, just as her disinherited heroine in *Stella of the North* had shared the author's unhappy origins in Dumfries.

Perhaps the otherwise unverifiable "Romance of Helen Craik" did emerge after all in these Minerva Press romances, in particular *Adelaide de Narbonne*'s more sensational Gothic elements (illicit love and murder). Regardless of the existence of a murdered lover, we know from her own account that Helen Craik left Arbigland for Cumberland in 1792, and that she remained unhappy about her exile, and bitter that she, as a woman, did not inherit Arbigland. She is "fatally authorised," she tells us in *Adelaide of Narbonne* (1: 216), to speak to the effects of paternal tyranny, and indeed her career as publishing author began after her exile, and seems to have been motivated by a related sense of justice. Women's lack of property rights, in the *ancien régime* and in the republic, emerged as her novel's central theme, as it was a central concern in the author's own life.

From Helen Craik's own published account of her father, as well as other accounts of William Craik, he appears to have been the model for Adelaide's "despotic and ambitious father" (1:1). William Craik was a well-connected gentleman farmer and agricultural innovator, possibly a smuggler, and a force to be reckoned with in Dumfriesshire. An 1811 "Account of William Craik" in *The Farmer's Magazine* reveals much about the man: "His character was firm and determined; his industry steady and persevering. In short, whatever he undertook, *that* he carried through, no matter who were his opponents" (150). One example cited as proof of Craik's industry was his idea that, instead of indulging in "idleness" during the evenings by talking round the fireside, his farm servants should clean grain at night; when his servants refused, Craik threatened them with jail, and "submission immediately ensued."[63] Craik was able to enforce submission because he was the Justice of the Peace, as well as the Inspector General of the Customs of Scotland (and simultaneously may have been a smuggler).

Helen Craik's central concern with justice in *Adelaide de Narbonne*, in particular the abuse of justice by those in power and acting in its name, again finds a parallel in her father's role as Justice and his authoritarianism and possible criminal activities. Thus Craik's warnings about the "practical part of immutable justice" (and Adelaide's warning to Corday that "the practical part of philosophy is not quite so easily accomplished as the theoretical" [3: 27]) are not simply examples of that British hostility to abstract theory and philosophy that David Simpson has persuasively described in *Romanticism, Nationalism, and the Revolt Against Theory*.[64] These warnings are, more accurately, the products of the author's experience (like Corday's experience) that justice and philosophy, in France as in England and Scotland, for all practical purposes, exclude women.

Craik was a woman of privilege who had the means to escape her father's injustices, whatever they were, and live the rest of her life as that most enviable of figures, the "old maid" of independent means and head of an all female household.[65] Adelaide de Narbonne's brief stint as a widow, after her father died and before her forced second marriage, is also an example of this precarious and privileged independence as a "free agent":

> that situation in which I now found myself placed—a single individual, indeed, in the scale of human beings, but at length a free agent also, uncontrouled by the hand of despotism or caprice, sole mistress of my own actions, and largely gifted with the means of rendering the wretched and needy essential service. (3: 124)

This model of charitable nobility is one that Craik seems to have embraced, in life and in her novels, and it is a position made possible by her class, and in spite of her sex. Throughout her novels similar old maid characters are held up as alternatives to the romantic heroines they often assist (as Corday assisted Adelaide) because these women "preserve [their] liberty, nor ever would be prevailed upon to renounce the reprobated title of *old maid*" (*Julia de St. Pierre,* 3: 398).[66]

Helen Craik's revolutionary heroine Corday remains a rare and unrepresentative possibility in women's Romantic fiction, as unrepresentative and remarkable as Craik's own life seems to have been. Yet her two other novels set during the Revolution bear some uncanny resemblances to Fanny Burney's *The Wanderer,* and I believe they probably influenced Burney's own remarkable novel, which looks in retrospect at the Revolution while focusing on the insurmountable and international difficulties all women face. Burney worked on the novel (also set in 1793) from the late 1790s until she published it much later and under safer circumstances in 1814; and as Burney's own exile (in France) did not begin until 1802, she could have read all three Craik novels in question. At the very least, and irrespective of any direct influence through comparison with *Adelaide de Narbonne, The Wanderer* can be restored to a larger field of women's writing on the subject.

Craik's first novel, *Julia de St. Pierre,* opens with "the ill-fated wanderer" (3: 79), Julia, abducted from France and brought to England under cover of darkness; mistrusted and slandered as an unchaste "adventurer" by secret letters, like Burney's Wanderer (also named Juliet), Julia is cast out of the home in which she had taken refuge; for the rest of the novel she tries to discover her true identity (she often laments, "I am not what I seem, I know; but who I am, I know not" [2: 316]), which of course is aristocratic. The heroine of *Stella of the North,* "our fair incognita" (1: 129), is similarly an orphan who struggles throughout her life to avoid rape and destitution, and to establish an identity and name. "I have been from my birth an outcast from society!" laments "the unacknowledged and finally forgotten Stella" (4: 107, 108). As in *Adelaide* and *Julia, Stella* ends with the beleaguered French women emigrating to Britain, where they establish an idyllic genteel community of women who engage in charity, as Craik herself did.[67]

Like Burney's *Wanderer,* Craik's revolutionary novels illustrate women's political and economic vulnerability, as "fair incognitas" and "wanderers" (Burney's terms as well) so "unfortunately situated," as Adelaide de Narbonne had described herself, according to both French and British laws. Also like Burney, Craik does not ultimately support the French Revolution (though she does create some sympathetic republicans, like Corday), but rather removes her characters from "the increasing anarchy prevalent in France" to "the more peaceful island of Great Britain" (*Julia* 3: 368), and within Britain, to utopian emigrant communities of independent genteel women, rather like postrevolutionary Millennium Halls. As in *The Wanderer,* however, nothing in these French women's experience as unnamed wanderers in Britain suggests that their safety and peace are any more secure under British laws; rather, these gestures of escape at each novel's close, like the conventional marriage plots which also conclude as expected, are signs of the author's inability (perhaps unwillingness also, but I do not think so) to imagine a new narrative for women in Revolution-era Britain. Burney's struggle in *The Wanderer* is a similar one, on a larger scale, leading Claudia Johnson to describe it as a novel of "gigantic ambition and bewildering failure."[68] A new Corday, had she survived, would have demanded such a revolutionary narrative of gigantic ambition, and indeed in Craik's novel, Adelaide intended for Corday to escape with her to Britain, but instead she was caught and executed. That story of the new Corday remains unwritten.[69]

Notes

1. *Citoyenne Lacombe's Report to the Society of Revolutionary Republican Women,* in *Women in Revolutionary Paris 1789–1795: Selected Documents Translated with Notes,* ed. Darline Gay Levy et al (Urbana & Chicago: University of Illinois Press, 1980) 186–96; 193,192.

2. Dorothy Blakey's *The Minerva Press 1790–1820* (London: Bibliographic Society at the University Press, Oxford, 1939) is the original bibliographic source for attributing these novels (and two more, *Henry of Northumberland* [1800] and *The Nun and Her Daughter* [1805]) to Helen Craik (Blakey bases her attribution on a Minerva Press catalogue of 1814). Based on my readings of these three Revolution-era novels, I can independently confirm that they are Craik's. *Julia de St. Pierre* includes a long poem titled "The Maid of Enterkin"; a manuscript book containing this poem (now lost) was referred to at length in an essay published in 1919 by Helen Craik's descendant, George Neilson, in the *Glasgow Herald,* where he included facsimiles of other poems by Helen Craik in his possession, and thus her authorship of *Julia de St. Pierre* is confirmed. *Adelaide* and *Stella* are clearly the work of the same author, in style and content; they quote the same passages from recurring sources, use recurring plot lines and character types (especially her independent "old maid" characters), and are similarly concerned with women's economic and political injustices. Craik's obituary in *The Dumfries Weekly Journal* stated that Craik published anonymously

in English and French, but I have been unable to locate any French publications, although it is clear she knew French, since all her novels quote in French.

3. Margaret Anne Doody, "English Women Novelists and the French Revolution," (*La Femme en Angleterre et dans les Colonies Americaines aux XVIIe et XVIIIe Siècles* (Lille: L'Université de Lille III, 1975) 176–98, 195.

4. In 1848, *Julia St. Pierre; a Tale of the French Revolution* was anonymously published in London by E. Lloyd, and because of its title it continues to be cataloged as the work of Helen Craik, although it is not. The 1848 *Julia St. Pierre* is actually a novella based on J.C. Cross's dramatic spectacle *Julia of Louvain; or, Monkish Cruelty,* first performed at the Royal Circle Theatre in Southwark, 1797. On *Julia of Louvain,* see Jeffrey Cox, ed. *Seven Gothic Dramas* (Athens: Ohio University Press, 1992) 139–47.

5. "Reflections on the Novel, " originally published in *Les Crimes de l'Amour* (1800). *The 120 Days of Sodom and Other Writings,* trans. Austryn Wainhouse and Richard Seaver (New York: Grove, 1966) 109.

6. François Furet, *Revolutionary France 1770–1880,* trans. Antonia Nevill (Oxford: Blackwell, 1988) 139. Helen Maria Williams describes some of the Vendée massacres in detail, including the mass drownings, in vol. 3 of *Letters . . . of the Politics of France* (1795).

7. Simon Schama, *Citizens: A Chronicle of the French Revolution* (New York: Vintage, 1990) 791. The Vendée remains one of the most divisive and contentious subjects for historians of the French Revolution; estimates of deaths range from a "minimal" 40,000, to Reynald Sécher's characterization of the repression of the Vendée as "genocide." Charles Tilly examines this dispute in "State and Counterrevolution in France," in *The French Revolution and the Birth of Modernity,* ed. Ferenc Fehér (Berkeley: University of California Press, 1990) 49–68. Historians typically emphasize one of three different causes for the uprisings as the most important: religious resistance to the Jacobin secularization and repression of the church, the rural peasants' antagonism toward urban policies and administration, and the Vendéens' loyalty to the monarchy (the royalist explanation, favored by British conservatives in the 1790s). But all agree, as does Craik's novel, that resistance to conscription was a central, and the most immediate, cause of the revolts (specifically, the Convention's decree of February 24 1793 to conscript 300,000 men).

8. *Adelaide de Narbonne, with Memoirs of Charlotte de Cordet. A Tale. In Four Volumes. By the Author of Henry of Northumberland* (London: Minerva Press, 1800). As far as I know no modern account of British writings on the Revolution discusses Craik except Allene Gregory in *The French Revolution and the English Novel,* who devotes two pages to *Adelaide de Narbonne,* and of Craik's politics says that "Her own attitude towards the

Revolution is a Whiggism, conservative when compared with even so mild as a radical as Bage, very liberal in contrast to that of the country at large. . . . She quotes Hume with approval; but she nowhere falls into the popular error of dividing her characters into sheep and goats on the basis of their political convictions" (Port Washington, N.Y.: Kennikat Press, [n.d.]) 184–5. M.O. Grenby names *Adelaide* in a list of "conservative" anti-Jacobin novels, in "The Anti-Jacobin Novel: British Fiction, British Conservatism and the Revolution in France" (*History* 83 (1998): 445–71).

9. "Adelaide" also echoes the historical Mme. Adélaide (1732–1800), aunt of Louis XVI. Narbonne (Louis, Comte de Narbonne-Lara (1755–1813)) was also the name of the war minister from 1791–92, a monarchist, who accompanied Mmes. Adélaide and Victoire to Rome in 1791, and who was helped by his friend Mme. de Staël to escape to London after the monarchy was overthrown in August 1792.

10. Horace Walpole, *The Castle of Otranto,* ed. Robert Mack (London: J.M. Dent, 1998) 82.

11. Craik's reworking of the storming of Versailles into a Royalist mob attack is probably based on the most infamous Vendéen massacre: on 11 March 1793, Vendéen rebels killed over 500 inhabitants of Machecoul, a small Vendée grain market town near the Atlantic. Craik tries to distinguish the men responsible for this massacre from the official policy of the Royal Army, saying that Charette, the military leader of the army, had no knowledge of this rogue attack. The historical Charette was actually in charge of the Royal Army in the Machecoul region, and participated in the massacre.

12. Craik echoes Williams's account of the republican attack on the Vendée in Vol. 3 of *Letters . . . of the Politics of France* (1795) (*Letters from France,* ed. Janet Todd, in vol. 2 (Delmar: Scholars' Facsimiles, 1975) 2: 3: 17–18. Hereafter cited in the text by the volume in the Todd edition (1 or 2), and the text's original volume number (1 to 4) and page number.

13. "Insurrection in La Vendée," *The Times,* 8 July 1793, p.3. The term "banditti" was specifically used in reports in *The Times* to refer to the Vendée rebels, and *The Times* repeatedly tried to dismiss this characterization. For example, it printed what it described as "what the chiefs of the Royalists published in justification of their principles," beginning with their complaint that "We are called,' say they, 'sanguinary banditti" ("Treatment of Insurgents in La Vendée," *The Times,* 2 August 1793, 3).

14. Craik's Victorine may be based in part on the aunt of Louis XVI, Madame Victoire, who with her sister Madame Adélaide (1732–1800), fled from Paris to Italy in 1791. Like Victorine in Craik's novel, Madame Victoire was helped to evade arrest by a prominent republican (historically, Mirabeau).

15. Ann Radcliffe, *The Italian,* ed. Fred Garber (Oxford: Oxford University Press) 39.

16. Sade, "DISCOURS PRONONCÉ à la fête décernée par la Section des Piques, aux mânes de Marat et de Le Pelletier, par Sade, citoyen de cette Section, et membre de la Société populaire" (1793) (*Oeuvres Complètes du Marquis de Sade,* vol. 11 (Paris: Cercle du Livre Précieux, 1967) 119–22; 121 (translations from this text are my own).

17. Michel Foucault, Introduction to *Herculine Barbin,* trans. Richard McDougall (Brighton: Harvester, 1980) vii–xvii.

18. Chantal Thomas, "Heroism in the Feminine: Charlotte Corday and Madame Roland" (*The Eighteenth Century: Theory and Interpretation* 30 [1989]): 69.

19. Qtd. in Chantal Thomas, "Heroism in the Feminine," 74.

20. *The Times,* 3 August 1793, p. 2; 10 August 1793, p. 2.

21. *The London Chronicle,* July 23–25 1793 (vol. 74) 86.

22. *Histoire Parlementaire de la Révolution Française,* eds. P J.-B. Buchez and P.-C. Roux, vol. 28 (Paris: Paulin, Librairie, 1836) 315; translation as quoted in Schama 739.

23. Needless to say, *The Times* did not quote this or other republican statements in its lengthy account of Corday's trial and execution (published 10 August 1793); *Histoire Parlementaire* v. 28: 319; translation as quoted in Schama, 740.

24. Letter to Charles Barbaroux (this line omitted in *Times*), *Histoire Parlementaire* vol. 28: 330; trans. as quoted in Schama, 740; transcript of Corday's trial, *The London Chronicle,* July 25–27, 1793 (vol. 74) 89.

25. "The heroic Charlotte la Cordé, upon her Trial at the bar of the Revolutionary Tribunal of Paris, July 17th 1793" published 29 July 1793 by H. Humphrey. On this and other popular visual images of Corday, see Claudine Mitchell, "Spectacular fears and popular arts" in *Reflections of Revolution,* ed. Alison Yarrington and Kelvin Everest (London: Routledge, 1993) 159–81.

26. [Louis] Du Broca, *Interesting anecdotes of the heroic conduct of women previous to and during the French Revolution* (first American edition, Baltimore 1804). Du Broca includes Corday in his chapter on "Self-Devotion for Great Objects," a catalog of feminine self-sacrifice, and perpetuates the story of Corday's supposed lover, an aristocratic officer M. de Belzunce, who had been denounced in Marat's journal and killed.

27. Shelley's poem was published in his *Posthumous Fragments of Margaret Nicholson* (*Poetical Works of Percy Bysshe Shelley,* ed. Newell Ford [Boston: Houghton Mifflin 1975] 558–59). Southey's poem was published in *The Morning Post,* 14 July 1798 (*The Contributions of Robert Southey to the* Morning Post, ed. Kenneth Curry [University, AL: University of Alabama

Press, 1984] 74). Corday killed Marat on July 13, but was herself executed on July 17. The undated "Charlotte Corday," by "Miss Day" is included in Mary Russell Mitford's *Reflections of a Literary Life,* (London: Richard Bentley, 1852) vol. 2 of 3: 127–30.

28. Jeffrey Cox, "Ideology and Genre in the British Antirevolutionary Drama of the 1790s," *ELH* 58 (1991): 579–610; 602. *The Maid of Normandy and the Death of the Queen of France* was published in 1794 by Longman and claims performances in Dublin, Cheltenham, and three other cities, but it had been denied a license. I am grateful to Jeff Cox for drawing my attention to Eyre's play.

29. Edmund John Eyre, *Death of the Queen of France,* MS: dated, by Larpent, Norwich, 7 May 1804, and marked "Refused" (Readex Microfiche series in Nineteenth Century English Drama) 3.ii.

30. "Tabitha Bramble" to Robert Dundas, 23 January 1794, Public Record Office: HO/102/10 f. 121.

31. Vivien Jones, "Women Writing Revolution: Narratives of History and Sexuality in Wollstonecraft and Williams" (in *Beyond Romanticism,* ed. Stephen Copley & John Whale [London: Routledge, 1992], 178–99. See also Deborah Williams, "Spectacle of the Guillotine: Helen Maria Williams and the Reign of Terror," *Philological Quarterly* 73 (1994): 95–113.

32. As quoted. in M. Ray Adams, "Helen Maria Williams and the French Revolution," *Wordsworth and Coleridge: Studies in Honor of George McLean Harper,* ed. Earl Leslie Griggs (New York: Russell and Russell, 1962), 114.

33. *Gentleman's Magazine,* 1798, as quoted in Chris Jones, "Helen Maria Williams and Radical Sensibility," *Prose Studies* 12 (1989): 3–24; 11.

34. "Mad. Marie Ann Char. Corday," *The Times,* 10 August 1793, 2.

35. Williams also mentions "a friend" in connection with Corday when she tells the story of Adam Lux, who fell in love with Corday and died because of it; when Lux was in prison for publishing his pamphlet on Corday, Williams writes that "a friend of mine often saw him, . . . where he talked of nothing to him but of Charlotte Corday and the guillotine" (1: 1: 134–5). Woodward confirms that "Sans doute, Stone assista au procés de Charlotte Corday" (*Une anglaise amie de la Révolution Française: Hélene Maria Williams* [Paris: Honoré Champion, 1930] 79).

36. Cf. chapter 8, "The British Club," in David Erdman, *Commerce des Lumières* (Columbia: University of Missouri Press, 1986) 230.

37. Toasts two and four delivered at the British Club (Erdman, 230).

38. Louvet's description of Corday also appears in his *Narrative of the Dangers to Which I have been exposed since the 31st of May, 1793* (London: Joseph Johnson, 1795).

39. For other discussions of Corday's sublime and beautiful qualities, see Steven Blakemore, *Crisis in Representation* (Madison: Fairleigh Dickinson University Press, 1997); Nina Corazzo and Catherine Montfort, "Charlotte Corday: *femme-homme,*" *Literate Women of the French Revolution,* ed. Catherine Montfort (Birmingham, Ala.: Summa, 1994); Vivien Jones, "Women Writing Revolution: Narratives of History and Sexuality in Wollstonecraft and Williams," *Beyond Romanticism,* ed. Stephen Copley and John Whale (London: Routledge, 1992), 178–99.

40. Sade, "Reflections on the Novel," 109.

41. Stuart Curran, "'The Cenci': The Tragic Resolution," *Percy Bysshe Shelley: Modern Critical Views,* ed. Harold Bloom (New York: Chelsea House, 1985) 75.

42. Williams here refers to Liberty as a fury specifically in the Vendée counterrevolutionary war (2: 2: 212). Vivien Jones also notes Williams's use of Robespierre as a villain, and Liberty as a heroine ("Femininity, Nationalism, and Romanticism," *History of European Ideas* 16 [1993] 299–305; 303).

43. Du Broca also refers to Corday as the "voluntary victim" (194), and mentions the Lux legend (196).

44. Adam Lux, *Charlotte Corday. Par Adam Lux. Député extraordinaire de Mayence* [1793]: 6, 5 (my translation).

45. The closing of the convents in France was a pivotal moment in all of Craik's Revolutionary-era novels, signaling the expulsion of her women characters from their convent homes (where they did not always live voluntarily). Monastic vows were abolished in February 1790, and by November 1790 clergy had to take an oath of allegiance to the Constitution.

46. Review of *Adelaide de Narbonne, The Anti-Jacobin Review* (January 1801) 59, original emphasis.

47. This passage, identified as being "from Mrs. Robinson's Walsingham," is the epigraph for volume 3 of *Adelaide,* and is also quoted in volume 2, p. 23. The passage quoted is spoken by an increasingly defiant Sydney, cross-dressed as a man, to her mother, protesting her need to masquerade as a man in order to assure her inheritance of her family estate (*Walsingham, or The Pupil of Nature,* 4 vols. (London: Routledge/Thoemmes) 1: 313–4). Craik also quotes a different passage from *Walsingham* in vol. 2, 152.

48. In this respect, both Robinson and Craik draw on Wollstonecraft, who in her two *Vindications* had connected paternal and political tyranny, and opposed both, in direct contrast to Burke's support of the "organic," or natural, authority of kings and fathers.

49. I.e., in this passage when Corday views a majestic cataract: "The sensation it occasioned was similar to that produced by the Aeolian harp,

when seated alone, and reading Ossian's poems, its deep-toned strains vibrate on the heart with a sweet but undefinable effect" (1: 78–79).

50. Anne Mellor, *Romanticism and Gender* (London: Routledge, 1993), 3.

51. Mary Robinson, *Letter to the Women of England on the Injustice of Mental Subordination [1799]: A Romantic Circles Edition,* ed. Adriana Craciun, Anne Close Irmen, Megan Musgrave, and Orianne Smith (1998) <www.rc.umd.edu/editions/robinson/cover.htm>. For a full discussion of Robinson's and Wollstonecraft's responses to women's physical violence and strength, see Adriana Craciun, "Violence Against Difference: Mary Wollstonecraft and Mary Robinson," in *Making History: Textuality and the Forms of Eighteenth-Century Culture,* ed. Greg Clingham (Bucknell: Bucknell University Press, 1998), 111–41.

52. Miss Day, "Charlotte Corday," quoted in Mitford 128. In the American Sarah Pogson's play about Corday, *The Female Enthusiast* (1807), Corday says: "A woman's arm, when nerved in such a cause,/ Is as the arm of the avenging angel" (3.iii) (*Plays by Early American Women,* ed. Amelia Howe Kritzer [Ann Arbor: University of Michigan Press, 1995], 159).

53. *The London Times* 9 August 1793, 3; (*Histoire Parlementaire* 332).

54. Helen Craik, *Julia de St. Pierre* (London: Minerva Press, 1796) 3 vols.; 1: iii. A similar authorial intervention occurs in *Stella of the North*: "it has more than once been my lot to see the innocent condemned on the most fallacious appearances, and the guilty supported, when living proofs of their criminality were actually present" (2: 247).

55. Craik was the daughter of William Craik and Elizabeth Stewart, and died on 11 June 1825 at age 74, meaning she was probably born in 1750. Arbigland remains known today solely as the birthplace of John Paul Jones (1747–1792), the American naval hero considered by the British to be a pirate, who was born in a gardener's shed on the estate, and may have been one of William Craik's illegitimate children. One of Craik's acknowledged illegitimate children, Dr. James Craik, became George Washington's personal physician (Helen Craik discusses him in her letters to the *Farmer's Magazine*).

56. Two of Burns's letters to Craik survive: in the first, from 1790, Burns thanks Craik for sending him a "manuscript volume of Poems," and famously compares those two "QUEENS OF THE HEARTS OF MEN," poetry and Woman: "Bewitching Poesy is like bewitching WOMAN: she has in all ages been accused of misleading Mankind from the counsels of Wisdom and the paths of Prudence" (*Letters of Robert Burns,* ed. G. Ross Roy [Oxford: Clarendon, 1985] vol. 2 [1790–96], 46–47). In 1792 Burns wrote again to thank Craik for her work "HELEN," possibly a long poem (now lost) which he promised to read and help revise. Several of her poems were published in the *Glasgow Herald* in 1919 by her descendant, Dr. George Neilson, as "Burnsiana," from a manuscript book of her poems (also now lost) in his

possession. Craik also wrote a poem in Burns's copy of his Edinburgh edition *Poems,* dated October 1789.

57. Samuel Arnott, "The Romance of Helen Craik of Arbigland," *Transactions of Dumfriesshire and Galloway Natural History and Antiquarian Society* 11 (1923–24), 77–83.

58. George Neilson's account of Craik's poetry is almost all that remains of it, since the manuscript book of her poems from which he quotes has not turned up in any archive containing his papers. Several poems exist at present: "The maid of Enterkin" in *Julia de St. Pierre,* and "To Captain R[iddell]" and "To Captain R[idde]ll with the maid of Enterkin," the latter two reprinted in Neilson's *Glasgow Herald* articles, along with fragments of other poems by Craik. Neilson suggests that Craik's "Helen," which she had sent to Burns, was based on the traditional ballad of Helen of Kirkconnell. I quote part of Neilson's description of her poems because they have not survived: "A noteworthy characteristic is the recurrent Werterism of Miss Craik's poems.[. . .] My manuscript includes verses 'written by Charlotte at Werter's grave, 1779,' and another of Miss Craik's pieces bids us 'the sorrows of Werter deplore.'[. . .] Whether fostered by 'Werter' or not, a kindred tragic sentimentality appears in Miss Craik's preference for suicidal and murderous subjects. Verses on the Earl of Caithness who shot himself in 1789, on Hackman's murder of Miss Ray in 1779 and on the mutual murder-suicide of Faldoni and Theresa in 1770 are instances of this painful taste" ("The Maid of Enterkin. Burnsiana I.," *Glasgow Herald,* 8 March 1919, 7).

59. E.g., Alan Temperley, "The Groom of Arbigland," *Tales of Galloway* (Edinburgh: Mainstream, 1979), 266–8; Dane Love, *Scottish Ghosts* (London: Robert Hale, 1995), 61–2.

60. *The Farmer's Magazine* published two letters by Helen Craik giving a biographical account of her father William Craik (*The Farmer's Magazine* 46 [June 1811]: 154–63; 161). When William Craik succeeded to the family estate in 1736, the estate was worth approximately £170; he had Arbigland built, possibly after his own design, and when his designated heir, his nephew, took possession of the estate in 1799 "the property was then valued at 1161 yearly rent for taxation, and the whole estate mentioned as one farm in the valuation roll, which no doubt arose from the owner having all the farms in his own hands" (P.H. McKerlie, *History of the Lands and Their Owners in Galloway,* vol. 4. [Edinburgh: William Paterson, 1878], 155).

61. In her second letter published in the *Farmer's Magazine,* Craik wrote: "the fact is, the female part of his family were never permitted to interfere, in the smallest degree, with those occupations and pursuits, which he considered as more particularly his own. The natural consequence was, we were kept in total ignorance of every transaction that came under this prohibited denomination" (156). This letter goes on to give great economic, genealogical and agricultural detail, however, demonstrating Helen Craik's

knowledge of both her father's public business activities and farming methods, and his private indiscretions, i.e., his "hard drinking, hard riding, and
every other youthful excess" (158) and his illegitimate son.

62. After Julia is thrown out of the Stanleys' house under suspicion of
being an unchaste "adventurer," she goes to live with a servant's family, and
there we hear the tragic story of their daughter, Charlotte: Charlotte had
been secretly married to a man whose father disapproved of her because of
her lack of wealth. One night, a shot rang out, and Charlotte ran out to find
her husband shot dead. The murderer was her own brother, apparently
tricked into the murder by their family; upon his death, and as in Craik's
case, "the family estate went to the heir male, a distant relation" (3: 49).

63. "Account of William Craik, Esq. of Arbigland," *The Farmer's Magazine* 46 (June 1811): 145–54; 152. Helen Craik's letters about her father and
her own life follow this account, and she also discusses this account her
father's encounter with the farm workers. Another example of William
Craik's "resolute behaviour" (153) took place while he served as Justice of
the Peace, and ordered that a "notorious ruffian accused of murder" be
restrained: "Mr. Craik, observing that the constables were terrified by the
ruffian's threats, jumped from the seat of Justice, and snatching a rope from
one of the constables, first wrenched the knife from the fellow, and then
forcibly tied his hands behind him, without any assistance whatever" (153).

64. *Romanticism, Nationalism, and the Revolt Against Theory* (Chicago:
University of Chicago Press, 1993).

65. After Helen Craik's uncle James died, leaving her £400, Flimby
Lodge, Cumberland, the ancestral home of this branch of the Craiks, seems
to have become an all-female household; Margery Neilson and Barbara
Craik both named Helen Craik as executrix in their wills, and when the
former died in 1809, the estate was sold for £16,504, and the proceeds split
between the male heir of Arbigland, Douglas Hamilton Craik, and Helen
Craik (Wills of James and Barbara Craik, GGD 159/14 and GGD 159/16,
Dumfries and Galloway Libraries, Information and Archives).

66. Craik here echoes Robinson in *Sappho and Phaon,* where she wrote
that after she was widowed, Sappho "never after could be prevailed on to
marry" (*Sappho and Phaon,* in Duncan Wu, ed., *Romantic Women Poets: An
Anthology* [London: Blackwell, 1997], 188). The old maid in question in *Julia*
is Miss Rutland, who bears some similarity to Craik: "her fortune was large;
but painful occurrences, in the early part of her days, had given her a dislike
to the world, and had rendered seclusion from it her choice" (3: 116). In
Stella of the North, the "old maid" is Miss Adair, "comparatively a free agent
in the world" (4: 157), who "though addressed by men of the first rank and
merit in their country, has hitherto declined all proposals of marriage, and
appears determined to retain the reprobated appellation of 'an old maid,' in
spite of the numerous opportunities which daily occur" (4: 340–1).

67. Craik's obituary makes reference to her charitable works, as does the memorial plaque dedicated to her inside the Church of St. Nicholas, Flimby, which reads in part: "Respected in life and lamented in death, she was to the afflicted a kind and consoling friend and to the poor an indulgent and liberal benefactress."

68. Claudia Johnson, *Equivocal Beings: Gender and Sentimentality in the 1790s* (Chicago: University of Chicago Press, 1995), 165.

69. I was able to complete the research for this essay thanks to a grant from the National Endowment for the Humanities. I am grateful to Donna Landry, John Logan, and Kari Lokke for their helpful comments on earlier drafts, and to Peter Eyre of the Whitehaven Record Office and Marion Stewart of the Dumfries and Galloway Archive Centre for their help locating archival sources. My thanks also to the New York Society Library for access to their Hammond Collection.

Mary Hays's "Female Philosopher": Constructing Revolutionary Subjects

෴

Miriam L. Wallace

While the Revolution in France opened up possibilities for representing the poor and women as political and active subjects (at least initially), in England these very possibilities were quickly recontained as the post-1792 backlash set in. The insistently gendered terms in which public debates on liberty and tradition, parliamentary reform, and the state of the monarchy were framed made women's nature a particularly invested topos of these debates. English women in the early 1790s were caught between the conflicting demands for extending liberty and self-determination to (middle-class) women and for proper feminine restraint of public display and speech. One effect in England of the French Revolution was to solidify a particular model of gendered identity as a sign of England's difference from France. Nevertheless, for a brief period in the 1790s many English women participated actively in linked debates about the position of women and the possibility of political reform at home and abroad.

In particular, the realm of writing—fiction, political essay, book reviews, drama, letters to the editor, and letters to sympathetic friends—was the site in which British women fought their own revolution. Grounding their arguments in the philosophical and political discourse which exploded in England surrounding the French uprisings, British women were able to extend arguments about the rights of French citizenry and to borrow from French women's public actions to describe and argue for their own escape from social oppression. However, as a plethora of late eighteenth-century texts reveal, and critics have well-documented, English women were also trapped by these discourses which enabled their opponents in England to align

"French ideas" with uncontrolled sexuality and sensuality, and so return these women's stories to the merely "personal."

In a collection on women writers in the French Revolution, Mary Hays's letters and her novel *Emma Courtney* (1796) may seem initially to stretch the terms of "Revolutionary writing." *Emma Courtney* famously tells the partially autobiographical story of an individual British woman's romantic and emotional history as a warning to her adopted son who stands on the brink of committing similar errors. Emma recounts her passion for Augustus Harley and her epistolary efforts to persuade him that women have as much right as men to declare their feelings, until her belated discovery of Harley's secret marriage silences her outpourings. Subsequently, she tells her son, she married another suitor, but the fatal effects of her husband's jealousy poisoned this marriage and led to her husband's death. Restricted to England and focused on personal passions and their effects on familial relationships, the novel is at first glance barely related to the ferment of Revolution.

Particularly in the 1790s, however, ideas were a key site of English engagement with the French Revolution. Public debates about "French ideas" in England during the 1790s were extensive and incendiary, leading to serious material consequences for many dissenting religious thinkers and the so-called "Jacobin" writers.[1] These included Hays's friends: William Frend, who was forced to leave Cambridge University, Thomas Holcroft, who was called to trial for treason in 1794 and dismissed without charges being preferred, and Mary Wollstonecraft, who was vilified after her death as an example of an "unsex'd female" or "amazon."[2] Although Hays was not herself an observer or direct participant in actual events in France, her engagement with and propagation of "French ideas," particularly in *Emma Courtney,* earned her much public censure.[3] Arguably deriving from particularly English renditions of "French systems," Hays's contributions to the founding debates of Anglo-feminism in her personal writings and her published work are worthy of more attention than they have generally received. The French Revolution has cast long shadows; the significance of its events and theoretical arguments are still being debated.[4] It remains an important site for modern feminist exploration as well, and bears on how feminism continues to struggle with the relation of theory to experience, mind to body, and rationality to sensibility.

David Simpson has argued that opposing common sense experience as a British national trait to abstract theory as a French national trait was a common strategy of the anti-Jacobins.[5] Importantly, Mary

Hays attempted to link experience with theory in her writings, as did all the "Jacobins." The separation of abstract theory and the power of its grand view from experiential authority and authenticity which circulated in the political debates of the 1790s, has also haunted feminist claims from the 1970s on. Simpson traces twentieth century suspicion towards "French theory" back to the revolution in an attempt to account for the British and Anglo-American theory debates in the 1970s and 1980s. I suggest that this anxiety is perhaps even more pressing for Anglo-American engagements with English and French branches of feminist theory, where the opposition between Anglo and French modes of theorizing have emerged as an important, if oversimplified, binary opposition.[6] Primarily, this essay explores the specific efforts to create a viable feminine subject position, a "female philosopher," in Mary Hays's first novel and the letters which precede and are incorporated into that novel. Secondarily, the trajectory of my argument gestures toward a prefiguration of 1970s (and contemporary) Anglo-American feminist debates which Hays's work, taken in tandem with Wollstonecraft's, performs.

Finally, I want to argue for English Jacobinism as a "structure of feeling,"[7] named and codified into apparent coherence by its opponents, the self-styled "anti-Jacobins." Given that it was the conservative and anti-Jacobin backlash that named these writers as a coherent group, we should be suspicious and hesitant about accepting their terms uncritically, although the term may be nearly unavoidable.[8] Rather than identifying those writers through their allegiance to particular political groups within France, I propose to consider the conjunction of these writers who are generally interested in the question of environment over inheritance ("necessarianism" as propounded by William Godwin), female rationality (as propounded by Wollstonecraft), and individual merit marked by sensibility and rationality rather than birthright (clear in the novels of Hays and Holcroft) as the growth of a particularly English "structure of feeling."

Raymond Williams suggested that emergent cultural forms, or a change in cultural hegemony signaled by an extreme and different mode of thought, feeling, and philosophy can best be denoted a "structure of feeling," and thus recognized long before and more clearly than traditional Marxist notions of "emergent class" systems would enable us to identify such social and cultural developments (Williams, 131–2). Specifically, Williams's formulation allows us to recognize a shift in shared social thought before it is reified through institutional practice. Because "Jacobinism" becomes recognizable and nameable through its institutionalized opponents (such as the government sponsored

Anti-Jacobin Magazine), conceiving of "Jacobinism" as a structure of feeling allows us to recognize its manifestations both earlier and over a longer period than the institutionalized parodic version identified by the anti-Jacobins (Williams, 134). I suggest further that fiction acts as a particularly rich site for tracing this emergent "structure of feeling" as a site of ideological intervention and imaginary exploration, particularly of "feelings" or "sensibility," which may in part account for why despite the Jacobin's allegiance to reason, their novels all incorporate an extensive rhetoric of sensibility. Williams notes that conceiving of the "social" as merely the institutionalized allows the "personal" of subjective experience to escape analysis (Williams, 128). Where we in 2001 may see system, genre, and coherent ideological groups, these writings from the 1790s exhibit the struggle to explore new conjunctions of ideas and to find coherent forms in which to express those ideas. One important site for tracing the development of Jacobin feeling is both the personal and published writing of those later castigated as Jacobins; among the women of this group, Mary Wollstonecraft and Mary Hays were particularly well-known as public figures of the "Jacobin woman" and "philosophess."

While Wollstonecraft has received a great deal of (feminist) critical attention, Hays has received comparatively little, although she wrote two important novels in the 1790s: *The Memoirs of Emma Courtney* (1796) and *The Victim of Prejudice* (1799). She also published the *Appeal to the Men of Great Britain in Behalf of Women* in 1798, anonymously. By then, arguing for women's rights was considerably more dangerous and unpopular than when Wollstonecraft published *A Vindication of the Rights of Woman* in pre-Terror 1792.[9] Finally, Hays left behind a legacy of letters and periodical essays in addition to several fictional and historical works published in the early nineteenth century; among her periodical writings are two obituaries of Mary Wollstonecraft, whose deathbed she attended.

Like her friend Mary Wollstonecraft, Mary Hays grapples with the special problems and challenges which female sensibility presents to the claims of philosophy. Unlike some of the writing of Wollstonecraft, however, in both fiction and autobiographical work Hays consistently casts passion and sensibility as central to "female philosophers" and as a corrective to the abstract reasoning of her mentor, William Godwin.[10] This represents a departure from the increasing valuation of reason over passion in late eighteenth century thought. In part, Hays's argument, although tentative and inconsistent, also prefigures a continuing critical dilemma within feminist thought, and may be understood as an explicitly feminist strategy. Hays is ultimately suggesting that what we know as "reason" is formed by experience, by personal history, and hence by feeling. Echoing Williams's "structures of feeling," she implies that feeling as personal is not opposed to history as abstract and impersonal, but that feeling is *part* of historical location and knowledge. As she says in her letter of 9 February 1796, "I cannot love mankind collectively—they are a mere abstraction to me—why should I love them?"[11]

The problem of individual sensibility that the later eighteenth century identified is that it appears to invite quiescence and self-indulgence rather than "active virtue" or political and moral action, hence the peculiarly ambivalent status of sensibility among both revolutionary and antirevolutionary writers in the 1790s. Even current critical debates surrounding the history of sensibility in the late-eighteenth century are fraught with the same worries. From delineations of sentimentality and sensibility as inherently bourgeois, individualist, and socially conservative, to accounts of sensibility's potential for expanding the individual realm of self-interest, sorting out the ideological implications of sensibility throughout the eighteenth century and into the nineteenth remains extremely vexed.

Wollstonecraft scholars have argued that Wollstonecraft's own relation to sensibility and rationality, passion and reason, feeling and thought is a complex and continuing negotiation throughout her work.[12] Certainly her essays are particularly ambivalent, while her novels participate in some of the tropes of privileged feeling in order to create heroines and celebrate their ability to forge connections across social lines. Wollstonecraft's final novel treads remarkably unstable ground, evoking both liberal feminist claims for women's legal autonomy and right to paid labor and radical feminist arguments for women's natural bond through shared oppression by masculinist social institutions to effect a sentimental connection between middle-class Maria and working-class Jemima. Perhaps most interestingly, *Wrongs of Woman* moves towards gendering the question of sensibility's potential for social justice, suggesting that sensibility may function to overcome the prejudices of class between women, but that between men and women it can only fall again into the prison of heterosexual marriage or libertinage. If Wollstonecraft is not simply anti-sensibility, she manages to throw serious question on its potential for female liberty and knowledge.

By contrast, sensibility and emotional susceptibility, while dangerous, remain necessary attributes for Hays's ideal "female philosopher." Even more than Wollstonecraft's, Mary Hays's arguments for reason and rational control are tempered by appeals to the importance of strong feelings as the motivation for self-improvement, the development of virtue, and learning the proper use of reason. Hays's writing conjoins sensibility with reason to imagine a specifically "philosophical" female subject. Her heroines (including herself in her personal letters, Emma Courtney, and even Wollstonecraft in the obituaries which Hays wrote) are thinking, rational beings whose highly developed sensibility exists in dynamic tension with reason as they struggle to understand and control their circumstances, choices, and actions. Viewed in the context of Hays's celebration of sensibility, Wollstonecraft's work displays a consistently greater ambivalence towards sensibility .

As with Wollstonecraft, Mary Hays's life has been used both as the exclusive key to her work, and as the reason for dismissing her writing as that of a "neurotic"[13] or an "a thing, ugly and petticoated."[14] This tendency to return political feminist writers' work to the realm of the personal replicates antirevolutionary backlash, often in a particularly misogynistic and virulent strain, and has persisted as a strategy for silencing female voices to the present day. How individual women writers negotiate the double trap of claiming a public voice while portraying themselves as not sexually suspect "public" women is tied to generic experiment. Like Mary Wollstonecraft's *Historical and Moral View of the French Revolution,* and Helen Maria Williams's *Letters from France,* which as Vivien Jones has argued mixed "masculine" history with the "feminine" novel form,[15] *Emma Courtney* mixes "philosophy" (by which Hays also means politics) with the sentimental novel through the traditional narrative medium of an individual emotional history. Thus, without situating her novel explicitly in the context of the Revolution in France, Hays nevertheless was able to reiterate ideas and arguments which were current in the debates of the London corresponding societies and which became dominant "structures of feeling" through the debates engendered by the American, Haitian, and especially the French, revolutions.

If Vivien Jones is correct in suggesting that the historical tenor of the times both enabled women writers to expand the genres which they might explore, and made the debates about the propriety of those genres part of a larger debate about the proper role of women, Hays's own novel and its mixed reception are telling. While *Emma Courtney* is squarely within the dominant genre for women writers at the time (the life history, sentimental novel), its author was castigated as a "Jacobin philosophess" whose enthusiasm for French philosophy and Godwinian system lead her into embarrassing and illicit sexual extravagances. Conflating the author Hays with her fictional and philosophical heroine, some readers of the novel reduced its philosophical argument to illicit sexual content.[16] Modern readers have only too frequently repeated this move, either conflating the author with the character, or straining to read the novel as simply the warning against excessive sensibility which Hays's preface claims it is. Such critiques often fail to note the complex and subtle negotiations that the novel itself performs in separating the usefulness of passion and sensibility as principles of active virtue from their dangers for a female philosopher.[17] Critics have consistently misrecognized Hays's novel, then, as either a thinly veiled account of and excuse for her own passion along the lines of earlier eighteenth century scandalous memoirs, or as a clear argument for reason as the legitimate controlling force of passion. Marilyn Butler, for instance, argues that the "theme of *Emma Courtney*—at least at the conscious level—is that women will never be free unless they learn to submit their passions to the control of reason," and she argues that it is a "revolutionary novel about the need for self-control" (*Jane Austen,* 44, 54). While Butler is not completely inaccurate, the novel performs a more complex and ambivalent negotiation than this account recognizes, marked here by the parenthetical "at least at the conscious level." By overtly questioning the dangers of feminine sensibility and arguing for women's rational abilities, *Emma Courtney* is able to explore the models of psychological and social subjectivity available for female-gendered subjects and to propose a new model. The novel's "tendency" (in Godwin's terminology from "Of Choice in Reading") is to celebrate women's potential for using sensibility to develop reason, thereby becoming "female philosophers."

Sensibility is particularly at issue in the autobiographical roots of Hays's first novel. From 1794 to 1796 Mary Hays carried on a rich and detailed correspondence with William Godwin.[18] In 1796 she published her first novel, *The Memoirs of Emma Courtney,* drawn in part directly from her correspondences with William Godwin and William Frend.[19] When at Godwin's suggestion, she attempted to turn her painful failed love affair into a novel, she turned to her own letters for material, asking Frend to return them to her for that purpose.[20]

Fiction and (auto)biography were privileged forms for the English revolutionary writers generally. The history of a life, in particular, following the "Jacobin" philosophy that traced adult characters as developed through past impressions and experiences, helps to explain the prevalence of autobiography and fictional life histories among these writers. From Godwin's account of Wollstonecraft's life to Thomas

Holcroft's incomplete account of his own, and from Godwin's *Caleb Williams* to Holcroft's *Anna St. Ives,* each Jacobin was as interested in telling historical and fictional lives to illustrate moral points as any moralist of the century. Moreover, as predominantly "feminine" forms of writing, novel and life-story enabled Hays to enter into the masculine discourse of "philosophy." Where educated male writers like Godwin began with politics and philosophy and then moved to narrative fiction in an effort to reach a wider and different audience, female writers and the educationally less-privileged male writers (specifically Holcroft), frequently began with either novels or translations. Hays, of course, begins with letters, that ultimately feminine and feminized form, although her letters are inherently "philosophical."[21]

Hays not only writes her life into fiction, but argues for reading fiction as a particularly important site of women's education—both as philosophers and as fashionable women. The fear that women might mistake fiction for reality and model their lives on dangerous literary models haunts discussions of the novel and its "tendencies" throughout the century. While both Hays and Wollstonecraft (like many other eighteenth century thinkers) display concern with appropriate reading for girls in their essays and book reviews, their approaches and judgements differ.

Wollstonecraft in *A Vindication of the Rights of Woman* argues against allowing girls to read novels without guidance, including mocking the ridiculousness of novelistic portrayals of feminine behavior. Yet she also suggests that reading novels is better than reading nothing, and that even novels may be turned to beneficial use with the right guidance. Wollstonecraft then makes her point through telling the story of two girls, cousins, educated by a benevolent father-uncle. While his own daughter has been spoiled by an indulgent mother and cannot concentrate on the more solid intellectual fare of history and moral essay, the niece's more established pleasure in reading enables her to graduate to the more demanding and substantial reading that Wollstonecraft and the uncle value. Acknowledging that novel reading has been the primary source of most women's education, Wollstonecraft admits that for weak-minded and undisciplined girls novel reading may still be a requisite, if lamentable first step. She bolsters this argument with this illustrative story, aligning herself as rational educator with the "sagacious" father and uncle, and against the "fond, weak mother" who has spoiled the daughter, thereby reiterating the gendered terms in which genre is cast.[22]

Conversely, in *Letters and Essays* Hays writes at length to a mother concerning why novel reading is appropriate for her daughter and how to encourage her to read rightly, moving from lively sensations to rational thought, from fiction to history and philosophy. She supports her contentions by appealing to her own readerly experience and responses; thus, Hays considers *Clarissa* an admirable novel while remaining cautious about Rousseau's *Julie*:

> You ask if I would advise you to put Richardson's Clarissa [sic] into the hands of your daughters . . . If we may judge of the merit of a work by the effects which it produces on the mind, I confess, this is a book, which I would recommend to the attention of any young persons under my care. I read it repeatedly in very early life, and ever found my mind more pure, more chastened, more elevated after the perusal of it. The extreme youth and beauty, fine talents, and exalted piety of the heroine, render the character . . . something like the fine ideal beauty of the ancients. . . . in contemplating the perfect model [Clarissa herself], the imagination is raised, and the soul affected; we perceive the pencil of genius, and while we admire, catch the glorious enthusiasm . . . Rousseau is not a writer equally pure.[23]

Hays here values novels not as a makeshift substitute for weak-minded women but as the natural beginning place for female education, assuming an innate propensity to sensibility in the best female minds. While Wollstonecraft critiques *Clarissa*'s portrayal of chastity and female honor, Hays admires that same novel for the elevation of mind and purity of thought that it encourages. Hays further aligns Clarissa with the "ancients," and so with philosophy and history filtered through a modern Christian sensibility; Wollstonecraft, focusing on Clarissa as a model of passive virtue and will-lessness, can find only dangers here for women. Both Hays and Wollstonecraft are searching for models of feminine education and subjectivity, and each situates *Clarissa* differently in this effort.

Hays's allegiance to fiction led her to read Godwin's *Enquiry Concerning Political Justice* (1793). In her first letter to William Godwin, asking to borrow his copy of *Political Justice,* she gives a flattering description of her first encounter with Godwin's own first novel, *Caleb Williams; or Things as They Are*:

> The affecting struggle between prejudice and principle in the finely sketched character of Falkland; . . . the soul harrowing catastrophe of the unfortunate Hawkins, the protracted

persecutions and sufferings of the intrepid and ingenuous Caleb William—alternately excited in my mind a sensibility almost convulsive! Hurried along by the interesting and impassioned narrative, I had scarcely time, till a second perusal to pay a proper attention to the variety of excellent remarks, political and moral with which these memoirs abound.[24]

Here Hays presents herself as both the right reader of Godwin's novel and an able interpreter of the political function of literary sensibility. As a reader, she is drawn into the novel's design to form the reader's political ideas through his or her emotional involvement with the narrative. She is first "excited [into] a sensibility almost convulsive," and only on the second reading becomes the reasoning reader who consciously grasps the intended political messages. The mind is prepared to receive philosophical arguments through emotional involvement and connection, that is, through sensibility. Sensibility and reason are conceived here as working together to achieve the correct interpretation of social critique, a dynamic which her own novel two years later explored further.

William Godwin was a particularly complex choice for Hays's mentor at this point in both their lives. His *Political Justice* in many ways explicitly rejects the doctrine of sensibility as it was popularly understood. "Sentimentalism has many critics in the period, but no one who is juster, more penetrating, or, for a while, more whole-hearted, than William Godwin," in Marilyn Butler's words (33). In this context, Mary Hays's refusal to relinquish the power of feeling despite her allegiance to rational control appears more daring than Godwin's more dismissive attitude toward feeling as nonrational. Her writing, beginning with her letters and developing through her first novel, attempts to find a way to adhere to the politically motivated emphasis on rationality without relinquishing the claims of sentiment and passion as powerful political forces. Her letters to Godwin negotiate this difference, alternately bemoaning her inadequate knowledge of philosophy ("I shall, I doubt, never be a philosopher—a barbed and invenomed arrow rankles in my bosom—philosophy will not heal the festering wound")[25] and arguing that surely her powerful feelings must have importance ("Oh! how impotent is *mere* reasoning against reiterated feeling!").[26] Although this is largely a one-sided correspondence, Hays's letters reveal strong tensions between her intellectual allegiance to William Godwin and her reluctance to abandon her own experiential and emotional knowledge. *Emma Courtney* should be read as Hays's final effort to master her own intellectual and emotional arguments with Godwin, encapsulating her letters and his responses in her fictional creation.

Despite his reputation as a confirmed rationalist, Godwin's own relation to sensibility is far from simple. Even the champion of reason in *Political Justice* was not above (perhaps inadvertently) casting Mary Wollstonecraft as a model of feminine sensibility in his *Memoirs of the Author of* A Vindication of the Rights of Woman (1798). Wollstonecraft's tragic and unforeseen death appears to have invited her friends to sentimentalize her as a suffering heroine. Hays's own obituary of her friend, which preceded publication of Godwin's *Memoirs,* uses the language of sensibility heavily, echoing Hays's epistolary efforts to construct herself as a heroine of sentimental tragedy. Likewise, Hays's obituary of Mary Wollstonecraft in *The Monthly Magazine and British Register for 1797* contains this description of Wollstonecraft as female philosopher and sensible feminist heroine:

> Quick to feel and indignant to resist the iron hand of despotism, whether civil or intellectual, her exertions to awaken in the minds of her oppressed sex a sense of their degradation, and to restore them to the dignity of reason and virtue, were active and incessant: by her impassioned reasoning and glowing eloquence, the fabric of voluptuous prejudice has been shaken to its foundations, and totters towards its fall: while her philosophic mind, taking a wider range, perceived and lamented in the defects of civil institutions, interwoven in their texture, and inseparable from them, the causes of those partial evils, destructive to virtue and happiness, which poison social intercourse and deform domestic life.[27]

Wollstonecraft's qualifications as a "philosophic mind" consist here of "impassioned reason" and quick feelings. In Hays's obituary of Mary Wollstonecraft in *The Annual Necrology for 1797–8,* she reiterates her assertion of sensibility's importance as a first cause for developing into a female philosopher: "persons of the finest and most exquisite genius have probably the greatest sensibility, consequently the strongest passions, by the fervor of which they are too often betrayed into error. . . . If by her quick feelings, prompt judgements, and rapid decisions, she was sometimes betrayed into false conclusions, her errors were expiated by sufferings, that, while they disarm severity, awaken sympathy and seize irresistibly upon the heart."[28] The language of the obituary follows Hays's argument that women develop reason out of an originary sensibility. This selection from the obituary says as much about Hays herself and her efforts to recontain and re-create her own self-presentation as it does about her dead friend and erstwhile critic. In fact, the language is remarkably similar to that of Hays's letters to Godwin and her novel.

Beginning with her own sufferings in her letters, fictionalizing and recontaining the meaning of her experience in *Emma Courtney,* and then moving to narrate other women's lives, this concern with public meaning of seemingly private, feminine domestic events remained a central concern for Mary Hays throughout her written work. Hays would go on in the first decade of the nineteenth century to write a six volume *Female Biography* (1803), noting for what ideas and actions these numerous women ought to be admired and remembered, hence continuing her project of teaching women to read rightly.[29] Here, in the *Annual Necrology* obituary, Hays takes Godwin's writing not only as a model (as Watson has noted), but as material for her own efforts to build the idea of a "feminine philosopher." Unlike the rational male model, the female philosopher works with the materials at hand—her life, her feelings, her body—and is thus sensitive to change, but also susceptible to error. Hays's female philosopher is a working model, not an ideal and fixed star as are many of the heroines and heroes of sentimental and English Jacobin literature.[30] Mary Hays preferred, instead, the "unhappy friend" of her 11 January 1796 letter to Godwin, imagining Mary Wollstonecraft as a "subject-in-process" rather than a paragon of either radical sensibility or pure cold reason. Her heroine, Emma, likewise struggles to become a female philosopher.

Hays's writings—fictional, political, philosophical, and personal—all work to construct a mode of female subjectivity in language. Superficially similar to Samuel Richardson's heroines (her early letters to Eccles contain displays of eyes rolled up to heaven, speechlessness, hysterical tears, and debilitating illness, while her later letters insist with some regularity that the "fatal blow has been struck" and anticipate an early death), Hays's feminine subject represents an extension and further elucidation of mid-century feminine sensibility. Hays avoids Wollstonecraft's dilemma in *A Vindication of the Rights of Men* (privileging reason as the only mode of full agency and thus denying the sole mode in which feminine subjectivity is recognized, sensibility, while paradoxically using it) by refusing to dismiss sensibility ever.

Hays conceived of an epistolary novel as particularly accessible to her effort to translate her experience into narrative. Linked explicitly with sensibility by some critics, letters are a discursive form which encourages and demands excessive and expanding discursivity, either in the form of letters in response, or, as is the case with Emma's and Mary Hays's later letters, in the form of ever more demanding letters of self-display and self-creation (c.f. Watson). Letters demand more letters, reworking and reiterating in an effort to clarify and fix meaning for reader and writer. Epistolary novels, then, are a hybrid literary form, particularly available for women writers as a less culturally valued genre (versus formal poetry, for instance), and especially one which explicitly explores the act of constructing a self. Hays replied to Godwin's encouragement in her efforts to turn her failed love affair into a novel thus:

> Accept also my acknowledgements for the encouragement you have given me to prosecute my projected work. . . . The epistolary form I conceived the most adapted to my style and habits of composition, but I could not please myself—fictitious correspondence affords me not the stimulus which I ever feel when addressing my friends. Should I ever . . . proceed I could wish to produce a work that should do me some credit, that should be written under your auspices, and that you should conceive not unworthy of being publically addressed to you.[31]

Again, there is a reference to the power of human connection and the authenticity of personal experience; her letters to real people are more stimulating than fictional letters. Hays was ultimately, of course, to include excerpted portions of her letters to Godwin and Frend in her novel, hence adding the stimulus she claims to lack here. This inclusion also blurs the generic boundary between fiction and biography both intentionally and strategically.

Hays's project in *Emma Courtney* is to use emotionally compelling fiction and personalized narrative to refigure philosophy, claiming the power of revolutionary discourse for women, and linking women's experience with philosophical knowledge. This connects Hays's work to 1970s' "cultural," "radical" and/or "difference" feminist emphasis on women's shared experiences of oppression. "In defending her novel," Gary Kelly notes that "Hays connects feminist politics and aesthetics by implying that women may not be disabled from sublime experience by 'retirement' in domestic life, but rather empowered subjectively and thus artistically."[32] Hays, then, is in part arguing that women bear special knowledge and that that knowledge is a valuable addition to rational philosophy. This argument surfaces explicitly in *Emma Courtney* when Emma attempts to explain her position to Augustus Harley:

Of what then, you may ask, do I complain—Not of the laws
of nature! But when mind has given dignity to natural affections; when reason, culture, taste, and delicacy, have combined to chasten, to refine, to exalt, (shall I say) to sanctify
them—Is there, then, no cause to complain of rigor and
severity, that such minds must either passively submit to a
vile traffic, or be content to relinquish all the endearing
sympathies of life? Nature has formed woman peculiarly
susceptible of the tender affections. "The voice of nature is
too strong to be silenced by artificial precepts." To feel these
affections in a supreme degree, a mind enriched by literature and expanded by fancy and reflection, is necessary—for
it is intellect and imagination only, that can give energy and
interest. . . . I wish we were in the vehicular state, and that
you understood the sentient language; you might then com-
prehend the whole of what I mean to express but find too
delicate for *words*.[33]

Emma argues that she is not challenging the laws of nature, hence
the laws of sexual difference, but rather that in declaring her love and
in loving where both feeling and reason concur, she is, in fact, following natural law. Augustus Harley, rather, is the one who violates both
reason and sensibility by his reticence which, she presumes, comes
from a concern for social propriety and "artificial precepts." He is the
one, in a word, who is artfully concealing his feelings and desires, not
she, reversing the common eighteenth-century accusation of feminine
artfulness from the heroine onto him. Instead of Wollstonecraft's
critique of a certain effeminacy in both women and men in favor of a
dissenting model of manliness,[34] Hays celebrates sensibility as an
active site of female virtue and casts Harley's refusal to respond as
neither sensible nor natural.

The passage, then, depends upon essentialist ideas about femininity (special access to feelings, closeness to nature) in order to argue
against the prevailing social idea of feminine nature as "delicate."
Here, feminine nature is truly delicate when it insists upon speaking
internal truth rather than covering such truth with artful and false
modesty. Rather than being indelicate in declaring her feelings, Emma
argues that she is displaying true delicacy—such delicacy in fact, that
human language is incapable of carrying her true meaning, but tends
to leave itself open to grosser interpretation. Echoing the language of
sensibility, she wishes they were in the "vehicular state" in which souls
leave the body and communicate through direct association of ideas.

Similarly, Hays writes to Godwin in her second letter after reading *Political Justice* that:

> Strong passions, or a capacity of receiving lively impressions are said to accompany strong mental powers. We may thank for almost every stable principle (says an admirable writer) the force of our passions, permitted to overleap the boundaries of content. It was happily observed, by a deceased and respected friend of mine, that the rock must be *convulsed* ere it produced the diamond. Symptoms of such convulsions I think I can trace even in the calm philosophical principles of the author of political justice![35]

Hays here flatters Godwin as the "philosopher" who wrote *Political Justice,* while at the same time insisting that his ideas of rational control and happiness miss the importance of passion's force, referring to a dead authority as her support.[36] She further notes that Godwin's work is itself not free of the "convulsions" of passion. This strategy of argument by analogy and citation (typical of philosophical writing, including Godwin's), and of flattery masking a strong critique is common in her letters to Godwin, and forces us to reconsider *Emma Courtney.* This novel is more than a polemic against uncontrolled passion in favor of reason as some critics have claimed. Gary Kelly has argued that *Emma Courtney,* though "not as political as Godwin's *Things as They Are,* Holcroft's *Anna St. Ives* (1792), or Wollstonecraft's *The Wrongs of Woman,*" is "like them, a 'philosophical romance,' or fictionalization of 'philosophy'—the rationalist social and political criticism held . . . to be responsible for the Revolution" (*Women, Writing* 95). I suggest that further, Hays's novel is a subtly different sort of political and philosophical argument, aimed at correcting and compensating for an elision of feminine experience in Godwin's own revolutionary philosophy.

In her second letter to Godwin, Hays calls on him to act as her mentor. She demands that he criticize and correct her ideas honestly and baldly, without softening his opinions:

> From you I shall expect truth, truth, which by sexual prejudices, voluptuous and impertinent precautions, has hitherto been prevented, like the winds of heav'n, from visiting us too roughly! "I have been in the habit of flattering women, (says Mr. H. Tooke on his trial) but I will not flatter men!". . . "Opinion (is declared by Rousseau) to be their [women's]

throne, but the grave of men." All the indignation, the honest scorn which a Necessarian may be allow'd to feel, these insulting paradoxes have received in my mind. I own myself weak—frequently very weak—but I trace it to a different source. Let not those who, with barbarous usurpation, have endeavored by brute force to monopolize the chief good—knowledge—aggravate injustice by contempt: Or let them recollect, to humble a pride so mean, how long the boasted reason of man has been held in subjection by the wiles of the interested and the tyranny of prejudice and prescription![37]

This letter attributes the power and insight of a philosopher to Godwin, but then it goes further. Hays also critiques Godwin's radical compatriots (Horne Tooke) and his philosophical antecedents (Jean-Jacques Rousseau). She suggests that men, even well-intentioned politically radical men, have monopolized knowledge and reason in the same way as kings, aristocrats, and slave-holders have oppressed other men. Hays takes back the position of the unjustly oppressed from the male victims of the treason trials and situates women as doubly oppressed, by their radical brethren as well as by Kings, laws, and husbands. This paints male philosophical reason as inherently limited and itself blinded by prejudice which it fails to recognize. Finally, her critique places pressure on Godwin to become the *kind* of mentor that she requires him to be and to recognize the limits of his own reasoning powers. Six months later, another letter extends her critique of reason's limitations:

> Philosophy, it is said, should regulate the feelings, but it has added fervor to mine—What are passions, but another name for powers? The mind susceptible of improvement, from whatever causes, either moral or physical, is the mind having capabilities of receiving forcible impressions; such minds . . . are prone to enthusiasms.[38]

Hays here links minds which are "susceptible" to philosophy with feminine sensibility. Her novel repeats and develops this idea further, repeating her letter nearly word for word, but situating it as a fictional letter from the heroine, Emma, to her mentor, Mr. Francis:

> Philosophy, it is said, should regulate the feelings, but it has added fervor to mine! What are passions, but another name for powers? The mind capable of receiving the most forcible

impressions is the sublimely improvable mind! Yet, into whatever trains such minds are accidentally directed, they are
prone to enthusiasm, while the vulgar stupidly wonder at the
effects of powers, to them wholly inconceivable: the weak and
timid, easily discouraged, are induced, by the first failure, to
relinquish their pursuits. . . . But the bold and the persevering, from repeated disappointment, derive only new ardor
and activity. (*EC* 86)

From correspondence to fiction, Hays consistently argues that
those minds which are most susceptible to the errors of sensibility are
also those most likely to become philosophers. In fact, this is also the
purport of her obituary of Wollstonecraft in the *Annual Necrology;*
this makes Hays more than merely a mouthpiece for Godwin's own
forthcoming *Memoirs,* as some critics have suggested. The implication in this passage from *Emma Courtney* is that female minds contain
both propensities, and are particularly worthy of reclaiming. Rewriting her letter to Godwin as a fictional letter to Mr. Francis, however,
allows her to place these sentiments in the mouth of Emma Courtney.
She thereby distances herself as author from the enthusiasms of her
character, and moves from a notion of writing direct and unmediated
experience to a more carefully mediated and politicized version of
that initial experience. In addition, the characters of Mr. Francis and
Augustus Harley give the author-Hays a fictional mode in which to
contain and represent both William Godwin and William Frend, turning the tables of public representation on them.

Emma Courtney serves, then, as a mode of philosophical control
for the raw material of sensibility, precisely echoing Hays's model of
sensibility as a first response which through the mediation of rational
reflection develops into true philosophy. Hays rewrites her life experience and her relations to her mentor and her beloved into a site for her
own self-creation as philosopher. Her first novel enacts the conjunction
of sensibility and rational control as philosophical exploration through
the conscious recontainment of narrative form.

Even in her most self-effacing anxiety about her claims to be a
"philosopher," Hays holds to her claim of privileged emotional knowledge. Her complaints about her inability to achieve her own intellectual standards of reasoning function doubly; both to make her claim
to be a "philosopher" less threatening and at the same time to use her
passionate desire to mark her as a true philosopher struggling against
an unjust oppression based upon sex. This kind of double linguistic
and narrative strategy takes into account sympathy's emotional claims

to knowledge and active virtue, while also allowing her to claim modestly that she waits for Godwin's instruction as to why this project should be abandoned. Hays, then, imagines a specifically feminine philosophy, composed of reason (associated with a male principle) and sensibility (imagined as a female principle) working together. Not only does she accuse her male mentors, from her early lover-mentor, John Eccles, to her later mentor, William Godwin, of being too "abstract," but she suggests that exquisite sensibility is not only a liability, but a gift, and a gift more commonly found in women. Her heroine, Emma Courtney, argues that "[n]ature has formed women peculiarly suscep-tible of the tender affections. . . . To feel these affections in a supreme degree, a mind enriched by literature and expanded by fancy and reflection is necessary, for it is intellect and imagination only that can give energy and interest" (*EC* 85). Similarly, Hays herself explains to Godwin: "do you not perceive that my reason was the auxiliary of my passion—or rather, my passion the generative principle of my reason? Had not these contradictions, these oppositions roused my mind into energy, I might have continued tamely domesticating in the lap of indolence and apathy."[39] By contrast, in her two *Vindications,* Mary Wollstonecraft refuses to imagine women as essentially different, and so waivers on the brink of dismissing women as active agents alto-gether. Rather, Wollstonecraft urges men to develop into proper citi-zens who will lead women from error into appropriate citizenship.

Despite the gendered essentialism of her statements, then, what Hays achieves is to represent female philosophy as the true philoso-phy, of which male philosophy is the incomplete echo. Further, she makes the gendered basis of general, universal claims of political philosophy visible. Sensibility of the sort Hays employs is located not just in the body or the inner psychical self, but is rewritten, reworked, and reiterated through different forms of writing, acting as a sort of "situated knowledge"[40] which circulates among women as each other's writers and readers. Her letters do not claim that her own misery is true for all women, but that it is true for her; at the same time, she claims that her own unhappiness and frustration are linked to a condition shared by women generally. Hays's letters and essays argue that women share training in useless and mentally unchallenging work, limited education with an overdetermined emphasis on feeling and sensibility as the only challenging mental arena open to them, and that all female knowledge takes on a sexual character because women's education has been in service of supporting a male monopoly on intellectual work and rationality. It is in her recognition that sensi-bility represents an arena of specifically feminine intellectual power that she differs most overtly from the Mary Wollstonecraft who wrote *A Vindication of the Rights of Men* and *A Vindication of the Rights of Woman.* While Wollstonecraft appears to be alive to the dangers of essentialism for women, and hence cautious about this sort of move, Hays uses an essentialist move to create a feminine space.

Sensibility in its political form functions finally as a strategy for evading the isolation of a purely individual self. As autonomous individuality becomes the model for the psychological and political subject (and a masculine model at that), the sensible subject troubles both the coherent isolation and the proud masculinity of that subject.[41] While the association of femininity with sensibility has been used historically to contain female desire and autonomy, it has also created a cultural space for female writing and marked instabilities in the dominant institutions of gender and gendered subjectivity.

Despite its tendency to solipsistic isolation, sensibility may also serve as a powerful counter to the limitations of a mechanistic or skeptical model of human psychology. Chris Jones points out the radical implications of the late eighteenth-century version of sensibility, which he argues has been effectively lost due to the success of the Anti-Jacobin movement in defining their enemies as uncontrollably sensible and passionate, noting that "[t]hey especially attacked the efforts of feminists to claim rights based equally on reason and feeling" (ix). As Syndy Conger argues further, "[s]ensibility as a metaphor has its own limitations, but at the same time, it eases many limitations present in the Lockean mind-as-entity model. . . . The mind of sensibility frequently vibrates as a result of experiences, rather than breaks; it not only succumbs to experience, it grows as a result of it" (*Mary Wollstonecraft,* xxviii–xxxix). If sensibility contains a progressive political thrust, it is in the potential which it holds for linking personal experience to systemic analysis. Despite the dangers of self-indulgent and patronizing modes of sensibility, mediated sensibility offers the possibility of shared ground for political and social action. This is central to the later project of twentieth-century feminisms, both theoretical and activist. From the limitations of identity politics' assumption of experience as unproblematically immediate, to post-structuralism's suspicion towards the individual agent, returning to earlier theories of sensibility seems a promising first step towards exploring this early refusal to dissociate the private from the public.

Mary Hays records her own misfortunes as a profoundly alienating and personal story in her letters, both the leather-bound collection of letters later published as *Love Letters of Mary Hays* and the still largely unpublished collection written to Godwin between October

1794 and June of 1796 (in the Pforzheimer Collection). Her attempts through her first novel to link this story with the stories of others, and to use her own emotions for political and philosophical analysis, is an effort to overcome the painfully isolating experience of private emotion. Within the novel, Emma tells her adopted son, Augustus, the tragic story of her frustrated desire for his father, in an attempt to make her own personal story take on social significance. Emma opens her tale with an invocation of the emotional power of shared experience as a basis for philosophical learning:

> The victim of my own ardent passions, and the errors of one whose memory will ever be dear to me, I prepare to withdraw the veil—a veil, spread by an importunate, but, I fear, a mistaken tenderness. Learn, then, from the incidents of my life, entangled with those of his to whom you owe your existence, a more striking and affecting lesson than abstract philosophy can ever afford. (*EC* 9)

While "abstract philosophy" may enable the analysis, Emma is confident that the personal emotional pain she reveals will make the lesson more affecting and thus more effective.

Through fiction and self-fictionalization Hays was able to recognize her personal experience and feelings as socially significant. The public reactions which she provoked, ranging from fictional representations as "Bridgetina Botherim"[42] and public accusations that she had improperly offered herself to her poet-friend, Charles Lloyd, in the manner of Emma Courtney,[43] suggest that the culturally hegemonic response to the threat which her work's conjunction of emotion and politics represented was to return her story to the private idiosyncrasies of one woman, and a scandalous one at that. Like Wollstonecraft's life story as recounted in the *Anti-Jacobin Magazine's* review of Godwin's *Memoirs,*[44] Hays's history is isolated first as merely personal, and second as dangerous to imitate, thus containing its revolutionary threat. The reductive public conflation of fiction and biography, using each to discredit the other and then isolating each genre, represents a conservative recognition of the power implicit in connecting personal and public, and an effort to contain that connection by representing both as improper. The connection itself, in fact, becomes an improper one, invoked to this day against feminist political work, and sometimes leading to the dismissive charge of "essentialism" rather than a more thoughtful engagement with the strategic structures of argumentation in some feminist writing. Ultimately, what

Hays portrays as her own private tragedy and then translates into fiction has social and political significance. This is an emergent valuation of women's feeling which may represent a particular "structure of feeling" within the "structure of feeling" I have identified as "Jacobin." As Williams explains:

> There is frequent tension between the received interpretation and practical experience. Where this tension can be made direct and explicit, or where some alternative interpretation is available, we are still within a dimension of relatively fixed forms. But the tension is as often an unease, a stress, a displacement, a latency: the moment of conscious comparison not yet come, often not even coming. (*Marxism* 130)

Thus, Mary Hays's ambivalent wavering in her letters and *Emma Courtney* between the competing powers of sensibility and reason, and between her reverence for masculine philosophy and her allegiance to the female heart, marks the unspeakable tension she experiences in her allegiance to Godwinian politics. Her novel's "tendency" to celebrate the very sensibility it was ostensibly written to critique reveals an unresolved tension between her allegiances to emotional experience and to rational analysis. This tension was resolved and simplified within dominant ideology as the danger of female sensibility and impropriety. It remains as an unnamed unease in this neglected novel.

Moreover, Hays's emergent argument for feminine sensibility within "philosophy," although tentative and inconsistent, prefigures a continuing critical dilemma within feminist thought. Her concern with sensibility at the precise historical moment when it becomes most politically suspect may be understood as feminist strategy of literary resistance within an increasingly constrained and gendered social context. Hays's work ultimately suggests that what we understand as 'reason' is formed by experience and personal history, and hence is informed at its root by feeling. In this she implies that feeling as personal is not opposed to history as abstract and impersonal, but that feeling is *part* of developing historical location and knowledge.

What is particularly intriguing about Hays's writing in light of later feminist developments is that what Hays is really theorizing as the root of her own development as philosopher is something akin to "consciousness raising" as it was practised in the 1970s. It is her passionate feelings and her immediate sense of the authenticity of her experiences which leads her to search for a more abstract way to understand them, in history and in political philosophy. In a clearly pedagogical model of self-discovery, the (female) mind is first stimulated by the personal experience, and is then motivated by the intensity of that original feeling to search for the analytical tools necessary to draw more general claims. It is this move to investigate experience as a valuable site for knowledge without necessarily insisting that experience is simply transparent and unmediated that makes much modern feminism so resilient (despite trendy claims of "post-feminism"). It is feminism's demand that one investigate what one "knows" which continues to make feminism a rich and complex system of analysis at the end of the twentieth century. Reading Hays and Wollstonecraft against each other not only reveals the richness of this early interaction but also may help us to understand the continuing debates within feminism over the role of the body, feminine desire, and the call to rational individualism.

Mary Wollstonecraft's attempt in the *Vindications* to claim manly rationality for women contrasts with Hays's sustained refusal to relinquish women's special claim to sensibility's potential power. However, the essentialism which Hays uses here cuts both ways. At this root of Western anglophonic feminism we find an earlier version of the debate between claiming political agency as individual rational subjects and valuing the specificity of women's difference (in some incarnations named as "liberal feminism" and "cultural feminism" respectively).[45] Wollstonecraft arguably preceded Simone de Beauvoir in naming women as trapped by biological function into immanent location as both site of desire and arbiter of the passions. Hays refused to relinquish women's claim to desire, but in so doing reified many of the historicocultural assumptions about "women's nature" in her own purely positive version. This problematic dynamic is still with us. As Donna Haraway notes in "Gender for a Marxist Dictionary," approaches which have tried to validate the specifically "feminine" (French Feminism, lesbian separatism, cultural feminism, radical feminism, etc.) have often risked cooptation and oversimplification by anti-feminists, while approaches which tried to evade the "natural" female body (liberal feminism, existentialism, socialism, and some followers of Foucauldian cultural studies or queer theory performativity) have risked collapsing feminine and feminist agency into other causes.[46] The battle over Wollstonecraft's importance, as either the forerunner of Beauvoir's call for women to subordinate the female body to the transcendent female subject or as the impassioned representative of maternal knowledge, indicates the danger of binary formations for feminism. Feminists in the first years of the twenty-first century cannot afford either to relinquish the hard-won rights which pragmatic, empirically grounded feminisms have spearheaded, nor to ignore the warnings about the limitations of political subjectivity grounded in western reification of the individual self.

Both Wollstonecraft and Hays were, in their own ways, believers in individual experience as a site for knowledge and rights, and yet both were also canny crafters of experience and self through literary rhetoric. The work of both, then, claims at once that women's experiences, while multiple, are distinctly different from those of the seemingly universal "man" whose rights were under debate in the last decade of the 1700s, and that those experiences can only take on communal and collaborative meaning through narrative shaping. Hays's particularly inventive approach to recreating and reimagining her own lived experience gestures toward a more nuanced approach to politicizing the personal than some of the initial twentieth-century feminist approaches to consciousness raising and identity politics. Even if the "personal is political" as the lives of these early feminist foremothers show, the personal is itself open to construction. It is in our best interest, as *Emma Courtney* reveals, for us to tell our own stories to our own ends while continuing to be self-critical about those ends. Hays's vindication of sensibility deserves further examination as a limited but engaged strategy for claiming and creating feminine subjectivity and agency. We cannot yet afford to dispense with the fictions we tell each other about our corporeal, psychological, and material lives.

Notes

1. The term "Jacobin" to designate these writers has some currency, and I will use it throughout this essay, although it is in some senses a serious misnomer. The so-called English Jacobins were so named by their political antagonists in the short-lived *Anti-Jacobin* and the subsequent *Anti-Jacobin Review and Magazine*. In fact, the English supporters of the French Revolution and of English political reform were more nearly aligned politically and personally with the Girondins. Mary Wollstonecraft, among others, attempted to clarify the differences among the various shifting interest groups of French revolutionaries, but was largely unsuccessful in combating the nationalist myopia which set in in England after 1792 when public opinion was increasingly unsympathetic to the Revolution. Retaining the term Jacobin participates in that historical blindness, and problematically lumps all who fought for political reform with the Montagnards or Jacobins, who, in fact, persecuted and put to death many of the Girondin leaders whom the

English Jacobins actually supported in both thought and action. Thomas Paine, Mary Wollstonecraft, and Helen Maria Williams were all endangered at various times by precisely the faction in France with which conservative English political scandal linked them.

2. See Thomas Holcroft's *A Narrative of Facts, Relating to a Prosecution for High Treason* (London: H. D. Symonds, 1795), for an account of his experience during the treason trials and his proposed, though never delivered, defense. See also Richard Polwhele's infamous *The Unsex'd Females* (London, 1798), for the claim of gendered misbehavior and for an account of Wollstonecraft as "amazon."

3. Gina Luria, introduction to *Letters and Essays, Moral and Miscellaneous,* by Mary Hays (1793, reprint New York: Garland Press, 1974) 8; hereafter *Letters.*

4. In particular, I am thinking here of the critical argument over the meaning of the French Revolution represented by François Furet's revision of the previously dominant Marxist line represented by Georges Lefebvre and Albert Saboul. For a succinct discussion of this debate, see Ferenc Fehér's introduction to *The French Revolution and the Birth of Modernity* (Berkeley: University of California Press, 1990).

5. David Simpson, *Romanticism, Nationalism, and the Revolt Against Theory* (Chicago: University of Chicago Press, 1993).

6. See for example, Toril Moi's *Sexual/Textual Politics* (New York: Methuen, 1985) and Domna Stanton, "The Franco-American Disconnect" in *The Future of Difference,* eds. Hester Eisenstein and Alice Jardine (New Brunswick, N.J.: Rutgers University Press, 1987).

7. See Raymond Williams, "Structures of Feeling," *Marxism and Literature* (Oxford: Oxford University Press, 1977), 128-135.

8. See for example, Gary Kelly, *The English Jacobin Novel 1780–1805* (Oxford: Oxford University Press, 1976),16.

9. As G. J. Barker-Benfield points out, at the time it was published, *A Vindication of the Rights of Woman* (1792) was largely favorably received (*The Culture of Sensibility: Sex and Society in Eighteenth-Century Britain* [Chicago: University of Chicago Press, 1992], 364).

10. See, for example, Mary Hays to William Godwin, MH 11, 11 January 1796, in the Carl H. Pforzheimer Collection of Shelley and His Circle, The New York Public Library, Astor, Lenox and Tilden Foundation (hereafter Pforzheimer Collection). I am grateful to the Carl H. Pforzheimer Collection for permission to quote from Mary Hays's personal letters.

For "abstract," Hays's meaning seems to have been close to the notion of "universal," as for instance philosophical and political writers thought of "man" as a universal ideal applicable to all political subjects, rather than recognizing their conception of "man" as a Western European, middle-class, raced and gendered construction.

11. Mary Hays to William Godwin, MH 13, 9 February 1796, MS Pforzheimer Collection.

12. See Markman Ellis, *The Politics of Sensibility: Race, Gender and Commerce in the Sentimental Novel* (Cambridge: Cambridge University Press, 1996); Mitzi Meyers, "Pedagogy as Self-Expression in Mary Wollstonecraft: Exorcising the Past, Finding a Voice," in *The Private Self: Theory and Practice of Women's Autobiographical Writings,* ed. Shari Benstock (Chapel Hill: University of North Carolina Press, 1988); Claudia Johnson, *Equivocal Beings: Politics, Gender and Sentimentality in the 1790s, Wollstonecraft, Radcliffe, Burney, Austen* (Chicago: University of Chicago Press, 1995); Nicola Watson, *Revolution and the Form of the British Novel, 1790–1825: Intercepted Letters, Interrupted Seductions* (Oxford: Clarendon, 1994); Chris Jones, *Radical Sensibility: Literature and Ideas in the 1790s* (New York: Routledge, 1993).

13. Marilyn Butler, *Jane Austen and the War of Ideas* (Oxford: Clarendon, 1975), 44.

14. Samuel Taylor Coleridge to Robert Southey, 25 January 1800, in *Letters of Samuel Taylor Coleridge,* ed. E. H. Coleridge (Boston 1895), 323.

15. Vivien Jones argues that the "conjunction of (feminine) novel paradigms with (masculine) history in both *Letters from France* [Helen Maria Williams] and *Historical and Moral View* [Mary Wollstonecraft]" articulated a growing ability for women writers under the pressure of the revolutionary moment to challenge paradigms of feminine propriety, generic decorum, and national political ideology, thus linking generic experiment with early feminism (Vivien Jones, "Women Writing Revolution: Narratives of History and Sexuality in Wollstonecraft and Williams," in *Beyond Romanticism: New Approaches to Texts and Contexts 1780–1832,* ed. Stephen Copley and John Whale [New York: Routledge, 1992], 179–180).

16. Mary Wollstonecraft defended her friend's novel to Mr. Barbauld, writing to Hays that she was perceived as an atheistical "philosophess" (Mary Wollstonecraft to Mary Hays, MW 44, no date, MS Pforzheimer Collection). Thomas Holcroft also wrote to Mary Hays to apologize for critical statements he made about her book which he had apparently not read (Thomas Holcroft to Mary Hays, (TH) MSC 2206, 20 September 1791, and TH 2207, 26 September 1797, MS Pforzheimer Collection).

17. For example, Jane Spencer's account of *Emma Courtney*'s initial reception takes critics of Hays's novel to task for "ma[king] the novel and its author bywords for immorality, despite Hays's careful claim that her heroine's story was meant 'as a *warning,* rather than as an example'" (*The Rise of the Woman Novelist: From Aphra Behn to Jane Austen* [New York: Blackwell,

1986], 130). Nicola Watson, by contrast, notes the novel's perverse tendency to support the very contention which it claims to be written against (*Revolution*, 46).

18. The original manuscripts of many letters are located in the Pforzheimer Collection of the New York Public Library. Some of the same letters, as well as many earlier ones, are published in *The Love Letters of Mary Hays (1779–1780)*, ed. A. F. Wedd (London: Methuen, 1925); hereafter *Love Letters*.

19. Frend is generally supposed to be the unnamed object of an unrequited passion about which she writes to Godwin; see Wedd, introduction to *Love Letters*, 1–14.

20. Mary Hays to William Godwin, MH 12, 6 February 1796, MS Pforzheimer Collection.

21. Hays's first published piece of writing was a letter on the efficacy of public worship in the dissenting tradition, written under the pen-name "Eusebia" (for accounts, see Luria, *Letters*, and Wedd, *Love Letters*). It was this letter which brought her to the attention of William Frend, the Cambridge Dissenter and later object of her affection, who first recommended Godwin's *Political Justice* to her. For Hays, entry into the public realm of writing was entry into a social circle as well.

22. Mary Wollstonecraft, *A Vindication of the Rights of Men with A Vindication of the Rights of Woman and Hints*, ed. Sylvana Tomaselli (Cambridge: Cambridge University Press, 1995), 283–4.

23. Folger Collective on Early Women Critics, *Women Critics 1660–1820: An Anthology*, Bloomington: Indiana University Press, 1995, 298–9. Wollstonecraft, by contrast, states explicitly, "When Richardson made Clarissa tell Lovelace that he had robbed her of her honour, he must have had strange notions of honour and virtue. For, miserable beyond all names of misery is the condition of a being, who could be degraded without its own consent!" (*Rights of Woman*, 149–50). Interestingly, Hays will return to precisely this problem in her second novel, *The Victim of Prejudice* (1799), both to support Wollstonecraft's claim and to reveal the pessimism which the social and political position of women calls up at the turn of the century.

24. Mary Hays to William Godwin, MH 1, 14 October 1794, MS Pforzheimer Collection. See also Wedd, *Love Letters*, 228.

25. Mary Hays to William Godwin, MH 11, 11 January 1796, MS Pforzheimer Collection.

26. Mary Hays to William Godwin, MH 8, 13 October 1795, MS Pforzheimer Collection.

27. Mary Hays, untitled obituary of Mary Wollstonecraft in the *Monthly Magazine and British Register for 1797*, July-Dec. Vol. IV. (1798), 232–3.

28. Mary Hays, "Memoirs of Mrs. Wollstonecraft," in the *Annual Necrology for 1797–8* (1800) 411–12.

29. In her introduction to that work, Hays restated her allegiance to sensibility and novelistic entertainment as the proper mode through which to instruct women readers (*Female Biography* (1803), iii–iv).

30. Such perfect heroes and heroines include Samuel Richardson's Clarissa, Harriet Byron, and Sir Charles Grandison, Thomas Holcroft's Anna St. Ives and Frank Henley, and Robert Bage's Hermsprong.

31. Mary Hays to William Godwin, MH 9, 20 November 1795, MS Pforzheimer Collection.

32. Gary Kelly, *Women, Writing and Revolution: 1790–1827* (Oxford: Clarendon, 1993), 95.

33. Mary Hays, *The Memoirs of Emma Courtney* (Oxford: Oxford University Press, 1996), 89; hereafter EC.

34. See Johnson, *Equivocal Beings.*

35. Mary Hays to William Godwin, MH 2, 7 December 1794, MS Pforzheimer Collection.

36. This source is identified as "My revered and deceased friend, Mr. Robinson of Cambridge" in Mary Hays, *Letters and Essays,* 88.

37. Mary Hays to William Godwin, MH 2, 7 December 1794, MS Pforzheimer Collection.

38. Mary Hays to William Godwin, MH 6, 28 July 1795 MS Pforzheimer Collection.

39. Mary Hays to William Godwin, MH 12, 6 February 1796, MS Pforzheimer Collection.

40. Donna Haraway, "Situated Knowledges: The Science Question in Feminism as a Site of Discourse on the Privilege of Partial Perspective," *Feminist Studies* 14.3 (1988): 575–599.

41. Syndy Conger, *Mary Wollstonecraft and the Language of Sensibility* (Cranberry, N.J.: Associated University Press, 1994), xviii.

42. See Elizabeth Hamilton, *Memoirs of Modern Philosophers* (London, 1801).

43. See Luria, *Letters,* and Wedd, *Love Letters,* for accounts.

44. The *Anti-Jacobin Review* responded thus: "We coincide with him [Godwin] in his opinion of the *utility* of a life of Mrs. W__; though for a very different reason . . . it manifests what it is wise to avoid. It illustrates both the sentiments and conduct resulting from such principles as those of Mrs.

W__ and Mr. G__. It also in some degree accounts for the formation of such visionary theories and pernicious doctrines . . . Her imagination and passions became her guides through life (*Anti-Jacobin Review and Magazine* 1 (July-Dec. 1798): 94).

45. See for example, Linda Alcoff's essay "Cultural Feminism Versus Poststructuralism: The Identity Crisis in Feminist Theory" in *Signs* 13.3 (Spring 1988): 405–436.

46. Donna Haraway, "Gender for a Marxist Dictionary," *Simians, Cyborgs, and Women: The Reinvention of Nature* (New York: Routledge, 1991): 127–48.

Indirect Dissent: "Landscaping" Female Agency in Amelia Alderson Opie's Poems of the 1790s

∽

Ann Frank Wake

Perhaps the only way for most late eighteenth-century British men and women to "experience" the French Revolution at all would have been through acts of sympathetic imagining. Ironically, Adam Smith had promoted an influential attitude of suspicion toward such efforts that would complicate already tenuous (British) literary responses to revolutionary events in France. Years earlier Smith had claimed that "the emotions of the spectator will still be very apt to fall short of the violence of what is felt by the sufferer." "Mankind," he wrote, "though naturally sympathetic, never conceive, for what has befallen another, that degree of passion which naturally animates the person principally concerned. That imaginary change of situation, upon which the sympathy is founded, is but momentary." "The thought of their own safety," he continued, "the thought that they themselves are not really the sufferers, continually intrudes itself upon them."[1] This view, of course, had consequences for well-intentioned authors who were distanced from actual scenes of revolutionary experience; in fact, the consequent gap in aesthetics between sufferer and imaginer would clearly challenge the legitimacy and authenticity of writing not based upon "real" experience. Steven Bruhm has argued that efforts to solve this obvious challenge to active, sympathetic imagining would change the very course of literary history, as the late eighteenth-century evolution of aesthetics is, in his words, "trying to find ways out of that [doubt regarding the legitimacy of sympathetic imagining] and to shore up the aesthetic of shared suffering." From these debates emerged a new "'aesthetic' definition of sympathy . . . the unified sympathetic body was invested with the power to close the

261

subject-object gap, and it heralded the migration from what we call the Enlightenment to what we call the Romantic" (*GB*, 16–17).

Amelia Alderson Opie, by coincidence of time, place, upbringing, interest, and talent, would become a significant, if overlooked, contributor to this developing "Romantic" aesthetic. She, too, would use physical landscapes to bridge the divides between real experience and imagined response to the "aesthetics of shared suffering" at the very heart of the Romantic movement. Several of Opie's poems written from 1792–95 provide a unique opportunity to explore how a woman with dissenting religious and political views responded to distinctly British social and political forces during the Terror. The tensions that emerged in the poetry would magnify the already tenuous terrains of gender roles, liberalism, patriotism, sensibility, and moral agency which typically labeled men as either "true" British citizens or seditious Jacobins, while either ignoring women or degrading them for political participation. Having no direct experience of the Revolution would set Opie at a further disadvantage compared to contemporaries such as Helen Maria Williams or Mary Wollstonecraft, both of whom wrote from first hand experience of events in France. Opie's poetic landscapes depict the metaphorical and formal dilemmas faced by someone very self-conscious of her female voice and the right to be political in her work.

Roxanne Eberle's examination of Opie's personal letters demonstrates her "commitment to radical politics" during the 1790s, and her enthusiastic participation in Jacobin politics and philosophy throughout the period.[2] Opie's poems show less enthusiasm for Jacobinism, however, than do her letters, and raise the question of why she hid or disguised her dissenting politics in the poetry. One clue may be found in a letter Opie, then Alderson, wrote to Susannah Taylor in 1794. Describing her sense of impending doom, "when *salut and fraternité* will be the watchwords for civil slaughter throughout Europe," she comments, "It will be an awful time; may I *meet it with fortitude!*" (Eberle 120 [italics mine]). Opie's conviction that she respond stoically to the violence at hand suggests why she might use indirect means to express her politics in the 1790s poetry. By 1808, when her poem "Lines on the Place de la Concorde at Paris" was published, Opie would overtly criticize France for "thy recorded cruelty."[3] During the Terror, however, events seemed frightfully ambiguous. Deborah Kennedy notes that in 1795, writing about the Revolution meant that writers found themselves "encumbered by what [Ann] Rigney describes as an anachronistic position, which in this case meant knowing how the Terror ended."[4] But not knowing also had its own price. If sites of the Terror could be interpreted in multiple ways by those actually in attendance, the ambiguity would seem magnified for those with indirect knowledge of events. Opie's poetic landscapes reflect the obliqueness and uncertainty of one who withholds judgment while events unfold, without knowing the end point; they also show that she meets, "with fortitude," the multiple, imagined sufferings of these landscapes.

Opie's landscapes also share important connections with many male visual artists who were pro-Revolution, foremost of which was a serious preoccupation with art as a means of exploring the very nature of sympathetic response to political events. Her path crossed with many visual artists; she had a love affair with Henry Fuseli, and she met the painter and radical Thomas Holcroft in 1794 during a trip to London that also introduced her to Horne Tooke, William Godwin, and Mary Wollstonecraft. She met and eventually married the portrait painter John Opie and, upon his death in 1807, contributed a memoir to his *Lectures on Painting* (published 1809).[5] In a poem she wrote to her husband, "To Mr. Opie, on his having painted for me the picture of Mrs. Twiss" (1799),[6] Opie depicts her heart as a landscape in which "pride and friendship" "war with equal strife" on a battlefield in which her own roles change—she first "exults" as her husband's "friend," then as "the wife." This poem not only suggests obvious connections between painter/painting, husband/wife, and poet/poetry, but also links the idea of "soul" with landscape more obviously than we see in earlier poems written in the same decade. Her increasing interest in visual aesthetics throughout the 1790s has been identified by Duncan Wu, who notes that Opie's poem "Ode to Borrowdale in Cumberland" particularly bears a connection to aesthetic theory and "recalls the landscape through the lens of someone well read in the works of the picturesque theorist William Gilpin."[7] If the untamed, picturesque landscapes in Opie's poetry may be understood to express souls in political disquietude, they also profit by comparison with strategies used by landscape painters sympathetic with her politics.

Of the visual artists most notorious for their sympathy with the French Revolution—Henry Fuseli, James Barry, George Romney or William Blake—David Bindman notes that while they were strongly influenced by the events of the Revolution, they did not refer directly to such events in their work. They covertly expressed a politics of dissent through their depictions of sublime natural scenes. Opie, Kennedy notes, developed landscapes that foregrounded already familiar connections between weather and politics.[8] If romantic landscapes on canvas attempted to metaphorically represent souls in torment or repose, Opie's poetry, too, "paints" a series of metaphorically expressed psychological responses to revolution and its impact in England and beyond. These projections, in turn, authenticate the woman poet's personal, feeling responses to sites of Revolution and Terror, using images which draw conscious attention to the very sites and acts of imagining. The imagery Opie used to depict the Revolution's influence without direct reference to events is similar to that of William Blake's mid-1790s visual art, with its "imagery of Bastille-like confinement . . . found everywhere," as Bindman describes it (69). In each of the four mid-1790s poems discussed in this essay, images of "Bastille-like confinement" choke the speaker, whether the "cloistered maid" who retires in "artificial gloom" in the poem "To Twilight," the forced memory of a "smiling scene" that soon becomes "sequestered" and solitary in "Ode to Borrowdale in Cumberland," the "wretched" lands of Europe in "Ode on the Present Times" faced with "War, who bids trembling Europe gasp, / With wild convulsions in his bloody grasp," or, finally, the speaker's bidding in "Stanzas Written Under Aeolus's Harp" to heal "ye whose hearts the tyrant sorrows wound."[9] In the absence of actual experience of the Terror, then, Opie imagined landscapes of suffering which, in turn, illuminate her search for agency on multiple levels, including those of the gendered, private body, the "feeling" body, the "body politic," and the national and global bodies/landscapes destroyed by "real" pain and suffering.

The popular use of landscapes to reflect political response in covert ways also would provide a useful strategy for Opie in her particular position in Norwich. Ironically, the liberal politics of religious Dissenters made visible resistance even more difficult for women within the fold, than outside of it. According to Chris Jones, "The relinquishing of patriarchal authority is too important to be ascribed to an extension of the religious tolerance demanded by Dissenters. Their claims for freedom of worship and equality of representation were accompanied by *an emphasis on the hierarchical relationships of the sexes and the family even stricter than the aristocratic norm.*"[10] Imagery that functions symbolically in the landscapes, then, provides a strategic outlet for indirect political response without exposing Opie to the ridicule or reprimand of her Dissenting father and his circle.

Political "Credentials"

Opie revealed her interest in, and commitment to, liberal politics through the extensive measures she took to involve herself in local and national political affairs. She maintained active involvement in the liberal antislavery movement throughout her life, often using her literary talents to provoke public opinion through such melodramatic poems as "The Negro Boy's Lament" (published 1802), which ultimately gave her widespread public recognition.[11] Opie's first biographer, Cecilia Lucy Brightwell, notes Opie's fascination with the English court system and the unusual fact that she often daily attended court in Norwich to observe cases, although she refused to attend trials for capital offenses. Opie wrote in the 1840s after her conversion to the Society of Friends, "Whatever be the cause of the pleasure I take in attending [court] on these occasions, I hope it is an innocent gratification . . . and it is my conviction, that whatever brings us acquainted with, and interested in, the affairs and well-being of our fellow creatures, in their varied stations and positions in society, may have a beneficial influence on our hearts, minds, and characters" (*Memoir,* 184). Opie reconfigured her earlier radicalism into a philosophy more compatible with the woman's role within the Society of Friends. As Mary Poovey has written of Mary Wollstonecraft, Jane Austen, and Mary Shelley, Opie showed interest in liberal politics her entire adult life, but did seem in middle age to consider herself in reformist rather than radical terms. To maintain her social dignity, Opie would utilize strategies that include "indirection, obliqueness, and doubling," which resulted when, according to Poovey, "women writers sought to express themselves while remaining respectable."[12] Both the Dissenting circle in Norwich and members of the Society of Friends would insist that women play supporting, rather than active, roles in political affairs—Opie even gave up writing poetry and fiction upon her religious conversion.

Opie's father, Dr. Alderson, Brightwell wrote, was "of the ultra-liberal party" so that his daughter's values "were naturally formed in accordance with them. She attended the famous trials of Horne Tooke, Holcroft, and others, for high treason, and wrote accounts of them to her father, full of passionate interest and zeal on behalf of the accused."[13] Significantly, Opie's publications of the 1790s were published primarily in Norwich's Dissenting periodical, *The Cabinet,* and Robert Southey's liberal *Annual Anthology.*[14] Opie's association with Dissenters would suggest a pro-Revolutionary poetry, in keeping with her father's influence, yet Opie's texts typically reflect, instead, a hierarchy of gender codes embedded within Norwich's religious Dissenting circle. Marlon Ross has explained that the "dissenters' unitarian concept of life," depends upon connections between *direct* experience and action, to suggest a "seamless thread [that] runs from practical experience through moral conduct to political action" so that "to cut that thread at any point would be to alter the character of all three spheres." Without direct experience of events, female religious Dissenters would find it difficult, if not impossible, to extend the "thread" of "moral conduct to political action" when they could not begin at the unitarian starting point of "practical experience." Using the example of Anna Letitia Barbauld when speaking on the education of young children, Ross finds that she is "in the same breath speaking politics" and that, for her, a "political lesson" would ultimately be to "link the morality of the state to the political responsibility of the individual citizen."[15] How would Opie participate in the discourse of Revolution within a paradigm dependent upon *direct* experience as it connects to morality and action? In depicting particular points of landscape on English or European soil, she would appear to substitute *imagined* experience as the means by which to draw upon the "seamless thread" begun by others that was so central to the dissenting religious view. Beginning with imaginative rather than lived acts, however, would again raise the question of credibility at a time when even acts of sympathetic response to actual events were considered inauthentic and, thus, suspect.

By diluting Opie's radical politics of the revolutionary period in the *Memoir,* Brightwell thought she did Opie a service; she was, in fact, preparing the groundwork for Opie's credible middle age "transformation" into a proper Quaker lady. This image radically contrasted with that of the young, Dissenting Unitarian who had idolized Charles Fox and Napoleon. From those days of "revolutionary ferment and unparalleled political excitement," Brightwell wrote of Opie's young adulthood:

> It is evident that a fellowship in political opinions was the only bond that united Miss Alderson to many of those with whom, at this time, she associated. Her good sense, and firm rectitude of moral principle, happily preserved her from the follies and errors into which not a few of those around her were led, by their extravagant zeal for a liberty that speedily degenerated into license; and although she might, sometimes, be betrayed by her native ardour into imprudence, her own standard of duty ever remained pure and high. (*Memoir,* 10)

Brightwell dutifully carved a "proper lady" one might expect to repent of her former "wicked" ways, although Opie herself later commented with nostalgia and enthusiasm rather than regret over her early politics. Opie relished visits she made with her father to London during the Terror in 1794 and 1795 and Brightwell notes that Opie was introduced to "many celebrated characters" on these trips. These included many French emigrants whom Brightwell describes as "the victims of the great Revolution" who were "men of high standing, and literary talent and repute." Opie much later described this scene in terms of a highly stratified, picturesque landscape—a *"wilderness* of pleasure, in which fruits and flowers disputed with *weeds."* The chief attraction was "intellectual intercourse" with a number of pro-revolutionary sympathizers, including Mrs. Barbauld, Godwin and Wollstonecraft (*Memoir,* 9–10). Some years later Opie would know Madame de Staël, General Lafayette, Sheridan, Southey and Byron.

Opie visited Paris three times; the first visit took place in 1802 with husband John Opie, and left a lasting impression on her life. Opie actually "beheld the great masterpieces of art then assembled at the Louvre by the victorious arms of Napoleon. She gazed with admiring eyes on that mighty conqueror himself, and conversed with her political idol, Charles James Fox" (*Memoir,* 13–14). To be a Foxite at that time was to be pro-revolutionary and anti-Pitt: according to Clive Emsley, reformers "branded Pitt as 'the English Robespierre.'"[16] Brightwell records that Opie returned to Paris in 1829 (then again in 1830–31) for the first time since 1802 when the Terror was still fresh in the minds of the British citizenry. She was by this time a member of the Society of Friends, but her comments on revisiting the sites of revolution reflect a paradoxical essence of historical landscapes; sites of tyranny can become sites of pleasure, and vice versa. Entertaining one minute, appalling the next, "real" landscapes intensify the dilemma for the poet confronted with imagined ravaged terrains that only Fancy might make beautiful. Opie wrote of her 1829 visit, "It was not without mixed emotions, in which, however, those of pleasure predominated, that I re-entered that France, which, in 1802, I had left a republic, but which, in 1829, was once more a monarchy, and under the government of the Bourbons." She commented that "while contemplating the Hôtel de Ville, as the frowning memorial of scenes of blood and horror, that I should, in the succeeding year, behold it with such different associations; that I should see the (comparatively) bloodless flag of the tricolour waving from its ancient roof, and that I should drive within its ponderous gates, and ascend its gloomy staircase" (*Memoir,* 78, 81). She would describe the Place de Grève, as "that spot so full of appalling recollections" that would "in future be sacred to the triumphs of constitutional freedom, and that the Hôtel de Ville would become the scene of entertainments given to Lafayette and the citizen-king."[17]

During the trip of 1829, she visited Lafayette's country residence, La Grange, noting that the general was "as usual, fresh, benevolent looking, and admirable in all ways." During the visit she notes that "The general gave us an account of the early events of the Revolution; the other gentlemen who were present, assisting." She writes of this extraordinary morning only that "the time passed only too quickly" and that she "sat up and read the memoirs of Segur; and with a curious feeling laid me down, knowing that I should see both him and Lafayette the next day" (*Memoir,* 82–83). Opie's awe in the presence of these men of history and power led her to "prepare" herself for the next day by reading the memoirs of Segur, who had been the Minister of the French Army in the mid 1780s and had resigned during the Dutch crisis in 1787, but had continued to work with Lafayette throughout the Revolution. Her radical years of pro-Revolutionary sympathy and admiration of the French Revolutionaries manifested themselves in middle age as hero-worship for men who had actually experienced the events that had so captured Opie's imagination in her young adulthood. These were the "sons of liberty" referenced in Opie's "Lines on the Place de la Concorde at Paris;" these were men who had conquered the "sons of anarchy" to bring a "smiling scene" to Paris once again. Their actions and their authenticity would challenge anyone, and Opie's self-conscious, giddy reaction contrasts with the poems written at the time the events actually took place. Opie would perhaps feel her own prior attempts to imagine these events as feeble and ineffectual in the presence of these "great" men, particularly given the gendered hierarchy she learned from her dissenting upbringing.

In the mid-1790s poems, Opie attempts to "translate" the dissenting context of liberal politics into everyday experience, using the landscapes to suggest a series of moral reactions to both revolutionary and non-revolutionary landscapes of pain, the latter the actual sites of most women's authentic experiences. She must abstract and imagine the pain of war, but she can particularize images of social chaos and personal terror. She literally creates this aesthetic of what Marlon Ross has called "double dissent," or what I describe here as a politically "indirect dissent," by defying expectations of both the political and religious Dissenters and the British status quo. Ross used the term "double dissent" to explain the impossible bind of the dissenting woman during the early Romantic period, in which "the only pure form of feminine action she can take in offering her (non)political support to the status quo is to be silent. The woman who desires to dissent, however, finds herself in an ironically fortuitous position, possessing a political voice without the drawback of belonging to the corrupt interests of established power. For her, to speak politics is automatically to assault the status quo." Thus her "primary dilemma" is "how to speak politics without being contaminated by the moral compromises which characterize mainstream politics" (*Configurations*, 92).

Women dissented by writing, and they dissented by taking nonconformist positions which translated into a "formal dilemma" for the female poet with regard to issues of genre and form. The dilemma of form becomes a means by which to authenticate the work through the deliberate choice to use conventional forms. If the dissenting woman poet's "politicized generic forms" are "notoriously conventional—requiring author and reader to identify already legitimated political discourses," then she may find in these forms ways to "unbalance the form's links to established power" given that she has "no formal authority within that structure." Her power, having been constructed within the Dissenting moral framework, she must serve by "regulat[ing] the moral temperament of a nation and by being 'instrumental to the good of others'" (*Configurations*, 92–93). The woman poet thus ultimately occupies the status of "double dissent"— "as a political female and as a female within a nonconforming community deprived of civil liberties."[18] Religious Dissenters in Opie's circle would expect a challenge to the status quo, but would not allow women to act on their moral responses. Non-Dissenters would expect nationalism and patriotism from an English "proper lady," but only through appropriate expressions of sensibility, rather than action. By acting/imagining on moral grounds in defiance of both sides, Opie takes a path of self-directed agency that seems, however, less to empower her writing than to exhaust its landscapes of the mind and body politic. The speakers in Opie's poems typically find themselves on oblique paths—paths of indirect dissent—that challenge through subtext rather than through overtly political critique. These landscapes can be beautiful and pleasurable one moment, and menacing and violent the next; they echo the paradoxical memory contained in actual sites of historical meaning, bloodshed and reverence.

Indirect Dissent, Fancy, and the Feminine

If all writers in the late eighteenth century were pressured by moral imperatives in an age of sensibility, the problem emerged as significantly less complicated for male writers who commanded, with confidence, the public voice by which to pursue moral political response.

While William Wordsworth and Edmund Burke no doubt wrestled with how one produces genuine *personal* (or in their view, feminine) response to a tragic scene, Meena Alexander reminds us that for Wordsworth, it was, ironically, this feminine principle which "granted sympathy" and secured "centrality for the poet."[19] The burden for women poets hinged upon producing a morally conscientious response in the reader that drew upon familiar forms to legitimate the female poet's authority, while even her legitimacy as a reader proved complex within this culture. Andrew Ashfield suggests that eighteenth-century canon formation led to an understanding of literature itself as "no longer the best vehicle for moral precepts," but rather as "the actual site of moral activity itself." The language used to describe intense emotional responses to literature frequently included the terms 'ravishment' and 'transport'; readers "were ravished into a more refined being and transported to the site of romance." Of woman as reader Ashfield asks several essential questions regarding her position within this ideological framework: "What would it mean for a woman to be 'ravished and transported' in the reading scene? What would it mean for a woman to recover mastery in the moment of the sublime" (*RWR*, xii, xvii)? As Opie drew upon conventional uses of Fancy and sensibility, the 1790s poems suggest that formally and ideologically she could not "have it both ways." Rather, she trudged through a complex terrain in which the female poet paradoxically assumes inappropriate power or agency over her readers simply by writing, while simultaneously being expected to demonstrate appropriate "feminine" sensibility in the text that she should not write. Joel Haefner describes this strategic maneuvering to find an outlet for self-expression as the effort to map out a "literary location" in order to "situate herself clearly for the reader."[20] But it would be the woman writer's understood relationship to Fancy, in particular, that would or would not generate the necessary space for authentic poetic voice, form, and feeling.

Julie Ellison has described ways in which the "always gendered" aesthetics of sensibility "cannot depend on simple gender dichotomies. It becomes a process, rather, of discerning how sensibility can become, under certain circumstances, an idiom of female ambition and citizenship, invested in national success, as well as a means of resistance."[21] It is through the implied inferiority of Fancy, then, that Opie would negotiate "indirect dissent." It was understood that compared to Imagination, Fancy—not coincidentally the medium associated with women poets—was considered the "inferior but therapeutic faculty" (Ellison, 228). Opie's struggle to position her speakers in "appropriate" relationships to the landscape suggests this mingling of confidence and eventual exhaustion as confidence in her (unsupported) agency wanes. Male writers such as Burke and Wordsworth, by contrast, could assume their right to appropriate the "superior" faculty—Imagination—when confidence wavered. In moments of greatest despair they managed to produce a public literature perceived as moral and that legitimized itself by conveying an essential authentic personal response to suffering. Wordsworth describes his recollection of the events of 1793–94 in Book X of *The Prelude,* finding "ghastly Visions" of "despair / And Tyranny, and implements of death" (10. 402–3)—the nightmares engendered by the Reign of Terror.[22] At nightmare's peak, "where the dust was laid with tears" (10. 408–10), the poet's voice restores visionary power which, if it cannot transcend the horror, creates poetic function rather than self-exhaustion: "Then suddenly the scene / Changed, and the unbroken dream entangled me / In long orations which I strove to plead / Before unjust tribunals" (10. 409–12). With a voice "Labouring, a brain confounded, and a sense / Death-like of treacherous desertion" in the *"last place of refuge, my own soul"* (10. 413–15 [italics mine]) we see the great poet's dilemma and his power, interfused, to transfix the scene and literally and needfully to talk his way out. Wordsworth follows this "sense" of "Death-like, of treacherous desertion" (10. 414) with a scene that returns us to his youth and the origins of prophetic calling, when he would first "yield [him]self to Nature, when that strong / And holy passion overcame me first" (10. 416–17). He identifies his prophetic role: "So did a portion of that spirit fall / On me uplifted from the vantage-ground / Of pity and sorrow . . ." (9. 448–450). Wordsworth has effectively "proven" and legitimated his authority: "Wild blasts of music thus could find their way / Into the midst of turbulent events; / So that worst tempests might be listened to" (10. 461–463).

Echoing Wordsworth's compelling need both to respond to, and to legitimate his response to, the Terror, Burke wrote to Lord Fitzwilliam in 1793 that he had "fallen into a state of the world, that will not suffer me to play at little sports, or to enfeeble the part I am bound to take, by smaller collateral considerations. I cannot proceed, as if things went on in the beaten circle of events, such as I have known them for half a century. The moral state of mankind fills me with dismay and horrors. The abyss of Hell itself seems to yawn before me. *I must act, think, and feel according to the exigencies of its tremendous reason.*"[23] Prior to this bold claim, Burke already had stood at the "abyss of Hell" and produced *Reflections on the Revolution in France* (published 1790). Writing to Dupont, the "very young gentleman in

Paris" referred to in the original extended title page, Burke began the
Reflections with a concern that he express appropriate humility over
the exercise: "I will not give you [Dupont] reason to imagine that I
think my sentiments of such value as to wish myself to be solicited
about them. They are of too little consequence to be very anxiously
either communicated or withheld. It was from attention to you, and to
you only, that I hesitated at the time when you first desired to receive
them . . . my errors, if any, are my own. My reputation alone is to
answer for them" (12). Although Burke set out to convince his audience that he wrote his opinions at Dupont's request, Dupont never
saw the *Reflections* until published and, according to Russell Kirk,
was "astounded by it" (4).

By inventing a solicitation for his public response to the Revolution, Burke had mapped out his literary location and justified why, by
1793, the "little sports" would no longer content him. Burke could
confidently claim his literary location in aggressive terms: he had previously written in *A Philosophical Enquiry into the Sublime and the
Beautiful* (1757), "I know of nothing sublime which is not some modi-
fication of power."[24] The "little sports" would be for others (women)—
for the sites distinct from Burke's identification with "tremendous
reason," which would become, for Opie, the very sites of female agency
and moral activity. Hers were landscapes in which politics and
psychodrama would self-consciously become linked. Opie would draw
attention to the imaginary features in her landscapes as a way to invest
her readers in the process of authenticating her response to indirect
experience. She would inspire a sympathetic reaction that would transcend boundaries of nationalism and patriotism, while enabling her to
critique flawed political landscapes characterized by oblique terrains
and paradoxical weather emblematic of a failed body politic.

"Landscaping" Female Agency

In the *Memoir,* Brightwell records a fragment written in Opie's
adulthood that describes a powerful early childhood recollection. The
passage both suggests the self-doubt that emerged when Opie
confronted sites of pain, and the corresponding need to authenticate
her experience through artistic self-expression. Opie writes,

> One of my earliest recollections is, of gazing on the bright
> blue sky, as I lay in my little bed, before my hour of rising
> came, and listening with delighted attention to the ringing of

a peal of bells. I had heard that heaven was beyond those blue skies, and I had been taught that there was the home of the good; and I fancied that those sweet bells were ringing in heaven. What a happy error! *Neither illusion nor reality, at any subsequent period of my life,* ever gave me such a sensation of pure, heartfelt delight, as I experienced, when, morning after morning, I looked on that blue sky, and listened to those bells, and fancied that I heard the music of the home of the blessed, pealing from the dwelling of the Most High. Well do I remember the excessive mortification I felt when I was told the truth, and had the nature of bells explained to me; and though I have since had to awake often from illusions that were dear to my heart, I am sure that I never woke from one with more pain than I experienced when forced to forego this *sweet illusion of my imaginative childhood. (Memoir,* 6–7, [italics mine])

I quote this recollection in its entirety because I find that it echoes a significant, distinguishing feature that would characterize Opie's mid-1790s poetry; for Opie, the process of distinguishing "illusion" from "reality," and her painful, even mortifying associations with that process, convey the chronic problem of inauthenticity. In the passage, Opie assigns freedom to a specific location—"there," in the bed, while gazing at the "blue sky"—which she connects with "delight" and "the good." Learning "truth" becomes "mortifying." If the passage suggests a telling pattern, it may be that in adulthood the poignant desire for serene blue skies—a landscape of desire—would confront self-perpetuated illusions as "real" as the pain of discovery. Desire occupies the spaces between illusion and reality which, extended to the poetry, become literalized landscapes where illusion and reality meet, but where desire always remains painfully compromised by "real" experience and threatening actual events. Landscapes mediate Opie's political outrage and the sensibility required in imagining pain indirectly. They distinguish her poetry in significant ways from, as we shall see, contemporary fellow poets Anna Letitia Barbauld, Mary Robinson or Charlotte Smith, who typically focused their attention directly on politics and the body politic rather than on a particular body and soul imagined in a landscape of pain.

When the physical body experiences "real" pain with heroic dignity, "real" bodies are authenticated. Whether factual or imagined, the recorded stoicism of women in France "going to execution," writes Deborah Kennedy, "was meant to be viewed by survivors as an important act of resistance" (103). While the courageous acts of French women were constructed and understood differently from those of men by both the French and the British, British women's responses were typically dismissed by their male peers as inauthentic or inconsequential.[25] We saw two techniques employed by British male writers focused on the problem of authenticity: one from Wordsworth, who simply assumed the legitimacy of his response to the Terror (because he had been in France?), and one from Burke, who used false humility to generate an occasion by which to express his political and moral indignation at early stages in the Revolution. In the first mid-1790s poem addressed here, "To Twilight," Opie's speaker struggles to find a voice that proves appropriately stoic for the enactment of "virtue in distress"[26] when confronted by moral reprehension.

"To Twilight" (written 1792) describes the speaker's states of mind in terms of weather that blows in and out with every changing political influence and reaction. The speaker longs for a state of "twilight," which she describes as the time of day most fit to maintain a stoic, tempered response to extreme fear. Both Night and "mimic day" prove harsher and expose deeper, more chilling reasons to fear the future with horror. The poem universalizes an imagined fear of annihilation that names no country but provides a covert response to the early days of the Terror as well. Opie uses a series of comparable landscapes as the vehicles by which to reflect the speaker's imagined pain and sympathetic response to the ever-present "danger, sorrow, frenzy, and despair" in a landscape of terror. Opie's speaker ultimately retreats from both the scene of horror and from pity itself (perhaps an imitation of England's repressive, pitiless reaction against French sympathizers). She thus responds in a way that would have been understood as less heroic, or properly, stoically feminine by comparison with reports that reached England of actual women participants, including that of the speaker in Anna Letitia Barbauld's poem of the same year "On the Expected General Rising of the French Nation, in 1792" (published 1825; *RWR*, 16–17).

Barbauld's poem overtly expresses political views that Opie would treat covertly through a paralyzed speaker's insufficient response to overwhelming fear, but Barbauld's poem was not published until more than a generation after the events took place. Barbauld's speaker imagines French victory—a bold France that conquers, repents its cruelties, and rises in pity and from a noble tradition to become "the model of the world." The speaker in Barbauld's poem acknowledges the oxymoronic qualities of war—heroism coupled with cowardice, national security coupled with corrupting power—but hopes for an

outcome in which "Virtue struggles with Despair," class struggle ultimately equalizes, and violence generates freedom. A new, "imagined"
France emerges phoenix-like from the ashes, complete with "faith"
and "reverence" for "ancient laws."

In Opie's "To Twilight," Twilight is executed by the inevitable
arrival of Night and "mimic day." At this imagined site of routine,
inevitable violence, the speaker retreats, neither able to act nor sleep.
Refusing to take sides, the speaker's limbo culminates in tensions
expressed in a series of images that suggest a paralysis of the feminine within the revolutionary context. Futurity, like Twilight, wraps
itself in a "chilling veil of gloom and mists." By contrast, Twilight's
"simple garb," her "veil of grey" proves, like the speaker's own wraps,
"Meet for the cloistered maid." "I am Sorrow's child," claims the
speaker, and Twilight's "cold showers, / Thy mist-encircled forms, thy
doubtful shapes, / Wake a responsive chord / Within my troubled soul,"
to become physically manifest in the speaker's "pale," "cold, sunk
cheek."[27]

The speaker in "To Twilight" rejects the possibility of political
compromise within this landscape: "dewy Eve," "Night's fire-embroi-
dered vest," and the "unwelcome moon" cause spite and envy for both
their intensity and their contextualized associations with power and
destruction. Of the moon, the speaker claims to "loathe the cheerful
sight, as still my fate, / O Twilight! bears a hue resembling thine; /
And envy-struck, I shun / The scene I cannot share." Unable to find
relief in "mimic day," true sympathy cannot emerge from *unshared or
unrecognized* suffering or pretense. Physical and emotional numb-
ness characterize the unshared scene, but the speaker's is not a stoic
act characteristic of male and female revolutionaries in France, but
rather an effort that shifts the emphasis to authentic perception and
response. Shunning the "cheerful sight" brought on by the moon—the
"scene I cannot share"—magnifies the extreme significance of the
private body's moral obligation to act itself out on the body politic. In
the poem's final stanza, the speaker retreats in despair to her couch,
but she does so not to seek tranquility in the "rapture" of recollection,
as might Wordsworth. Rather, she conjures a mental landscape of
"artificial gloom" fit to "suit my soul / And e'en from pity hide / My dim
and sleepless eyes." She, in turn, acts out global suffering on her own
metaphoric body and on the imagined body politic.

The fusion of the numb "sleepless" physical body and the unpitied
restless "soul" at poem's end challenges the extent to which, and
how, pain might be shared in a war-torn landscape. Steven Bruhm
explains that,

> The literature of sensibility, and by extension Romantic
> fiction fostered the myth that pain could be shared through
> the medium of the sympathetic body. Thus pain became a
> proclamation of ontological presence both for the victim and
> the spectator of pain; the distinction between them could no
> longer be said to exist. As Elaine Scarry argues, pain is "so
> incontestably and unnegotiably present . . . that 'having pain'
> may come to be thought of as the most vibrant example of
> what it is to 'have certainty.'" (*GB,* 19)

The suffering experienced by Opie's speakers might be said to reveal
her confidence in female perceptions of pain which, to quote Ellison,
helps in "discerning how sensibility can become, under certain circumstances, an idiom of female ambition and citizenship, invested in
national success, as well as a means of resistance" (230). By numbing
the imagined physical body Opie's speaker manifests a sympathy
which rejects pain that cannot be "shared," thus the speaker feels most
vulnerable and alone when most imaginatively sympathetic to the
pained bodies of revolution.[28] Opie's ontology of pain, then, contributed to the emerging aesthetic of sympathetic response identified with
the new movement in poetry at the same time that it helped to formulate the early mythology of the isolated Romantic poet. The isolated
writer, whose hope is to broaden the sympathetic response of the body
politic, faces, in "To Twilight," the envy of what cannot be shared.
Disconnection punishes the female body and mind, making them
undeserving of pity—inauthenticity has been exposed through this
metaphoric gap between body and soul. The revolutionary landscape
becomes both the vehicle by which the woman poet achieves a certainty or confidence in the personal voice and, paradoxically, the means
by which that voice and body numb themselves from "unshared
scenes" that can only be imagined, but nonetheless have the power to
metaphorically destroy the speaker's imagined body and soul.

Opie's poem from 1794, "Ode to Borrowdale in Cumberland,"
concentrates completely on the speaker's personal need to draw psychological relief or escape through an intense effort to absorb the self into
the changing weathers of a single landscape. Bruhm notes that if pain
"'presses too nearly' or 'too close,' it freezes the sensibilities and closes
us off from feeling anything whatsoever for anyone else" (*GB,* 34).
"Borrowdale" contains both the site of individual pain and reflects
escape from that pain; Duncan Wu has described the poem as "revolutionary in its content" (349). The speaker beholds in nature's cycles
a transformation of sublime terror into a landscape of ecstasy, which

finally occupies the speaker's emotionally tortured body and transforms into a "physical" pain. The speaker crystallizes the scene of pleasure into a memory, as if to literalize a "place" of freedom and escape. Tracing a full day's natural cycle, which includes the passing of a frightening thunderstorm, becomes a way for the speaker, who calls herself "the mourner" by poem's end, to metaphorically "sequester" the sublime scene so that she can "fly to" an imagined landscape for healing and sustenance. The process anticipates Wordsworth's later poem, "I Wandered Lonely as a Cloud," in which the speaker's "vacant" and "pensive mood" becomes transformed by a past recollection of extreme beauty. If the speaker in "To Twilight" "freezes" from having too nearly imagined the pain of future sufferers, in "Borrowdale" the speaker beholds nature, uses it as the vehicle to traverse the psychodrama of creative process, and manipulates the transformation, as will Wordsworth's later poem, to "paint" a "smiling scene" of consolation, albeit an arguably superficial, inauthentic response.

While on a literal level "Borrowdale" describes a particular landscape while seeming to ignore the impact of revolution on that place, the poem provides insight into the female poet's methods of emphasizing psychological restoration in the midst of a debilitatingly frightening atmosphere. The mingling of pleasure and pain, a conventional feature of sublime experience for the Romantics, cordons off the poem's "sequestered scenes," described as "varied, wild" and "formed to soothe Affliction's child." Nature, of course, bears the "heart-healing balm." In 1794, "the long hours are told by sighs / And sorrow steals health's crimson dyes." Wordsworth could talk himself out of his despair in "Tintern Abbey" by having learned

> To look on nature, not as in the hour
> Of thoughtless youth; but hearing oftentimes
> The still, sad music of humanity,
> Nor harsh nor grating, though of ample power
> To chasten and subdue.
>
> (lines 88–93)

Opie's speaker, by contrast, draws attention to her doubt. Her emotional pain manifests itself in the "tortured breast's alarms," and only a recollection of Borrowdale might save her:

> Yes, scene sequestered, varied, wild,
> So formed to soothe Affliction's child,
> Sweet Borrowdale! to thee I'll fly,

To hush my bosom's ceaseless sigh.
If yet in Nature's store there be
One kind *heart-healing balm for me,*
Now the long hours are told by sighs,
And sorrow steals health's crimson dyes,—
If aught can smiles and bloom restore,
Ah, surely thine's the precious power!
(RWR, 149 [italics mine])

While this penultimate passage suggests the power of psychological escape into a subliminal, "varied, wild," landscape akin to
Wordsworth's process of using memory to present a moment ripe for
psychological restoration, the passage in "Borrowdale" undercuts the
speaker's confidence that she can transcend landscapes of horror. The
passage culminates in the speaker's effort to convince herself that
"surely" Nature contains the "precious power" to "restore" "smiles and
bloom." The passage moves from the certainty of "Yes," to twice
repeated "Ifs," that Nature actually holds the "heart-healing balm."
In 1798, with the Terror well over, Wordsworth could place faith in
the power of his own mind. With the Terror's end still unresolved,
Opie wrote "Borrowdale" using a creative process that influenced
Wordsworth's but that resists his reconciled happy ending. Rather, we
see the female poet's desire, hope, and consciously superficial effort to
rescue a "heart healing balm" from a now quiet landscape that awaits
the sutures of war. In "Borrowdale's" final stanza, the speaker refers
to herself in the third person as a "mourner" with a "sick soul" who
might, finally, "on Heaven repose." Turning her back on a landscape
that holds no certainty, the speaker yields her "tortured breast's
alarms" to conventional religion for a blessing that will fulfill, in the
poem's final line, a prayer for "Health, peace, and hope in Borrowdale." The shift away from the poet's ability to transcend the pain of
personal and shared suffering and move toward Heaven suggests the
poet's failing confidence in her own poetic voice.

If nature's restorative powers momentarily, then superficially,
and then, finally, no longer, heal the "sick soul" in a tortured landscape in "Borrowdale," then Opie's "Ode on the Present Times, 27th
January 1795" collapses that crisis of poetic function altogether by
destroying Fancy itself. The poem confronts the paradoxes of continued war in Europe given that the Terror finally ends. That the Terror,
with its outcomes known, did end, would make a multinational war
seem even more absurd. 1794 had stood out for the very real threat
of famine from a bread shortage, high prices, and riotings which

frequently involved participation by British soldiers (Emsley 47–48). 1795 began with no sign that circumstances would improve; hence Opie's exhausted message of apocalyptic horror and fear acted on a landscape that will not restore vision to its inmates. Rather, the poet now blames, universally, the perpetrators of the Terror and continental war.

Marlon Ross explains that universalizing messages in women's poetry have a particular significance based upon the calculated response that the poet shapes for, and elicits from, the reader. Describing some poems as deliberately "uncircumstanced," Ross shows how a decontextualized message will necessarily jar the reader in expected ways, and into a universalized circumstance. He uses the example of Barbauld's "The Mouse's Petition" to explain that Barbauld's strategy,

> remind[s] us that a topic is a figure (of speech, mere talk) that points us to a place necessarily outside of its own figuration. Her humble topic drives us outside of the poem and into circumstance, away from the diversionary pleasure of reading as a singular politicized moment (the expected occasion) and toward the duty of living as a morally conscientious, ongoing, and outgoing activity. In other words, the more universal and ubiquitous the poem aspires to be through its moralizing sentiment, the more "uncircumstanced" it becomes, threatening to abstract the process of reading from the experience of actual circumstance itself. (*Configurations,* 100)

While Barbauld used a "humble" subject to pull the reader outside of individual particularities, Opie chose a subject guaranteed to draw a sympathetic response. But rather than build on England's circumstances, Opie decontextualizes the suffering precisely to implicate the reader and draw attention to a citizenry's culpability. The imperative to universalize permeates Opie's "Ode on the Present Times," as it does Barbauld's poem, by presenting imagined images of suffering and death that extend beyond England's landscapes and into all of Europe. The speaker seeks to generate fellow-feeling—again, a "shared" suffering—that draws all Europeans into a struggle for a freedom that itself has been corrupted through abuse of power and bloodshed. While the poem's specific references to Poland, Britain and "Gallia lower" contextualize events in sociohistorical terms, the poem necessarily becomes ideological.[29] The speaker hyperbolizes the extreme moral urgency with which the reader must respond, by removing something most dear to her—by actually killing Fancy at the poem's end—

a shocking and powerful strategy which portions out culpability and punishment for crimes against humanity.

Nature and the horrors of war in "Ode on the Present Times" become inextricably linked by their sublime effects on the poet's psyche. The speaker must universalize the experience in order to create personal space by which to negotiate the language for imagined famine and violence. Mary Robinson's poem of the same month, "January, 1795" (1795, repr. 1806; *RWR,* 121–122), provides a scathing commentary on England's misdirected public policy, using couplets in quatrain stanzas to underscore the nonchalance of the enterprise. Opie's "Ode," by contrast, uses the serious, conventional form of the ode to universalize, and thereby "uncircumstance" the particulars, the effect of which is to disseminate the effects of the landscape into the reader's conscience; the reader then must share blame. Opie's poem spreads responsibility for competing, but equally devastating, ideologies that span all European national landscapes.

The England of Robinson's "January, 1795" promotes the worst in its people. Class division, vanity, a failed economic system, and empty, insincere rhetoric culminate in the final stanza's harsh indictment of exposed cunning and insincerity:

> Honest men who can't get places,
> Knaves who show unblushing faces;
> Ruin hastened, peace retarded;
> Candour spurned, and art rewarded. (*RWR,* 122)

The allusion to repressive measures taken to silence protesters and the "unblushing faces" of those "rewarded" for their "art" overtly demonstrates Robinson's political position: she will have "candour" if no one else does. Opie, in "Ode on the Present Times," will implicate everyone for destroying the chance for peace. The weight of such "candour" will destroy the poem's speaker. Opie uses a quintessential Romantic landscape of the mind to stand in for the horrors of war, which one must presumably have a "mind of winter" even to contemplate. The poem begins with Winter driving his "horrors round," over a "rugged soil," while "Each sign of Spring's gay beauty fades." The speaker will ultimately implicate herself for such dire imaginings: she will punish herself both as spectator and as agent of universal, shared pain.

Ceri Crossley and Ian Small remind us that in both post-Revolutionary France and in Britain, "certain terms, such as 'mass' or 'terror', became charged with new meanings."[30] The "Ode" seems particularly to depend upon charged, coded language to deliver its message.

Words used in the poem such as "riot," "despot," "blaspheming," "horrors," "Freedom," "bloody strife," "bloody laurels," "Slaughtered Man," and "lurking fiend" would remind the reader of the Terror, and transpose reminders of actual events onto multiple, imagined landscapes. Distinctions that Bruhm draws between "terror" and "horror" in the Gothic fiction of Ann Radcliffe also suggest the difficulty Opie might have had in making "real" the horror of actual events never experienced. One way to draw attention to this dilemma of authenticity was to hyperbolize the effects on the audience through killing off Fancy. Bruhm paraphrases Ann Radcliffe's depiction of terror as an emotion which "occupies and expands the mind, and elevates it to high expectation, is purely sublime, and leads us, by a kind of fascination, to seek even the object, from which we appear to shrink." Terror is "that carefully regulated aesthetic experience that can use intense feeling to seek objects in the world, objects which can include people in distress." Horror, by contrast, in the words of Radcliffe's character Mr. W., referring to Emily's experience in *The Mysteries of Udolpho,* "'contracts, freezes, and nearly annihilates' the passions which lead to community, and forces the horrified spectator to enclose and protect the self." Opie's ending to the "Ode" seems similarly preoccupied with the speaker's voyeurism, placing both self and other spectators of war on the theatre of European annihilation. Simultaneously, she draws attention to, in Bruhm's words, "how the ingenuous spectator [the poet] imagines a scene of physical suffering" (*GB,* 32, 37).

While Opie imagines the scene as Winter, Charlotte Smith's *The Emigrants,* book 2 (published 1793; *RWR,* 38–40) uses a spring scene to emphasize the subject's paradoxical position in the act of "gaz[ing]" at landscapes of pain. Her speaker "Feels not the joy reviving Nature brings" and "shrinks from horrors such as War." Violets take on sinister aspect, "lurking in their turfy beds / Beneath the flowering thorn, are stained with blood . . . while War, wide-ravaging, annihilates / The hope of cultivation." Opie's speaker in "Ode on the Present Times" cannot imagine spring arriving at all and complicates the subject position by acknowledging how easy it would be to succumb to popular views of justice, patriotism, loyalty. The gendered social boundaries and limits become inseparable from the political site itself, at "safe" distance from the observing poet, who implicates France, Russia, and ultimately England for crimes against humanity served in the name of the seductress Freedom. This "Form sublime" stands for the imaginative limits of an exhausted mind. Freedom becomes subject to seductive "charm" and "beauty to inspire," until it, too, becomes corrupt. Freedom's triumphs, when unshared, cause the speaker to weep for the presumed foe, described as "Slaughtered Man!" Blakean in her depiction of the circularity of corrupting power, to which even Freedom itself becomes a cheerful seducer, Opie refuses the seduction on moral grounds: "I see thy [Freedom's] form sublime, acquire / New power to charm, new beauty to inspire; / I cannot smile; I cannot join / The song of triumph! though thy foes, / Celestial power! are also mine" (*RWR,* 150). England's future, "Forbidding Man to weep for Slaughtered Man!" would mock true human value and liberty. On either side of war, "Are they not Men?," the speaker asks.

In "the time for Woe to reign" in "Ode on the Present Times," Opie isolates and describes political (male) power, the sublime, the true nature of freedom and humanity, and nature itself, and, as in "To Twilight," remains separate and alone: "I cannot join," the speaker claims. Within the poem's context, this isolation stems from both the formal dilemma of authenticating an imagined response, but also from the moral dilemma generated by misappropriated female agency. The poet isolates herself from future visions—from landscapes of pain and from the need to respond, and from the moral imperative to devise and control the reader's response to horror. If terror governed the landscapes in "To Twilight" and "Borrowdale," with its corresponding effect of sublime "high expectation" and "fascination"—to borrow Radcliffe's description—then the horrors of the "present times" indeed "contract, freeze, and nearly annihilate" the speaker in the "Ode," as they did Emily in *Udolpho.*

The poet, however, humanizes the foe, as if it was her duty as Europe's moral agent. Has not England the same potential for seduction by that great "form sublime" ("Freedom") which can culminate in reigns of terror? In lines crucial to illuminating the poem's central tensions, the speaker asks, "For who are they that madly bear / Against thy sons the venal spear? / *Are they not men?*—then say, *what power / Can bid my bosom mourn no more; O where's the fiend-delighting ban / Forbidding Man to weep for Slaughtered Man!"* (*RWR* 150–51 [italics mine]). This rhetorical question effectively distances the poet from the very moral implications raised by being an imagined spectator. She imagines becoming intoxicated by a "fiend-delighting ban" which would "forbid" her from the moral imperative to weep for all of humanity—a bold response in its desire to reject the moral agency or sensibility assigned to the female spectator. Opie envisions a universe absent of the moral implications assigned to the woman poet negotiating status quo politics and the politics of form. In effect, such imagining in turn collapses the very space in which the female poet can manipulate her "indirect dissent" altogether. Just as the anticipated horrors of famine will sweep over England to fill in the hollow space of victory should England triumph over a blighted Gallia, so the mind of winter, itself "the scene with horrors fraught," would "fade" from the poet's own sight—its desolation yielding to ultimate terror and horror which leaves only a space to collapse unto itself, with no possible return of spring and, worse yet for the poet, no Fancy.

Opie's vehicle, desolate Winter, precludes imagining a rebirth through Spring whose "gay beauty fades." Without a consoling vehicle the poet imagines a temporarily safe moral space—"the present ill / *Appears* to lose its power to kill," while "*future* scenes" leave no space for moral, political, or personal response, thus "pale Fancy flies / Lifts her dim Tearful eyes to heaven, and dies." At this moment Wordsworth sought his "last place of refuge, my own soul" and uttered "long orations" of protest and despair. The magnitude of a Blake's, Wordsworth's, Coleridge's, Shelley's, Keats's imagined terror at losing imaginative power—the source of future writing—collapses in Opie's poem. She constructs here not only the political scene of moral instruction but also a "hideous progeny" as deeply political and sublime as Mary Shelley's future creatures who hunt each other over the landscapes of an icy, cold, and boundless ice in and of the mind. Opie's voice of dissent must implicate itself, not merely for giving language to the ultimate human horrors—slaughter and famine—but for having sustained so long a space by which to utter the unthinkable, undoable act—not merely writing itself, but imagining a space in which the female might be "stoic" with her "virtue in distress." But rather than feeling consoled to "drink the milk of paradise" or "think of the Leech gatherer on the lonely moor," Opie's speaker punishes herself for her demonic, if momentary, vision of abandonment. There is no "last place of refuge" here, but "pale Fancy," dead, a poet's complete and utter loss—a recognition of the speaker's failure to provide the appropriate moral agency as well as the proper stoic response at the moment of most dire imagining.

To attribute women's socially sanctioned power (her only) to moral agency as did Opie's society, and to view Europe in 1795, was, for Opie, to imagine the utter moral failure of humankind, but, more fundamentally, womankind, to fulfill the quintessential role of energized reactivity. Opie's "Ode" exposes the void at the core of a politics in which women, in dissent, implicate themselves in a moral Catch 22 with no political or poetic escape. By exposing the failures of self and humanity on a European battlefield, Opie simultaneously exposes the failures of a body politic which would assign moral agency to its least politically significant and powerful members—to the seer with no authority to "see"; to the agent with no authority to share suffering or to act out her duty. In the political ruins, no transforming female voice can be heard—the soul bears no "last place of refuge" from a task it cannot complete, a revolution it cannot win, a poem it writes, at least metaphorically, at the risk, and failure, of future utterance.

Also written in 1795, Opie's "Stanzas Written Under Aeolus's Harp," may be viewed as a final step of active survival for the female poet's voice. The poem emphasizes the restoring image of the Aeolian harp to conjure visions and generate a voice when Fancy dies, as it did in "Ode on the Present Times." The language gives double meaning to words that serve as blatant reminders of the Terror and war, such as "tyrant," "frenzy," "gathering throng," and "rapt enthusiast." This time, these words serve Fancy through the mediating Aeolian lute; Fancy, not Robespierre, becomes the "rapt enthusiast" who would return dignity to humanity and give "regret's sad tribute" to "lost friends" subject to "tyrant sorrows" and "tyrant passions." The poet's solution at the point when "art's laboured strains my feelings tire," will be the familiar lyre. The poem begins with a healing plea that the harp "hear" the "tyrant sorrows," "tyrant passions" of heart and breast in response to "fond griefs" and lost souls. The double reference to "tyrant" suggests that these are imposed, rather than natural, losses that echo the imagined horrors of the Terror. The speaker's mind interacts with the harp's tones and cadences, and its "regular progression" of sounds "wake thy trembling nerves" into "warmer life," gradually giving way to a plea for continuous self-restoration and consolation.

"Stanzas Written Under Aeolus's Harp," like the "Ode on the Present Times," uses coded language to create a climate desperate for grand scale rejuvenation that revives "enchantress Fancy" from grief and dormancy. At first startled by the "wild disorder" in the physical and emotional landscape, "Pale Frenzy listens . . . kindred wildness owns, / And starts appalled the well known sounds to hear." Fancy herself eventually "with most rapture hears" the "first rising strains melodious poured / Untouched by mortal hands," as if again to 'free' herself from inauthentic moral agency by shifting to a religious explanation. Now a "rapt enthusiast" whose "wild creative eye" responds to extremes of the "gale" and "soft zephyrs," Fancy transforms the frenzied landscape into a place of quiet. The harp, a "breathing instrument," can then hear the "softest call" of the "inmost soul." The poet ends the invocation in a benediction to the harp for returning voice to

Fancy with even "thy faintest breath." The speaker ultimately (re)claims female agency, unlike in the "Ode on the Present Times," by recognizing the nobility embedded in the very struggle to find peace within an internalized act of imagined suffering. No particular place on a map can contain the transcending process of the healing poet: the "grand illusion of romantic *ideology*," writes Jerome McGann, "is that one may escape such a world through imagination and poetry. The great truth . . . is that there is no escape, that there is only revelation" (589). When "art's laboured strains" "tire" the poet, the harp's "simple music" gives strength and desire for this "revelation." But there is no confidence that revelation brings restoration. The poet's voice enables, but, as McGann suggests, does not promise success or even revelation. The chaos of England's tired political landscape(s) mirrors Fancy's ambiguous, desperate workings on a soul that imagines, suffers, and barely survives the imagined torture of the bruised body and soul.

While Opie helped to make the uses of landscape a conventional means by which to enact the speakers' psychodramas in poetry, her visions always bear the marks of a woman writer hesitant to challenge overtly the body politic. At a time when anyone who spoke out in support of the Revolution risked charges of treason, and when women were judged by newly reentrenched conservative gender codes of behavior, Opie negotiated a way to address these dilemmas in formally conventional and, thus, universal terms. The crisis of confidence suggested in these poems would drive her speaker into complete retreat from imagined pain in "To Twilight" and to superficial consolation in "Ode to Borrowdale in Cumberland." In "Ode on the Present Times" she would risk a vision of Gothic horror so extreme as to exhaust and finally obliterate Fancy itself, but she would try again, as poets do, to generate a strategy to enable future utterance in "Stanzas Written Under Aeolus's Harp." The quintessentially Romantic Aeolian harp—the now passive, now active, metaphor for poetic salvation—becomes a critical legitimating medium for Opie's self-revelation at the site of "real" or "imagined" suffering. Opie ultimately authenticates her voice through a symbol of active suffering *shared* with her fellow (male) poets. In appropriating this conventional stand-in for the poet's mind, Opie secures her own poetic function by reasserting her ability to sympathetically connect with the 'foe'. She, in effect, "shun(s) the scene / I cannot share," thereby transcending the gender codes that prejudiced her audience while exhausting her own mental battlefronts, domestic and foreign.

Notes

1. Quoted in Steven Bruhm, *Gothic Bodies: The Politics of Pain in Romantic Fiction* (Philadelphia: University of Pennsylvania Press, 1994), 16. All subsequent references will be cited within the text and notes as *GB*.

2. Roxanne Eberle, "Amelia Opie's *Adeline Mowbray:* Diverting the Libertine Gaze; Or, The Vindication of a Fallen Woman," *Studies in the Novel* 26: 2 (Summer 1994): 121–152. Eberle concentrates primarily on Opie's writing after 1798.

3. From *The Warrior's Return, and Other Poems,* 2nd ed. (London: Longman, Hurst, Rees, and Orme, 1808), 125–29. Written several years before its publication, the poem explores the anachronistic dilemma suggested by beautiful landscapes metaphorically defiled by the horrific human activities which take place on them. The Seine's banks, in the poem, seem "formed for jocund revery," yet trigger the memory of "that spot" "dark with blood." The imagined landscape contains the horror of lived events remembered by those who "mourn," but still appears innocent to the physical eye.

4. Deborah Kennedy, "Spectacle of the Guillotine: Helen Maria Williams and the Reign of Terror," *Philological Quarterly* 73.1 (Winter 1994): 106; Ann Rigney, *The Rhetoric of Historical Representation: Three Narratives of the French Revolution* (Cambridge: Cambridge University Press, 1990), ix, 50–51, 60.

5. In C. L. Brightwell, *Memoir of Amelia Opie* (London: The Religious Tract Society, 1855), 1–17. The *Memoir,* published only two years after Opie's death and drawing primarily upon letters and Brightwell's friendship with an aged Opie, is the major source of Opie's environment as a child and young woman. It provides essential information about Opie's life, particularly given that a number of Brightwell's sources were sold at Sotheby's, 22 June 1953, and remain "untraced," according to Andrew Ashfield, ed., *Romantic Women Poets, 1770–1838* (Manchester: Manchester University Press, 1995), 309. Citations from Brightwell are referred to within the text and notes as *Memoir.* References to the Ashfield edition are cited within the text as RWR.

6. *Romantic Women Poets, An Anthology*, ed. Duncan Wu (Blackwell, 1997), 100.

7. Wu, in the introduction, "Amelia Opie (*née* Alderson)," in Wu, ed., 345–350. Wu notes that the poem was "inspired by Amelia's visit to the Lake District," makes reference to "the anxious response of radicals to the repression of Pitt's administration," and "anticipates" Wordsworth's "Tintern Abbey" "in reposing its faith in the powers of memory to soothe one's anxieties." I will suggest later in this essay a distinction between Opie and Wordsworth's uses of memory and nature to console their anxious speakers.

8. David Bindman in *The Shadow of the Guillotine: Britain and the French Revolution* (London: British Museum Publications, 1989), 30; Kennedy, 108. The Bindman text provides an extensive catalog of visual images which reflected and influenced both French and British culture during and after the Terror.

9. *RWR*, 146–152. Because Opie used her birth name, "Alderson," until her marriage to John Opie in 1798, Ashfield identifies her as "Amelia Alderson" in this edition.

10. Chris Jones in *Radical Sensibility: Literature and Ideas in the 1790s* (London and New York: Routledge, 1993), 7 [italics mine].

11. See Donald H. Reiman's Introduction to Opie's *Poems*, ed. Reiman (New York and London: Garland Publishing, 1978), v–xv. Reiman provides a brief, critical overview of highlights of Opie's literary career, but claims that "most of Opie's poetry, when assayed, would be cast into the scrap heap, though her humanitarian concerns give some historical interest to her poems on West Indian slavery and on the British poor and social outcasts suffering the ravages of want and war" (viii). Reiman's Introduction makes no specific mention of the poems discussed in this essay in his appraisal of Opie's poetry, none of which were included in Opie's 1802 collection, *Poems*. Of related interest in *Poems* is Opie's "Lines Written at Norwich on the first News of Peace." According to Reiman, this poem was, along with "The Orphan Boy's Tale," the "most popular with early nineteenth-century readers" (viii).

12. See Mary Poovey's *The Proper Lady and the Woman Writer* (Chicago: University of Chicago Press, 1984), 144, for a summary of this argument. I prefer Eberle's view that "too often literary criticism has erred in assuming that the eighteenth-century revolutionary woman immediately became the Victorian angel in the house. Modern critics often focus on conservative Regency voices because in retrospect they seem to have won the ideological battle waged over the construction of femininity" (122).

13. *Memoir*, 9; Eberle notes that Dr. Alderson was "so disturbed by his daughter's outspoken objections to the [Horne Tooke, Thomas Hardy and Thomas Holcroft] trials [for treason] that he destroyed many of her letters" (121).

14. See *RWR*, 310, endnotes 98, 100, and 101. Wu also summarizes a large and wide-ranging number of reviews of Opie's later volumes, *Poems* (1802) and *The Warrior's Return* (1808), in the Introduction to Opie in *Romantic Women Poets*.

15. Marlon Ross, "Configurations of Feminine Reform: The Woman Writer and the Tradition of Dissent" in *Re-Visioning Romanticism: British Women Writers, 1776–1837*, eds. Carol Shiner Wilson and Joel Haefner (Philadelphia: University of Pennsylvania Press, 1994), 97. Further references to Ross are cited within the text as *Configurations*.

16. Clive Emsley, "The Impact of the French Revolution on British Politics and Society" in *The French Revolution and British Culture,* eds. Ceri Crossley and Ian Small (Oxford and New York: Oxford University Press, 1989), 54.

17. *Memoir,* 78, 81. Opie was drawn to and intrigued by the paradoxes of association embedded in Paris's sites of the Revolution and the Terror. In "Lines on the Place de la Concorde at Paris" from *The Warrior's Return,* she emphasizes that this particular scene which "formed the eye of taste to please!," was once a place of terror and bloodshed. The poem's epigraph notes that the spot was "Originally called the Place de Louis Seize," and that it is "next the *place de la Revolution,* where the perpetual guillotine stood" (126). Later in the poem, Opie describes that "once that spot was dark with blood," it "wakes the inmost soul to pain / And prompts the throb of agony." The now "smiling scene" proves a "horrid contrast" to the spot where "awful guilt" "stains thy [France's] shore." The poem ends in a warning that this place dare not be forgotten, for "danger lurks in every gleam, / And death's appalling agency."

18. *Configurations* 93. Ross finds that "Neither the earlier nor the more recent kinds of criticism apply very well to dissenting women poets, who heavily rely on the conventionality of forms and whose politics and writing practices exploit these forms in ways quite different from the canonized Romantic poets. Rather than trying to transgress, explode, or empty the form of its authority, as the Romantics are seen to do, the women dissenters are more interested in remotivating the form's conventionality to capitalize on its authority in order to legitimize their voices and views" (110, note 4). Susan Wolfson has more recently addressed the problem of gaps in formal considerations of Romantic aesthetics in her article "What Good is Formalist Criticism? or; Forms and Storms and the Critical Register of Romantic Poetry," *Studies in Romanticism* 37.1 (Spring 1998): 77–94.

19. Meena Alexander, "Romantic Feminine" in *Women in Romanticism* (Savage, MD: Barnes & Noble Books, 1989), 23, 27.

20. Joel Haefner, "The Romantic Scene(s) of Writing" in *Re-Visioning Romanticism,* 271.

21. Julie Ellison, "The Politics of Fancy in the Age of Sensibility" in *Re-Visioning Romanticism,* 230. Ellison continues: "Through the geography of prospect, fancy temporarily fuses imperial and lyric consciousness in key episodes of poems by women. The activities of 'fancy,' 'reflection,' 'meditation,' and 'imagination' that structure the reader's progress through a text have different meanings depending on the gender and position of the speaking subject" (230).

22. *The Selected Poetry and Prose of Wordsworth,* ed. Geoffrey Hartman (New York: Signet, 1970), 301–302. All further references to Wordsworth's poetry are cited from this edition by line references.

23. Burke in Russell Kirk's Introduction to *Reflections on the Revolution in France* (Chicago: Henry Regnery Company, 1968, 4th printing), 9–10 [italics mine].

24. Quoted in Alexander, 29. Alexander notes that "Terror for Burke underlies the sublime, and with it comes an instinctive sense of human vulnerability, a simultaneous withdrawal from and fascination with what is awe-inspiring, even violent and dangerous in its claims on our own selves. The feminine however is clearly distinguished from this perceived source of power: it is small, delicate, pleasing to the eye in its proportions. It seems to Burke quite clear that 'the beauty of women is considerably owing to their weakness, or delicacy, and is even enhanced by their timidity, a quality of mind analogous to it'" (from Burke's *Sublime and Beautiful*). Alexander continues, "The feminine then must be held quite clear of all that goes into the welter of power defining sublimity" (29).

25. See Dorinda Outram, *The Body Politic and the French Revolution* (New Haven and London: Yale University Press, 1989), 72, 81, 84.

26. I have borrowed the term Kennedy uses in her discussion of Helen Maria Williams's imagined responses to "images of [female] victims [in France] before the moment of execution, in postures that might be called 'virtue in distress'" (104).

27. Bruhm enhances this point by adding to the physical dimension, a cultural bias, noting "If nothing exists in the *mind,* to modify Berkeley's claim, but as it is perceived by the physical body," then "by the late eighteenth-century the physical had become one with the metaphysical"; "what comes to be valorized by late eighteenth-century moralists as 'sympathy,' then, is physiologically based." Consequently, the "well-ordered, harmonious and sympathetic eighteenth-century body . . . provided a model for the social body as well" (*GB,* 12, 14).

28. Bruhm explains how the sharing of pain "deconstructs its own community, since by centering itself in the observer who shares it, it becomes 'the most vibrant example' of an *individual* experience, one that is not communal at all" (*GB,* 56).

29. From as early as 1793, France had designs on Holland and Belgium, Russia on Eastern Europe. The reference to "Gallia" in the poem could refer to the territories of both France and Belgium, as it did in antiquity, or it could simply mean "Frenchman." Jerome McGann argues on the point of ideology that, in the case of Wordsworth's "Intimations Ode," the poem "generalizes—I'd now like to say mythologizes—all its conflicts, or rather resituates these conflicts out of a socio-historical context and into an ideological one." See "Romanticism and Its Ideologies," *Studies in Romanticism* 21.4 (Winter 1982): 581.

30. Introduction to *The French Revolution and British Culture,* xi.

Revolutionary Representation

Elizabeth Inchbald, Joanna Baillie, and Revolutionary Representation in the "Romantic" Period

Terence Allan Hoagwood

And put the case hee should enjoy them, since he is so stupid that hee cannot wish any thing truly good, he did but please himselfe under his burden, and deceive his understanding with glittering misery, and then what better were he than some jovial madde man.

(John Hall, *Paradoxes* [1650], 34)

Were there no fooles, badd ware would not passe.

(George Herbert, *Outlandish Proverbs* [1640], no. 66)

I think of Marcuse's *Eros and Civilization*: the doomed hope that libidinal freedom is cognate with political freedom and with justice on a civilizational scale. The irresistible machinery of what Marcuse calls "repressive desublimation" trivializes libido as the computerized advertisement trivializes Jesus— the figment does not go away, the praxis carries on, but these things are made into one more engine of money-funneling and mass somnambulism.

(Simone Lecour, *Pénetré et Périr,* 1997)

I begin with three facts about *Natural Born Killers* (directed by Oliver Stone, 1994), facts that will already be familiar to those who teach courses in film: (1) the direction, photography, and editing of this movie involve rare technical and artistic accomplishments; (2) the movie is a critique of a society in which people are shaped by commercial television and its spectacles of simulated violence; and (3) college students enjoy learning about these matters, having arrived in the course sharing the false belief that this critique of the culture of violence must be a *commercial* for a culture of violence. In a perceptual environment that is mostly language and artificial imagery, and in which *most* discourse is advertisement, it is understandable that the most widespread habits of mind involve the tacit assumption that the only thing to do with a spectacle is to enjoy it without thinking.

In the society of the sales pitch, the default setting of a commercially programmed life is the pleasure-quest, with its uncritical focus on one's own feeling-states. Whether a particular book is a forgery is a question of fact; how one feels about oneself when one reads it (not even wondering whether it is a forgery) is a different question. Concentrating attention on how one feels and controlling how others feel are projects consistent with the marketing imperatives of a society organized according to sales and profit.[1] Scholarship is not. Customers' passive receipt of manufactured pleasure is the social or antisocial result of life conducted according to the marketing imperative. That form of pleasure is not an activity consistent with the aims of scholarship. Method acting (based on emotional recall and affective memory) takes into Hollywood what the society of advertising installs in all of us: an artificially induced preoccupation with manufactured passion which we find it rewarding (temporarily) to believe. These circumstances pose dangers to the knowledge industry; in the information society, "Information was not the precursor to knowledge; it was the tool of the salesman."[2]

The small subset of that society which consists of literary scholars (the MLA reports that the association has 30,552 members[3]) is not immune to the power of advertising and the mentality of its customers. The November 1996 issue includes 182 pages of text and 172 pages of commercial advertisements. To think of our perceptual environment as an artificial discourse of manufactured desire, made with an ulterior motive of monetary gain, does not induce uncritical personal pleasure. Because such pleasure is the *de facto* teleology of American life, many literary scholars probably prefer to regard the *PMLA* issue as a reference tool, and not as a vessel of advertisements, which it manifestly is. To interpret the circumstance under the assumption of widespread sincerity, what preoccupies us, most of the time, is the question of whether we are personally interested (an apt question for a society of customers), and not the question: What is the nature of the thing we're noticing? In less ingenuous cases, *cretensis cretensem* ("one false marchaunte deceiveth another").[4] However congruent with the imperatives of marketing, the currently popular interest in our own "appetite" has effects upon the scholarly value of our work:[5] to discuss one's own (or others') likes and dislikes may be different, in scholarly outcome, from discussion of true and false.

In this essay I will be suggesting that the mental or discursive habits of marketing (focusing on personal feeling-states, on one's own or others' likes and dislikes) are not always advantageous for scholarship. Not all literary questions are matters of fact, but some are, and these market-centered habits, with their discourse of affective states, may promote the adoption of false beliefs about matters of fact. My examples will be two romantic-period plays—*The Massacre* by Elizabeth Inchbald and *Constantine Paleologus* by Joanna Baillie— but the essay's larger argument concerns scholarship, criticism, and their relationships with two things: (1) the object of knowledge, and (2) the artificial discourses of manufactured desire that constitute our ordinary perceptual environment, inside the academy and out, with the mental and discursive habits that are thereby manufactured for the audiences of commercials, including us.

At the outset I will state as clearly as I can an important distinction that qualifies the ensuing arguments: I am not concerned with the question whether people (including academic professionals) should have pleasure in their lives and works; one need not be a hedonist or even a utilitarian to wish to promote human joy. My concern is rather with the manufacture of certain artificial concepts of pleasure, and with some forms of obsessional subjectivity that pass for pleasure in a society of commodity advertising. My essay seeks to do what I suggest might well be among the goals or consequences of scholarship broadly considered—demystification; I am concerned to demystify what passes for passion or pleasure under the conditions of artificial manufacture and commodity culture. As Andrew Bowie has said in a different connection, "The apparently immediate is in fact mediated."[6] I suggest that it should not be the business of scholarship to conceal its mediations. An artificial appeal to appetite or passion or pleasure may be a feature of authors' promotions of their literary products (as in Wordsworth's case, to which I will turn momentarily); to suspend disbelief, in such a case, will be to miss (rather than to reveal) the truth of the matter; if the author's work is a fabrication of texts and not of feelings, it will be a scholarly activity to find and point out that fact—not to encourage delight in the faking of passion. Alternatively, an appeal to passion may be a feature of professors' promotions of their own occupational projects: "One of the most exciting developments in literary and cultural studies is the dramatic reevaluation of the British Romantic scene";[7] "The emotional impact of this sort of personalized historicism depends on its sensational theatricality. . . . Students are delighted to test the arresting stageworthiness of this scene by mounting it in class as a *tableau vivant*."[8] There may be unreasonable confusion between those two sets of ulterior motive: that is, a professor's wish to provoke delight (professionally) might lead him or her to indicate erroneously that poets are correspondingly interested in their own personal feelings. In the preface to *Lyrical Ballads* Wordsworth begins by declaring his intention to impart "pleasure"; his customers' feelings are his actual or rhetorical topic: "I flattered myself that they who should be pleased with them would read them with more than common pleasure."[9] To put the matter bluntly: if a poet's emotions have to do with his or her occupational success, then it is not in the interest of scholarship to pretend that the emotions pertain to something else, even if the poet authorizes the pretense. As the classroom exercise of the *tableau vivant* suggests, however, it may be increasingly difficult to clarify a scholarly alternative to delighted acts of pretending. In a society of simulation it can appear as if there is no object or subject other than a momentary simulacrum and the artificial feelings attendant upon it. More that four decades ago, Erich Fromm observed that "in the nineteenth century, inhumanity meant cruelty; in the twentieth century it means schizoid self-alienation"; and

> the modern, alienated individual has opinions and prejudices but no convictions, has likes and dislikes, but no will. His opinions and prejudices, likes and dislikes, are manipulated in the same way as his taste is, by powerful propaganda machines which might not be effective were he not already conditioned to such influences as advertising and by his whole alienated way of life.[10]

The recent decades' revival of interest in Romantic-period drama, expressed often in the popular rhetoric of a neo-realism (in terms of political power, historical conditions, and anger about oppressed groups) is in many ways a cause for celebration. When I say that this scholarly development simultaneously represents a degradation in scholarly thought and writing, I write with the embarrassed ambivalence of one working within the movement that I describe.[11] The thought-forms that I shall be describing are not unique to studies of drama (appearing with equal clarity in studies of the nineteenth-century novel), or even nineteenth-century studies, which is simply the sub-discipline I happen to know best. Because examples will be necessary to make clear this essay's central critical point, I choose two recent studies—one of nineteenth-century drama and one of a nineteenth-century novel—not because these particular essays are the most prominent or influential, but rather because they seem to me exemplary, representative, and worthy of serious critical reflection.

In "Domestic Drama and Drama of Empire,"[12] Fred Radford writes of the Victorian theater and its reflection of a "self-image" for "its audiences," involving the "stress of doubt" (1). When I say that those terms present a subjectivized impression of what the Victorian theater was, I mean to contrast the internalized and personalized constructs ("self-image," "stress of doubt") against the way that one sort of materialist would see the Victorian theater as a structure of boards and plaster, and another would see it as a commercial enterprise. Radford's definition sees it as a set of subjective feeling-states, and that is a surprising way to describe the actuality of a theater. Radford adumbrates his argument with a commentary on a painting, Sir Joseph Noel Paton's *In Memoriam* (1862), in which some Sepoys in violent rebellion, intruding into a prison where women pray, are overpainted by Paton and replaced by images of Scottish soldiers coming to the women's rescue. "In effect, the correction of the painting erases the victory as the triumph of the avenging imperial troops was supposed to erase the shame of the early defeats in the 'Great Mutiny' itself" (2). "Triumph," "avenging," "shame"—the vocabulary indicates the pitch at subjectivities. This focus on subjective states suggests a lack of interest in material reality. Further, Radford corroborates the remark by an illustration, a photograph which is not in fact a photograph of the painting at all, but rather a photograph of an anonymous "contemporary engraving" of it. Artists often exploit simulations (the toy ape used in the filming of *King Kong* was eighteen inches tall), but scholarship is more normally *about* simulation rather than another instance of it. The fact of the matter—and plays, paintings, and engravings are factual matters—disappears from view when the spotlight is on the attitudes-in-themselves, feelings for feelings' sake, and a mere rhetoric of realism.

Radford's interesting essay includes the appeal of melodramatic anecdotes (usually involving murder, rape, suicide). Responsibly, Radford mentions that these anecdotes flatly falsify "the true outcome" of their heroine's stories, but the essay's point is not the truth of what happened but "the paradigm" that enters "the national consciousness" (4). The essay discusses Dion Boucicault's melodrama *Jessie Brown* without including a single fact about the play: was it produced? when? where? Was it printed? published? by whom? and when? Instead, Radford focuses on feeling-states and attitudes in the imaginary characters ("bloody-minded henchman"; characters "driven by desire"; and a character named Geordie who "is tainted with military cowardice until he renounces his inappropriate desires" [5, 8]). Apparently quite content with that narrative of feeling-states, and without any reference to facts about the work (was it ever published before it appeared in 1984 in the book that is Radford's source?), the essay goes on to the next melodramatic example. Very clearly—and the essay is admirable for its clarity of style—the object of the essay's investigation is no book or play production that ever existed in the material world, but rather an imaginary experience, a disembodied set of subjective states amenable to Radford's paraphrase.

An essay by Anne Weinstone in an earlier issue of the same periodical begins with an epigraph (from Teresa de Lauretis) that declares a ruling (even exclusive) interest in feeling-states: "The [project] is, as I see it, to articulate the relations of the female subject to representation, meaning, and vision, and in so doing to set out the terms of another measure of desire, the conditions of presence of another social subject."[13] The essay that takes this epigraph subsequently presents an argument that "the motive force that propels the narrative progression of *Villette* in toto . . . is Lucy Snowe's drive to decenter heterosexual union and its implied construction of family as the locus of both personal and narrative fulfillment, and her concurrent attempt to bring into existence 'another social subject' (de Lauretis's term), one who would enter into a chaste relationship of diffused eroticism with a male brother-mate: a relationship of what Lucy calls "passionate solicitude" (367). I observe that this essay's points of reference are subjective ("fulfillment," "eroticism," "passionate solicitude") and counterfactual. (Lucy Snowe, the character, does not really exist, and the propositions of the argument *about* her are as imaginary as the sentences of the novel— "*drive* to decenter . . . ," "*attempt* to bring into existence . . . ," "one who *would*. . . .") Sentences like those cannot be true or false; they do not refer to anything in the world outside fictitious ideation. And the use of the phrase "in toto" suggests a belief in the scholar's mind that this attempt to evoke subjective feeling-states exhausts all there is to be known about the novel. But the essay is not about the novel (which was, in fact, a book published in 1853); the essay's points of reference are in you, dear reader, and in me: "I agree with Alexander Doty that one does not have to be gay or lesbian, or even bisexual, to see from a queer vantage point or to take queer positions. In my view, queer also must include, for example, celibates, straight 'effeminate' men, and straight people who, as Sandra Harding allows, are engaged in the process of 'giving up the spontaneous consciousness created by their heterosexual experience in a heterosexist world'" (368). Thus the essay declares that it is not about a book (published in 1853) but rather about its own niche market in 1995. The social goals of the project and its insights concerning desire may be of considerable human value, and they should perhaps be released from the bondage of scholarly convention. The product, which is the essay and the learned journal, is not faulty scholarship about *Villette,* but rather no scholarship about it at all. It is an essay on feeling-states and not an essay on what Bronte and her publishers actually made in 1853, while many real things were actually going on.

In contrast, recent work by Catherine B. Burroughs emphasizes historically specific problems in the public world in which plays and their theatrical performances were, in fact, made.[14] Burroughs represents "the closet play" not as a set of feeling-states for you and for me, but as a set of actualities in real places: "The closet play comes into view as a genre especially well suited for providing women with a forum for dramatic experimentation within the privacy of their homes" (125). In contrast to numerous studies of Romantic-period "mental theater," Burroughs points out that "closet" was a physical thing in actual houses: "a small, private room, often used for meetings" (145n).[15] She notices Baillie's purposive use of a calculated rhetoric of "passions," and she indicates much about the public and commercial actualities of the theater in which Baillie contrived that rhetoric (126). Similarly, Sarah Siddons's public career indicates that acting was "a profession in which women could make quite a bit of money" (130); Mary Russell Mitford spoke and wrote not only of her inner states of feeling but very specifically about the size of audiences and observable nature of the public response (131). In contrast, studies that have so far been more influential than Burroughs's (and her book has just now appeared, so this may change)—studies that I will be mentioning below—have preferred to accept Baillie's manufactured rhetoric of "passion" as if it were passion rather than manufactured rhetoric.

As I have suggested, professionalized criticism in other literary fields has taken a turn in the same subjectivizing direction, similarly cloaking its interest in feeling-states with a rhetoric of illusory reference to the realities of history. In an issue of *PMLA,* Jaimie Hovey begins an article by asking: "How 'essential' is national identity to the modern subject?"[16] and then goes on to explain "the psychic constraints of gendered national belonging" (394). The "constraints of national, racial, and sexual inclusion" (403) sound quite materialistic, even biological in their reference, but in Hovey's essay they are no such thing; these terms and topics are reduced to "psychic" attitudes, to inwardly felt states in a "subject." In the same issue of *PMLA,* the next article explains how a poem by Derek Walcott "vivifies" an "inheritance" of "injury and at the same time deconstructs the uniqueness of suffering" (405). Though the essay mentions "violent colonial imposition" (407), which sounds at first like a reference to the real world, in fact the essay's topic and emphasis is an inwardly felt state of an imaginary subject—"his exquisitely elaborated pain" (407); and the critic concludes that Walcott's poem, after all, "poeticizes pain" (415). The putative emotions supposedly *meant* by the language of the literary artifact, and whose inner experience the critic narrates for the customer, furnish an example of "the soul of the commodity which Marx occasionally mentions in jest" but which does not exist except as a fiction used by the marketing industry.[17] I could multiply examples of this subjectivizing tendency, accompanied by a rhetorical pretense of real-world reference, but perhaps the familiar pattern has already been made clear.

Referring to a different but related example, Bruce Handy has recently characterized the exploitation of supposedly real reference for profit via entertainment values: "Marketing is everything."[18] The gendering of this issue—the treatment of personal subjectivity as feminine and factuality as masculine—has, of course, a long history, including important episodes in the Romantic period and continuing into the marketing ventures of current academic writing and publishing. Currently popular foci for the issue of marketed gender stereotypes (chiefly a feminine focus on feelings) include saliently the poetry of Felicia Hemans, perhaps because she marketed the stereotype of the affective female more successfully than any other writer of the nineteenth century. Duncan Wu has recently explained the issue by comparing Romantic-period reviewers with some late-twentieth-century commentators: An anonymous reviewer in *The British Critic* for 1823 writes that Hemans "is especially excellent in painting the strength and the weaknesses of her own lovely sex, and there is a womanly nature throughout all her thoughts and her aspirations, which is new and inexpressibly touching. A mother *only* could have poured forth [Hemans's] deep and passionate strain of eloquence"; and Wu observes that "the modern line, articulated by [Anne K.] Mellor, is remarkably similar; she says that Hemans 'constructed her self and poetry as the icon of female domesticity, the embodiment of the 'cult of true womanhood.'" Only the jargon has changed;

the substance remains the same. It is a line that both relegates the feminine to a second division category . . . and distorts our understanding of what women writers were trying to achieve."[19] As Wu knows, Mellor is not alone in the reproduction of the gender-stereotyping against which many Romantic period women (e.g., Mary Wollstonecraft and Mary Robinson) struggled. For example, Stuart Curran's claims that Jane Taylor's poetry is to be admired for "Taylor's capacity to reveal the inner life" and that "Charlotte Smith made a virtual career out of self-pity" perpetrate the same invidious substitution (putting the *woman* for the *poem*) as Richard Polwhele, Francis Jeffrey, Felicia Hemans, John Wilson Croker, and other Romantic-period salesmen of the belittling trademark with a large marketing niche, the stereotypically affective female.

What Wu does not mention is the commercial value of marketing stereotypes of demographic groups: textbooks in marketing that have been widely used in American universities during the past couple of decades are explicit about the procedures: "Demographic segmentation divides a market into subgroups on the basis of age, sex, income, education, occupation, social class, ethnicity or race, or other similar factors. Customer demography is the most commonly used segmentation base."[20] "Astute marketers look closely at the demographic aspects of the population and target their marketing accordingly"; one "demographic aspect of the marketing environment is the number of women versus the number of men in the population. Women in the United States form an important and a changing market. . . . Marketers have realized that women outlive men, that they share housekeeping duties with their husbands, and that they work in increasing numbers outside the home. Marketing campaigns must be adjusted accordingly."[21] Demographic niche marketing depends on the identification of the subject with the mass-produced image (the identity-traits) which is a marketer's tool. The supposed affectivity of women is such a trait: to focus on "the interior lives of the individual subjects" and "to prioritize emotional sympathy as the basis for a feminine ethic of care" and "to insist on the 'feelings'" are the trademarks of femininity when it has been made into a marketing tool.[22] The goal of marketing is to cause its audience to identify with these trademarks.

Two plays on the French Revolution, *The Massacre; taken from the French* by Elizabeth Inchbald and Baillie's *Constantine Paleologus,* are independently interesting works, and they are also valuable for thinking about those issues in literary scholarship that I have tried to illustrate above. These plays can help to show what difference it makes for interpretations whether one focuses on customer-satisfaction (subjectively felt attitudes like pity or fear or *jouissance*), or whether instead one focuses on the actual production and reception of the theatrical or literary business—stage production, which Aristotle called the art of the prop-master, or (in print forms) composition, typography, printing, bookbinding, and sales. I have suggested that the product that is sold by appeal to a subjective state (pleasure) is often described by critics as if it *were* itself a species of enjoyment, and I have suggested that there really is a difference between a book and a state of mind, and that a confusion of those two different sorts of thing does not help scholarship. Outside professional literary studies (and perhaps sometimes within literary studies too), the confusion of commodity with desired feeling-state is a deliberate operation which, when it reaches the scale of the mass market, enables producers and distributors of entertainment-commodities to install attitudes at long range. This production and installation of command models for the mind depends on a rhetoric of pleasure, and it is performed by corporations; that is the point of Jean Baudrillard's important essay "The Precession of Simulacra."[23] I will suggest, by way of my examples, that processes of textual and theatrical production, which are *not in minds* but which are, instead, material events, are themselves machines productive of meanings.

The *Massacre* is a stage play that has never been staged. *Constantine Paleologus* is a verse drama written for publication in a book but soon staged, several times. Both plays represent the French Revolution: Inchbald's *The Massacre* is set in Paris in 1792, and Baillie's play (like Shelley's epic *The Revolt of Islam*, or like Coleridge's play *Osorio*) represents the French Revolution figuratively, shifting the action to an historically removed setting (the fall of Constantinople in 1453). William St. Clair has described Godwin's *Abbas, an Historical Tragedy* (a play surviving only in manuscript) and commented briefly and wisely: "The curtain rises to reveal a mob of exulting Sunni Persians outside the smoking ruins of Medina where they have just destroyed the religious shrines of the Shiite Ottomans. . . . In *Vaurien*, one of the earliest of the anti-Jacobin novels, d'Israeli mocked philosophical writers who, to avoid the censorship laws, wrote Constantinople when they meant London and Mahometanism when they meant Christianity."[24] Baillie's resituation of the French revolutionary violence backward into fifteenth-century Constantinople and her execration of the infidel hordes who threatened the blessed security of the monarch were conventional. The dangerous hordes (atheist French revolutionaries) appear in the garb of invading Moslems, and Church and King appear not as Louis XVI or George III but rather the Emperor Constantine. This procedure of symbolic substitution (putting current events in ancient costume) enabled writers to represent revolutionary content when more direct enactments were not permitted on the London stage.[25] As Borges has said, censorship is the mother of metaphor.

In contrast, Inchbald's play represents directly the September Massacres of 1792. The play's characters repudiate the violence and call for peace, but that fact about the text could not protect the play from censorship. As he was banning conservative Mary Russell Mitford's royalist play, *Charles I,* the King's censor, George Colman the Younger, Examiner of Plays, said that the meaning of the author or of the play did not matter: "the morbid matter," Colman said, "lies in the very bones and marrow of the historical facts."[26] The *Massacre* was kept off the stage for fear that its violence would be a danger to the public or to the crown, and so Inchbald set out to have it printed as a book; after the proofs were printed, political pressure then prevented the publication of the printed play, and it did not appear at all, in any form, until James Boaden published it in his volume of *Memoirs* in 1833.[27] The analogy with contemporary films—e.g., *Pulp Fiction* and *Natural Born Killers*—is clear: people will believe that a critique of violence is a commercial for violence.

In an essay on *Julius Caesar,* Inchbald raises the issue of censorship, political suppression, and their effects on the drama: "when the circumstances of certain periods make certain incidents of history most interesting, those are the very seasons to interdict their exhibition."[28] Thus, revolutionary conflicts have been suppressed in two very different ways in these two dramas of violent revolution: censorship, in Inchbald's case, and symbolic substitution, in Baillie's. A paradox emerges: the play by Inchbald, a stage professional, was never produced on stage (to the best of my knowledge, it has *still* never been produced on a stage); the play by Baillie, who was a literary (rather than theatrical) professional, *was* produced on the stage. The irony is deepened because Inchbald's essays include observations about plays (like *The Winter's Tale*) which are better read than staged, and Inchbald remarks specifically (in her essay in *The British Theatre* on Baillie's *DeMonfort*) that Baillie's playwriting would benefit from more study of the stage. However, owing to political conditions (rather than skill) it was Baillie's play on the Revolution that was staged many times in the period, whereas Inchbald's remained suppressed in page proofs until 1833.

To notice some facts about the stage history of *Constantine Paleologus* will help to indicate how meanings are made for literary and dramatic works outside authorial intention, and certainly outside the author's feeling-state. The play opened first in Liverpool, on 7 November 1808, and the playbill for that performance says that the play "was altered by Mr. Terry, whose benefit it was [and who played Constantine]." Later in 1808, *Constantine Paleologus* was performed in London, at Surrey Theatre, re-titled *Constantine and Valeria.* It was produced again in 1820 in Edinburgh, where, according to a review in *Dublin University Magazine,* Baillie's play was again rewritten by the theatre manager, who informed the author that it had been necessary to adapt the play to "the taste of the present day," which demanded "the delineation of vehement passion." It is important that the theater manager asked Baillie to fabricate an illusion of passion, not to undergo passion. The theatrical company thought that Baillie's version included too much "didactic composition." And because the company was small, it was further necessary to reduce the number of characters. Baillie attended the production, and (in the words of the reviewer, who was also the theater manager) "the house was crowded, the audience liberal of applause, and the authoress delighted." Evidently playwrights in Baillie's lifetime, like teachers in insecure fields now, could be pleased by audiences' approval of their simulations of emotion. Several times in 1825 the play was performed in Dublin, and (according to its advertisement) "altered and adapted for representation in this theatre." The consequences of Baillie's drama coming out of the closet included its being rewritten by others, losing meanings, gaining meanings, and (in the way of theater) becoming an altogether corporate production.[29]

Burroughs's essay that I have already cited argues that Baillie's rendering of domesticity on a public stage has profound gender-political implications (*Closet Stages,* 11–12). I agree, and I too would suggest that the material means of dramatic production (or literary production) have a great deal to do with social and human meanings. In contrast, in a brilliant new essay Philippe Lacoue-Labarthe and Jean-Luc Nancy disjoin the artistry and value of dramatic texts from the physicality of performance. Later they complicate this judgment, as I shall show in a moment, but here, approvingly, they cite Aristotle who "declares that the *opsis* [stagecraft, spectacle, performance] is . . . foreign to art"; "the reading (aloud, of course; this is very important) suffices to cause the catharsis" so that "the [staged] representation — from the exclusively Aristotelian point of view . . .—is not at all necessary." During a theatrical performance, "one remains there to listen to a text."[30]

To listen to these texts, I suggest, is to be led out of them and into a specifiably conflicted social world. One exemplary trope within the plays will help to show how this is so. In *The Massacre,* Eusebe Tricastin escapes from the September Massacres in Paris, with the blood of his wife's mother on his clothes; even when he is home, sixty miles from Paris, his mind is disordered by the violence that he witnessed: for example, he saw "infants, encouraged by the fury of their tutors, stab other infants sleeping in their cradles" (9). In *Constantine Paleologus,* a Citizen rushes into the palace to warn the Emperor and his family of the mob violence in the city: "I come to tell your highness that the city / Is in commotion; e'en with flesh-forks arm'd"—not only adults engage in this mindless slaughter in the streets, but "The very children too" (451).

This circumstance of the murderous children links both plays to a larger discourse of the Revolutionary years. Inchbald adds a note to that sentence: "Shocking, even to incredibility, as these murders may appear, the truth of them has been asserted in many of our public prints during the late massacre at Paris." Inchbald refers to the massacre on St. Bartholomew's Day in 1572: "the same extravagant wickedness is attested to have been acted at the massacre on St. Bartholomew, by almost every historian of that time" (9n). This note demythologizes the action. Permitting these annotations on the page, the printed text allows what a staged performance of the script alone would not: this is what Pierre Macherey has called an "irruption of the real,"[31] and what Lacoue-Labarthe and Nancy have called an "interruption of the myth" (274). Material and social effects dispel the illusion of merely imaginary action. Imagine the projector's stopping in the middle of a movie, and the director's turning on the lights and making, in person, a speech about a factual matter. In both cases, it is not only the *content* of the discursive note that achieves this "irruption of the real." The printed footnotes—as physical features on the page—are a machinery for importation of factuality. The ideological difference between Baillie's play and Inchbald's is represented by Baillie's burial of the reference to the real as opposed to Inchbald's making that reference into a typographical object. This entirely bibliographical fact, the presence on the page and the function in the reference—invade the imaginary space of the dramatic illusion.

A precursor-play can help to clarify the difference: Jeff Cox has suggested to me that Marie-Joseph Chenier's play, *Charles IX* (1788), may be the French play to which Inchbald's subtitle refers. Chenier's play also includes a massacre in Paris followed by counsel against massacre. In both plays a leader of the violence undergoes a conversion and advocates peace. Chenier's play is in five acts, and its action is set in 1572, whereas Inchbald's play, set in her present (1792), contains three acts. But by her own account (in an essay on her adaptation of other plays from the German), Inchbald preferred free deviation from the original in her adaptations.[32] Chenier's *Charles IX* ends in the tragedy of the king; in contrast, Inchbald's play ends in the moralized optimism of those who were once violent rebels becoming benevolent protectors of the innocent. In its use of historical displacement, in its versification, and in its conclusion in despair over national degradation, Chenier's play resembles Baillie's *Constantine Paleologus,* which ends in the misery and horror of the infidels' victory over Christian patriarchy, more than it resembles Inchbald's *Massacre.*

The issue of gender politics is related, in these women's writings, to the dramaturgy of the closet. In *Closet Stages* Burroughs compares Baillie's plays with Wollstonecraft's nonfictional writing which refers in theatrical terms to social acting.[33] Her plays often do not appear feminist even by eighteenth-century standards, but Burroughs says that in general the theory of Romantic-period women writers emerges "from women's experiences of performing gender on the public stages of 'social theaters'" (17). This is an astute point because it does not rest on a claim about subjective intention—Burroughs does not resort to the tempting rhetorical posture of claiming that Baillie had political goals similar to those of late-twentieth-century American academics.

Like the poetry of Felicia Hemans, Baillie's plays can be said to make gender domination visible, which is a critical function, whether it was intended critically or not (and there is no cogent evidence whatsoever that Hemans or Baillie devoted any of their writings to feminist political goals). However, Baillie's explicit and popular endorsements of patriarchal concepts of femininity and her use of traditional sex-role stereotypes might be said to expose, with political significance but without political intent, the artificiality of the social scripts that dispossess and demean women. In this way, the artificially staged simulation of personalistic attitudes is an occasion for purchased pleasure, for those who prefer not to think—particularly, those who prefer not to know that the spectacle and the feelings are fake. For critical reflection, however, such a simulation is an exhibit of reactionary and patriarchal patterns—gendered domination by remote control—even though it means to be (rather) a commercial venture.

In this connection, Baillie's professedly opportunistic fabrications of the illusion of "passion" are germane. In contrast to an emerging consensus in Romantic-period studies,[34] Baillie does not say, and her writings do not suggest, that "passion" is intrinsically good, morally worthy, or politically useful. She says that it is a popular commodity. In the "Introductory Discourse" in her *Series of Plays, In Which It Is*

Attempted to Delineate the Stronger Passions of the Mind: Each Passion Being the Subject of a Tragedy and a Comedy (1798), Baillie writes of the fabricated spectacle of "passion"—its power to interest people, not its moral or political value or truth. She says that all persons "not deficient in intellect" derive "pleasure" from "curiosity" about other peoples' feelings.[35] Her point is that the public spectacle of "passion" has power to "excite . . . curiosity and interest" (10), at a "public execution" (10) no less than an artificial enactment on a stage (11). Adam Smith's *Theory of Moral Sentiments* (1759), William Hazlitt's *Essay on the Principles of Human Action* (1805), and Percy Bysshe Shelley's "A Defence of Poetry" (1821) do make moral arguments about emotional sympathy as an engine of ethical action, but Baillie does not—she writes of show business. She says that, even in others' writings that *are* moral and philosophical , the function of affecting "images and examples" involves *appeal* to emotional appetites rather than moral or philosophical values or truth (13). Not only does Baillie state her intent to exploit audiences' appetites for "passion," but she also explains that it works by way of creating a false belief, in the audience, that the author felt something. Robert Young, star of the long-popular television show *Marcus Welby, M.D.,* regularly received letters from TV viewers asking him for medical advice. As Baillie says, "when we meet in some scene of a good play a very fine stroke of this kind, we are apt to become so intoxicated with it, and so perfectly convinced of the author's great knowledge of the human heart, that we are unwilling to suppose the whole of it has not been suggested by the same penetrating spirit" (14). That plan goes beyond inducing a suspension of disbelief; in show business, a dramatic display of "passion" is a spectacle contrived with an intent to deceive; "it's a trick," as the character played by Juliette Lewis says of her own stories in the movie *Husbands and Wives* (directed by Woody Allen, 1992). Whereas Baillie *explains* the spectacle of "passion" in terms of the salesmanship of show business, much recent scholarly writing about the literature of the period, and about Baillie in particular, *perpetrates* (with or without intention) such salesmanship rather than explanation.

In his contribution to "Joanna Baillie: Stagecraft and the Politics of Performance," Greg Kucich has recently said that Baillie's social goals (contrary to the evidence) included equality across classes and gender, and that the staged simulation of personalistic passion to which *dramatis personae* are subjected somehow promotes this goal. Kucich cites Baillie's "Introductory Discourse" to support this claim, which is consistent with Anne Mellor's canonical gloss on Baillie[36] and with Marjean Purinton's characterization of Baillie's social goals in

Purinton's excellent commentary on *DeMonfort* in her book *Ideology Unmasked.*[37] Such a view would surely help to make Baillie's plays more popular now; further, if Baillie is right about the appeal of "passion," then making "passion" a theme of our own rhetoric, without putting much of a critical edge on it, could be a valuable resource for threatened academics in a dwindling job market; and it can also interest and comfort us. But in fact the "Introductory Discourse" does not say that the simulation of personal passion promotes equality; it says that the simulation of personal passion promotes commercial entertainments. It is also a matter of documentary fact that Baillie's plays lost some rhetorical didacticism to gain some simulated passion not because of her social or political goals, but rather because of theater managers' attempts to draw crowds. This is the sales appeal of which Robert Phillip Kolker has written, in connection with the use of close-ups in popular movies: close-up photography is used "to narrow the narrative field to concentrate attention inward," excluding the context of life outside to focus on "the emotionally charged human face."[38] It may be that, as another critic has written, "a multitude of causes, unknown to former times, are now acting with a combined force to blunt the discriminating powers of the mind" and "to reduce it to a state of almost savage torpor," producing "a craving for extraordinary incident" and a "degrading thirst after outrageous stimulation"—passion, in short, as in "frantic novels" and "extravagant stories in verse."[39] To moralize that operation would be a scholarly mistake. And the putative feminism of Baillie's antirevolutionary drama likewise calls for some careful analysis rather than hasty (if happy) presumption.

Constantine Paleologus celebrates the subordination of women in domesticity, a subordination that is part of the conservative morality or propaganda in Edmund Burke's *Reflections on the Revolution in France.* According to Burke, love of the patriarchal arrangements at home in one's cottage nurtures a loving obedience and reverential submission to the monarch. Devotion to domestic patriarchy is practice for submission to a national system of patriarchy. In Baillie's play, the revered Emperor's benevolence at home in the palace and the Queen's devotion to him are produced as models in a Burkean propaganda of domesticity. In act 1, Constantine is described in terms of his "domestic habits."[40] Nobles arrive to meet with the Emperor when he returns from surveying the battle, but Constantine goes first to give his dear devotions to his wife. The men discuss "death and carnage" (450) while Valeria tries to distract Constantine's thoughts from the disagreeable fact of the fall of their civilization, and to recall her husband's thoughts to home and to private feeling—"The hour of thy heart's sorrow . . . The hour of thy heart's joy" (451). Valeria repudiates the entire public sphere: "Our nature suits not with these worldly times" (451). In act 5, when Constantine dies, Valeria asks of the conqueror nothing but "A place in the quiet tomb with my fall'n lord" (476). That is exactly what she achieves, by committing suicide (477). This role, then, is a script for conventional femininity, an image of gender-essentialism that diminishes women and justifies by ideological means their total subordination to men. In this way, *Constantine Paleologus,* with its dramatic acceptance of the destructive effect of these stereotypes on women's lives, anticipates (or models for) Hemans's *Records of Woman:* there, in almost every poem, but most obviously in "The Bride of the Greek Isle" and "Properzia Rossi," Hemans memorializes the destruction of a woman who subordinates herself to a man, in a lovingly womanly way.

Gender is typified (or even stereotypified) in Inchbald's *The Massacre* as well. Inchbald's play rehearses a conventional script in the tradition of sentiment: when asked whether Madame Tricastin had told him of her distress, her benevolent old father-in-law replies, "Tell!—is there cause for telling when a woman of sensibility loves or hates? When she feels hopes or fears, joy or sorrow? No—the passions dwell upon her every feature—none but the female hypocrite need fly to the tongue to express them" (3). Perhaps (like Mary Hays's novel *Emma Courtney*) this play exhibits that belief about women to expose it to critique. In the *Massacre* as in Baillie's play, the woman dies—a paragon of wifely and maternal devotion. Perhaps (though I do not think so) codified scripts of speechlessly emotive women function in a revolutionary way by recentering value in the body, in finite time and physical space, as Jerome J. McGann has recently suggested.[41] Baillie's gender-image is womanly removal from the world; Inchbald's gender-image is immediate immersion in the action here and now—but it is action scripted for the sentimental subordination of women. In such scripts, women are prisoners of their supposed feeling-states, their artificially posed attitudes.

In the literature of the period, the portrayal of horrid French revolutionary violence is often (though not always) royalist:[42] Burke's sensationalistic rhetoric, in *Reflections on the Revolution in France,* about the brutal ruffians disturbing the elegant queen and her children in the palace is an obvious example. This Burkean rhetoric of domestic loveliness for the royalty, intolerably threatened by the invasion of savages, is a common (and very conservative) topic in Baillie's play, as it had been in Burke's polemic. But in the *Massacre,* the repudiation of violence is couched in the terms of a democratic and revolutionary group.

The plays' representations of the crowds—obviously a common topic in representations of the Revolution—dramatize vividly this distinction between Inchbald's politics and Baillie's. In *Constantine Paleologus* (1.i), a disguised Turk has infiltrated the palace to give the spy Petronius some gold with which to bribe crowds to rise in insurrection. Even during this sordid interaction, the crowds to be enlisted by such bribery are called (by those who bribe them) "rabble." Only slightly later in the play (1.ii), the Emperor Constantine consults one of his noble friends for news, and Othus, an aristocratic and learned Greek, tells him that the imperial city is populated by a "degraded herd."

In act 2, a little mollifying of the raging crowds takes place, but in a patrician and extremely belittling way. In a street before the palace, a crowd arrives with torches and clubs, shouting threats to Constantine (2.i). When the Emperor appears, he complains that the crowd do not behave like good children. At this rebuke, some of the crowd are heartwarmed by this anamnesis of their own dependency and filial duty. Reformed by the Emperor's moral superiority (dramatized merely by his rebuke that they are not good children), some among the crowd actually cheer Constantine. Some remain hostile, but the crowd of supporters grows, and the Emperor's loyal followers drive the grumbling remnant away.

The Moslems (Baillie's costumed version of the Reign of Terror) are no better, but actually worse, in their contempt for the crowd. Mahomet's vizir points out that Mahomet's vanguard "is of a motley class, / The vile refuse and garbage of the camp." Mahomet says "Garbage, I trust, / Is good enough for filling ditches up" (3.i). Nothing on either side of this war, in Baillie's play, ever mitigates this patrician contempt for the common multitude.

In the *Massacre* the common topic of the mob in the streets is central to the action from the start. A friend bursts into the house of Tricastin to warn him that some raging adversaries from the capital are here. Young Tricastin is "proscribed; a price is set upon your life . . . rabble are at the gate" (2.i). But these rabble undergo conversion to peacefulness by the play's end, coming to protect the threatened gentry, not to attack them; it is the citizen's battalion of protectors at the end of the *Massacre* who say, "amongst the whole battalion, we have not one hangman" (3.ii). It is the "rights of man" that inspire this love of peace and popular benevolence, and not, as in *Constantine Paleologus,* a reminder that an unruly mob is behaving like bad children. Further, it is the public citizens' own sensibility that awakens their moral justice, and not, as in Baillie's patrician fantasy (or Burke's), instructions from their betters. In the *Massacre,* Glandeve, one of the revolutionaries, voices the moral turn for the better in these terms: "'tis liberty to do good, not ill—liberty joined with peace and charity." In Baillie's play, the people of the crowd, "the vile refuse and garbage" of the city, are still human garbage at the play's end, subjugated now and ruled by a Moslem, but not otherwise changed, ennobled, or dignified.

To compare the political engagements of Inchbald's play with Baillie's is thus simultaneously to contrast two ideologically loaded images of the French Revolution (one reformist, the other reactionary) and also two forms of suppression undergone by writings on revolutionary themes—censorship, and symbolic substitution. The reactionary propaganda of Baillie's play, in the service of political domination (monarchy) and gendered domination (patriarchy), will not be visible to an audience that has suspended its disbelief in order to enjoy an artificial spectacle of passion. Further, the vicarious enjoyment of faked passion is incompatible with the reflection that this show is an example of manipulative profiteering. It does not cease to be such a thing, in fact, when customers forget the fact. Even if a playwright (or poet) had said that passion is universally good for you (which Baillie did not say), or if she had said that she would like for audiences to be trapped inside the artificial emotions of a phony spectacle, it would not be in the best interest of scholarship to confine itself within the contrived parameters of a staged pretense. It cannot be a scholarly obligation to suspend disbelief of a falsehood on the grounds that a writer found it profitable to promulgate that falsehood. Similarly, the claim that faked feelings are enjoyable is not a good reason to accept a scholarly mistake or a failure of critical intelligence. Even if an appeal to passions sells theater tickets (which is what Baillie did say), or if such an appeal sells garments or beer, to use such appeals in that way is marketing and not scholarship. When a salespitch is successful the result is sale, not knowledge or truth or any of the other goals of what still purports to be a sciential enterprise.

I do not mean to close in a celebration of the figurality of these dramas. At this point the complications of Lacoue-Labarthe and Nancy, which I mentioned earlier, arise: they advise "suspicion . . . toward . . . a figural and fictional . . . presentation of the . . . truth'" (280). From a meaning-theory point of view, surrogation and figuration may be an impoverishment of truth, a curse rather than a blessing—"figuration is in fact the bad luck of . . . the 'human world' in general,"

Lacoue-Labarthe says (280). I would rather suggest that figuration and symbolic displacements do not impoverish a work of its truths, though they cannot constitute those truths. Some truths remain *outside* the sentential and symbolic meanings of the figural construct (whether an enactment or a text), *outside* your subjective feeling-states, dear reader, but in the material form of that enactment or a text. A text is not a thought or a feeling: it is a made thing in the world. It is marketing that produces the confusion between things and one's attitude about the things, because marketing works precisely on attitudes. In human works there are and always were meanings that are larger than their own ideation, and larger than the enjoyment of them. Further, and finally, I suggest that interpretation of these writings, and critical description of those meanings, should probably take these larger-than-authorial meanings into account.

Notes

1. See Alison Schneider, "Jane Tompkins's Message to Academe: Nurture the Individual, Not Just the Intellect," *The Chronicle of Higher Education* (10 July 1998): Schneider reports that some of Prof. Jane Tompkins's classes at Duke University "stayed overnight on an island" to "feel the magic" of the sea, and "they tried to figure out what the books meant to them on a personal level, and what they, as classmates, meant to one another" (A8). The same article reports that Prof. Tompkins has secured a new position in which she "will teach one course a year," and that "she is spending less and less time teaching and says she may retire from university life altogether in the not-too-distant future" (A10).

2. Earl Shorris, *A Nation of Salesmen,* quoted in Thomas Frank, "The New Gilded Age," in *Commodify Your Dissent,* ed. Thomas Frank and Matt Weiland (New York: Norton, 1997), 23.

3. "Association statistics," *PMLA,* 112. 4 (September 1997): 605.

4. Richard Taverner, *Proverbes or Adagies, Gathered Out of the Chiliades of Erasmus* (London: William How, 1569), 9.

5. For a recent example of this interest in appetites, see Stephen C. Behrendt and Harriet Kramer Linkin, preface to *Approaches to Teaching British Women Poets of the Romantic Period,* ed. Behrendt and Linkin (New York: MLA, 1997), xii: "All this activity points to the very real appetite for the work of these neglected writers."

6. Andrew Bowie, "Non-Identity," in *Intersections,* ed. Tilottama Rajan and David L. Clark (Albany: State University of New York Press, 1995), 252.

7. Behrendt and Linkin, preface to *Approaches to Teaching British Women Poets of the Romantic Period,* xi.

8. Greg Kucich, "Staging History: Teaching Romantic Intersections of Drama, History, and Gender," in *Approaches to Teaching British Women Poets of the Romantic Period,* ed. Behrendt and Linkin, 93.

9. Wordsworth, Preface to *Lyrical Ballads,* in *William Wordsdworth: Selected Prose,* ed. John O. Hayden (Harmondsworth: Penguin, 1988), 279–80.

10. Erich Fromm, *The Sane Society* (New York: Holt, Rinehart and Winston, 1955) 360, 339.

11. See Terence Allan Hoagwood, "Prolegomenon for a Theory of Romantic Drama," in *The Wordsworth Circle,* 23. 2 (Spring 1992): 49–64; and "Romantic Drama and Historical Hermeneutics," in *British Romantic Drama: Historical and Critical Essays,* ed. Hoagwood and Daniel P. Watkins (Cranbury, N.J.: Fairleigh Dickinson University Press, 1998), 22–55.

12. Fred Radford, "Domestic Drama and Drama of Empire: Inter-textuality and the Subaltern Woman in Late Victorian Theatre," *Nineteenth-Century Contexts,* 20 (1997): 1–25.

13. Teresa de Lauretis, "Oedipus Interruptus," *Wide Angle,* 7 (1985): 38; quoted in Anne Weinstone, "The Queerness of Lucy Snowe," *Nineteenth-Century Contexts,* 18 (1995): 367. The bracketed interpolation is Weinstone's.

14. Catherine B. Burroughs, "The English Romantic Closet: Women, Theatre Arts, Joanna Baillie, and *Basil,*" *Nineteenth-Century Contexts,* 19 (1995): 125–49. See also Burroughs's important new book, *Closet Stages: Joanna Baillie and the Theater Theory of British Romantic Women Writers* (Philadelphia: University of Pennsylvania Press, 1997).

15. Burroughs quotes the definition of "closet" from Martin Harrison, "Closet Drama," in *Theatre* (Manchester: Carcanet Press, 1993), 56.

16. Jaimie Hovey, "'Kissing a Negress in the Dark': Englishness as a masquerade in Woolf's *Orlando,*" *PMLA,* 112. 3 (May 1997): 393.

17. Walter Benjamin, *Charles Baudelaire: A Lyric Poet in the Era of High Capitalism,* trans. Harry Zohn (London: New Left Books, 1973), 55. Robin Jarvis applies this remark by Benjamin to urban "strollers [sharing] the nature of the commodity, surrounded by a surge of 'customers'" and compares "the peddling of imaginative sympathies" with "'the prostitution of the commodity-soul'" (*Romantic Writing and Pedestrian Travel* [Houndmills, Basingstoke: Macmillan; New York: St. Martin's, 1997], 210).

18. Bruce Handy, "Buzz Buzz Buzz," *Time* (20 July 1998): 50. Handy observes that "optioning" magazine and newspaper articles has been a growing trend in Hollywood.

19. Duncan Wu, in *Romantic Women Poets: An Anthology,* ed. Duncan Wu (Oxford: Blackwell, 1997), xxiii. Wu cites Mellor's *Romanticism and Gender* (New York and London: Routledge, 1993), 123.

20. William H. Cunnigham, Isabella C. M. Cunningham, and Christopher M. Swift, *Marketing: A Managerial Approach,* 2nd ed. (Cincinnati: South-western, 1987), 284.

21. Stewart W. Husted, Dale L. Varble, James R. Lowry, *Principles of Modern Marketing* (Boston: Allyn and Bacon, 1989), 78–79.

22. Greg Kucich, "Staging History: Teaching Romantic Intersections of Drama, History, and Gender," in *Approaches to Teaching British Women Poets of the Romantic Period,* ed. Behrendt and Linkin, 91.

23. Jean Baudrillard, "The Precession of Simulacra," in *Simulations,* trans. Paul Foss, Paul Patton, and Philip Beitchman (New York: Semio-text(e), 1983), 1–80.

24. St. Clair, *The Godwins and the Shelleys* (Baltimore: Johns Hopkins University Press, 1989), 234.

25. The machinery of censorship was powerful, efficient, and very busy, and its effects were crucial for the dramatic literature of the period: see L. W. Conolly, *The Censorship of English Drama 1737–1824* (San Marino: Huntington Library, 1976); and Hoagwood, "Prolegomenon for a Theory of Romantic Drama," 49–64.

26. George Colman, Examiner of Plays, to Mary Russell Mitford (1825), quoted by Kenneth Johnston and Joseph Nicholes, "Transitory Actions, Men Betrayed: The French Revolution in the English Revolution in Romantic Drama," *The Wordsworth Circle,* 23. 2 (Spring 1992): 87.

27. James Boaden, *Memoirs of Mrs. Inchbald: Including Her Familiar Correspondence with the Most Distinguished Persons of Her Time. To Which Is Added "The Massacre," and "A Case of Conscience"; Now First Published from Her Autograph Copies,* 2 vols. (London: Richard Bentley, 1833). Boaden's preliminary note to *The Massacre* says that "This play was suppressed, though printed, before publication, in deference to political opinions" (2: 356). My text for the play is a copy of the 1792 proofs which is located at the Library of Congress.

28. Inchbald, "Remarks" prefixed to her edition of *Julius Caesar: A Tragedy, in Five Acts; by William Shakespeare. As performed at the Theatre Royal, Covent Garden, Printed Under the Authority of the Managers from the Prompt Book* (London: Hurst, Robinson and Co., 1808), 3. This work appeared among the twenty-five volumes that Inchbald edited under the general title *The British Theatre.* Inchbald's prefaces from this collection have been reprinted with an introduction by Cecilia Macheski (Delmar, N.Y.: Scholars' Facsimiles, 1990).

29. Margaret Carhart, *The Life and Work of Joanna Baillie* (1923. Rpt. n.p.: Archon Books, 1970), 154–57.

30. Philippe Lacoue-Labarthe and Jean-Luc Nancy, "Scene: An Exchange of Letters," trans. Maiko Behr, in *Beyond Representation: Philosophy and Poetic Imagination,* ed. Richard Eldridge (Cambridge: Cambridge University Press, 1996), 273–302.

31. Pierre Macherey, *A Theory of Literary Production,* trans. Geoffrey Wall (London: Routledge and Kegan Paul, 1978), 39.

32. Inchbald, "Preface on the First Publication of *Lovers' Vows,*" in *Lovers' Vows; A Play in Five Acts; Altered from the German of Kotzebue, By Mrs. Inchbald, As Performed at the Theatre Royal, Covent-Garden, Printed Under the Authority of the Managers from the Prompt Book* (London: Longman, Hurst, Rees, Orme, and Brown, 1808), 3.

33. Burroughs, *Closet Stages,* 19.

34. This consensus was in eloquent evidence at the fascinating session "Joanna Baillie: Stagecraft and the Politics of Performance," organized by Donelle R. Ruwe and held at the MLA Convention in Washington, D.C., in December 1996.

35. Baillie, "Introductory Discourse" to *A Series of Plays* (1798), in *The Complete Poetical Works of Joanna Baillie* (Philadelphia: Carey and Lea, 1832), 9.

36. See Anne K. Mellor, "Joanna Baillie," in *British Romantic Literature 1780–1830* (Fort Worth: Harcourt Brace, 1996), 430–32.

37. Marjean Purinton, *Romantic Ideology Unmasked: The Mentally Constructed Tyrannies in Dramas of William Wordsworth, Lord Byron, Percy Bysshe Shelley, and Joanna Baillie* (Newark, Del.: University of Delaware Press, 1994), 125–62.

38. Robert Kolker, *A Cinema of Loneliness,* 2nd ed. (New York: Oxford University Press, 1988), 309.

39. William Wordsworth, preface to *Lyrical Ballads,* 2nd ed. (1800), 284.

40. Joanna Baillie, *Constantine Paleologus; or, The Last of the Caesars. A Tragedy, in Five Acts,* in Baillie, *Dramatic and Poetical Works* (London, 1851), 449.

41. See McGann, *The Poetics of Sensibility* (Oxford: Oxford University Press, 1996), 113–16: Mary Robinson's sequence of sonnets, *Sappho and Phaon* (1796) is here said to illustrate an "enlightened sensibility" valuing simultaneously "intellectual beauty" and "the fully liberated body" in a way that somehow has political importance: "Robinson's and Sappho's histories come to reflect each other's. . . . It is the poetic sensibility that exposes these

relations, according to Robinson, and the poetry of sensibility that puts them into most effective (social) action. Not that the more polemical views and approaches [of Wollstonecraft, e.g.] are unimportant or ineffective. But for Robinson the poet is especially favoured with the power to wed the longest kind of philosophical view ('the whole') with full, intense, and immediate awareness ('passion')," though the "passion" is entirely a "rhetorical convention" (4). In contrast, Rebecca Jackson and Terence Allan Hoagwood have pointed out that Robinson's *Sappho and Phaon* "exposes the fatal consequences that real women suffer when they 'learn to love' in ways dictated by the fictions of female desire" (Introduction, *Sappho and Phaon, In a Series of Legitimate Sonnets* (1796 [Delmar, N.Y.: Scholars' Facsimiles, 1995]), 6.

42. For examples of such portrayals on the radical side, see James Mckintosh, *Vindiciae Gallicae: Defence of the French Revolution* (1791), new ed. (London: W. H. Cox and J. Chidley, 1838), 70–71; Thomas Paine, *The Rights of Man* (1791), in *"Reflections on the Revolution in France" and "The Rights of Man"* (New York: Doubleday, 1973), 296; Coleridge, "On the Present War" (1795), in *Lectures 1795 on Politics and Religion,* ed. L. Patton and P. Mann, in *The Collected Works of Samuel Taylor Coleridge,* gen. ed. Kathleen Coburn, 14 vols. to date (Princeton: Princeton University Press, 1970–95), 1: 69; and Shelley, preface to *Laon and Cythna; or, The Revolution of the Golden City: A Vision of the Nineteenth Century* (1818), in *The Complete Works of Percy Bysshe Shelley,* ed. Roger Ingpen and Walter E. Peck, 10 vols. (London: Ernest Benn, 1926–30), 1: 240–41.

Benevolent Historian: Helen Maria Williams and Her British Readers

ᓚ

Deborah Kennedy

Traditionally, the areas of politics and history have not been regarded as a woman's proper sphere of study or activity. If, even in the twentieth century, as Joan Wallach Scott has observed, the involvement of women in those fields has been problematic, then how much more so was that the case for women in the late eighteenth century,[1] when Catharine Macaulay was the only female historian of stature,[2] and Angelica Kauffman perplexed critics by surpassing her male contemporaries in the genre of history painting.[3] What, then, did readers think of Helen Maria Williams (1761–1827), a well-known poet of sensibility, with many friends in London's politically active Dissenting circles, who became famous for her books on the French Revolution? Her eight volumes of *Letters from France* (1790–1796) trace the development of the Revolution from the period of the Festival of the Federation in July 1790, when she visited France for the first time, to the aftermath of the Reign of Terror. Taking up permanent residence in France in 1792, Williams identified with the progressive principles of her Girondin friends, and continued to write in defence of liberty until her death in 1827. Her *Letters from France* became an important source of information for the British reading public at a time when the rights of men (and to a lesser degree the rights of women) were the subjects of vindication and vilification in the British press. The involvement of French women in the Revolution gave them a place in the political and historical record that challenged traditional definitions of their roles. Likewise, it was an age when the literary women of England who wrote about the events in France could be scorned as "strumpets," laughed at as politicians in "petticoats," or revered as "benevolent" historians. Each of these phrases was used to describe Williams at one point in time.

The responses to Williams's writing reflected the political divisions accentuated by the revolutionary debates and are thus characterized by their political allegiances and gender expectations. Williams's British reviewers reacted in one of three ways: they either refused to accept that she or any other woman was capable of writing on matters touching political affairs; or they accepted that a woman could write on such subjects, but they demanded that her work conform to traditional modes of political and historical discourse; or, finally, they championed the *Letters from France* as a unique and valuable work whose epistolary style and appeal to pathos set it apart—in a positive sense—from standard history.[4] Such divergent positions are reflective of Williams's own ambivalence about how to classify her work. She shied away from the presumption of calling it history—a masculine category—and yet the very raison d'être of her books was to provide a record of experiences and events of lasting historical and political importance.

In the opening to her first volume of *Letters from France,* Williams explained why she had become such an ardent supporter of the Revolution: "this was not a time in which the distinctions of country were remembered. It was the triumph of human kind; it was man asserting the noblest privileges of his nature; and it required but the common feelings of humanity to become in that moment a citizen of the world."[5] Although she claimed for herself the identity of a "citizen of the world" (echoing Richard Price in his "Discourse on the Love of Our Country"—the speech that provoked Edmund Burke to write his great counterrevolutionary book, *Reflections on the Revolution in France*), Williams realized that for an English woman to publish such jubilant support of the newly reborn French nation would expose her to charges that she was both unpatriotic and unfeminine.[6] She tried to reassure her critics that she was not usurping the role of a male political observer; rather, she was reading the Revolution as a woman, or responding with her heart to the events in France: "my political creed is entirely an affair of the heart, for I have not been so absurd as to consult my head upon matters of which it is so incapable of judging" (1.1.66). Lacking the political knowledge and education that a male writer might possess, Williams stakes her claims instead on the power of a woman's ability to be moved by scenes of happiness, suffering, or injustice, and to judge them accordingly, even if she did not understand all of the political issues involved. Her assertion of the traditional view of women's emotional nature was not simply a rhetorical strategy used to deflect criticism: Williams's emotional sensitivity and her ability to express it were fundamental parts of her own self identity and her public identity as a poet of sensibility.

Over the course of the six years that she published the *Letters from France,* Williams became more knowledgeable and politically astute, but her signature, as it were, was still that of the "woman of feeling," and favorable reviews of her work consistently emphasized its "feminine" ethos. For instance, the *Analytical Review* stated explicitly that "Her reflections on the French Revolution are truly feminine."[7] The statement (which implies a comparison to Burke's *Reflections*) registers the uniqueness of a historical moment when a reviewer could combine in the same sentence the words "revolution" and "feminine." The *Analytical Review* went on to say that her *Letters* "confirmed the very favourable opinion we have entertained of the goodness of the writer's heart. . . . As the destruction of the Bastille was an event that affected every heart—even hearts not accustomed to the melting mood, it was natural to suppose that it would particularly touch a tender one—and every page of Miss Williams's book tells us, in an unequivocal tone, that her's is true to every soft emotion."[8] In the political climate of 1790, events like the fall of the Bastille were viewed from a perspective shaped by a culture of sensibility. Readers expected Williams to respond to scenes of injustice with her exemplary tender-heartedness.

Her literary persona formed a striking contrast to Mary Wollstonecraft's in a *Vindication of the Rights of Men.* While the first volume of Williams's *Letters* was partly a travel book and was written before Burke's book appeared, Wollstonecraft's *Vindication* was a direct and forceful reply to Burke.[9] The *English Review* praised Wollstonecraft by saying, "The language may be thought by some too bold and pointed for a female pen; but when women undertake to write on masculine subjects, and reason as Miss Wollstonecraft does, we wish their language to be free from all female *prettinesses,* and to express with energy and perspicuity, the ideas they mean to convey."[10] Wollstonecraft seems to have succeeded in using the "rational forms of inquiry" that Greg Kucich has called a "crucial strategy" for "women historians seeking acceptance in a closed field of masculine activity."[11] However, not all reviewers were pleased with Wollstonecraft's masculine persona: the *Gentleman's Magazine* ridiculed her as a gender-crossing military combatant, "armed cap-à-pied."[12] On the other hand, according to one writer, Williams was a wholly feminine opponent to Burke. In the poem "On reading 'Letters written from France in the summer of 1790 to a Friend in England, by Helen Maria

Williams,'" Edward Jerningham depicts Burke as a knight with all the benefits of his masculine armor to protect him, and yet he is vanquished by Williams, a "lovely Maid," dressed in a "flowing robe," who

> ... tries no formal refutation
> Of his elab'rate speculation,
> Nor raves of Governments and Laws,
> For she to Nature trusts her cause;
> Makes to the heart her strong appeal,
> Which all who have a heart must feel.[13]

Jerningham follows Williams's own argument in asserting that her strength resides in her rhetoric of sensibility, which enables her to retain her femininity even though she is writing about politics.[14]

However, by 1792, and certainly after the September Massacres of that year and the overthrow of the French monarchy, the tide of opinion in England turned against the Revolution—and against those, like Williams, who persisted in supporting its principles. Conservative propaganda flourished throughout England, and it is perhaps best represented by the popular visual design known as *The Contrast* (1792), which was engraved by Thomas Rowlandson.[15] Simply put, it depicted British liberty as a virtuous woman in contrast to the bloodthirsty hag that represented French liberty. *The Contrast* would have been anathema for "a citizen of the world" like Williams who thought no nation should have the monopoly on liberty. Certainly Jerningham's poetic description of Williams in her flowing robes defending liberty illustrates in a telling way the distinction between her internationalist position and the divisive images represented in *The Contrast,* especially once political loyalties hardened after the outbreak of war between the two countries in 1793. It soon became clear that a woman's compassionate response to the events in France was no longer sufficient to excuse her from taking an interest in revolutionary politics. As we shall see, opponents of the Revolution argued that it simply was not proper for a woman to write about anything political at all, and they should instead devote themselves to their traditional roles as wives and mothers.

Many women writers took sides in the revolutionary debates, including Hannah More and Frances Burney. In her popular poem *Village Politics* (1792), More argued that women's interest in the French Revolution was as unthinking as their passion for French fashion; they were dazzled by anything French. In that poem, the loyal Sir John admonishes his wife when she asks him to tear down their good old English mansion and replace it with one in the French style. The political analogy is clear, and Sir John's lady, who likes "to do everything like the French," needs to be kept in her place by her patriotic husband.[16] *Village Politics* and Hannah More's conservative tracts made a significant contribution to Church and King propaganda, but because she wrote as a Royalist, she did not think of herself as a political writer. Even when writing about the French Revolution she denied any interest in "entering far into political principles."[17] There was no contradiction in this for More, who insisted in *Strictures on the Modern System of Female Education* (1799), that "I am not sounding an alarm to female warriors, or exciting female politicians: I hardly know which of the two is the most disgusting and unnatural character."[18] A similar position was held by Frances Burney who believed that politics was "not a *feminine* subject for discussion,"[19] but that did not prevent her from writing her last novel *The Wanderer* (1814), set during the French Revolution, nor from publishing a pamphlet in 1793 to raise money for emigrant French clergy.[20] Burney and More were compelled to write about the critical events around them, even if it meant they were encroaching on subjects they believed women should normally avoid.

But Williams had no such reservations and had found her life's work in writing about revolutionary politics. Because of her high profile, she announced her return trip to France in a poem entitled *A Farewell to England for Two Years* (1791). When events in France became more violent, her situation was discussed openly in the press, and some writers used her example as a warning to others. In early 1793, a very public attempt was made to persuade her to return to England when her friend Anna Seward published a letter in *Gentleman's Magazine,* addressing her as a type of prodigal daughter.[21] Calling her the "amiable, the benevolent Helen Williams,"[22] Seward seemed to be speaking on behalf of the nation in appealing for the return of Britain's well-loved poetess. But Williams did not come back, and Seward's letter was followed by the publication of an entire book addressed to Williams, which was far more critical in tone. Laetitia Matilda Hawkins's two-volume *Letters on the Female Mind, Addressed to Miss H. M. Williams, with Particular Reference to Her Letters from France* (1793) urged Williams to give up politics and resume writing elegant (i.e., apolitical) poetry. Though using the inclusive phrase "let us," she was concerned less with reforming Williams than with reinforcing women's traditional roles: "Let us, my dear madam, in the mean time take care of our homes; let us discharge *our* duties."[23] According to Hawkins, not only was the subject of government one that women could not "discuss with propriety," but women lacked the capacity and the experience to understand such subjects.[24] Whatever Williams's eyewitness status and the authenticity of her sources, the fact that she was a woman would continue to be held against her. In 1804 the *British Critic* maintained that Williams was "not destitute of intellectual ability, but we unequivocally deny her being possessed of those qualities of mind which are essential to decide on the profound subjects of the political affairs and constitutions of nations."[25] Such arguments became standard components of conservative discourse, in which "pert misses" were disparaged for presuming "to pass judgement on the political rights and conditions of nations."[26]

Among contemporary writers, this view was sharply opposed by Charlotte Smith, who defended women's interest in political affairs in the defiant Preface to one of her own novels on the Revolution, *Desmond* (1792).[27] The continuing success of the *Letters from France* was itself evidence that, despite resistance, a woman could demonstrate an interest in these matters and become something of an authority on them. Williams was determined to write a comprehensive account of the French Revolution. The eight volumes chronicle changing events, but her characteristically compassionate yet dignified narrative voice gives coherence to the *Letters,* as she implores her readers to embrace the ideals of the "friends of liberty" (1.4.117, 1.4.152, 2.4.1). Though her mood can veer from enthusiasm to indignation, she maintains a decorum in her writing that contrasts with the graphic imagery used by many of those who wrote about the Revolution. For instance, Mary Wollstonecraft, in the conclusion to the first volume of the unfinished *Historical and Moral View of the French Revolution* (1794), compares revolutionary violence to a necessary purging of the bowels, in which "excrementitious humours [exude] from the contaminated body."[28] Lewis Goldsmith describes the rancid food in French prisons as "a little putrescent meat, and vegetables full of dirt, hair, and worms."[29] In contrast, the problem of hunger in the prisons is daintily depicted by Williams using figurative language in the following manner: "famine scowled along these gloomy mansions" (2.2.112). Her *Letters* possess the politeness of an eighteenth-century Bluestocking, which enables her to retain a ladylike distance from the horrors she must recount. This was in keeping with her own self-presentation as a spokesperson for the civilized ethos of an "enlightened" age (1.2.205). Frequently reasserting the importance of this period in world history, she regarded her own work as necessary to correct the misleading accounts written by counterrevolutionary writers (4.4.181). She continued her appeal to sensibility, alternating between tearful vignettes and almost business-like accounts of military actions. Her desire in 1793 for "equal laws, wise instruction, rational faith, and virtuous conduct" (1.4.154) was no different from her wish in 1796 "to trace humanity pouring balm into the wounds of the oppressed" (2.4.2). Such words epitomise the nature of this "benevolent historian." These are enlightenment ideals rendered in the discourse of sensibility.

Williams had many advocates in England, and, since the political alliances of individual journals were sharply drawn in the 1790s, Whig periodicals reviewed Williams's work much more favorably than Tory journals. Supportive journals like the *New Annual Register* regarded Williams with respect for having the initiative to write about the important events of the Revolution. That journal angrily dismissed Laetitia Matilda Hawkins's book for its contemptuous efforts to discredit Williams and its "endeavour to excite [others] against an ingenious and lively female, for having spirit enough to think for herself, and to write on topics, with which the greater part of her sex are precluded from being acquainted by their confined and defective education."[30] This review registers the fact that, at least for some readers, Williams's work on the Revolution was a pioneering effort that opened up the possibility that women could write about subjects which had traditionally been reserved for men.

The more conservative reviews campaigned against women's involvement in politics by arguing that they were transgressing proper codes of female behavior. In France itself, the year 1793 saw a backlash against female activists,[31] and many prominent women suffered unrelenting attacks in the French press, as Elisabeth Roudinesco has shown in her study of Théroigne de Méricourt;[32] and Mary Seidman Trouille in her work on Madame Roland.[33] An analysis of the English reviews of Helen Maria Williams's books shows that conservative British journals maintained a certain decorum in the early 1790s, while much harsher comments appeared only in the postrevolutionary period. This review from the Tory *British Critic* is typical of the tone of the earlier period:

> When a young lady writes, with dogmatical decision, upon subjects which have divided the sentiments of the best, wisest and most experienced of mankind, we think it by no means detracts from our gallantry, or good humour, if we confess it to be our opinion that she might easily have been occupied in better and more fruitful employments.[34]

While the *British Critic* here sounds rather like a disapproving but concerned father, it became less patient with Williams as the years wore on, though the worst name that they used for her was "misguided female" in a review of February 1796.[35] *Gentleman's Magazine* tended to be more scornful and sarcastic but stopped short of outright vitriol. However, attacks on Williams in the press worsened over the next few years, a period of continued government suppression of radical activities in Britain.[36] The *Anti-Jacobin; or, Weekly Examiner,* founded in 1797, and its successor the monthly *Anti-Jacobin Review* hurled vicious insults at Williams and other British men and women who could in any way be described as radicals or as reformers, and the tone of other conservative attacks degenerated as well. For instance, while the liberal *Analytical Review* had referred sympathetically to "the elegant pen of Miss Williams," in 1801 the conservative *British Critic* gave up its own decorous tone and chastised Williams for what they called her "polluted pen."[37] Whether her pen was "elegant" or "polluted" had more to do with the journal's politics than Williams's style of writing.

The insults directed against women who took an interest in the French Revolution were typified by those in the book *Unsexed Females* (1798), by Richard Polwhele. As the term "unsexed" implies, and as critics such as Steven Blakemore and Eleanor Ty have documented, women interested in politics were by definition "fallen" women.[38] "Unsexed" really meant "oversexed," as Claudia Johnson has pointed out.[39] Critics were alert to any suggestion of sexual impropriety, and frequent references were made to Williams's relationship with John Hurford Stone. In a vicious attack on her book about Switzerland, the *Anti-Jacobin* registered its shock that the papers should rely on Williams, whom they called "Mrs. Stone," as a source of information, since she was, in their words "a Poissarde more bloody, . . . a st—mp-t more shameless, than any which . . . Paris ever vomited forth."[40] Such vile sexual insults were typical of the *Anti-Jacobin,* which sometimes deprecated women writers en masse as the "Wollstonecraft School," even though Wollstonecraft had died in 1797.[41] In one instance, Williams was paired with Madame de Staël, as we see in this quotation from a poem published in the *Anti-Jacobin* in May 1798, where Williams and Germaine de Staël are depicted as "[working] their fingers to the bone, / And cutting their Petticoats to rags / To make . . . bright Three Colour'd Flags."[42] The startling image of the women writers using their petticoats or undergarments to make French flags exposes their bodies to the public eye, and implies that they would sacrifice feminine modesty or chastity for their political cause. Furthermore, the roughness and violence attributed to Staël and Williams in this depiction is of a kind usually associated with lower-class female radicals in Paris. The author ignores Williams's middle-class status and Staël's aristocratic status (by marriage), implying that their political writings make them of a piece with transgressive women of a lower class, with whom neither Staël nor Williams would have been pleased to be compared. This blurring of differences in class and politics was also a feature of the attacks on women in the French press, as Trouille has observed in her study of the comparisons made between Madame Roland and the more militant Olympe de Gouges.[43]

It served the purpose of conservative propaganda to simplify revolutionary politics by ignoring such differences.[44] While such remarks about Williams in the press were, in general, only made in the post-revolutionary period, earlier examples occur in the private correspondence of both Horace Walpole and Edmund Burke. The following comment is among Walpole's many vituperative remarks about the British women who supported the French Revolution; it is from a letter dated 26 July 1791, in which he refers disparagingly to Williams and Anna Laetitia Barbauld, comparing them to poissardes who were "invited to the Crown and Anchor, and had let their nails grow accordingly; but somehow or other no poissonnières were there, and the two prophetesses had no opportunity that day of exercising their talents or talons."[45] Here Williams and Barbauld, both middle-class women writers, are once again categorized among the "poissonnières" or poissardes, terms used for fishwomen, marketwomen, or lower-class women in general. Walpole's deliberate play on the words "talents" and "talons" implies that what they think of as their literary talents are no better than the bestial "talons" or claws attributed to the unruly French women, who themselves were often caricatured in the French press. Poissardes were frequently represented in satirical prints as well, one of which James Gillray used to warn British women away from revolutionary politics. His didactic cartoon was based on an anonymous French print depicting incidents that occurred in France in the spring of 1791, when groups of nuns were beaten by bands of women who broke into their convents.[46] Gillray's print is dated June 1792 and entitled *A Representation of the horrid barbarities practised upon the nuns by the Fish-women on breaking into the nunneries in France.* Its inscription reads: "This print is dedicated to the Fair sex of Great-Britain & intended to point out the very dangerous effects which may arise to Themselves if they do not exert themselves to" stop the mob from gaining power.[47] The poissardes are oversized figures—giantesses—attacking the nuns whose bodies are exposed in an indecent manner. The analogy is clear: female modesty itself is threatened by revolutionary politics.[48]

Edmund Burke, whose writings contributed to the alarmist climate of the counterrevolutionary period, addressed the issue of female transgression directly in an important private letter of 1795, where he warned his friend Mrs. Crewe about the dangerous influence of women like Helen Maria Williams and Mary Wollstonecraft. He began by admonishing Mrs. Crewe for not taking seriously enough the danger these women represented: "this is no trifling game they are playing":

> I hope and supplicate, that all provident and virtuous Wives and Mothers of families, will employ all the just influence they possess over their Husbands and Children, to save themselves and their families from the ruin that the Mesdames de Staals and the Mesdames Rolands, and the Mesdames de Sillery, and the Mrs. Helena Maria Williams, and the Mrs. Woolstencrafts &c &c &c &c &c and all that Clan of desperate, Wicked, and mischievously ingenious Women, who have brought, or are likely to bring Ruin and shame upon all those that listen to them. The Sex has much influence. Let the honest and prudent save us from the Evils with which we are menaced by the daring, the restless, and the unprincipled.[49]

Five of the most prominent English and French women writers of the 1790s have made Burke's list of female offenders: Staël, Roland, Genlis (Sillery), Williams, and Wollstonecraft. By using their names in a plural form and adding several "etceteras," he even augments the threat by making them seem part of a growing army of dangerous women, evoking a fear of the mob, like a many-headed hydra.[50] In opposition to this monstrosity are the "honest" and "prudent" mothers and wives, who are a source of stability, unlike the "restless" "clan" of "Wicked" women who support, in whatever way, the politics of the Revolution. Burke's women, defined by their perceived virtue, belong to one of two categories, like those used in the popular design of *The Contrast*.

Similar oppositional imagery was used by the Scottish writer Anne Grant in a poem of the postrevolutionary period entitled "A Familiar Epistle to A Friend," which sought to chasten radical women. Although her poem revealed some of the difficulties of her own life as a female poet, Grant accepted her traditional role and subordinated her literary career to her family responsibilities. She acknowledged

Williams's spotless early reputation as a poet of "the chaste classic Muse" (177), but, as far as Grant was concerned, everything went wrong once Williams went to France and became so drunk with liberty that she joined the revolutionary "demons" (183), threatening social order:[51]

> With virtues, and graces, and beauties beside,
> The delight of her friends, of her country the pride,
> Say, who could to ******** their suffrage refuse,
> Or who not be charmed with her chaste classic Muse?
> To the passion for liberty giving loose rein,
> At length she flew off to carouse on the Seine;
> And growing inebriate while quaffing the draught,
> Equality's new-fangled doctrines she taught;
> And murder and sacrilege calmly surveyed;
> In the new pandemonium those demons had made;
> Seine's blood-crimsoned waters with apathy eyed,
> While the glories of old father Thames she decried.[52]

This passage from Grant's poem is like a compendium of negative images of the Revolution, a mix of drunkenness, murder, and madness. She believed that contact with France immediately turned Williams into a "loose" woman, who transgressed sexual and moral codes of behavior. Grant's before-and-after pictures act as a warning to her female readers and vividly recall the images of virtuous English liberty juxtaposed against evil French liberty in *The Contrast,* as if the story of Williams's life during the revolutionary decade were emblematized by the contrasting iconography of that design.

The proliferation of warnings, pronouncements, and images of "unsexed" females at the end of the eighteenth century and into the beginning of the nineteenth century demonstrates the efforts to control women's literary and political activities. They often consisted of gross personal insults, distortion of facts, and fearmongering. However, Williams was somewhat shielded from the attacks against her because she had little access to British publications while living in Paris during the war years. When she did respond to her critics, she took the moral high road, proclaiming in the preface to a book published in 1801 that she would continue to write despite "the censure which has been thrown on writers of the female sex who have sometimes employed their pens on political subjects."[53] She settled into an authorial persona that she felt was justified by her role as an "eyewitness" to events in France, and in fact hoped that her books would "make a part of that marvellous story which the eighteenth century has to record to future times."[54]

Williams would make no claim for the title of historian, however, even though she was "treading on the territory of History,"[55] because:

> In the serious annals of history, all is told with calm and with method; but I am not a historian, I have only hazarded in the preceding pages to express my own sentiments during the course of the revolution. Many others will search for the revolution in books, but I remember it; the incidents of this recital are in my memory and the emotions that they produced are also in my heart.[56]

From the beginning of her career to the end, Williams argued that her presence on the scene and her emotional commitment to revolutionary ideals gave legitimacy to her work, and her reviewers acknowledged her credibility as a reliable, if partisan, eyewitness of events in France: "Few English women, or even English men, have enjoyed a more ample opportunity of observing . . . the revolutions in France."[57] But what could these observations be called, exactly? A reluctance to accept the title of politician or historian is understandable when we consider that no proper titles or categories existed for a woman who did the type of writing that Williams did. After all, "female politicians" were viewed as monstrous, and by definition historians were, to quote one of her reviewers, "grave old men."[58] A similar problem faced Madame de Staël whose work *Considerations of the Principal Events of the French Revolution* (1818) has resisted categorization since it is, in Charlotte Hogsett's words, "more than memoirs," but not "a political work in the traditional sense."[59] Praising it as subversive of genre, Linda Orr has sought to reclaim Staël's book, which, with elements like "autobiography, satire, travelogue, [and] political philosophy," has a "diversity" that "pushes the limits of history."[60] Two hundred years ago, Sophie Grandchamp said something similar about Williams's political writing: "Turn by turn, you are a friend, a historian, a novelist, a poet, a statesman, a politician, a critic, even a theologian."[61]

The fact that the *Letters from France* did not fit easily into any traditional categories frustrated some reviewers. For instance, although the *English Review* wrote favorably of her work, praising its philanthropy, they were disappointed that it lacked the clarity and structure of "historical composition,"[62] which should follow closely the "chain of events."[63] They criticized the emotional content and what they and the *European Magazine* called the "florid" qualities of her style: "it would have been still more interesting had Miss Williams confined herself more to facts and circumstances, and been sparing of heightening of words and of her own emotions and opinions."[64] For some readers, then, Williams's sensibility and anecdotal narrative diminished the value of her historical accounts. The *English Review* had criticized her in 1792 as writing not for "sagacious politicians" but only for women, or "politicians in petticoats,"[65] an image that had been used earlier in the eighteenth century to satirize the women in Queen Anne's court who seemed to be usurping male power, and, prior to that, to describe female activists of the English Civil War period as "petticoat petitioners."[66] In this case, however, the *English Review* uses the term "politicians in petticoats" to relegate Williams's writings to the superficial realm of "female *prettinesses*" that they had disparaged earlier.[67]

While some reviewers criticized the *Letters from France* for lacking structure and clarity, the *Critical Review*, in an article in 1801, sympathized with the problems Williams faced regarding readers' expectations of historical writing:

> it is well known with what difficulty the historian is prevented from becoming a partisan in his narration, even of events long since elapsed, and in which he could have no personal interest. But if this be true with respect to grave old men, how can it be supposed with the refinement of feeling and the delicacy of organization of the fair writer before us, that her imagination should not occasionally be a little too much exalted, and her colouring a little too vivid?[68]

This reader argued that if impartiality is difficult even for an educated historian, it is unfair to expect it of a person without such a background. But that should not preclude her from writing about history and politics:

> If [the *Letters from France*] want the profound investigation of the statesman or legislator,—if they are destitute of those political discussions, in which historians of the higher order are fond of indulging,—they will be found to contain what is more valuable,—a picture of the times. What they lose in stateliness, they gain in interest; if they plunge not deeply into the intrigues of cabinets, or the views of politicians, they delineate correctly the fluctuations of popular sentiment; and if they enter but little on the disgusting and generally tiresome

details of senatorial debates or military exploits, they paint the manners, and, by variety of engaging anecdotes, expose the human heart.[69]

The *Critical Review* gave Williams the acceptance she had hoped to gain. She was not criticized for lacking the education of a male historian, nor was she criticized for being a woman writing on politics; instead, her work was valued in a journal (albeit a like-minded one) that allowed her to join their ranks as a "friend of liberty."[70]

In 1796, the liberal *Analytical Review* referred to her both as a "historian" and as "our benevolent historian."[71] This presents an image of Williams that is far removed from the degrading caricatures promulgated in the later conservative press, where even terms like "benevolence" and "humanity" were ridiculed because of their association with revolutionary discourse. The complimentary adjective "benevolent" is one worth reclaiming, and it was intended in the *Analytical Review* as a tribute to the way that Williams wrote about the French Revolution, as she drew her readers' attention to scenes of pathos involving the victims of the Reign of Terror. We don't know if Williams would have preferred being called simply the "English Historian of the French Revolution," as her nephew described her after her death.[72] But perhaps she would have been willing to accept the title "benevolent historian" from her peers, for, with its qualifying adjective, it acknowledges the deeply felt concern for humanity that first prompted her to write about the French Revolution and that sustained her as she recorded its dramatic history in the eight volumes of her *Letters from France*.

Notes

1. See Joan Wallach Scott, *Gender and the Politics of History* (New York: Columbia University Press, 1988), 15–27, 178–98.

2. See Bridget Hill, *The Republican Virago: The Life and Times of Catharine Macaulay, Historian* (Oxford: Clarendon Press, 1992), 130–38.

3. See Wendy Wassyng Roworth, "Kauffman and the Art of Painting in England," in *Angelica Kauffman: A Continental Artist in Georgian England,* ed. Wendy Wassyng Roworth (London: Reaktion Books, 1992), 86.

4. For a brief overview of Williams's critical reception see Jack Fruchtman, Jr., Introduction, *An Eye-Witness Account of the French Revolution,* by Helen Maria Williams (New York: Peter Lang, 1997), 1–30.

5. All references to Williams's multivolume *Letters from France* will be to the modern reprint *Letters from France,* eight volumes in two, intro. Janet Todd (Delmar, New York: Scholars' Facsimiles & Reprints, 1975) and will be cited in the text, indicating the series number, the volume number, and the page number. The eight volumes are divided into two series of four volumes each. Reviews of the *Letters from France* (*LF*) will cite the series and volume number. This passage is taken from 1.1.14.

6. Richard Price, "A Discourse on the Love of Our Country," in *Richard Price: Political Writings,* ed. D. O. Thomas (Cambridge: Cambridge University Press, 1991), 181. Price gave his speech celebrating the French Revolution at the meeting for the 1688 Revolution Society, a club of Whigs and Dissenters, where the year before Helen Maria Williams's mentor Reverend Andrew Kippis had been the guest speaker.

7. Rev. of Williams's *Letters written in France in the summer, 1790* (*LF* 1.1), in the *Analytical Review* 8 (September-December 1790): 431.

8. Rev. of Williams's *Letters written in France in the summer, 1790* (*LF* 1.1), in the *Analytical Review* 8 (September-December 1790): 431–432.

9. See Gary Kelly, *Revolutionary Feminism: The Mind and Career of Mary Wollstonecraft* (London: Macmillan, 1992), 90, and Janet Todd, introduction to *Mary Wollstonecraft: Political Writings* (Toronto: University of Toronto Press, 1993), xii.

10. Rev. of the second edition of Wollstonecraft's *A Vindication of the Rights of Men,* in the *English Review* (January 1791): 61.

11. Greg Kucich, "Romanticism and Feminist Historiography," in *The Wordsworth Circle* 24 (Summer 1993): 136.

12. Rev. of Wollstonecraft's *A Vindication of the Rights of Men,* in *Gentleman's Magazine* 61 (February 1791): 151.

13. Jerningham's poem was published in the *Universal Magazine* 18 (December 1790): 472.

14. This was something that Williams admired most in her friend Madame Roland: her ability to discuss "the most important political questions" without any loss of feminine dignity. See Helen Maria Williams, *Souvenirs de la Révolution française,* trans. Charles Coquerel (Paris: Dondey-Dupré, 1827), 72.

15. See Jan Wellington's essay in this volume for a copy of this engraving. *The Contrast* was designed by Lord George Murray and engraved by Thomas Rowlandson. See David Bindman, *The Shadow of the Guillotine* (London: British Museum, 1989), 119.

16. This passage from Hannah More's *Village Politics* is referred to in Prickett, *England and the French Revolution,* (London: Macmillan, 1989),

160. The entire poem is printed in the anthology *British Literature 1780–1830,* eds. Anne K. Mellor and Richard E. Matlak (Fort Worth: Harcourt Brace, 1996), 210–216.

17. See Hannah More, *Remarks on the Speech of M. Dupont* (1793) from *The Works of Hannah More,* 11 volumes (London: Henry G. Bohn), 2: 407. Hannah More was also one of many women who found a "socially acceptable" way to be involved in the politics of the day by contributing to the British war effort through fundraising and sewing for British troops. See Linda Colley, *Britons: Forging the Nation 1707–1837* (New Haven: Yale University Press, 1992), 261.

18. Hannah More, from Chapter One, *Strictures on the Modern System of Female Education* (1799), in *Selected Writings of Hannah More,* ed. Robert Hole (London: Pickering & Chatto, 1996), 126.

19. This is quoted in a letter dated 6 July 1796 from Frances Burney to Dr. Charles Burney, *Journals and Letters of Fanny Burney,* volume 3, ed. Joyce Hemlow (Oxford: Clarendon, 1973), 186.

20. Entitled *Brief Reflections Relative to the Emigrant French Clergy: Earnestly Submitted to the Humane Consideration of the Ladies of Britain* (1793), the pamphlet was preceded by a two-page apology justifying "on the grounds of benevolence for the entry of a female into public affairs." It seems, then, that the defence of "benevolence" was employed by female writers of various political persuasions. See Burney, *Journals and Letters of Fanny Burney* 3: 18, note.

21. Seward's letter to Williams, dated 17 January 1793, can be found in the *Letters of Anna Seward,* 6 vols. (Edinburgh, 1811), 3: 202–209. It was published in the *Gentleman's Magazine* (February 1793): 108–10.

22. Anna Seward, letter to Helen Maria Williams, 17 January 1793, in *Letters of Anna Seward,* 3: 204.

23. Laetitia Matilda Hawkins, *Letters on the Female Mind, Its Powers and Pursuits. Addressed to Miss H. M. Williams,* 2 vols. (London: Hookham and Carpenter, 1793), 1:117.

24. Laetitia Matilda Hawkins, *Letters on the Female Mind,* 1:5, 1:25.

25. Rev. of Williams's edition of *The Political and Confidential Correspondence of Lewis the Sixteenth,* in *British Critic* 23 (April 1804): 430–431.

26. William Beloe, *The Sexagenarian; or the Recollections of a Literary Life,* 2 vols. 2nd. ed. (London: Rivington, 1818), 1: 363.

27. For this passage from the preface of *Desmond,* see the introductory essay to this volume, 16, 18–19.

28. Mary Wollstonecraft, *Mary Wollstonecraft: Political Writings,* ed. Janet Todd (Toronto: University of Toronto Press, 1993), 386.

29. Lewis Goldsmith, *Female Revolutionary Plutarch* (London, 1806), 3: 268.

30. See the review of Hawkins's *Letters on the Female Mind,* in the *New Annual Register* (1793): 277.

31. In October 1793, women's political clubs in France were outlawed by the Jacobin government in a campaign to suppress women's political activity. See Ruth Graham, "Loaves and Liberty: Women in the French Revolution" in *Becoming Visible: Women in European History,* ed. Renate Bridenthal and Claudia Koonz (Boston: Houghton Mifflin, 1977), 236–54. In England the stability of the family was asserted as an essential component of political stability.

32. Elisabeth Roudinesco, *Madness and Revolution: The Lives and Legends of Théroigne de Méricourt,* trans. Martin Thom (London: Verso, 1991).

33. See Mary Seidman Trouille, "Revolution in the Boudoir: Madame Roland's Subversion of Rousseau's Feminine Ideals" in *Sexual Politics in the Enlightenment: Women Writers Read Rousseau* (New York: State University of New York Press, 1997), 163–92.

34. See the review of Williams's *Letters from France. . . and Particularly Respecting the Campaign of 1792,* (*LF* 1: 3 and 4), in the *British Critic* 2 (November 1793): 244–252, 244.

35. Review of Williams's *Letters Containing a Sketch of the Scenes* (*LF* 2: 3), in the *British Critic* 7 (February 1796): 210.

36. The last years of the eighteenth century saw the naval mutinies of 1797 and the Irish revolt of 1798; habeas corpus was again suspended (April 1798 to March 1801) and legislation passed to outlaw radical societies and unions. See H. T. Dickinson, *British Radicalism and the French Revolution 1789–1815* (Oxford: Basil Blackwell, 1985), 40–41.

37. See the review of Williams's *Letters Containing a Sketch of the Scenes* (*LF* 2: 3), in *Analytical Review* 23 (January 1796): 19, and the review of Williams's *Sketches of . . . the French Republic* in the *British Critic* 17 (1801): 583.

38. See Steven Blakemore, "Revolution and the French Disease: Laetitia Matilda Hawkins's *Letters* to Helen Maria Williams" *SEL* 36 (1996): 673–691; and Eleanor Ty, *Unsex'd Revolutionaries* (Toronto: University of Toronto Press, 1993).

39. Claudia L. Johnson, *Equivocal Beings: Politics, Gender, and Sentimentality in the 1790s: Wollstonecraft, Radcliffe, Burney, Austen* (Chicago: University of Chicago Press, 1995), 9.

40. See the *Anti-Jacobin; or, Weekly Examiner,* 30 April 1798: 233.

41. Williams was also mentioned in a review by William Heath of Mary Hays's *Memoirs of Emma Courtney* and *The Victim of Prejudice* in the *Anti-Jacobin Review,* 3 May 1799: 55–58. According to one critic, Heath denounced many radical works, but it was "the works of the feminist writers of the 1790s that Heath most often singled out for condemnation." He called them the "Wollstonecraft School." See Emily Lorraine de Montluzin, *The Anti-Jacobins, 1798–1800* (New York: St. Martin's Press, 1988), 106.

42. This was part of the poem "A Consolatory Address to His Gun-Boats, by Citizen Muskein," printed in the *Anti-Jacobin; or, Weekly Examiner,* 14 May 1798: 312–13.

43. Mary Seidman Trouille, "Revolution in the Boudoir," 187.

44. As Albert Goodwin has shown, even reformers who were "pillars of middle-class respectability" were depicted as "anarchists" plotting "the violent overthrow" of church and state. Albert Goodwin, *The Friends of Liberty: The English Democratic Movement in the Age of the French Revolution* (Cambridge: Harvard University Press, 1979), 25.

45. Horace Walpole, letter to Mary Berry, 26 July 1791, in *Horace Walpole's Correspondence with Mary and Agnes Berry,* ed. W. S. Lewis and A. Dayle Wallace (New Haven: Yale University Press, 1944), 11: 320.

46. The anonymous French engraving *La discipline patriotique* is reprinted as illustration number 33 by Catherine Marand-Fouquet, who explains that 9 April 1791 was the height of this disorder. See *La femme au temps de La Révolution* (Paris: Stock/ Laurence Pernoud, 1989), 151, 410–411.

47. The Gillray print is found in David Bindman, *Shadow of the Guillotine: Britain and the French Revolution* (London: British Museum, 1989), 103.

48. For a discussion of the French print see Madelyn Gutwirth, *The Twilight of the Goddesses: Women and Representation in the French Revolutionary Era* (New Brunswick: Rutgers University Press, 1992), 312–14.

49. Edmund Burke, letter to Mrs. John Crewe, 11 August 1795, in *The Correspondence of Edmund Burke,* vol. 8, ed. R. B. McDowell (Cambridge: Cambridge University Press, 1969), 304.

50. Another print entitled *Women's Political Meeting in a Church,* by Chérieux, particularly conveys the idea of women's political activity as wild, threatening, and dissolute. See Madelyn Gutwirth, *The Twilight of the Goddesses,* 325.

51. Stephen C. Behrendt discusses Grant's poem briefly in his essay "British Women Poets and the Reverberations of Radicalism in the 1790s," in *Romanticism, Radicalism, and the Press,* ed. Stephen C. Behrendt (Detroit: Wayne State University Press, 1997), 88.

52. Anne Grant's poem "A Familiar Epistle to a Friend" (1802) is reprinted in *Women Romantic Poets 1785–1832: An Anthology,* ed. Jennifer Breen (London: Dent, 1992), 86–93. This passage is from lines 178–85.

53. Helen Maria Williams, preface to *Sketches of the State of Manners and Opinions in the French Republic towards the Close of the Eighteenth Century. In a Series of Letters* (London: Robinson, 1801), n. p.

54. Williams, *Poems on Various Subjects* (London: Whittaker, 1823), x.

55. Williams, *Poems on Various Subjects,* x.

56. Williams, *Souvenirs de la Révolution française,* 199–200.

57. Rev. of Williams's *Sketches,* in the *Monthly Review* 35 (1801): 82.

58. Rev. of Williams's *Sketches,* in the *Critical Review* 31 (February 1801): 184.

59. Charlotte Hogsett, *The Literary Existence of Germaine de Staël* (Carbondale: Southern Illinois University Press, 1987), 140, 141.

60. Linda Orr, "Outspoken Women and the Rightful Daughter of the Revolution: Madame de Staël's *Considérations sur la Révolution Française,*" in *Rebel Daughters: Women and the French Revolution,* ed. Sara E. Melzer and Leslie W. Rabine (New York: Oxford University Press, 1992), 134.

61. Sophie Grandchamp, "Lettre à l'auteur," in *Aperçu de l'état des moeurs et des opinions dans la République française vers la fin du XVIIIe siècle* (Paris, 1801), vi.

62. Review of Williams's *Letters Containing a Sketch of the Politics of France (LF* 2: 1 and 2), in the *English Review* 26 (October 1795): 248.

63. Review of Williams's *Letters from France* (LF 1: 2), in the *English Review* 20 (July 1792): 57.

64. Review of Williams's *Letters Containing a Sketch of the Scenes (LF* 2: 3), in the *English Review* 26 (November 1795): 363 and in *European Magazine* 28 (Nov. 1795): 341.

65. Review of Williams's *Letters from France (LF* 1: 2), in the *English Review* 20 (July 1792): 57.

66. The term "petticoat government" was used in 1702 to describe both the reign of Queen Anne and a matriarchal household, the latter of which was objected to in a rebuttal entitled *The Prerogative of the Breeches (Oxford English Dictionary).* On the large numbers of female petitioners in the Civil War period see Patricia Higgins, "The Reactions of Women, with Special Reference to Women Petitioners," *Politics, Religion, and the English Civil War,* ed. Brian Manning (London: Edward Arnold, 1973), 204.

67. See the review of the second edition of Wollstonecraft's, *A Vindication of the Rights of Men,* in the *English Review* (January 1791): 61.

68. Rev. of Williams's *Sketches,* in the *Critical Review* 31 (February 1801): 184.

69. Rev. of Williams's *Letters Containing a Sketch of the Scenes (LF* 2.3), in the *Critical Review* 16 (January 1796): 1.

70. The term "friend of liberty" is used in a review of Williams's *Letters Containing a Sketch of the Politics of France (LF* 2.1 and 2), in the *Critical Review* 14 (August 1795): 361. The appellation "friend of liberty," also refers specifically to British radicals associated with English reform and revolutionary societies such as the London Corresponding Society. See Goodwin, *The Friends of Liberty: The English Democratic Movement in the Age of the French Revolution* (Cambridge: Harvard University Press, 1979).

71. See the review of Williams's *Letters Containing a Sketch of the Scenes (LF* 2.3), in the *Analytical Review* 23 (January 1796): 22, 23.

72. Athanase Coquerel, "Reply to Dr. Strauss's Book 'Life of Jesus,'" in *Voices of the Church, in Reply to Dr. D. F. Strauss,* ed. Rev. J. R. Beard (London: Simpkin, Marshall, 1845), 27.

The Politics of Truth and Deception:
Charlotte Smith and the French Revolution

༭

Judith Davis Miller

Perhaps there cannot be a subject of greater political importance, or better calculated to lead us in safety through the
mazes of controversy, than that of the value of truth.[1]

—William Godwin,
An Enquiry Concerning Political Justice, 1793

In the above introduction to chapter 4, "Of the Cultivation of
Truth," William Godwin asserts the place of truth in the republican
philosophy that informed radical politics in England during the
1790s. He later stipulates that truth results from knowledge of the
arts and sciences filtered through a sound reasoning process. And
truth has as its own result the improvement of political institutions,
he suggests in section 1, "Of Abstract or General Truth," because "if
politics be a science, the investigation of truth must be the means of
unfolding it" (4:4:1: 218). He goes on to argue, with the absolutism
that characterizes his 1793 treatise, that "there cannot be a more
unworthy idea, than that truth and virtue should be under the necessity of seeking alliance with concealment" (4:4:1: 232).[2] Godwin
shares the radical vision of political philosophers such as Condorcet,
who, directly involved in the French Revolution (and victim of its
shifting political winds), prophesies in his "Sketch for a Historical
Picture of the Progress of the Human Mind" (1793) that the principles
and practice of "liberty, knowledge, and reason" will eventually
spread throughout the world as a result of the revolution in ideas
taking place in France and sweeping across Europe.[3]

In her five French Revolutionary novels, Charlotte Smith reveals herself to be the philosophical companion of Godwin and Condorcet. While Smith's radical sensibility and linking of gender and politics have been the subject of much recent commentary, most critics posit the absence of a political philosophy as a reason for placing Smith at the margins of the republican movement. Florence Hilbish first suggests this evaluation in discussing the influence of the Revolutionists on Smith's work, maintaining that "her subordination of theory to plot removes her from within to the edges of the Revolutionary circle."[4] In *Jane Austen and the War of Ideas,* Marilyn Butler agrees with Hilbish, asserting that Smith, like Mary Robinson, is not a "conscientious polemicist," but would "intermittently . . . reveal liberal sympathies."[5] Gary Kelly essentially continues this reading in *The English Jacobin Novel, 1780–1805,*[6] while in her recent critical biography Loraine Fletcher complains that "though (Smith's) dissatisfaction with the established order was extreme, she had only the haziest ideas about how it might be changed," adding that "(t)he lack of a consistent criterion of value other than Sensibility . . . is her weakness as a satirist."[7]

I propose to read Smith's novels in the context of Godwin, whose *Enquiry* permeated the discussions of radical philosophy during the 1790s. This reading reveals in her novels a consistent concern with political philosophy that implies the "philosophically motivated search for 'unity of design'" (4) Kelly finds lacking in them.[8] As she progresses from *Delmont* (1792) through *The Young Philosopher* (1798), Smith's concerns parallel those of Godwin, effectively testing the applicability of his abstractions on individual lives, much as Godwin was to do in his own *Caleb Williams* (1794). In the abstract philosophy of the *Enquiry,* Godwin can be something of a Platonist; his writing suggests, as Butler has noted, that "Truth and Right Reason awaits outside us, ready to be found if only our efforts towards rationality and mental independence are strenuous enough" (47). Indeed, Godwin argues that the honest man must be "contented to offer himself up a victim to the shrine of veracity" (4: 4: 225), dying if necessary rather than seeking "to obtain a desirable object by vile means" (4: 4: 226). Smith's protagonists wrestle with the issue of the difficulty of establishing truth as the basis for both personal and public life in a society that is filled with deception and disguise. In the world of these novels, social forms, national prejudice, intrigue, disguise, superstition, and rumor become tropes for the obfuscation of knowledge and impediments to the perfection of the truth necessary for good government urged by Godwin.

Smith complicates her exploration of the political and social role of truth by implicating herself as author in various disguises, addressing the vexed issue of women as writers of the developing genre of the novel. Mary Anne Schofield applauds Smith for her ability to "cast herself, together with her foibles and adventures, as the heroine," in her novels, adding that "Smith's honesty is brutal at times;"[9] emphasis upon this ability and the resulting conflation of her life and work have been staples of Smith criticism from the earliest period. Contemporary reviewers often chastise her for creating characters who seem clearly to represent herself and people with whom she has come into contact. In his 1810 *Imaginative Biography*, Sir Egerton Brydges actually uses this similarity to defend Smith's virtues, connecting them with those of her heroines: "It appears to me scarcely possible that in such a multitude of volumes, many of them written in haste, the same prominent features should materially vary from those of the author."[10] After exhaustive research, Florence Hilbish bases much of her now legendary 1941 biography of Smith on information she draws from details in the novels—details that, in the main, have proven to be true based on subsequent findings. And as recently as 1991, Sarah Zimmerman argued convincingly that Smith carefully crafts a persona in her letters to her publishers and her prefaces to the public that echoes the heroine of sensibility so prevalent in the cultural consciousness of her time.[11]

The inevitable politicization of this persona in the highly charged cultural and political climate of the French Revolutionary period in England becomes a further motivation for the layers of meaning and codes of secrecy and disguise in Smith's texts. Thus Smith herself becomes the proof of Godwin's insight that "Persecution cannot persuade the understanding, even when it subdues our resolution. It may make us hypocrites but cannot make us converts. The Government, therefore, which is anxious above all things to imbue its subjects with integrity and virtue, will be the farthest in the world from discouraging them in the explicit avowal of their sentiments" (2: 5:110). Her dilemma bears witness that the politics of deception calls everything into question; if the author becomes an issue by self-inclusion in the text, it is easy then for her to become the issue in her writing—a pitfall Smith must avoid at all costs. The dilemmas into which she places her protagonists mirror her own need to strike a balance between representing herself as a poignant and sympathetic figure to increase the sales of her books and expressing the deeply felt political convictions that her personal experiences and the repressive political climate had only strengthened.

As a result, Smith's focus on the problem of truth and deception anticipates the connections between disguise and issues of identity, gender, and (self-)representation in a patriarchal society illuminated by recent feminist critics Terry Castle, Mary Anne Schofield, and Catherine Craft-Fairchild.[12] These representations of disguise and deception also make clear her connection to the tradition of the courtship novels of her time as they have been treated by these recent feminist critics. Not only does she examine the gendered need for deception on the part of her main characters; she also explores its roots in the multifarious deceptions of the society in which they live and goes further to extrapolate from cultural mores their political and philosophical implications. In providing what is essentially commentary on and exemplification of Godwin's philosophy, Smith adopts various rhetorical strategies, most of which function apophastically. One such strategy involves a practice that I will characterize as "open concealment," in which she openly involves her characters in behaviors that challenge form and yet conceals the challenge to convention by insisting on their virtue both in the preface and in the text itself. In effect, this technique tells her readers, "These are my true opinions, but I insist they are not, I can't be accused of impropriety." She also uses a "species of ventriloquism,"[13] speaking the politics a woman cannot directly address through a male protagonist, while at the same time, as Craft-Fairchild has noted in commentary on other women novelists, endowing him with a feminized sensibility that firmly places him alongside the heroine in opposition to the patriarchy that victimizes both.[14] And she further blunts the edge of criticism by blurring the line between fact and fiction with her prefaces, authorial intrusions, thinly veiled autobiographical references, and use of actual historical events interspersed with fiction. As she writes her way through the 1790s, these strategies ultimately engage her in an exploration of the fundamental epistemological issues of the nature of knowledge and its relationship to the construction of identity that are at the root of the radical political agenda.

Influenced by Fanny Burney's popular *Evelina* (1778) and *Cecilia* (1782), Smith stayed true to the genre expectations of the courtship genre in her first novels. Despite their seemingly traditional plots, however, *Emmeline* (1788) and *Ethelinde* (1789) introduce social themes that lay the groundwork for her subsequent politics, challenging some accepted mores regarding women, such as the social rejection of a woman who bears a child out of wedlock. And with *Celestina,* Smith begins that engagement with contemporary political events that strikingly characterizes her subsequent novels. Smith wrote this novel during the momentous years of 1789–1790, and in it she responds positively to the events in France, describing Willoughby, Celestina's beloved, passing through the south of France during the summer of 1789, and "hearing, but hearing, at a distance, the tumults, with which a noble struggle for freedom at this time agitated the capital, and many of the great towns of France."[15] Through the story of the French Bellegarde, whom Willoughby encounters in his quest for Celestina's true lineage, Smith takes aim at the infamous *lettres de cachet* and other repressive policies of the *ancien régime*. This brief lapse into politics did not lead to negative criticism from the reviewers, probably because the main emotional thrust and the structure of the novel are still strongly within the courtship genre. Furthermore, because England at this time was not yet threatened by the events occurring in France, it was still possible to interpret the uprising of the French people optimistically, as a correction of the French political system in the direction of a constitutional monarchy like that of England.

Smith's incipient radicalism developed as a result of a lengthy period spent in Brighton in early 1792 on the advice of her doctors, nursing the arthritis that was to plague her for the rest of her life. This seaside town was already receiving French émigrés and taking on a political as well as a social cast; Hilbish writes that Smith's sister, Catherine Dorset, "assigned the radical influences that later brought much censure upon her sister" to this town, adding that "here . . . her talents introduced her to many distinguished and literary people, some of whom were the most violent advocates of the French Revolution" (146). While Smith was inhaling the air of a radicalism inspired by the great rallying cry of Richard Price's speech to the London 1688 Revolution Society in November of 1790, and further inflamed by Mary Wollstonecraft's *A Vindication of the Rights of Woman* and Thomas Paine's *Rights of Man* in early 1792, much of England was reacting with sympathy for the French King as it heard the news of his flight to Varennes in June of 1791, his capture, and his subsequent virtual incarceration at the Tuileries. Horace Walpole expressed the feeling of many of his compatriots when he wrote, "The escape of the King and Queen of France came merely time enough to double the shock of their being retaken. An ocean of pity cannot suffice to lament their miserable condition."[16] Such differences of opinion set the stage for the polarization of political feeling that was to characterize the rest of the 1790s and compel Smith to develop her strategies of deception.

In response to the intense political atmosphere, Smith embarked on her program of open concealment. First, she discarded her previous practice of naming her novels after their heroine and named this novel after the main male character, Desmond, placing the strong political statements with which the novel abounds in his voice and distancing them from the author to protect her from the criticism that feminine engagement in politics would inevitably earn. To further forestall the anticipated criticism, her preface admits to her own knowledge of politics, urges the need for women to know what is happening politically, and protests that she has come by her knowledge legitimately, compelled by her circumstances to work in the world to support her children through writing. She insists upon the objectivity of Desmond's directly stated radical politics. This strategy worked; despite the timing of reviews of the novel between July (*European Magazine*) and December (*Monthly Review*), a period of mounting concern as the Paris crowd invaded the Tuileries and the September Massacres occurred in the prisons of Paris, contemporary critics generally accepted the novelist's right to discuss politics and even seemed to find the discussion refreshing.[17]

Smith's employment of her strategy of open concealment in the love relationship between Lionel Desmond and Geraldine Verney met with less success. Smith attempts to defuse this challenge to convention by insisting in her preface that "in representing a young man, nourishing an ardent but concealed passion for a married woman; I certainly do not mean to encourage or justify such attachments," adding that there is no "story more moral, than one that represents the existence of an affection so regulated. . . ."[18] Smith had her defenders, such as Sir Egerton Brydges, who pointed out the purity of Desmond's devotion and of Geraldine's response (97–98). Nonetheless, as Hilbish notes, "*Desmond* by many was thought to encourage wives to desert their husbands, and Mrs. Smith's own separation was recalled" (151). These detractors seemed to understand that Smith was rebelling against a society that represented the parental pressure that had circumscribed her life through her early disastrous arranged marriage while providing a further apologia for her own life; as Pat Elliott has suggested, the character of Geraldine "serves Smith's purpose in her criticism of arranged marriages."[19] What was more threatening, however, was that Smith linked the personal with the political by paralleling this emotional break in the matrimonial bonds with arguments in favor of the French Revolution. In the context of the radical politics of the novel, as Diana Bowstead has convincingly argued, "the radicalization of the heroine is complete by the end of the novel, and must be taken as its central action . . . ."[20] This creates an emotional thrust that subverts any conservative social or political reading.

Smith is most Godwinian in her association of the political decep-tion that prevents a nation from ascertaining the truth with the personal rumor that prevents society from accurately assessing an individual's moral character. In the *éclaircissement* at the novel's end, Desmond's French friend, Jonville de Montfleuri, clarifies recent events in a letter to Desmond's mentor, Mr. Bethel, who has served as a rather benign representative of and vehicle for society's perspective on his actions. While in France, Montfleuri and Desmond have become aware of a rumor that Desmond had been seen to accompany his alleged lover, Geraldine, who is married, while she gave birth to their illegitimate child. Montfleuri explains that it was he, not Desmond, who had been seen, accompanying his sister, Josephine, who was about to deliver the child born of a brief affair she had with Desmond—an affair that Montfleuri responds to rationally, endeavoring "to conceal what could not be amended" (4: 340). Dispelling the further anti-Jacobin rumor that Geraldine's husband had been killed by French national troops, he merges the personal into the public by commenting wryly, "thus it is, that, throughout the revolution, every circumstance has, on your side the water, been exaggerated, falsified, distorted, and misrepresented, to serve the purposes of party; and thus I, as well as Desmond, fear it will continue to be" (4: 340).

As a part of her strategy of open concealment, Smith uses the constraints of modesty imposed by the genre of the courtship novel to begin her examination of the impediments social deception and con-straint present to her characters' clear understanding of the truth of their own feelings. She does this by establishing in the characters of Desmond and Geraldine a denial to the self of the self in love that will characterize many of her later figures. Ruth Yeazell has pointed out the culture of modesty's support of the notion that "if women remain modestly unaware that they love until they are asked to marry, their desires will remain safely in the keeping of their husbands."[21] According to genre expectations, as long as Geraldine insists that her love is pure, and that she has had no thought inconsistent with her marriage vows, its material existence can be denied—to herself, as well as to others. It is true that Desmond admits his love, but he insists on its Platonic nature, protesting that his disinterested passion for Geraldine is an ideal that does not require materializa-tion. While these postures are intended to allow them—and Smith's readers—to rest easy in the assurance of the purity of their love, she goes on to demonstrate how this habit of suppression may prevent them from a full understanding of themselves and of each other, for the novel ends on a note of some doubt. Desmond's final epistle to

Bethel paints an idyllic portrait of the perfect country life he and Geraldine will share when her mourning for her conveniently dead husband is over, but his letter also reveals a great deal of anxiety; he admits that "I sometimes frighten her by my restless and vehement temper" and that I "weary her with my apprehensions and enquiries," closing by asking Bethel to soothe his "agitated heart." (4: 347–348). Thus, despite the conventionality of their happy ending, Smith portrays characters who have not yet reached the condition of perfect truth and perfect mutual understanding, providing a kind of proleptic commentary on the Platonic absolutism that Godwin was soon to express in his *Enquiry.*

When Smith turned to her next novel, her working conditions were ideal; according to George Romney, she began *The Old Manor House* while visiting William Hayley at Eartham in August, 1792.[22] The picture painted by Romney's letter suggests a rural retreat far from the political conflict intensifying in her country's capital, where the London Corresponding Society had been formed by Thomas Hardy; King George issued a proclamation for the Prevention of Seditious Meetings and Writings that led to the December government trial of Paine in absentia on the basis that the *Rights of Man* was a seditious libel. The battle lines were being clearly drawn between the suppression of information to maintain the status quo and the dissemination of knowledge as essential to reform, for Hardy had formed the London Corresponding Society in order to dispel the "gross ignorance and prejudice of the bulk of the nation."[23] The situation in France was deteriorating; the Tuileries had been invaded in June 1792, and Louis XVI was executed in January of the following year, just four months before Smith published her novel.

Perhaps most important to Smith, Godwin published the *Enquiry* in February 1793, giving philosophic voice to the connection between the personal and the political that was one of her main concerns. In response to the increasingly conservative politics of those in power, Smith clearly felt unable to be open and explicit about her own sentiments; her defense of her republican principles "went underground" in *The Old Manor House.* She distanced herself from the criticism leveled against *Desmond* by establishing her plot in another time, 1776–79, avoiding the direct political statement and engagement of her previous work. However, as Fry and others have suggested, her choice of the American Revolutionary War as a locus gives her an opportunity to criticize contemporary British policy under the guise of comments about that war; for instance, she could make anti-war statements about the American Revolution that had obvious implications in 1792 for Britain, which was about to declare war against France.²⁴ This time she titled the novel with the house rather than the main character, suggesting indirect commentary on the house of England that was, like the old manor house, in a state of decay, and using the character of its owner, Mrs. Rayland, as a emblem of patriarchal tyranny.

The parallels Smith sets up between England and the manor house background her further parallels between the social and the personal. For the first time Smith directly demonstrates how social repression prevents the very formation of an individual identity, at the same time pursuing her policy of open concealment by pushing her protagonists to the brink of decorum and form. Monimia's identity problems begin with her descent from the mercantile world Smith satirizes so often and the suggestion that her deceased mother was a woman "to whom report imputed uncommon beauty; and scandal too intimate connexion with the noble patron of her father."²⁵ Her social marginality is further emphasized by the response to her name of Mrs. Rayland, her aunt's employer, who mutters, "Monimia! I protest I don't love even to repeat the name; it puts me so in mind of a very hateful play, which I remember shocked me so when I was a mere girl, that I have always detested the name. Monimia!—'tis so very unlike a Christian's name, that, if the child is much about me, I must insist upon having her called Mary" (1 :12).²⁶ By insisting on the priority of a social construct, Mrs. Rayland is precluded from knowing the real Monimia until the end of her life.

Smith's novel exemplifies Godwin's connection of repression with hypocrisy by bringing this political issue to the personal level as she contrasts the secrecy of Monimia and Orlando imposed by society with their personal desire to be honest and sincere. Their relationship begins in childhood, and Orlando realizes his love early in the novel, when Monimia is only fourteen. However, Mrs. Rayland's determination to keep them separate forces them to hold secret meetings in Monimia's bedroom in the turret and in Orlando's private study. Smith was well aware of the impropriety of this situation; the (unacknowledged) lovers meet during the night, sometimes all night, with Orlando leaving at dawn. As with Desmond and Geraldine, Smith emphasizes the purity of the lovers' relationship in the face of their seeming descent into vice. At their first turret meeting Orlando declares, "I protest to heaven that I mean nothing but the purest friendship towards you . . . " (1: 30); yet he already has acknowledged to himself that he loves her. Their need for deception causes Monimia emotional anxiety; she agonizes, "It must be wrong to carry on a clandestine correspondence" (2: 196).²⁷ These overt protestations are belied by the metaphoric weight of these passages as the consummation of love through the intrusion of the male into the private place of his beloved, a reading supported by Orlando's characterization of Mrs. Lennard, Monimia's guardian, as a "dragon" of "unwearied vigilance" (1: 28). The intimacy evoked by their meetings is undeniable, but deny it Smith does, and readers such as Hilbish have felt compelled to defend Monimia ever since.[28]

The patriarchal forms symbolized by Mrs. Rayland and Mrs. Lennard create an atmosphere that involves even Orlando's well-intentioned father in the general repression, compelling Orlando and Monimia to careful, fine-line interpretations of what can be said while maintaining a posture of honesty. In an encounter with his father, after Orlando has angered Sir John Belgrave by protecting Monimia from his advances, and has been challenged to a duel, he treads this fine line. He tells the partial truth: that he had accosted Belgrave because he was shooting in Mrs. Rayland's woods. When pushed by his father to explain more fully, he equivocates, asserting that he has "no reason to be ashamed of telling the truth." His father sees through this: "Come, come, Orlando! . . . (Y)ou would not tell it, if you could, without being guilty of the meanness of a direct falsehood, conceal it." And when his father pursues the question by asking if he knows Monimia, he replies, "certainly I am—acquainted with her; that is—I know her, to be sure, a little . . ." (1: 97). He is, of course, splitting hairs; since the world, including his father, would inevitably call into question the purity of his relationship with Monimia if he told the truth, he convinces himself that only prevarication can protect their virtuous relationship.

Just as Godwin insists that "superstition and ignorance are the support of despotism" (IV:4:229), Smith's protagonists challenge the despotism of social form by engaging in a quest for the knowledge that is crucial to truth. Monimia has been the victim of the superstition that ignorance, prejudice, and avarice have made rampant at Rayland Park, where the noises that a ring of smugglers make on dark and stormy nights are interpreted as the actions of ghosts. Orlando takes particular interest in educating Monimia against such superstition; furthermore, in a gesture that is typical of Smith's heroes, he intends "to fortify the mind of Monimia against whatever *might* happen, by giving her a taste for reading, and cultivating her excellent understanding" (1: 161).

Smith widens and intensifies the scope of her portrait of a society whose duplicities obscure the truth that is necessary to political health by contrasting Orlando and Monimia's "virtuous" disguising of the truth and their quest for knowledge in this novel with the various duplicities of the villains, Mr. Woodford, Sir John Belgrave, Doctor Hollybourn, and Roker, representatives respectively of the merchant class, the aristocracy, organized religion, and the law. Woodford is simply engaged in the duplicity of hypocrisy, making his way from petty merchant to successful businessman with links to the politics of power through bribes, insider trading, rotten boroughs, and obsequious posturing in the styles and appurtenances of the rich and famous. Sir John Belgrave pretends marriage to Monimia while intent upon seduction; having bribed Orlando's erstwhile go-between to reveal the secret entrance, he sneaks into her turret room, an invasion of her privacy that suggests rape and clearly functions as a negative parallel to the welcome entry of Orlando earlier in the novel. In an echo of *Clarissa,* Belgrave pretends to discontinue his advances but works with Roker and Mrs. Roker (Monimia's Aunt Lennard) to move her to the home of a Mrs. Newhill, whose actions regarding Monimia are little better than those of the madam of a house of prostitution.[29] It is appropriate to Smith's disdain for the degenerate aristocracy that Monimia is saved by their opposite, Mrs. Newhill's son, a common English sailor who represents the stalwart yeoman class and behaves with courage and respect, providing Monimia the "safety and protection" (4: 469) that all women need. For Roker and Hollybourn, the lawyer and the clergyman, the most heinous crime is reserved; they have hidden the last will and testament of Orlando's Aunt Rayland written in his favor and thereby kept in effect an earlier will in favor of Hollybourn. The discovery of their duplicity allows the novel to come to its happy end: the recognition of Orlando's true right to inherit the old manor house. Social justice triumphs over despotism.

When Smith turned to *The Banished Man,* published in 1794, both her personal situation and the political environment had worsened. During its writing, Smith would have read reviews of her long poem *The Emigrants,* published in May of 1793 shortly after *The Old Manor House,* reviews criticizing her allusions in this poem to her personal life. If *The Old Manor House* had at least been partially written at a time of respite, *The Banished Man* was written at a time of incredible emotional stress and economic duress. Her son, Charles, was wounded at Dunkirk, had his leg amputated below the knee, and was being nursed at her home. Her daughter, Anna Augusta, was ill, leading her mother to great medical expense. Pressed by her need for money, she had already written one novel, *The Wanderings of Warwick,* and as she finished writing *The Banished Man,* was already proposing her children's book, *Rural Walks,* to her publisher so that "as I am reduced to four or five pounds, I may take immediate measures accordingly before famine stares me in the face."[30] In the meantime, events in France had been exploding. Louis XVI had been executed on 21 January 1793, to be followed by Marie Antoinette in October. The chaos into which France was to burst had begun, with the executions of the Girondists, the Hébertistes, and the Dantonistes, leaders replacing leaders in a dizzying apocalyptic maelstrom. The war between England and France had also intensified, and in May, Pitt's government arrested and tried the leaders of the Society for Constitutional Information and of the London Corresponding Society for treason.

Against this background, the avoidance of confrontation by Smith might have been understandable. On the surface, she does that; implicitly agreeing with English conservatives that the current course of the Revolution is lamentable, she writes a main character, D'Alonville, who is a French aristocrat banished from his birthright by war. This was not a completely ingratiating subject, however; as she was aware, by this time the political atmosphere was beginning to turn against the French émigrés living in England. Furthermore, she took this opportunity to provide commentary on the views on prejudice Godwin expressed when he inveighed against national education as invidious to the advancement of knowledge and truth because it will "actively restrain the flights of the mind, and fix it in the belief of exploded errors" (6.8: 209). Smith challenges contemporary patriotic sympathies by writing a novel whose thesis is essentially a plea against narrow national prejudice and in behalf of principles that transcend national boundaries. Thus she once again embodies his political philosophy in the lives of her characters, for the unstated theme of the novel deals with the limitation on knowledge that is willingly self-imposed, as people see others only through the lens of prejudice and therefore cannot "know" them at all as real individuals. Returning to the technique she used in *Desmond,* Smith places *The Banished Man* in recent history, late 1792 to mid 1793, appealing to the public with a boldly topical subject that is on everyone's mind.

Smith's two prefaces to *The Banished Man* expand on Godwin by addressing the issue of truth as it relates to the role of the writer. In the first, she employs her open concealment strategy by emphasizing the connection between the events of the novel and her own life, while denying the existence of that connection. She insists that hers is a work of fiction: "I have in the present work, aimed less at the wonderful and extraordinary, than at connecting by a chain of possible circumstances, events, some of which have happened, and all of which might have happened to an individual, under the exigencies of banishment and proscription; but I beg leave to add, that my hero resembles in nothing but in merit, the emigrant gentleman who now makes a part of my family; and that though some of the adventures are real, the characters are for the most part merely imaginary."[31]

Smiths' second preface, appearing at the beginning of volume 2 as "Avis au Lecteur," addresses more directly the role of the fiction writer, in effect linking this role with her battle against national prejudice and implying that both are a form of seeking *le vrai,* or *le vrai semblance.* Smith's insistence on using French in a preface to a novel that has a French hero directly challenges a political atmosphere that was beginning to turn against the French émigrés living in England. Thus, when she laments that *le vrai* "seems not to be the present fashion" (2: ix), the statement has multiple resonances. For Smith, the current taste for the Gothic is not *le vrai semblance,* and she suggests that she only uses Gothic touches in the novel in order to sell books. At the same time, by emphasizing that she is a highly conscious author, creating characters and incidents, and chafing under the need to come up with new material and to be responsive to her audience, she seeks to remind the reader of the distinction between fiction and reality, between the author and her work.

Echoing the atmosphere of increasing political repression as well as her own personal trauma, Smith creates in *The Banished Man* a fallen world whose repression impinges even more dramatically on the construction of identity. The greater power of their adversaries compels her protagonists to extensive subterfuge; they must disguise their virtue, their true nature, and seem otherwise in order to be able to assert that identity in a noble action. D'Alonville must use the disguise of a peasant in order to rescue the important papers of the Rosenheim family from their destroyed home in territory now controlled by the French "patriots," whose name belies their treachery to their country's principles. He uses a similar disguise when he later returns to France in order to take part in the underground fight against the new regime, experiencing a sense of relief when he is discovered anyway and can reassert his own identity, even if it will lead to execution. And in the novel's last volume, D'Alonville and Mrs. Denzil conceal his marriage to Angelina so that he will be able to support himself by working as a tutor to the sons of Lord Aberdore.

Smith continues to contrast such virtuous concealments with the actions of her villains, who use deception out of weakness or in order to achieve nefarious ends. The vicious Abbé Heurthofen is almost pathologically incapable of telling the truth. When he saves himself after a fall in a stream rather than coming to the aid of the women in the coach, he ludicrously fabricates an elaborate tale of his heroic swim downstream, only to be immediately found out by Madame Rosenheim and Madame D'Alberg. Heurthofen's deception and lack of a fixed identity are underscored by his apostasy; not only does he abandon his calling; his avarice leads him to join the revolutionary cause, change his name, and ultimately marry the widow of D'Alonville's brother, who also had changed identities by changing his name in the revolution and fittingly died as a result of Heurthofen's betrayal.

Perhaps nothing signals Smith's sense of despair at the changing political climate of England more clearly than her exile of characters in this and her succeeding novels. As a final act of repudiation of the repressive atmosphere of England and a gesture of liberation, she takes her now happily married international couples, D"Alonville the Frenchman and Angelina the Englishwoman, and Ellesmere the Englishman with his Polish Alexina, out of the repressive environment of England to Italy. She uses this exile as an opportunity to engage them in a working out of Godwin's philosophical tenet that "discussion is the path that leads to discovery; that "unrestrained communication of men's thoughts and discoveries to each other" is necessary to the quest for truth (2:5:117). In doing this, she characteristically affirms the relativity of truth when Ellesmere and D'Alonville agree to disagree about whether the French Revolution had merit in its original design. Their example illustrates Smith's developing philosophy that political differences openly expressed can lead to a life of harmony and continual discovery; Ellesmere learns that independence is more important than wealth, while D'Alonville the urbane Frenchman learns to appreciate "the unadorned beauty of nature"(4:334). Most importantly, his adversity has taught him lessons of fortitude and resolution; as he says, it has "instructed me to conquer prejudice, and to feel for the sufferings of others. In losing everything but my honor and my integrity, I have learned, that he who retains those qualities can never be degraded, however humble may be his fortune" (4:340). No reader familiar with the personal history of Charlotte Smith can doubt that, by that species of ventriloquism possible in the narrative form, D'Alonville speaks for the author as he summarizes the triumph of truth over deception.

The reviews that followed the publication of *The Banished Man* in the autumn of 1794 and spring of 1795 indicate that Smith's strategy of open concealment was working; overlooking the novel's Godwinian resonance, reviewers focused instead on Smith's change of position in regard to the French Revolution in the light of the Reign of Terror, either praising it (*European Review*) or suggesting that it was written to amend the opinions she had expressed in *Desmond* (*Analytical Review*). More hostile criticism was reserved for her inclusion in the novel of herself in the character of Mrs. Denzil; once again, her attempt to distance herself by insisting in the preface that she drew upon characters she met only as any novelist must draw from experience had failed, for, as Janet Todd remarks, "women's writing was not . . . alienable . . . , as Charlotte Smith well knew, and observation could not so easily become an autonomous commodity for a woman writer."[32] Tired from the fray, and overwhelmed by the critical illness of Anna Augusta, Smith turned to writing a novel that escaped entirely from direct comment on the contemporary political scene and returned to her earlier style: *Montalbert*. But as this escape from contemporary reality was being published, France was continuing to fall apart, enduring the White Terror that followed the Reign of Terror and the chaos that was to lead to the establishment of the Directory. England was experiencing heightened public unrest and political polarization as a result of the extended war and the weakened economy that accompanied its expense. The summer of 1795 saw food riots in Birmingham and other major cities; in October of that same year, the London Corresponding Society held a public meeting remonstrating George III; three days later George's coach was attacked as he rode to the opening of Parliament. The Pitt government tightened its grip, introducing a "Bill for the Safety and Preservation of His Majesty's Person and Government Against Treasonable and Seditious Practices and Attempts" and a "A Bill for the More Effectually Preventing Seditious Meetings and Assemblies," soon followed in early 1796 by the act suspending *habeas corpus*. The literary war between the so-called Jacobin and anti-Jacobin forces was at its height. In the meantime, the death of Anna Augusta in July of 1795 shortly after the publication of *Montalbert* left her mother with a grief that burdened her until her death. Smith's preface to her next novel sums up her trials: her "murdered happiness," her weakened health, her literary and social isolation as she is told that she has "made enemies by personality," and her continuing failure to bring her lawsuit to a settlement due to the chicanery of the lawyers whom she blames for the poverty that prevented her from providing effective care for the critically ill Augusta.[33]

Smith's personal torment and vulnerability in the increasingly repressive political atmosphere inform the pages of *Marchmont,* published toward the end of 1796. She had suggested mockingly in her second preface to *The Banished Man* that it might have been better to have "earthed my hero, and have sent him for adventures to the subterraneous town on the Châtelet mountain in Champagne, or even to Herculaneum," in search of the novelty that would preclude charges of plagiarism (2: iv). In this "going to earth" Smith foreshadowed the emotional direction to which she moves in *Marchmont*. Godwin had argued that "truth was calculated in the nature of things to discipline the mind to fortitude, humanity and virtue" (4:4:224), and Smith's stated purpose, to "enforce the virtue of fortitude" (1: xvi), points to its necessity on both the personal and public level. As Marchmont and Althea (whose name is reminiscent of the Greek word for "truth") embark on their mutual quest for their rightful inheritance, symbol of their rightful identity, their society forces them into situations of isolation, concealment, and imprisonment, emphasizing their utter marginalization and victimization. Perhaps no gesture in the novel is more emblematic of this vulnerability and of the denial of individual rights than Smith's description of Lord Mohun, who, when he first meets her, begins by "surveying Althea with the sort of look that a sagacious jockey puts on when he is about to purchase a horse" (1:134). Mohun's scopophilia, his "rude and insolent manner of staring, which was cruelly distressing to Althea" (1: 204), becomes a visual metaphor for rape. This is later reified in his literal attempt to seduce/rape her when she comes to his house to reason with him about giving her the money coming to him from her inheritance, over which he has control as a trustee.

While the emotion of victimization is clearly connected with Smith's personal circumstances, she also uses it to continue her examination of the close relationship between the individual and larger sociopolitical issues, as the conflict between Althea, a marginalized and virtually orphaned heroine, and Mohun, representative of the unbridled power of government, suggests. Smith continues to use the power of rumor to destroy reputation as a trope for the obstruction of truth through inaccurate knowledge and malice. A Mrs. Gisborough, clearly representative of the Bluestocking circle Smith often parodies for its pseudo-intellectualism, writes to Sir Audley, Althea's father, to recommend Marchmont as tutor to his eldest son in preparation for the latter's projected tour of Italy and Germany, the "grand tour" that formed the finishing touch to a young gentleman's education. Sir Audley replies in the negative, giving no reason for his rejection of Marchmont, which Smith is careful to make clear to her readers actually derives from the guilt he feels about his role in causing the family's unpayable debt by taking unfair advantage of Marchmont's father. Misinterpreting this letter as a sign that "something was undoubtedly wrong in the character of this young man" (2: 16), Mrs.

Gisborough and her circle of friends drop their attempt to help him. Althea becomes a similar victim of rumor when she takes the indecorous step of moving in with her acknowledged lover's indigent family; society gossips proceed to give the worst interpretation to Althea's move, which Smith has carefully justified as a response to the enmity, selfishness, and jealousy of her stepmother, and to the "purity of female friendship" (4: 244) she has with Lucy, Marchmont's sister.

Again, Smith uses the patterns of female modesty inherent in the conventions of the courtship novel as part of a strategy of open concealment. It is clear from the beginning that Marchmont and Althea are destined for each other, yet their acknowledgment of their love is unusually slow; Althea epitomizes the "blankness of mind" that Yeazell suggests is the result of such repression of knowledge (51). Althea's first encounter with Marchmont is brief: "hardly venturing to look at the stranger, (she) walked on—but she saw, in the transient glance she had of him, that he was a young man of genteel appearance" (1: 98). Their next encounter takes place shortly after, when Althea is leaving the meeting with her father in which he responds to her resolution to refuse Lord Mohun's proposal of marriage by threatening to disown her. Smith takes pains to make clear to the reader that Althea is at this point "(f)ree from every preference, and uninfluenced by every motive but native integrity" (1: 151). Marchmont is on his way in to beg her father for some relief from the debt the latter is pursuing, forcing Marchmont's family into poverty; this time, Althea and Marchmont don't even speak. After this meeting, they encounter each other outdoors, striking up a conversation in which Althea's main emotion is pity for his plight. As the novel unfolds, Althea's thoughts recur to Marchmont, but she does not consciously acknowledge them; Smith emphasizes that "she would have started had she been told that she thought of particular favour of a young man whom she had seen only twice" (1: 201). It is especially important that Althea maintain the purity of any interest she shows Marchmont: "unwilling to acknowledge, even to herself, how frequently she thought of him, she endeavoured to persuade herself that it was his virtues and his misfortunes alone that had awakened these lively emotions in her mind, and that any other person, equally meritorious and equally unhappy, would be as often the subject of her thoughts" (1: 209–210). As before, the determined innocence of their relationship serves to offset the seeming impropriety of the situation into which Smith places her lovers, for during Althea's banishment to Eastwoodleigh, his father's ruined estate that is now in the hands of Sir Audley, Marchmont conceals himself in the interstices of the house; thus, they live under the same roof. Marchmont is a ghostly presence in the house who finally materializes in a revelatory encounter in one of the great rooms. Their relationship continues to develop in this pattern of evasion of self-knowledge and revelation, hesitation and resolution. They do not declare their love until the end of volume 2, when Marchmont leaves for his exile in France to escape debt.

In *Marchmont* Smith expands the complexity of her open concealment strategy; on the one hand, Marchmont's repeated sympathy with the fate of Louis served to assuage the political criticism of some of her readers, functioning as a counterbalance to the novel's censure of the British legal system, which, as Fry has pointed out, "considering the atmosphere of repression at the time, . . . is remarkably explicit" (102). On the other, it is a reflection of her deep and abiding philosophy of humanism that goes beyond class and nationality. And when Smith exposes her hero to some of the repercussions of the Reign of Terror, her comments directly link the occurrences in France with the condition of England. As Marchmont views the ruins of the royal palace, he makes an ironic connection between what the French have done to Louis and what the English power structure has done to him, noting that "the poor wandering individual, alone in a foreign and an hostile country, might have found objects of compassion, in reflecting on the fate of the late possessors of the immense pile I saw before me; and I might have said, 'The exile, once the owner and heir of Eastwoodleigh, is less wretched than the surviving owners of Versailles!'" (3: 189).

Any sense that sympathy for Louis indicated Smith's change of heart in the direction of social conservatism is further obviated by the events of the final volume of the novel. In a long discussion between Althea and Marchmont upon his return to England from France, Smith once again indicates the conflict between truth and deception brought about by social hypocrisy and form. Their love for each other has been openly declared; indeed, they are living under the same roof once again, with only his mother as her guardian, a clear breach of social decorum. Althea, who is under age, suggests requesting permission to marry from her stepmother, but Marchmont argues that such a request, once denied, as it inevitably would be, would force them into open rebellion; furthermore, it would make Marchmont's presence known to his pursuers. In their discussions, Marchmont contrasts the hypocrisy of the social world, the world of money and power, of *"les Gens comme il faut"* (4: 196) with "our world, which we shall find in our own hearts, in each other, and in our family" (4: 199), asking Althea how, as an honest person "who generally sees with judgement so true," she can "keep up forms of deference and affection where they do not exist?" (4: 194). Yet in response to the reality of the outside world, they are forced to celebrate their marriage after publishing the bans in the obscurity of out-or-season Margate, keeping their marriage a secret.

In this novel, Smith deepens the contrast between this "virtuous subterfuge" forced on her otherwise ingenuous characters and the vicious lies of her villains by exhibiting a new unity of purpose in these prevarications, for no other novel Smith wrote is more concerned with issues of money; the lies of her father, her stepmother, Mohun, and Vampyre, his minion, are all aimed at preventing Marchmont from investigating the skullduggery that took his father's estate away from him and preventing Althea from receiving her proper inheritances from her Aunt Trevyllian and her father and from pursuing her right to the larger inheritance from her cousin Trevyllian's estate. The *anagnoresis* at novel's end, brought about by the *deus ex machina* of Marchmont's distant relative, Desborough, a misanthropic do-gooder with republican sympathies, establishes to the world the protagonists' right to their inheritance. Their ability now to step into the roles for which their breeding destined them amounts to society's acknowledgment of their true identity. Thus the connection between personal and public identity is made, and the prevarications and labyrinthine intrigues in which their opponents have enmeshed them are understood to have done far more than keep them from their money and involve them in virtuous deception; they have sought to deny them their selfhood.

As Charlotte Smith turned to the writing of her last true novel, *The Young Philosopher,* the war with France continued; Napoleon kept England on edge with unsuccessful invasions into Pembrokeshire and Ireland and set up a puppet republic in Switzerland. Even radicals in England deserted the French cause. But publications like *The Anti-Jacobin* in November of 1797 ensured that the atmosphere of repression and political controversy continued. Meetings of the London Corresponding Society were disrupted by the authorities in July of 1797 and April of 1798, shortly before *The Young Philosopher* was published. On the home front, Smith was still trying desperately to bring the question of her children's inheritance to a successful conclusion. The reviews of *Marchmont* were favorable to a degree, but critics still complained that her inclusion of what they saw as personal vendettas was harmful to the design of the novels. Even worse, the subscription list to her second volume of *Elegiac Sonnets,* printed at this time, was much shorter than the first, damaging both her ego and her pocketbook.

Smith's response to the climax of anti-Jacobin sentiment during these years was to write a novel on a higher plane, one that represents the fullest development of a political philosophy that now openly echoes, parallels, expands upon, and sometimes critiques Godwin. In *The Young Philosopher* she chooses a title that must remind her readers of both the French *philosophes* and Godwin, especially since she creates a character, Armitage, who evokes the figure of Godwin. Involving her characters only tangentially with the French Revolution, she nonetheless addresses and refines the political philosophy it generated and to which Godwin gave voice, exploring the nature of truth and the limitations imposed on it in the contemporary climate more directly and fully than ever before. Thus she continues her policy of "open concealment," averting criticism of her personal politics by insisting in the preface that "(t)here may be many traits, many ideas, and even many prejudices, which may be necessary to support or render these characters natural, that are by no means those of the composer of the book."[34]

Delmont's character exemplifies Godwin's principle of independent judgment: "(t)o a rational being there can be but one rule of conduct, justice, and one mode of ascertaining that rule, the exercise of his understanding" (4: 112). Smith describes his early education at the hands of his mother: "the use she made of her power was to teach him to reason on everything he learned, instead of seeing all objects as they are represented, through the dazzling and false medium of prejudice, communicated from one generation to another" (1: 87). This education allows Delmont to develop social liberty; he is an open, sincere young man who eschews unnecessary social forms, having "for some months established his own liberty, so far as to shake off adherence to these forms, with which, under the name of politeness, men have agreed to fetter one another" (1: 120–121).

Delmont later emphasizes the association between truth and liberty on the political, moral, and religious plane in a key interchange with his unwanted guest, Dr. Winslow, a pompous clergyman, an interchange that boldly echoes the situation and language Smith had used in the openly political *Desmond* six years before. Delmont averts an argument about the infallibility of the church and the divine right of kings, although he clearly questions both. But when Dr. Winslow launches into invective against philosophers, charging them with having launched the recent bloodshed and misery in France, Delmont leaps to their defense, characterizing the philosophers as persons who have "sought and imagined they had found truth," who "endeavoured to emancipate the people from the fetters which galled and crushed them to benefit and enlighten the world," and expressing pleasure that "the gloomy and absurd structures, raised on the basis of super-stition, have toppled down headlong," while "the bastilles of falsehood, in which men's minds were imprisoned, are leveled with the earth, never to rise again!" (1: 146–47).

Delmont has the openness of social character that circumstances deny to Marchmont; he insists on his right to be open and sincere, to be himself. The only form of virtuous concealment used by the protag-onists arises from the conflict between honesty and consideration of others. In this, her final examination of Godwin's philosophy, Smith provides a critique of Godwin, who had insisted that it was always preferable to tell truths, even though they are "painful truths (being) disclosed to persons who are already in the most pitiable circum-stances" because falsehood would continue to keep them weak and because they might hear the awful truth under more destructive circumstances (4: 224). Smith differs from Godwin, showing her roots in the benevolent sensibility of earlier eighteenth century philosophy; Delmont, Medora, and Mrs. Glenmorris all at various times conceal from each other the truth of their situation in an attempt to protect the others in some way. Mrs. Glenmorris, for instance, conceals from Delmont the reason for her delay in his marriage to Medora; that she is at the moment impecunious and fears involving him with an indi-gent family. And he conceals Medora's abduction from her to protect her from fear.

Despite their general personal honesty, Smith's protagonists are still enmeshed in the deceptions of others. As in *Marchmont,* a primary target in this text is rumor, the misunderstanding of a char-acter's virtue through lack of complete knowledge. In her preface, Smith lists first among her moral purposes "the ill consequence of detraction," (1: vi), and she develops in the novel several misunder-standings of her main characters, particularly Medora. In order to illustrate her point, she once again places her heroine in situations that challenge rules of decorum; at one point in the novel she is living in the home of Delmont, her beloved, without the benefit of a proper guardian, and she is abducted, exposing her to the advances of George Delmont's brother, Augustus, of her abductor (who has been careful to provide a guardian in the person of his mother), and finally of Sir Harry Richmond. All of these characters initially disguise their villainy from Medora, and, indeed, from society in general. However, once again real virtue and real principles with-stand the vicious attacks of those who are blinded by avarice and concupiscence.

Smith's response in this final novel to the ultimate deception, the deprivation of Medora of her rightful inheritance and, thus her identity, by her grasping grandmother and the minions of the law, suggests the extent of her own despair about her children's inheritance and about the possibility for social change in England. At the same time, however, it confirms her philosophy of the relativity of knowledge and of identity. Eleanor Ty has pointed out that in this novel "the philosophers, thinkers, and all of the characters who do not share the materialistic and corrupt values of civilized society are outcasts," suggesting this as a final position in Smith's political trajectory from optimism to despair.[35] Yet when Glenmorris relates the story of his sojourn in America, the end of his travails that started with the pirates on the coast of Scotland, he connects the value of freedom with the best in English history; for the Americans, he says, "the noble flame of liberty seemed to have purified their minds from every narrow and unmanly prejudice, and when they found that my heart beat in unison with theirs, when they heard me declare that, Englishman as I was, I would never have drawn my sword against men struggling in that glorious cause for which 'Hampden bled in the field and Sydney on the scaffold;' they forgot that I was born a Briton, a North Briton too, and belonging to those whose legions were then carrying fire and sword through their country, and they embraced me as a brother" (2: 242). Glenmorris's reference to Hampden and Sydney underscores his radical politics even as he asserts that the value of liberty transcends national boundaries and national enmities. And Armitage is given ringing arguments in favor of constitutional reform rather than revolution at the opening of book 4, when he confronts Mrs. Crewkhern, exposing the hypocrisy of the piety she has used as an excuse for aiding in institutionalizing Mrs. Glenmorris. She accuses him of being a freethinker, an illuminé, a democrat, a Jacobin, and a republican, but he responds by deconstructing the terms, effectively defusing her politically charged labels, and stubbornly asserts his own allegiance to the monarchy and the nobility.

Thus when Smith ultimately sends her outcasts to America, which has stood throughout the novel for religious, social, and political freedom, she echoes the end of *The Banished Man,* carefully averting narrow prejudice and allowing both Glenmorris and Armitage the freedom to respond according to their independent judgment. Armitage and Glenmorris embody two acceptable possibilities for the British; Smith suggests that their differences of opinion reflect different experiences and temperaments and do not imply hostility. Glenmorris is careful to avoid narrow prejudice, accepting Armitage's decision to remain in England and placing him "among the moderates and quietists; you endure all things, you hope all things, you believe all things," adding that "[w]hile you can be tolerably happy yourself, my dear friend, in this country, or believe that you can do good to its people, it is very fit you should stay" (4: 393). He realizes that he and Armitage do not "differ in the great principles of our actions, and all the rest is mere verbal wrangling" (4: 393), adding "[y]ou agree with me, that true philanthropy does not consist in loving John, and Thomas, and George, and James, because they are our brothers, our cousins, our neighbors, our countrymen, but in benevolence to the whole human race" (4: 394).

The Young Philosopher concludes Smith's novelistic examination of the role of deception as an impediment to the quest for truth so necessary to the personal and public health of the English. Her concerns have been very much those of Godwin; the epistemology her characters espouse is essentially that of his eighteenth-century rationalism. She has worked out in her characters and their experiences the connection between the abuse of power on every level and in all of its manifestations and the repression and limitation of truth and knowledge. Smith does not propose specific political reforms; however, the political discussions in these novels suggest that her general tendency, like that of Godwin, is toward reform rather than revolution. Smith seems to accept the relativity of knowledge; in her later novels, characters work together in the construction of knowledge and accept differing perceptions. But perhaps her greatest contribution to the discussion may be her understanding of the threat that the repression of truth and knowledge represents to the formation of identity. Inevitably, her comments are peculiarly appropriate to the status of women. As she draws from and embodies in her characters her own experiences, she is her own best evidence of the challenges women faced in the formation of public and private identity, for in response to social pressures, Smith spent most of her adult life denying her identity as a writer of novels, insisting instead that she was a private poet who turned to publication and novel writing only as a last resort. Yet her skill as a novelist belies her assertion. Smith's novels do not merely replicate each other in the service of earning a living; they show a writer deeply engaged in using the novel to explore the most important issues of her time, developing and clarifying a political philosophy that is worked out through character and plot while attending to issues of audience. It is true that she turned after *The Young Philosopher* to other forms of writing, but, as Matthew Bray has shown, even in her final poem, *Beachy Head,* published posthumously, she continued the relational strategy embodied in her last two novels, linking England and France historically and geologically as antidote to the divisions that have plagued those two countries.[36] The final gesture in that final poem confirms the benevolent impulse that lies at the heart of this relational mode of being, as she portrays the lonely Hermit, "disgusted with the world," who nonetheless dies while trying to save fellow humans from drowning in a shipwreck.[37] It is not difficult to see Charlotte Smith and her novels in that final gesture.

Notes

1. William Godwin, *An Enquiry Concerning Political Justice* (London: G.G. J. and J. Robinson, 1793), 211. All references to Godwin apply to this edition of the Enquiry and will appear in the text.

2. In this, Godwin carefully distinguishes himself from the relativism of Voltaire, whom he paraphrases: "Truth taught by moderate degrees gradually enlarges the intellectual capacity, and insensibly prepares the equality and happiness of mankind; but taught without prudential restraint would either be nipped in the bud, or occasion national concussions in the world, that would be found premature and therefore abortive" (4: 230). The progress of the French Revolution and Godwin's own subsequent career suggest the wisdom of Voltaire's more moderate position.

3. Marie-Jean-Antoine-Nicolas Caritat, Marquis de Condorcet. *Condorcet: Selected Writings,* ed. Keith Michael Baker (Indianapolis: ghe Bobbs Merrill Company, Inc., 1976).

4. Florence Hilbish, *Charlotte Smith: Poet and Novelist* (Philadelphia: University of Pennsylvania Press, 1941), 297. Further on in her discussion, however, Hilbish seems to call this statement into question when she calls Smith's works "novels of theory," adding that "beginning with an underlying principle, she arranged the plot and portrayed characters for the purpose of exposing contemporary evils" (297–98).

5. Marilyn Butler, *Jane Austen and the War of Ideas* (Oxford: Clarendon Press, 1987), 31.

6. Gary Kelly's point is made in the introductory chapter to *The English Jacobin Novel,* 1780–1805 (Oxford: Clarendon Press, 1975).

7. Loraine Fletcher, *Charlotte Smith: A Critical Biography* (New York: St. Martin's Press, 1998), 122.

8. The extent of the friendship between Smith and Godwin and the exact dates of their meetings are still tantalizingly undocumented. Fletcher

suggests that in 1796 Smith "was now reading Godwin on progress and perfectibility, and probably met him first at this time," sharing Gary Kelly's belief that "he was a close friend by 1798" (261). In his 1876 biography of Godwin, *William Godwin, His Friends and Contemporaries* (London: H. S. King, 1876), Charles Kegan Paul alludes to a visit by Charlotte Smith to Godwin's second wife, and Smith is known to have written a preface to his tragedy, *Antonio* (1800). The little known letter from Smith to Godwin quoted in the introduction to this volume does make it clear that in September 1797, Smith claims to be reading *Political Justice* for the first time.

9. Mary Anne Schofield, *Masking and Unmasking the Female Mind: Disguise Romances and Feminine Fiction 1723–1799* (Newark, Del.: University of Delaware Press, 1990), 190.

10. Sir Samuel Egerton Brydges, *Imaginative Biography* 2 (London: Saunders, 1834), 93.

11. Sarah Zimmerman, "Charlotte Smith's Letters and the Practice of Self-Representation," *Princeton University Library Chronicle* 53 (1991), 50–77.

12. See Terry Castle, *Masquerade and Civilization: The Carnivalesque in Eighteenth-Century English Culture* (London: Methuen, 1986); Mary Anne Schofield, (quoted above); Catherine Craft-Fairchild, *Disguise and Female Identity in Eighteenth-Century Fictions by Women* (University Park, Pa.: Pennsylvania State University Press, 1993).

13. Samuel Taylor Coleridge coins this useful phrase in his criticism of Wordsworth's dramatic form in *The Excursion;* he protests that in such writing "(either) the thoughts and diction are different from that of the poet, and then there arises an incongruity of style; or they are the same and indistinguishable, and then it presents a species of ventriloquism, where two are represented as talking while in truth one man only speaks." (*Biographia Literaria* 12, ed. James Engell and Walter Jackson Bate (Princeton: Princeton University Press, 1985). Its successful use by Smith and others may suggest a key difference between dramatic poetry and the novel.

14. Catherine Craft-Fairchild suggests that the mentor who helps the heroine acquire knowledge can sometimes be dually seen as a patriarchal lawgiver, as in the character of Harley in Mary Hays's *Memoirs of Emma Courtney;* however, discussing this phenomenon in the context of Godwin's epistemology suggests rather the axis of heroine and feminized hero in search of knowledge in opposition to the patriarchal suppression of knowledge (16).

15. Charlotte Smith, *Celestina: A Novel,* 2nd Edition (London: T. Cadell, 1791), 4: 189.

16. Quoted in Margery Weiner, *The French Exiles, 1789–1815* (John Murray: Fifty Albemarle Street, London, 1969), 54.

17. Hilbish summarizes these responses in her discussion of Desmond (47).

18. Charlotte Smith. *Desmond.* (London: Printed for G.G. J. and J. Robinson, Paternoster Row, 1792). Subsequent references to this edition will appear in the text.

19. Pat Elliott remarks that "(t)he position of Geraldine Verney, a married woman, as the heroine is a major departure from convention," suggesting that this use of a mature woman better serves Smith's purpose in her criticism of arranged marriages. "Charlotte Smith's Feminism: A Study of *Emmeline* and *Desmond,* in Dale Spender, ed., *Living by the Pen: Early British Women Writers* (New York: Teachers College Press, 1992), 107.

20. Diana Bowstead. "Charlotte Smith's *Desmond*: The Epistolary Novel as Ideological Argument," in Mary Ann Schofield and Cecilia Macheski, eds., *Fetter'd or Free?* (Athens, Ohio: Ohio University Press, 1986), 261.

21. Ruth Yeazell, *Fictions of Modesty: Women and Courtship in the English Novel* (Chicago: University of Chicago Press, 1991), 51.

22. Hilbish quotes his letter in Charlotte Smith, 157.

23. Thomas Hardy, *Account of the Origin of the LCS,* 1799, cited in Marilyn Morris, "The Impact of the French Revolution on London Reform Societies," in Gail M. Schwab and John R. Jeanneney, eds., *The French Revolution and Its Impact* (Westport, Conn.: Greenwood Press, 1995), 212.

24. Fry, Carroll L., *Charlotte Smith* (New York: Twayne Publishers, 1996), 91.

25. Charlotte Smith. *The Old Manor House.* London and New York: Pandora Press, 1987, 1: 11. Subsequent references to this edition will appear in the text.

26. Fletcher traces Monimia's name to the heroine of Otway's *The Orphan,* in which Monimia is visited in her bedchamber by her secret husband's twin, making her guilty, unwittingly, of incest. See Fletcher (185). Smith counted on her readers to understand this allusion. This adds considerable irony to Mrs. Rayland's comment, since Orlando later visits Monimia secretly in her bedchamber.

27. Deborah Ross notes how Smith's style during Monimia's inner debate makes it "yield up its Gothic energy" *The Excellence of Falsehood: Romance, Realism, and Women's Contribution to the Novel* (Lexington, Ky.: The University Press of Kentucky, 1991), 154.

28. Hilbish finds it "surprising how anyone, even a reviewer, could misconstrue Mrs. Smith's portrayal of innocence" (159).

29. It is interesting to speculate whether the name of Smith's rake, Belgrave, is an echo of Lovelace's correspondent, John Belford, furthering

the reverberation of *Clarissa* in the reader's mind and emphasizing the parallels between the two heroines' circumstances.

30. Letter to Cadell and Davies, 20 August 1794. Cited in Judith Stanton, "Charlotte Smith's 'Literary Business,'" *The Age of Johnson,* ed. Paul J. Korshin (New York: AMS Press, 1987), 390.

31. Charlotte Smith, *The Banished Man: A Novel* (London: T. Cadell and W. Davies, 1794), xi. Subsequent references will appear in the text.

32. Janet Todd, *The Sign of Angellica: Women, Writing, and Fiction, 1660–1800* (New York: Columbia University Press, 1989), 232.

33. Charlotte Smith, *Marchmont* (Delmar, New York: Scholars' Facsimiles and Reprints, 1989), v–xvi. Subsequent references to this edition will appear in the text.

34. Charlotte Smith, *The Young Philosopher* (London: Printed for T. Cadell and W. Davies, 1798), 1:vi. Subsequent references to this edition will appear in the text.

35. Eleanor Ty, *Unsex'd Revolutionaries: Five Women Novelists in the 1790s* (Toronto: University of Toronto Press, 1993), 154.

36. Matthew Bray, "Removing the Anglo-Saxon Yoke: The Francocentric Vision of Charlotte Smith's Later Works," *Wordsworth Circle,* 24 (Summer 1993): 155–58.

37. Charlotte Smith, "Beachy Head" in *The Poems of Charlotte Smith,* ed. Stuart Curran (New York: Oxford University Press, 1993), 2: 675ff.

Afterword

∾

Madelyn Gutwirth

A dear friend and illustrious Frenchwoman scholar whom I told I was reading a text called *Rebellious Hearts,* concerning the writings of British women on the French Revolution, exclaimed, "How could I ever have imagined that such a thing existed!" Indeed, the wealth and complexity of the responses sagaciously explored in these pages have power to astonish, especially across the restless divide that is the Channel. This volume acquaints us with the dimensions of hope and fear that France's revolutionary turmoil across the waters aroused among women. For them, the violent disruptions of European social conditions presaged the possibility, sometimes embraced, sometimes rejected, of a sea change not only in class adjustments, but in gender arrangements, at home or out in the public arena.

But the Channel's metaphoric breadth, which in a sense seemed far smaller during the age of the Revolution and its aftermath than it does to us today, waxes and wanes, even in these pages. For these studies furnish a monitory example of the problematics of cross-national stories, as myths and considerations of huge import in one nation count scarcely at all in the other, and divergent social and religious traditions make for divergent understandings of the same "events."

The volume's editors have cannily melted down the huge complex of issues presented by the long obscured wealth of writings by British women in the Revolutionary and Romantic eras that have been newly reintroduced to the scholarly community since the 1970s, when studies like Margaret Anne Doody's "English Women Novelists and the French Revolution," and Katherine M. Rogers' *Feminism in Eighteenth Century England* began to appear. Kari Lokke and Adriana Craciun have shaped this collection as a fourfold construction:

Revolution and Nationalism; Revolution and Religion; Revolutionary Subjects; and Revolutionary Representations. These categories have proven useful in breaking down the multifacetedness of these essays, even though, as the editors are well aware, the first three overlap materially: these women's rethinking of female subjectivity could not help but interface with their positions on matters religious and national. Some previous influential analyses had already prepared this volume's audience to view the authorial freedoms of these British women as constrained by the dominant gender grid consigning women to domestic roles. What the editors of the present volume have sought to exhibit is rather the obverse of that manner of reading them. Here is a phalanx of female authors, inspirited by the fiery contentions revolution has loosed upon the Continent, grappling with war, with politics, with prophecy, and with conscientious dissent. Over an emphasis upon limitations to female freedoms among these authors, limitations reified by the Revolution that were underscored by earlier studies, our present critical mood favors the retrieval of an awareness of female agency. But what the essays here establish convincingly is the inadequacy of this dichotomy as a grid. Certainly the liberatory thrust of revolutionary concepts of freedom and equality aroused among women in both nations, as among other classes of the dispossessed, energies and ideas that could no longer be wholly controlled, by even the most repressive ideological or legislative means. But the omnipresence of misogynous opinion, even when gently proposed, as in the dogma dictating women's "natural" role as domestic partner and loving mother, impelled women actors to invent elaborate strategies of mediation with prevailing concepts of womanhood which, while modifying the force with which they could speak up, yet enabled them to say a great deal to further their own interests. It is the wealth and variety of this generation of British women's tactical measures to maintain and extend their agency of the mind that have been demonstrated here.

Certainly the French Revolution provided a spark that ignited and loosed their expressive powers as it momentarily lent greater credence to the egalitarian phenomenon of female political speech. Yet virtually all the writers treated here grapple with a distinctly English set of institutions and conventions, whether radical, Whig, or Tory, religious or secular, literary or rhetorical, all the while remaining subject to the deep division of opinion abroad in their society as to the value of women's authorship and/or speech, and the imperatives of female virtue.

At least three overwhelming distinctions between the two Channel nations greatly impinged upon the ability of their women (but not of them alone) to find suitable expression for their imaginations and beliefs. One was the entrenched centralization of administration in France, which Tocqueville observed to have long antedated the Revolution, but which Napoleonic reorganization would only systematize. Although the monarch's agents might tolerate a degree of free discussion, the slightest sign of any group in process of formation, under the Old Regime, gave rise to its immediate suppression, so that local control of affairs remained minimal. Indeed the drive toward the devolution of power from the center to the nation was one of the pressures creating revolution. Needless to say, this repressiveness toward local initiatives stifled the development of a sense of civic participation.

A second great difference was, of course, religious: it lay in the gulf between Protestant England's tradition founding selfhood in the individual conscience's encounter with God, and Catholic France's lack of such a religious tenet, coupled with its denial of religious toleration in the wake of the 1685 Revocaction of the Edict of Nantes. It was only in 1787 that French Protestants were "emancipated," an act which still occasioned riots in parts of the west and southeast. Hence, by the Revolutionary period, England enjoyed a plethora of sites for religious dissent, in a number of which women were able to find a toehold of respectability while expressing their beliefs, whereas France presented few similar sites of authorization for individual convictions. Hannah More's conservative appeal to support persecuted priests and resist the stench of revolutionary ideas with their promise of permanent chaos, and Joanna Southcott's defense of the just war against heathen Napoleonic France from a dissenting sociopolitical stance present strikingly disparate examples of religious empowerment of women. As Angela Keane presents her, More appears torn between the desire for approval of her appropriation of the feminine proprieties, and longing for a prophetic stature. Southcott's visionary millenarian rejection of the Godless Revolution, in Kevin Binfield's reading, visibly animates her prophetic campaign against it as evil. But almost all of the Englishwomen dealt with here, even those who materially dissent from dominant dogmas, seem to embrace some degree of piety. Christianity for them is often consonant with an egalitarian compassion, whereas those women who espouse revolutionary views in the French context, like Isabelle de Charrière or Germaine de Staël, like the revolution itself, remain resolutely secular during this decade. It is worthy of note that the most fully realized author among French women writing the Revolution was the Protestant Germaine de Staël.

The relatively liberating effect upon women of the tradition of English Protestant dissent came freighted down, however, with what

Ann Frank Wake (following Chris Jones and Marlon Ross) notes as its distinctly less favorable side: the "liberal politics of religious Dissenters made visible resistance even more difficult for women within the fold than outside it," because their claims for liberty of religion and equal representation were consistently informed by the framework of family hierarchy.

A third important factor distinguishing French from English society was the relatively closer social distance between women and men obtaining in the privileged classes of pre-Revolutionary France. It was, indeed, this unseemly French mingling of the sexes in public assemblies and at the theater against which Rousseau inveighed in his *Lettre à d'Alembert sur les spectacles* which made him call for a more "decent" separation between them. A debased remnant of the courtly tradition, the language of gallantry, dominated relations between the sexes, erecting a huge semantic barrier against attempts by members of both sexes to inflect gender paradigms. The omnipresence and influence of women in French society before 1789, so well described by Dena Goodman's *The Republic of Letters,* appears to have aroused bourgeois and popular misogyny. The Jacobins' repressive gender backlash would be followed by a protracted period of abandonment by women of direct expression of their needs and views as a collective group with interests of its own.

Despite these distinctions, an overwhelming cross-cultural trend surfaces: swamping most differentiations between the gender politics of England and France in this period, prevailing even in the new American republic, is the powerful tendency among even the most progressive classes, in despite of two ostensibly egalitarian revolutions, to maintain intact and even reinforce gender hierarchy. Indeed, it can fruitfully be argued that some roots of the specific gender conservatism espoused by both the American colonial and the French bourgeois revolutions were offshoots from the English rural domestic ideal, with its reassuring dream of a relatively orderly, pacific gender division into separate spheres. As Linda Colley has asserted, this gender dispensation was probably so aggressively insisted upon because, in fact, it was respected with diminishing urgency in actual practice.

A huge collateral factor adding to the differing authorial postures of women in England and in France during this period arose out of dread of contagion from the fever of Frenchwomen's revolutionary militancy. We recall the stinging rebuke to women's political aspirations visited upon them by Jacobin politicians, culminating in André Amar's successful motion in the Convention of October 1793 forbidding them to associate together in groups of more than five persons, consigning them to private space: "Do you wish women to be seen in the French Republic coming to the bar, to the tribune, to political assemblies like men, abandoning restraint, the source of all their sex's virtues, and the care of their families?" he asked. In the immediate aftermath of this propaganda and civil rights defeat, the climate for Frenchwomen's writing in the nineties chilled materially. Despite a directly related campaign to discredit Englishwomen's militancy, epitomized by Richard Polwhele's attempt to smear it as tainted by the dis-ease contracted from French "harpies," British women authors still enjoyed, as compared with their French counterparts, relative freedom of expression through the nineties and into the Napoleonic era. In a final blow, the Napoleonic Code of 1804, with its withdrawal of divorce legislation and inheritance rights mandated by the early Revolution, expressly subordinated Frenchwomen to husbandly tutelage. Its enactment served to reinforce their loss of standing as public persons, and as writers. This worsening of Frenchwomen's conditions as such seems not to find much explicit echo among the authors treated in this volume, yet a muffled sound of their defeat may still be distinguished across the Channel as open militancy à la Wollstonecraft, Smith and Hays goes into retreat, to be replaced by works featuring more oblique treatments of women's condition, in genres less openly political.

Adriana Craciun notes that among British Jacobin novelists, it was, intriguingly enough, the women (like Charlotte Smith, Mary Robinson, Elizabeth Hamilton, and Helen Craik) who actually set their fictions in present-time France. As percipient observers of the French scene, among those authors treated in this volume, Helen Maria Williams emerges as particularly observant and prescient with respect to the weighing of French trends and persons, while Fanny Burney, with her intimate acquaintance with both nations, makes cogent comparisons between the two cultures. Naturally, not all of these women exhibit knowledge of the intricacies of politics or the rawness of daily life in Revolutionary France. Indeed, some reflect remoteness, as they abstract elements relevant to their own culture from among the welter of imperatives of contemporary French history and society. The authors dealt with in the section on "Revolution and Religion," Hannah More, Joanna Southcott, and Mariana Starke, as well as Amelia Opie from a very different political perspective, may be said to illustrate such a detachment. Their approaches are a far cry from Williams's history, so vital in its portrayals of beleaguered Frenchwomen like Mesdames Roland, de Genlis, Cécile Renaud et al., or Craik's introduction of Charlotte Corday into the imaginary script of her *Adelaide de Narbonne, with Memoirs of Charlotte de Cordet,* or Charlotte Smith's novels, in all of which we are invited to process the direct impact of historical circumstances. But on issues raised by the Revolution, as distinct from events or personalities, like that of education, or emigration, or the reorganization of the family and of selfhood, or of inheritance laws, or the relative merits of England and France as national or religious communities, or of the reorganization of power and wealth, this volume testifies to an extraordinary plethora of views. Perhaps above all else, the Revolution provided these women commentators with an irresistible tool for mounting a set of searing critiques of British society and its institutions.

It is probably the primacy of these closer to home issues for these authors that dictates their inability, by and large, to engage with the eruption into political space of outright militant proto-feminists of the Revolution like the authors of the *cahiers de doléance,* or Olympe de Gouges, or Théroigne de Méricourt, or the Club of Revolutionary Republican Women. The near-burial of these activist women's history as a minor footnote to a Greater History, à la Michelet, has been rectified in the twentieth century, following the lead of Albert Soboul and Léon Abensour, by the works of Marie Cerati, Paule-Marie Duhet, and Dominique Godineau, among others. Of course Mary Wollstonecraft's *Vindication* in some important respects enacts in speech principles the militants were attempting to enact in the revolutionary arena. Whereas these Frenchwomen's engagement with acts would impel them, temporarily, to travel beyond gender categories, the imperative to virtue powerfully imbues the Englishwomen's speech, even that of the most militant among them. A Marie-Jeanne Roland, an apparently seemly *mère / épouse* (or mother/wife, to use the Jacobins' term), who never assumed an active role as spokesperson in revolutionary affairs, and thus died more purely a "feminine" victim of the Terror's afflictions, appears to have been far more *simpatica* to the mainstream of British opinion than outrageously outspoken and subversive figures like Théroigne de Méricourt or Olympe de Gouges, or a murderous one like Charlotte Corday (despite the attempts of Craik and others to recuperate her as hero, whether royalist or republican). Maintaining the sense of a necessary distancing from the perilous shoals of gender problematics presented by the French revolt, even as these are in fact addressed in substance, the works treated here suggest, in each case, the invention of a writerly rationale: mostly these feature the launching of a personal fantasy fashioned mainly from local materials, to which revolution has lent a vital charge of energy, whether of hate, of love, or of aspiration.

National and religious conflict endlessly elicit deep-dyed gender
or ideological posturings. The English tendency to regard France as a
"feminized" nation goes back to Shakespeare's *Henry V,* at the least.
But the Revolutionary decade renews this vein, as Linda Colley has
pointed out. Jan Wellington's essay generalizes the prevailing English
rhetoric: "English character [is depicted] as reserved (but impassioned), serious, deep, artless, original, and independent, in contrast
with the French character which was seen as effusive, lighthearted,
shallow, changeable, artful, and slavish." These vagrant adjectives
make sometimes odd gender/national transpositions, some of which
Wellington's study ferrets out: e.g., how Wollstonecraft's bitter critique
of women's inadequacies assimilates them to the inferior French, and
how her acceptance of the trope of French frivolity and deficiency
underwent alteration in the course of her travels in Scandinavia, so
that she would emerge less categorical in her denunciations. The
English, particularly those who opposed the Revolution, persisted in
undergirding their patriotism with a view of themselves as sincere
and straightforward, as against the hypocritical, foppish, unreliable
men of that neighboring land, awash in the chaos of revolution and
civil war. Marianna Starke's *machiste* patriotism impels her to attack
the French Enlightenment: ignoring or ignorant of his courageous
defense of the brutally murdered Protestant Jean Calas, Voltaire the
cosmopolite, registers for her as merely vain and un-Christian, in
contrast to her presumably modest, open-hearted Protestant British
countrymen. While at first dazzled by Bonaparte's qualities as warrior
and approving of his resistance to popishness, Starke, in Jeanne
Moskal's quotation from Gary Kelly, would conclude, as of 1801, that
the "achievements of the feminized Revolution [were] now guaranteed by the manly hero Bonaparte," a view which, to say the least, did
not stand the test of time. Clearly, "manliness" remained a prize term,
fought for by every side. After all, the Revolutionaries themselves
(who in Starke's book had feminized themselves), in tarring their
aristocratic enemies as *femmelettes,* had laid claim to their republic
by calling up the principle of brotherliness: "Fraternité!"

   In illustration of a more purely political level of cross-national
commentary, Terence Hoagwood contrasts Elizabeth Inchbald's and
Joanna Baillie's scenarios of Revolution, both tactfully displaced
geographically to more exotic sites. Whereas the monarchist Baillie's
play *Constantine Paleologus* depicts the *peuple* as a worthless mob,
needing to be led, Jacobin sympathizer Inchbald's *The Massacre*
presents the people in the streets as ultimately impelled by magnani-
mous impulses. Fanny Burney, whose familiarity with the French

allowed her to weigh the mores of the two nations more even handedly, explores the French and English peoples novelistically to denounce the social practices of her own nation. Maria Jerinic reads Juliet's fate in Burney's *Wanderer* as an implicit critique of an English commonplace: Burke's attack on the Parisian crowd's treatment of Marie Antoinette popularized the view among English conservatives that the French lacked delicacy in their treatment of women. Burney's Juliet, however, ends up faring no better among England's sexual predators than she would in France. Judith Miller underscores Charlotte Smith's arraignment of the British legal system in her *Marchmont,* but she also sees Smith as striving to transcend the traditional national rivalry in both that novel and in *The Young Philosopher* as she seeks to link "England and France historically and geologically as antidote to the divisions that have plagued those two countries."

Invoking (unintentionally) the Hobson's choice tendered women by revolutionary change, Terence Hoagwood contrasts Joanna Baillie's "gender-image" as a "womanly removal from the world," as against Elizabeth Inchbald's project of "immediate immersion in the action here and now." Yet both of them, he argues, remain "prisoners of their supposed feeling-states, their artificially posed attitudes." This is perhaps to divide too arbitrarily what is pose, what feeling, in the human construct. All escape hatches from rigidly prescriptive roles involve the carrying of some baggage on the way out. Yet the Revolution could breed some stunning new selfhoods. Kari Lokke emphasizes one such: Charlotte Smith's allegiance to a "politics of transcendence," her attempt to salvage from out of the revolutionary miasma an emancipatory stance, undoubtedly undergirded both by some "attitudes" of womanly charity, along with a new-minted feminist demand for justice. Her emigrants are outsiderly pilgrims seeking a republic utopian beyond any then imagined. In parallel fashion, as Adriana Craciun shows us, Helen Craik's *Adelaide de Narbonne* invites Charlotte Corday into her novelistic revision of the gothic script to act as an offsetting active female pole to her gothically virtuous-but-oppressed Adelaide. Craciun, in fact, demonstrates how Craik's novel revises Burke in transforming Corday into a chivalrous rather than murderous figure, thus positing the possibility of women combining endowments of beauty and sensibility with rationality and the power to act. Miriam Wallace paints us a Mary Hays similarly grappling with the artificiality of the imposed antithesis between rationality and sensibility and their ostensible gendering, especially problematic for those radical women, like herself and Wollstonecraft, who craved a greater degree of political agency.

The works of these authors certainly set into motion, as Lokke and Craciun claim, a tension between their professions of writing only as "mere" private persons and "the false universalism of the bourgeois public sphere that excluded women." But for most of them, that meant laying claim to a larger universalism. We find Wollstonecraft scrambling the national and gender stereotypes, as Wellington displays in showing her moving "away from the monolithic conceptions of character that nationalist polemics demand and towards a future in which free, enlightened citizens transcend the limitations of gender and nationality and become citizens of the world." So too, we find Burney, in Jerinic's account, "destabiliz[ing] the notion that there is an essential Englishness which is fundamentally different from an essential Frenchness," as she chides both nations, each for thinking itself "rather a distinct race of beings, than as merely the emulous inhabitants of rival states." And Wake finds Opie bravely posing her "Ode to the Present Times "in *universal* terms," risking more, in disseminating blame for the gathering violence of the Terror, than many another poet of politics. We see the protagonist Marchmont in Miller's study whose "repeated sympathy with the fate of Louis is a reflection of [Charlotte Smith's] abiding philosophy of humanism that goes beyond class and nationality." Or Williams, declaring herself a "citizen of the world," in emulation of the "false universalists," thereby demanding consideration, though later rather than sooner, of inclusion of the likes of herself.

Of course, it may well be asked, were these women heard, and by whom? Lokke discusses Rita Felski's stand that women's marginality throws up a critique of society, palpable in all of the works discussed, that posits a "self-consciously oppositional identity." One can only agree that this position, though liminal, has repeatedly recurred in history. The writings of a number of the women of this study were important to one another: this is one of the myriad phenomena evoked by this volume which deserve further research. So palpably was this the case that we find evidence for it in Deborah Kennedy's glorious quotation from the letter by Edmund Burke warning off his friend Mrs. Crewe not to listen to such as Staël, Roland, Sillery, Williams, Wollstonecraft "&c&c&c&c&c and all that clan of desperate, Wicked, and mischievously ingenious Women who have brought, or are likely to bring Ruin and shame upon all those that listen to them. The sex has much influence." Demonstrably, there were women who did listen. And even more will listen now, thanks to the restorative research of subtle and able scholars like those represented here.

As Jerinic points out, a number of Englishwomen, in the climate of the Revolution's expanded concepts of civic life, felt themselves to be "living in a country which trumpeted its love of freedom and liberty," while denying them to their sex. But all is relative. We may recall that in Mozart's *Abduction from the Seraglio,* the Pasha's chieftain Osmin rebukes the fair English Blonde, to whom he's paying fruitless court and who snappily and smartly parries his every undesired advance: "Englishwomen are the freeest," he laments. Such was their reputation, despite France's rivalrous claim to be "Le Paradis des dames." In fact, as this collection displays, so they were. Their collective ruminations in poetry, travel accounts, polemics, history, and fiction, portray them in the age of Revolution grappling with the fate of nations and of faith, as well as their own rise, on a level surpassing that of women in other lands.

Contributors

Kevin Binfield, Associate Professor at Murray State University, Kentucky, has researched and published widely on the Luddites, Joanna Southcott, and Romanticism and politics in *Romanticism, Radicalism, and the Press,* edited by Stephen Behrendt (1997), the *Keats-Shelley Journal* (1997), *Approaches to Teaching Women Poets of the British Romantic Period,* edited by Behrendt and Harriet Kramer Linkin (1997), and *Mapping Male Sexuality* (2000). His book, *The Writings of the Luddites,* is forthcoming from The Johns Hopkins University Press. Professor Binfield is also editing a collection of the works of Joanna Southcott and is writing a book on the aesthetics of working-class writing during the Romantic period.

Adriana Craciun, Prew-Smith Byron Lecturer in English Studies at the University of Nottingham, has recently completed a book manuscript, *The Fatal Women of Romanticism.* She has published essays on Mary Wollstonecraft, Mary Robinson, Mary Lamb, and Charlotte Dacre. She has also edited Charlotte Dacre's *Zofloya; or, The Moor* [1806] (Broadview, 1997), and Mary Robinson's *A Letter to the Women of England on the Injustice of Mental Subordination: A Romantic Circles Edition* (1998). She is currently at work on a new Routledge edition of Wollstonecraft's *A Vindication of the Rights of Woman,* and a monograph on British women writers and the French Revolution.

Ann Frank Wake is Associate Professor of English at Elmhurst College, Illinois, specializing in nineteenth-century British literature, literary theory, and, more recently, race, class and gender studies in the U.S. She has published articles on Mary Shelley and on multiculturalism in the classroom, as well as poetry and feminist memoir.

Madelyn Gutwirth is Professor of French at West Chester University, and Research Associate at the University of Pennsylvania's Alice Paul Center for the Study of Women. In addition to numerous articles on French literature and culture, Professor Gutwirth is the author of *The Twilight of the Goddesses: Women and Representation in the French Revolutionary Era* (Rutgers, 1992), and *Madame de Staël, Novelist: The Emergence of the Artist as Woman* (Illinois, 1978).

Terence Allan Hoagwood, Professor of English at Texas A&M University, has published numerous books on Romantic literature, including *Politics, Philosophy, and the Production of Romantic Texts* (1996), *Prophecy and the Philosophy of Mind: The Traditions of Blake & Shelley* (1985), *Skepticism and Ideology: Shelley's Political Prose* (1988), *Byron's Dialectic: Skepticism & the Critique of Culture* (1993), and *A.E. Housman Revisited* (1995). Professor Hoagwood has also edited scholarly editions of Charlotte Smith's *"Beachy Head" and Other Poems* (1993), Mary Robinson's *Sappho and Phaon* (1995), Elizabeth Smith's *The Brethren: A Poem in Four Books* (1991), Violet Fane's verse novel *Denzil Place* (1996), Mary Hays's *The Victim of Prejudice* (1990), and, with Kathryn Ledbetter, *The Keepsake for 1829 and L.E.L.'s "Verses": A Romantic Circles Edition.*

Maria Jerinic is Assistant Professor of English at the New Mexico Highlands University. She also serves as an Assistant Editor for *Topics for Victorian Literature and Culture.* Her essay, "How We Lost the Empire: Retelling the Stories of the Rani of Jhansi and Queen Victoria," appears in the 1997 collection *Remaking Queen Victoria* (Cambridge University Press), edited by Margaret Homans and Adrienne Munich.

Angela Keane is Lecturer in English, University of Sheffield, and has published essays on Burke and Wollstonecraft. Her monograph, *Women Writers and the English Nation in the 1790s: Romantic Belongings,* is forthcoming from Cambridge, and her edited collection of essays, *Body Matters: Feminism, Textuality, Corporeality*, co-edited with Avril Horner, is published by Manchester University Press.

Deborah Kennedy is currently completing a book entitled *Helen Maria Williams and the Age of Revolution.* She has published numerous essays on Helen Maria Williams and the French Revolution. Among her other publications are essays on Felicia Hemans, Charlotte Smith, and William Wordsworth, including "Hemans, Wordsworth, and the 'Literary Lady,'" in *Victorian Poetry* (1997). She teaches at Saint Mary's University in Halifax, Nova Scotia.

Kari Lokke is Professor of English and Comparative Literature at the University of California, Davis. Her book *Gérard de Nerval: The Poet as Social Visionary* examines the sociopolitical significance of Nerval's mystical conceptions of selfhood, gender, and history. Professor Lokke is the author of articles on the aesthetics of the sublime and the grotesque, and on women poets of the Romantic era. She is currently writing a book on gender and transcendence in the novels of Germaine de Staël, Mary Shelley, Bettine von Arnim, and George Sand, entitled *Romantic Abandon.*

Judith Davis Miller is an Associate Professor of English at Sacred Heart University in Fairfield, Connecticut who has published articles on William Wordsworth and Emily Dickinson. Most recently she has been working on a full-length study of Charlotte Smith, titled *The Bow of Ulysses: Art and Identity in the Writings of Charlotte Smith.*

Jeanne Moskal is Professor of English at the University of North Carolina at Chapel Hill. She is the editor of Mary Shelley's travel books, Volume 8 in *The Novels and Selected Works of Mary Shelley* (1996), and the author of *Blake, Ethics, and Forgiveness* (1994). She is currently researching a book on British women travel writers and the politics of the Napoleonic Wars, and is completing an edition of Mary Wollstonecraft's *Letters from Norway* for Broadview Press.

Miriam L. Wallace is Assistant Professor of British and American literature at New College of the University of South Florida. She has published essays on the novels of Virginia Woolf, Lawrence Sterne, and Sir Walter Scott. She is currently working on a manuscript on constructions of gender and early feminism in the English Jacobin novelists of late eighteenth-century England.

Jan Wellington is Assistant Professor of English at the University of South Alabama in Mobile. Her article on poet and critic Elizabeth Moody appears in *An Encyclopedia of British Women Writers* (2nd edition, Rutgers UP, 1999). She has recently completed an edition of Moody's collected works.

Index

Abbas (Godwin), 302

Abensour, Léon, 370

Account of Trials on Bills of Exchange (Southcott), 144, 149, 151

Act of Union (1707), 73

Address to the Privileged Orders (Barlow), 5

Adelaide de Narbonne (Craik), 20, 194–201, 212–215, 223*n2*, 370; Corday as Romantic heroine in, 22; critique of marriage, 197, 212–215; patriarchy and, 197, 198; royalist view in, 198

Aesthetic: definition of sympathy, 261; evolution of, 261; of sensibility, 270; of shared suffering, 261, 262, 279; theory, 263; visual, 263

Agency: female, 21, 261–285; individual, 201; "landscaping," 261–285; misappropriated, 282; moral, 262; political, 202, 372; public, 20; violent, 20, 194, 201, 202, 212

Alexander, Meena, 85, 270

Amar, André, 368

Analytical Review, 324, 330, 351

An Estimate of the Religion of the Fashionable World (More), 118

Andrews, John, 174

Anti-Jacobin Review, 213, 214, 324, 355

Appeal to the Men of Great Britain in Behalf of Women (Hays), 70–71

Aristotle, 302, 304

Arnott, Samuel, 219

Ashfield, Andrew, 270

Astell, Mary, 70

Aulard, Alphonse, 144

Austen, Jane, 11, 76, 84*n46*, 171, 265

Bage, Robert, 185, 204

Baillie, Joanna, 20, 371, 372; backward resituation by, 302; burial of references to the real, 305; *Constantine Paleologus* (Baillie), 295, 302–312; on domesticity, 304; gender domination and, 306; plays on the passions, 23; revolutionary representation by, 293–312; social goals of, 307–308; symbolic substitution by, 303

Bainbridge, Simon, 12, 161, 162

The Banished Man (Smith), 4, 347–351

Barbaroux, Charles, 203

Barbauld, Anna Letitia, 266, 267, 273, 274, 325; "The Mouse's Petition," 279

Barlow, Joel, 4, 5, 104*n24*

Barlow, Ruth, 41

Barry, James, 263

Baudrillard, Jean, 302

Beachy Head (Smith), 4, 98, 105*n25*, 359

Beauvoir, Simone de, 85, 254

Bicheno, James, 138, 140, 144, 151

Binfield, Kevin, 11, 22, 135–154, 366

Blake, William, 9, 263, 264

Blakemore, Steven, 324

Blood, George, 40

Blount, Martha, 45
Boaden, James, 303
Bonaparte, Joseph, 165
Boucicault, Dion, 297
Bowie, Andrew, 295
Bowstead, Diana, 342
Brandes, Helga, 23
Bray, Matthew, 359
"The Bride of the Greek Isle"
    (Hemans), 309
Brief Reflections (Burney), 74
Brightman, Thomas, 153
Brightwell, Cecilia Lucy, 265, 266,
    267, 272, 286n5
Britain: Act of Union (1707), 73;
    anti-Catholic feeling in, 73, 169;
    character and, 35–57; cultural
    war with France, 180; disenfran-
    chisement of women, 195–196;
    dismissal of women's opinions in,
    274; education in, 116; "essential
    Englishness" in, 63, 64; gendered
    politics in, 162; as "masculine,"
    34, 35–38; millenarian thought
    in, 136; national identity in,
    35–38, 58n4, 168–172; national-
    ism in, 70, 162; national superior-
    ity of, 64; nation–building, 34, 35;
    patriarchy in, 16, 67; political
    debates on Revolution, 4; political
    reform and, 92; Protestantism in,
    73, 172–176; public policy in, 280;
    reactions to French Revolution,
    69, 137, 139, 320; thoughts of
    France as enemy, 58n4; views on
    Napoleon, 161
British Club, 3, 4, 5, 7, 207,
    227n37
British Convention (1793), 204
British Critic, 322, 323, 324
Brothers, Richard, 140, 141, 142,
    144, 150, 153, 154n9, 156n22,
    156n24, 156n28
Bruce, Reverend Stanhope, 138
Bruhm, Steven, 261, 275–276, 281,
    289n27

Brydges, Sir Egerton, 339, 342
Burke, Edmund, 9, 27n15, 85, 91,
    95, 97, 270, 271; advocacy of
    Catholic emancipation, 117;
    conservatism of, 186, 327; criti-
    cisms of, 117; French émigré
    clergy and, 115; on French
    Revolution, 81n18; on French-
    women, 38, 58n7; on Marie
    Antoinette, 199; on Napoleon,
    184; *A Philosophical Enquiry into
    the Sublime and the Beautiful*,
    272; political discourse of, 111,
    112; political views, 272; *Reflec-
    tions on the Revolution in France*,
    19, 111, 114, 174, 271, 272, 308,
    309; views on Britain, 68
Burney, Fanny, 82n29, 320, 369,
    371–372, 373; *Brief Reflections*,
    74; on British liberty, 14; chal-
    lenge to English superiority, 65;
    on companionate marriage, 14,
    64, 65, 75, 76, 77, 78; criticism of,
    66, 69; critiques of British society,
    66; ecumenical views, 74; nation-
    alism and, 13, 14, 22; political
    neutrality, 63; on Protestantism,
    14; reader expectations of, 79n2;
    reconciliation message of, 12;
    refusal to condemn France, 63,
    65; on religion, 73; response to
    Revolution, 12; Romanticism and,
    15; transnational themes, 66; *The
    Wanderer*, 12, 14, 17, 20, 63–78,
    66, 67, 79n3, 81n27, 84n50, 321
Burns, Robert, 218, 229n56
Burroughs, Catherine, 299, 304, 306
Butler, Marilyn, 242, 338
Byron, Lord George, 86

Carpenter, Elias, 138
Castle, Terry, 340
Castle of Otranto (Walpole), 195, 197
Catholicism, 65, 72, 75, 82n30,
    82n37, 144, 168, 169
Celestina (Smith), 340, 341

The Cenci (Shelley), 209

Censorship, 110, 311, 314*n25*;
metaphor and, 303

Cerati, Marie, 370

Chandler, David, 166

Character: absolute existence of, 54;
acquired, 53; British, 34, 35, 42;
climate and, 52–53, 60*n24*; construction of, 44, 56; control of, 33;
defining, 33; determination of, 52,
54; fixed conceptions of, 19; fluid
nature of, 56; identity and, 33;
institutional, 53; national, 34, 35,
52, 54, 55, 58*n3*; need for stimuli
for formation, 46; political struggle
for, 33, 34; potential for change in,
43–44; privite nature of, 33; religion and, 53; sexualization of, 47;
as sociohistorical construct, 35,
54, 56; stereotypes of, 19; strength
of, 44; subjectivity and, 33; tyranny
and, 43; unity of humanity and,
56; Wollstonecraft's views, 33–57;
of women, 45, 47, 51, 59*n16*

Charles IX (Chenier), 305, 306

Charrière, Isabelle de, 366

The Cheap Repository (More), 127

Chenier, Marie-Joseph, 305, 306

Cisalpine Republic, 164, 165, 173

Cispadane Republic, 164

Clapham Sect, 118, 126

Class: acknowledgement of, 105*n28*;
ambition, 168; consciousness,
136; differences, 325; dynamics,
168; emergent systems, 235;
equality, 307; gender and, 7, 10;
laboring, 11; markers, 174;
middle, 172, 173, 176, 180, 233;
politics of, 173; prejudices of, 237;
status, 172; struggle, 275; working, 105*n28*, 109, 136, 193, 202

Cobbett, William, 115

Coleridge, Samuel Taylor, 9, 283,
361*n13*; abandonment of French
Revolution, 27*n15*; on Napoleon,
161; *Osorio*, 302

Colley, Linda, 11, 16, 34, 64, 69, 70,
73, 80*n10*, 81*n21*, 81*n24*, 82*n36*,
135, 136, 154, 176, 368, 371

Colman, George, 303

*Communication on the Temporal
and Spiritual Sword* (Southcott),
146, 148, 149

Compassion, 96, 97, 121

Conger, Syndy, 251

Constantine Paleologus (Baillie),
295, 302–312, 371

"The Contrast" (Rowlandson), 36,
37*fig*, 38, 327

Conventicle Act (1664), 130

Corday, Charlotte, 20, 58*n8*, 193,
370, 372; as "angel of the assassination," 202; as divine avenger,
211; as *femme fatale*, 209–212; as
goddess of death, 210; as heroine,
194, 1g5, 19g, 211, 212; individual agency of, 201, 202, 203;
Jacobin representations of,
200–205; "masculine" crime of,
202; mixture of masculine/femi-
nine qualities, 212–213, 217; as
political subject, 201; republican
views of, 203, 208, 214, 215; as
Romantic heroine, 22; sentimental portraits of, 201–205; trial of,
208, 226*n23*; as voluntary victim,
228*n43*; Williams on, 205–209

Cottrell, Stella, 65, 80*n10*

Cox, Jeffrey, 203, 305

Craciun, Adriana, 3–23, 193–223,
365, 369, 372, 373

Craft–Fairchild, Catherine, 340,
361*n14*

Craik, Helen, 9; *Adelaide de
Narbonne*, 20, 22, 194–201,
212–215, 223*n2*, 370; concern
with justice, 217; disclaimer on
violence, 215–218; feminist views,
195; *Julia de St. Pierre*, 194, 195,
217, 220, 222, 223n2, 224*n4*,
230*n58*; political views, 195;
relations with father, 218–223;

Craik, Helen (*cont.*)
  representations of Charlotte
  Corday, 193–223; *Stella of the
  North*, 194, 218, 220, 222,
  229*n54*; use of historical novel,
  19, 20; views of French
  Revolution, 222–223
Critical Review, 329, 330
Croker, John Wilson, 66, 69, 301
Crossley, Ceri, 280
Cultural: consciousness, 339; dislo-
  cation, 87; hegemony, 235; inter-
  vention, 20; roles, 21; values, 87
Culture: commodity, 23, 295; of
  modesty, 343; national, 60*n27*; of
  sensibility, 319
Curran, Stuart, 9, 85, 86, 209, 301
Cutting, Rose Marie, 63, 80*n9*

Davidoff, Leonora, 16
Deane, Seamus, 28*n20*
Declaration of the Rights of Man,
  168
"A Defence of Poetry" (Shelley), 307
Desire, manufactured, 295
Desmond (Smith), 4, 5, 16–17, 19,
  24*n5*, 91, 95, 104*n24*, 322, 342,
  343, 351; radical stance of, 96
Discourse: advertising, 294; of affec-
  tive states, 295; artificial, 295;
  moral, 154*n5*; nationalist, 82*n34*;
  political, 105*n28*, 120, 163, 318;
  religious, 21; revolutionary, 245,
  266; of sensibility, 323; women's,
  163
"Discourse on the Love of Our
  Country" (Price), 318
Dissenters, 21, 153, 184, 264, 265,
  268, 269, 317, 368
Doody, Margaret, 64, 66, 70, 77,
  79*n3*, 80*n8*, 80*n11*, 81*n27*, 82*n29*,
  194, 365
Dorset, Catherine, 24*n5*
Doulcet, Gustave, 207
Du Broca, Louis, 203, 228*n43*
Duhet, Paule-Marie, 370

Dundas, Robert, 204–205
Dupont, Jacob, 116

Eberle, Roxanne, 262, 287*n12*
Eccles, John, 250
Elegiac Sonnets (Smith), 4, 86, 87,
  88, 355
Eley, Geoff, 16
Elliott, Pat, 342, 362*n19*
Ellis, Kate, 82*n30*, 82*n31*
Ellison, Julie, 270
The Emigrants (Smith), 4, 14, 21,
  92–99, 104*n24*, 281; emphasis on
  justice in, 96; feminine conscious-
  ness in, 93; humanitarianism in,
  5; moon as emblem of female
  transcendence in, 14, 18, 96;
  republicanism in, 5; as response
  to plight of French émigrés, 92;
  strategy of open concealment in,
  18; universalism in, 18
Emmeline (Smith), 340
Empathy, 118
Emsley, Clive, 267
English Review, 319, 329
"Epistle to a Lady" (Pope), 45, 46
*Essay on the Principles of Human
  Action* (Hazlitt), 307
Essentialism, 252, 254; dangers of,
  251; gendered, 250
Ethelinde (Smith), 340
Ethic of care, 96, 97, 136, 215, 301
Ethic of justice, 96, 97, 215
European Magazine, 328, 342
European Review, 350
Eustace, John Chetwode, 178,
  189*n19*
Evans, Reverend John, 146, 147,
  157*n42*
The Excursion (Wordsworth), 14
Experience: authenticating, 272;
  direct, 265, 266; in formation of
  reason, 237; imagined, 266, 298;
  inner, 300; morality and, 266;
  narrative and, 244; personal, 245;
  practical, 265; of Revolution, 261;

shared, 252; as site for knowledge, 254; universalization of, 280
Eyre, Edmund John, 204; *The Maid of Normandy and Death of the Queen of France*, 203

"A Familiar Epistle to a Friend" (Grant), 327
A Farewell to England for Two Years (Williams), 321
Fascism, 101
Favret, Mary, 18
Felski, Rita, 86, 87, 373
Feminism: anti-Jacobin, 162; liberal, 254; relation of theory to experience, 234; utopian, 101; of Wollstonecraft, 13
Fleming, Robert, 140
Fletcher, Loraine, 338
Forsyth, Joseph, 178, 189*n19*
Fox, Charles, 266, 267
France: abolition of monarchy, 4; atheism in, 12; caricatures of, 36, 37, 38, 39; Catholicism in, 65, 72, 75, 169; character of, 35–57; Constituent Assembly in, 164, 168; Convention, 5, 207; cultural war with Britain, 180; disbanding of women's clubs in, 193–194, 333*n31*; education in, 116; as "effeminate," 34, 35–38, 40, 45, 58*n5*, 173, 371; as enemy of Britain, 58*n4*; execution of king, 9; lack of character in, 45; millenarian thought in, 136; moral issues, 42; national character of, 35–38, 58*n3*; political reform and, 92; presentation of women in, 70; religious tolerance in, 144, 367; renovation of political system in, 58*n3*; seen as inferior, 64, 66; stereotypes of, 64–65; stoicism of women in, 273; threat to Britain, 28*n20*, 35; treatment of Catholic clergy, 12, 74, 75; tyranny of, 65; war against, 11

Francis (Emperor of Austria), 165
Frankenstein (Shelley), 213
Fraser, Nancy, 16, 87, 102*n8*
French Revolution: British response to, 9, 69; as crusade against Christianity, 28*n20*; Cult of Reason in, 169; danger for women, 69; destructive passions released by, 47; development of, 317; dramatic representation of, 302; economic inequality and, 93; expansion of women in public sphere, 139; Gothic views of, 209; ideological debates on, 16; interpretations of, 263; nationalism and, 13; negative images of, 327; political reality of, 14; relevance for current political struggles, 22; Scandinavian support for, 55; significance of gender in, 15; social hierarchy and, 93; support for, 3, 24*n5*; women's armed militancy in, 24*n3*; women's interest in, 4, 13, 317
French Revolution (Wollstonecraft), 34, 40, 44, 46, 47, 50
Frend, William, 19, 234, 239, 245, 248
Friends of the Rights of Man associated at Paris. *See* British Club
Fromm, Erich, 296
Furet, François, 195, 224n6
Fuseli, Henry, 40, 263

Garrett, Clarke, 136
Gay, John, 180
Gender: class and, 7, 10; codes, 265; conservatism, 368; construction, 36; critiques of, 13; crossing, 319; dichotomies, 270; dispensation, 368; equality, 307; essentialism, 309; in French Revolutionary culture, 15; hierarchy, 368; marketing and, 300; nationalism and, 7, 10; plays, 293–312; politics, 12, 173, 195, 306, 368;

Gender (*cont.*)
  relations, 20; roles, 35, 135, 136, 163, 262; stereotypes, 38, 88, 300, 301, 373; transcending limitations of, 55
Genre: autobiography, 239; courtship novel, 340, 343; expectations, 343; historical novel, 19, 20; letters, 18, 20, 240, 244; memoirs, 19; as "mobile category," 20; periodicals, 20; plays, 20; poetry, 21, 27*n15*, 261–285; sentimental novels, 238; travel journals, 18, 19, 20, 161–187
Gentleman's Magazine, 319
George III (King of England), 344, 351
Gerbert, George, 293
Gilligan, Carol, 96, 215
Gillray, James, 38, 39, 203, 325
Gindman, David, 263
Glorious Revolution (1688), 175
Godineau, Dominique, 370
Godwin, William, 6, 162, 194–195, 204, 236, 239, 240, 241, 242, 243, 245, 247, 250, 263, 337; *Abbas* 302; influence on Smith, 6, 338, 356, 357, 359, 360*n8*; as mentor to Hays, 19; "On the Cultivation of Truth," 337; radicalism of, 186; relations with Wollstonecraft, 52, 60*n23*; views on French Revolution, 267; on Voltaire, 360*n2*
Goldsmith, Lewis, 322
Goodman, Dena, 368
Gouges, Olympe de, 193–194, 325, 370
Grandchamp, Sophie, 328
Grand Tour: access to by women, 178; "Frenchification" and, 177; as male tradition, 18, 177; redefining, 18; threats to, 180, 181
Grant, Anne, 327
Greenfield, Liah, 73
Günderrode, Karoline von, 23

Gutwirth, Madelyn, 15, 197, 218, 365–374

Habermas, Jürgen, 15, 16, 21, 97
Haefner, Joel, 270
Halhed, Nathaniel, 150
Hall, John, 293
Hamilton, Elizabeth, 154*n5*, 369; conservative beliefs of, 7
Handy, Bruce, 300
Haraway, Donna, 254
Harding, Sandra, 299
Hardwicke Act (1753), 82*n42*
Hardy, Thomas, 287*n13*, 344
Harrison, J.F.C., 136
Hawkins, Laetitia Matilda, 9, 321, 323; conservative beliefs of, 7, 8; *Letters on the Female Mind*, 7; political responses of, 8
Hayley, William, 344
Hays, Mary, 132*n3*, 162, 203, 233–255, 372; *Appeal to the Men of Great Britain in Behalf of Women*, 70–71; criticisms of, 234; on education for women, 76; experience and theory in writings, 235; female philosopher of, 233–255; *The Memoirs of Emma Courtney*, 18–19, 22, 234, 236, 239, 245, 247, 248, 361*n14*; Romanticism and, 15; use of letters by, 18
Hazlitt, William, 33, 66, 69, 161, 187, 307
Hemans, Felicia, 8, 300, 301, 306, 309
Hilbish, Florence, 338, 339, 341, 362*n19*
Hoagwood, Terence, 13, 23, 293–312, 371, 372
Hobhouse, John Cam, 161, 187
Hogsett, Charlotte, 328
Holcroft, Thomas, 234, 239–240, 263, 265, 287*n13*
Homans, Margaret, 9
Hopkins, Bishop Ezekial, 147

Hopkins, James, 146, 147
Hopkins, Mary Alden, 126
Hovey, Jaimie, 299, 300
Hubert de Sevrac (Robinson), 19
Hume, David, 53, 214
Hunt, Lynn, 15, 218
Hunter, William, 36, 58n6

Identity: British, 64, 65; character
    and, 33; economic underpinnings
    of, 9; female, 9; formation, 345,
    359; French, 65; gendered, 233;
    individual, 45, 345; issues of, 340;
    national, 34, 58n4, 98, 166,
    168–172, 299; oppositional, 87;
    public, 319; religious, 73; self,
    319; sexual, 34; traits, 301
Imagination: activities of, 288n21;
    appropriation of, 271; character
    of, 129; gender meanings of,
    288n21; "glutted," 111; popular,
    110, 111; suffering and, 285;
    sympathetic, 261; works of,
    122
Imlay, Gilbert, 19, 49, 50, 55–56,
    60n21, 60n23
Inchbald, Elizabeth, 185, 371, 372;
    The Massacre (Inchbald), 295,
    302–312, 314n27; references to
    the real of, 305; revolutionary
    representation by, 293–312
"Introductory Discourse" (Baillie),
    23, 307–308
Italy, 163–166; feminization of, 173,
    178; Grand Tour and, 181, 182;
    Napoleon in, 162–166
"I Wandered Lonely as a Cloud"
    (Wordsworth), 277

Jacobinism, 235, 236, 240, 255n1
Jeffrey, Francis, 301
Jerinic, Maria, 12, 14, 17, 63–78,
    372, 373, 374
Jerningham, Edward, 320
Johnson, Claudia, 64, 80n15, 81n21,
    84n50, 223, 324

Johnson, Joseph, 41, 47, 52, 54
Jones, Chris, 206, 251, 264, 368
Jones, Vivien, 228n42, 238
Jones, William, 137, 138
Julia de St. Pierre (Craik), 194, 195,
    217, 220, 222, 223n2, 224n4,
    230n58
Justice: abstract, 216; allegories of,
    217; dispensing of, 216; ethic of,
    96, 97, 215; immutable, 216, 221;
    moral, 311; political, 6; practical,
    216; social, 92, 94, 137, 237, 347;
    symbols of, 218
Kant, Immanuel, 85
Kauffman, Angelica, 317
Keane, Angela, 11, 17, 21, 109–132,
    366
Kelly, Gary, 13, 154n5, 245, 338,
    360n8, 371
Kennedy, Deborah, 11, 18, 262, 273,
    289n26, 317–330
Kenrick, Samuel, 184
King, John, 151
Kirk, Russell, 272
Kluge, Alexander, 16
Knowledge: acquisition of, 361n14;
    construction of, 359; emotional,
    248; experience as site for, 254;
    feeling and, 237, 253; limitations
    of, 359; monopoly on by men, 248;
    object of, 295; patriarchal sup-
    pression of, 361n14; privileged,
    248; relativity of, 359; repression
    of, 359; self–imposed limitations
    on, 348; sexual character of, 250;
    situated, 250
Kolker, Robert Phillip, 308
Kucich, Greg, 307, 319

Lacombe, Clare, 193
Lacoue-Labarthe, Philippe, 304, 305,
    311, 312
Lagarde, Chauveau, 207
Lamont, William, 136, 153
Landes, Joan, 15, 16, 18, 172, 173,
    197, 214

Landscape, 21, 110, 262, 263; defilement of, 286*n3*; imaginary features in, 272; of pain, 281; "real," 267; reflection of political responses in, 264

Language: coded, 280, 284; of domination, 90; of literary artifacts, 300; nationalist, 135; religious, 185; of sensibility, 243, 246; of struggle, 90

Larpent, John, 203, 204

Lawrence, Karen, 64, 82*n33*

Lecour, Simone, 293

"Letter Introductory" (Wollstonecraft), 42, 47, 51, 53, 54

Letters, 20; hybridization of, 19; ideological struggle and, 18; as means of self-expression, 18, 240; public/private spheres in, 19

Letters Containing a Sketch of the Politics of France (Williams), 205–209, 206

Letters from France (Williams), 317, 322, 328–330

Letters from Italy (Starke), 11–12, 161–187; response to Napoleonic invasion in, 18

Letters on the Female Mind (Hawkins), 7, 321

Letters Written during a Short Residence (Wollstonecraft), 19, 34, 49, 51, 53, 60n21

Levinson, Marjorie, 87

Licher, Lucia Maria, 23

Ligurain Republic, 165

"Lines on the Place de la Concorde at Paris" (Opie), 262, 268

Liu, Alan, 57, 60*n27*, 87

Lloyd, Charles, 252

Locke, John, 125

Lokke, Kari, 3–23, 85–101, 365, 372, 373

London Corresponding Society, 137, 138, 344, 348, 351, 355

London Society for Constitutional Information, 5

The Long-wished-for Revolution (Southcott), 145, 150

Lukács, Georg, 20

Lux, Adam, 210–211, 212, 227*n35*, 228*n43*

Lyrical Ballads (Wordsworth), 296

Macaulay, Catharine, 317

MacCunn, F.J., 161

Macfarlane, Alan, 75, 82*n42*

McGann, Jerome, 87, 285, 289*n29*, 309

Macherey, Pierre, 305

The Maid of Normandy and Death of the Queen of France (Eyre), 203

The Man of Sin (Jones), 137

Marat, Jean-Paul, 20, 58*n8*, 97, 195, 201, 202, 203, 204, 208, 209, 210, 211, 218

Marcet, Jane, 120

Marchmont (Smith), 351–355

Maria, or the Wrongs of Woman (Wollstonecraft), 213

Marie Antoinette, 97, 194, 199, 200, 202, 372

Marriage: companionate, 14, 64, 65, 75, 76, 77; critiques of, 197, 212–215; French, 77; for joining man's family, 77; prison of, 237; seen as sacrifice, 82*n42*

Martin, Biddy, 86

Martineau, Harriet, 120

Marx, Karl, 300

The Massacre (Inchbald), 295, 302–312, 314*n27*, 371

Mayer, Lewis, 145

Mellor, Anne, 9, 85, 96, 136, 215, 300, 301

Melzer, Sara, 15

The Memoirs of Emma Courtney (Hays), 18–19, 234, 236, 239, 245, 247, 248, 361*n14*; revolutionary subjectivity in, 22

Méricourt, Théroigne de, 24*n3*, 323, 370

Merry, Robert, 3

Metaphor: censorship and, 303; exile
for women's dispossession, 79*n3*;
reign of women/corruption of
society, 173; sensibility as, 251; of
slavery, 100; of sublimity, 87; of
transcendence, 87; true, 122
Metternich, Clemens, 164
Mies, Maria, 23
Millenarianism, 22, 135, 136
Miller, Judith, 6, 9, 17, 19, 337–360,
372
Milton, John, 91, 92
Minerva Press, 194, 215, 220, 223*n2*
Mitford, Mary Russell, 303
*Monody on the Death of the Late
Queen of France* (Robinson), 200
Montagu, Elizabeth, 130
Monthly Review, 342
Moon: depression and, 88, 275; as
image of mind of the poet, 90;
imperiousness of, 91; as spiritual
ruler, 91; as symbol of transcendence, 14, 88, 96, 99
Moral: action, 237; agency, 262;
causes, 53; conduct, 265, 266;
conservatism, 308; development,
42, 46; dilemmas, 282; discourse,
154*n5*; failures, 283; imperatives,
282; justice, 311; obligation, 275;
order, 216; reprehension, 274;
sentiment, 46; space, 283;
welfare, 115
More, Hannah, 21, 320, 366, 369;
abolishment of slavery and, 109;
*An Estimate of the Religion of the
Fashionable World*, 118; antipathy to autonomy for women, 130;
ballads by, 128; "Blagdon persecution" and, 125; call for national
Christian pedagogy, 119–121; *The
Cheap Repository*, 127; Clapham
Sect and, 118, 126; concept of
moral commercial society, 121;
conservative beliefs of, 7, 321;
control of press and, 122, 123;
corruption and, 115, 125, 129;

counterrevolutionary perspectives of, 11, 17, 109–132; criticisms of, 132; on democracy, 109;
disciplinary regime of, 121–125;
education and, 109, 116, 117,
123–125; establishment of
women's clubs by, 130; evangelicalism of, 21, 126–129; French
émigré clergy and, 115, 116, 118,
119; home economics and,
119–121; metaphysical faith and,
21, 113; nationalism and, 13; as
Pope Joan, 22, 131; popular imagination and, 110, 111; popular
media and, 112; practical piety of,
113–119; regulation of Britain's
sympathetic economy and,
121–125; relations with Walpole,
112, 114–115, 129; religious views
of, 13, 109, 113, 117, 126–129;
*Remarks on the Speech of M.
Dupont*, 115, 117; response to
Revolution, 12; Romanticism
and, 15; *Strictures on Female
Education*, 43, 111, 119, 122, 123,
162, 321; Sunday School movement and, 22, 129–132;
*Thoughts on the Manners of the
Great*, 118; utilitarianism of,
125; view of virtuous femininity,
11; on Wollstonecraft, 113,
123–124
Moskal, Jeanne, 11, 12, 13, 18, 136,
161–187, 371
"The Mouse's Petition" (Barbauld),
279
Murray, John, 18, 162

Nancy, Jean-Luc, 304, 305, 311
Napoleon: anti-Catholic support for,
12; as art collector, 176; as
"Beast," 145, 146, 149, 151;
British views on, 161; Concordat
with Papacy, 169i defeat of, 66; in
Egypt, 166; "free–thinking" of,
184–185; idolization of, 266;

Napoleon (*cont.*)
in Italy, 162, 163–166; as
Protestant hero, 172–176; as
"Saviour," 161
Napoleonic Code, 369
Nash, Michael, 117
National Convention, 3, 4, 5, 23*n1*,
116
Nationalism, 9, 12, 94; British, 7, 13,
70, 162; conservative visions of,
13; defining, 60*n27*, 60*n28*; freedom from, 100; gender and, 7, 10,
36; as imperfection, 58*n6*; overcoming, 96; politics of, 12; public
sphere participation and, 135;
rhetoric of, 35; transcendence
and, 96; virtue and, 58*n6*;
women's views on, 11, 13
The Natural Daughter (Robinson),
19, 20
Nature: appreciation of, 82*n31*; as
feminine, 90; power of, 90, 278;
wandering and, 71–72; worship
of, 116
"The Negro Boy's Lament" (Opie),
265
Negt, Oskar, 16
Neilson, George, 223*n2*, 229*n56*,
230*n58*
Neo-realism, 296
New Annual Register, 323
Newman, Gerald, 174
Nussbaum, Felicity, 75

Oakleaf, David, 33
"Ode on the Present Times" (Opie),
264, 278–281
"Ode to Borrowdale in Cumberland"
(Opie), 263, 264, 276, 277, 278
"Of Abstract and General Truth"
(Godwin), 337
The Old Manor House (Smith),
344–347
Oliver, W.H., 137
"On the Cultivation of Truth"
(Godwin), 337

"On the Expected General Rising of
the French Nation" (Barbauld),
274
"On the Sublime" (Schiller), 89
Opie, Amelia, 9, 60*n21*, 261–285,
369, 373; antislavery stance, 265;
covert expression of politics,
263–264, 274; indirect dissent by,
270; interest in visual aesthetics,
263; "Lines on the Place de la
Concorde at Paris," 262, 268;
"The Negro Boy's Lament," 265;
"Ode on the Present Times," 264,
278–281; "Ode to Borrowdale in
Cumberland," 263, 264, 276, 277,
278; in Paris, 267, 288*n17*;
political views of, 264–269; pro-
revolutionary views, 268; radicalism of, 262; Romanticism and, 15,
262; "Stanzas Written Under
Aeolus's Harp," 264, 284, 285; "To
Twilight," 274, 275, 276, 277; use
of illusion, 273; use of landscape,
21, 262, 263, 264, 267, 272–285;
use of memory, 286*n7*; use of
weather by, 274, 276, 283
Orr, Linda, 328
Osorio (Coleridge), 302
Oswald, John, 3
"Outsiders' Society," 100

Pacifism, 101, 136
Pain: emotional, 277; inability to
share, 21–22, 269, 270, 276; individual, 276; landscapes of, 281;
ontology of, 21–22, 269, 270, 276;
pleasure and, 277; sharing,
289*n27*; site of, 276
Paine, Thomas, 3, 5, 113, 255*n1*,
341, 344
Paradise Lost (Milton), 91–92,
104*n20*
Parthenopean Republic, 165
Passions, 307; artificial, 311;
attributed to women, 47; deception and, 307; fabricated, 307;

personalistic, 307, 308; public spectacle of, 307; rhetoric of, 299; staged simulation of, 307, 308

Paton, Sir Joseph Noel, 297

Patriarchy, 12; British, 16; codes of proper female behavior and, 21; concepts of femininity in, 306; criticisms of, 79n3; domestic arrangements, 308; economic threats and, 20; effect on women, 44; encouraged by Dissenters, 264; identity in, 340; outsider status of women, 29n28; sexual predation and, 20, 68–69, 198–199; tyranny of, 71, 345; workings of power in, 86

Patriotism, 135, 136, 163, 262, 348

Peace of Amiens (1802), 28n20, 80n10, 146, 184, 186

A Philosophical Enquiry into the Sublime and the Beautiful (Burke), 272

Piercy, Marge, 22

Pius VII (Pope), 165, 168, 183

Poetry, 21, 27n15, 261–285; as icon of female domesticity, 300; rhetoric, 122; of sensibility, 315n41, 317, 319

Pogson, Sarah, 210

Political: abstraction, 113; action, 265, 266; alliances, 101; compromise, 275; deception, 343; discourse, 163, 318; disenfranchisement, 12; dissent, 9, 268; domination, 311; economy, 120, 121; inequity, 141; intervention, 20; justice, 6; oppression, 44; participation, 135, 136, 163, 262; power, 296; reform, 12, 13, 92, 115, 359; relations, 20; suppression, 303; violence, 12, 202

Politics: of class, 173; conflict in, 91; counterrevolutionary, 154n5; of deception, 339; family, 135; feminist, 245; gender, 173, 195, 306, 368; of nationalism, 12; party,

29n28; partyless, 115; revolutionary, 201; of transcendence, 85–101, 372

Pollack, Ellen, 45

Polwhele, Reverend Richard, 70, 127, 132n3, 162, 163, 206, 301, 324, 369

Polygamy, 75–76, 82n43

Poovey, Mary, 265

Pope, Alexander, 45, 46, 47, 59n16

Popular Commotions to Precede the End of the World (Jones), 137

Porteus, Bishop Beilby, 127

"The Precession of Simulacra" (Baudrillard), 302

The Prelude (Wordsworth), 9, 89, 90, 94, 271

Prevention of Seditious Meetings and Writings (proclamation), 344

Price, Richard, 68, 318, 341

"Properzia Rossi" (Hemans), 309

Prophecies Announcing the Birth of the Prince of Peace (Southcott), 152, 153

Protestantism, 12, 14, 64, 73, 82n36

Public sphere: boundaries of, 17; conflictual nature of, 16; feminist, 86–87; gendering of, 213; inseparable from private sphere, 98; in letters, 19; morality in, 21; nationalism and, 135; notion of, 15; partial, 87; participation in, 135; relation to private sphere, 103n11; religion and, 21; secular understanding of, 21; women's actions in, 8, 9; women's place in, 136; women's writing and, 6

Purinton, Marjean, 307–308

Rabine, Leslie, 15

Radcliffe, Ann, 82n29, 82n31, 110, 170, 171, 195, 281, 282; anti-Catholic views, 170; critiques of British domestic space, 71, The Italian, 200; A Sicilian Romance, 198

Radford, Fred, 297, 298
Realism, rhetoric of, 297
Reason: cultivation of, 116; formation by experience, 237; impassioned, 243; limitations of, 248; proper use of, 238; sensibility and, 238; virtue and, 47
"Records of Woman" (Hemans), 309
Redemption: Catholicism, 168; spiritual, 145
Reeves Association, 137
Reflections on the Revolution in France (Burke), 19, 111, 114, 174, 271, 272, 308, 309
Religion, 9; Catholicism, 72, 75, 82n30, 82n37, 144, 169; character and, 53; conflicts over, 174; dissent and, 9, 131; French atheism, 12; as means into political commentary, 163; Protestantism, 64, 73, 82n36; relevance for public sphere, 21; respect for, 64; Sabbath observances, 50; tolerance and, 21, 367; treatment of Catholic clergy, 12, 74, 75, 115
Remarks on the Speech of M. Dupont (More), 115, 117
Republicanism, 4, 5, 7
The Revolt of Islam (Shelley), 302
Rhetoric: manufactured, 299; of passions, 299; of realism, 297; of sensibility, 320
Riddell, Maria and Robert, 218
Rigney, Ann, 262
Robespierre, Maximilien, 20, 169, 184, 196, 209, 210, 228n42
Robinson, Mary, 19, 185, 273, 369; *Monody on the Death of the Late Queen of France* (Robinson), 200; *The Natural Daughter*, 20; political views, 280; radicalism of, 205; *Sappho and Phaon*, 315n41; as Tabitha Bramble, 204–205; *Walsingham*, 214
Rogers, Katherine, 365

Roland, Marie-Jeanne, 193–194, 327, 370
Romney, George, 263, 344
Ross, Marlon, 9, 85, 87, 90, 266, 268, 279, 368
Roudinesco, Elisabeth, 323
Rousseau, Jean-Jacques, 14, 124, 203, 248
Rowlandson, Thomas, 36, 38, 320

St. Clair, William, 302
Sappho and Phaon (Robinson), 315n41
Scandinavia: character of, 49; civilization in, 55; manners in, 54; public spirit in, 55; restrictions on women, 49; support for French Revolution, 55
Scarry, Elaine, 276
Schiller, Friedrich, 85, 89
Schofield, Mary Anne, 339
Scholarship: advertising and, 294; confusion of commodity and, 302; simulation and, 297; suspension of disbelief of falsehood and, 311
Schor, Esther, 91
Scott, Joan Wallach, 317
Scott, Sir Walter, 18, 19
Sealed people, 140, 143, 144
Sensibility, 96; aesthetics of, 270; ambivalent status of, 237; appropriate expressions of, 269; culture of, 319; discourse of, 323; encompassing, 19; female ambition and, 270; for female philosopher, 237; feminine, 248, 251, 340; ideological implications of, 237; individual, 237; language of, 243, 246; as metaphor, 251; poetry of, 315n41, 317, 319; political form of, 251; potential for social justice, 237; private expressions of, 21–22; reason and, 238; rhetoric of, 320
September Massacres, 3, 4, 9, 207, 303, 320
Seward, Anna, 321

Sharp, William, 138, 151
Shelley, Mary, 213, 265, 283
Shelley, Percy Bysshe, 9, 189n19,
    203, 209, 302, 307
A Sicilian Romance (Radcliffe), 170,
    198
Siddons, Sarah, 299
Simpson, David, 87, 221, 234
Slavery, 96, 99, 100, 104n21, 109,
    130, 248, 265
Small, Ian, 280
Smith, Adam, 120, 261, 307
Smith, Charlotte, 132n3, 185, 273,
    369, 372; The Banished Man, 4,
    347–351; Beachy Head, 4, 98,
    105n25; Celestina, 340, 341;
    compassion and, 96, 97;
    Desmond, 4, 5, 16–17, 19, 24n5,
    91, 95, 104n24, 322, 342, 343;
    detachment from male–domi-
    nated political struggles, 86;
    displacement and, 87; egalitarian
    sentiments of, 94; Elegiac
    Sonnets, 4, 86, 87, 88, 355; The
    Emigrants, 4, 12, 14, 18, 21,
    92–99, 104n24, 281; Emmeline,
    340; encoding of political ethos
    by, 87; Ethelinde, 340; female
    readership, 97; feminist under-
    tones in works, 92; fulfillment of
    domestic duties, 17; influence of
    Godwin on, 6, 338, 356, 357, 359,
    360n8; influence of Wollstone-
    craft on, 6; marginalization of, 93;
    maternal perspectives, 97,
    104n24; nationalism and, 13, 14,
    22; political views of, 86, 322,
    337–360; radical politics and,
    24n5; republican beliefs of, 4, 5;
    Romanticism and, 15; on slavery,
    96; sociopolitical position, 93,
    104n19; "Sonnet 4," 88; "Sonnet
    59," 87, 91, 92, 93, 94, 103n13,
    104n20; "Sonnet 83," 92; strategy
    of open concealment by, 17–18,
    340, 341, 342, 343, 345, 350;

transcendence and, 14, 85–101,
    104n20; use of historical novel,
    19; use of irony, 96; The Young
    Philosopher, 4, 214, 338, 355–360
Smith, Olivia, 127
Soboul, Albert, 370
Social: acting, 306; bondage, 68;
    boundaries, 281; change, 86, 358;
    conservatism, 354; deception,
    343; hierarchy, 93; hypocrisy, 354;
    institutions, 237; justice, 92, 94,
    137, 237, 347; marginalization,
    345; oppression, 233; reform, 130;
    repression, 345; virtue, 154n5
Society for Constitutional
    Information, 348
Society for the Reformation of
    Manners, 130
Society of Friends, 265, 267
Society of Revolutionary Republican
    Women, 193, 370
Southcott, Joanna, 11, 135–154, 366,
    369; Account of Trials on Bills of
    Exchange, 144, 149, 151; Com-
    munication on the Temporal and
    Spiritual Sword, 146, 148, 149;
    education of, 147; on French
    Revolution, 143, 144, 145; just
    war theory, 137, 141, 146, 148,
    149, 150; The Long-wished-for
    Revolution, 145, 150; militant
    writings, 136; millenarianism of,
    135–154; nationalism and, 13,
    140; opposition to House of
    Hanover, 144, 146, 148, 156n28;
    opposition to Napoleon, 145, 146,
    149, 151; pacifism of, 136; politi-
    cal commentary of, 163;
    proclaimed pregnancy, 22, 139,
    153; Prophecies Announcing the
    Birth of the Prince of Peace, 152,
    153; prophecy and, 20, 21,
    137–154, 156n22, 157n31,
    157n32; public role of, 22; radical
    views, 137; religious views of, 13,
    21, 162, 163; ridicule of, 138;

Southcott, Joanna (*cont.*)
  scandals involving, 139, 150;
  "Sealed People" and, 140, 143,
  144; *The Strange Effects of Faith*,
  142, 149; support of war against
  France, 11
Southey, Robert, 9, 212, 217, 265;
  abandonment of French Revolu-
  tion, 27*n15*; on Corday, 203
Spence, Sarah, 136
Spencer, Edward, 131, 132, 134*n23*
Staël, Germaine de, 60*n24*, 324, 325,
  327, 328, 366
"Stanzas Written Under Aeolus's
  Harp" (Opie), 264, 284, 285
Starke, Mariana, 9, 21, 161–187,
  369, 371; anti-Catholic views,
  11–12, 170, 171, 172; antiquarian
  issues and, 182–183; attacks on
  atheism, 169, 172; conservative
  beliefs of, 11–12, 18, 162; Grand
  Tour and, 176–183; *Letters from
  Italy*, 11–12, 18, 161–187; on
  Napoleon, 166–176, 183–187;
  nationalistic views, 12, 13; patriotic views, 166–168; Protestant
  identity of, 12; religious views,
  162; as representative of Britain,
  166–168
Stereotypes: character, 19; of demographic groups, 301; destructive
  effects of, 309; of France, 64–65;
  gender, 38, 88, 300, 301, 373;
  marketed, 300, 301; sex-roles,
  306
Steuart, James, 120
Stone, John Hurford, 3, 206, 207,
  324
The Strange Effects of Faith
  (Southcott), 142, 149
Strictures on Female Education
  (More), 43, 111, 119, 122, 123,
  162, 321
Subjectivity: character and, 33;
  disallowance of, 45; female, 9, 20;
  lack in women, 45; personal, 300;

revolutionary, 22; sociocultural
  perspective, 98
Sublimity: defining, 89; feminine
  consciousness and, 89; metaphors
  of, 87; power defining, 289*n24*
Sunday School Movement, 22,
  129–132
Sutherland, Kathryn, 120
Suu Kyi, 101
Sweet, Nanora, 85
Sympathy: acquisition of, 121; cultivation of, 121 defining, 261;
  emotional, 301, 307; true, 275

Taylor, Jane, 301
Taylor, Susannah, 262
Theory of Moral Sentiments (Smith),
  307
Thomas, Chantal, 201
Thompson, E.P., 136, 154n9
Thomson, James, 94
Thornton, Henry, 118
*Thoughts on the Manners of the
  Great* (More), 118
Three Guineas (Woolf), 99, 100, 101
"Tintern Abbey" (Wordsworth), 277,
  286n7
Todd, Janet, 351
Tompkins, Jane, 3121
Tooke, Horne, 113, 248, 263, 265,
  287*n13*
"To Twilight" (Opie), 274, 275, 276,
  277
Townley, Jane, 138, 155*n17*
Transcendence: of conflict, 88;
  detachment from historical reality and, 87; of limitations of
  gender, 55; as masculine
  construct, 85; metaphors of, 87;
  moon as emblem of, 14, 88, 96,
  99; of national prejudice, 21; overcoming of nationalism of, 96; of
  party spirit, 21; poetics of, 85; in
  political context, 95; politics of,
  85–101, 372; Romantic, 87, 98;
  self-awareness and, 95

Travel literature, 18, 19, 20, 161–187

Treaty of Campo Formio (1797), 165

Treaty of Tolentino (1797), 165

Trimmer, Sarah, 120

Trouille, Mary Seidman, 323, 325

Truth: as basis for life, 338; deception and, 354; fictional presentation of, 311; improvement of political institutions and, 337; intellect and, 360n2; internal, 246; limitations of, 359; place in republican philosophy, 337; religious, 21; repression of, 359; symbolic displacements and, 312; value of, 337

Tucker, Josiah, 120, 121

Turner, George, 138

Ty, Eleanor, 324

Tyranny: character and, 43; patriarchy and, 71, 345

Universalism, 18, 373; Enlightenment, 57

"The Unsex'd Females" (Polwhele), 70, 132n3, 162, 324

Vallon, Annette, 9

Victor Amadeus III (King of Italy), 164

Villette (Brontë), 298, 299

Vindication of the Rights of Woman (Wollstonecraft), 42, 45, 46, 112, 341, 370

Virtue: active, 237; development of, 46, 49, 238; nationalism and, 58n6; reason and feeling in, 47; social, 154n5; of women, 172

Voltaire, François, 179, 180, 214, 360n2

Wake, Ann Frank, 15, 21, 261–285, 368

Wakefield, Priscilla, 120

Walcott, Derek, 300

Walker, Joseph Cooper, 86, 102n5

Wallace, Miriam, 15, 19, 22, 233–255, 372

Walpole, Horace, 110, 111, 195, 325, 341; Castle of Otranto, 195, 197; private fantasy and, 133n7; relations with More, 112, 114–115, 129; on Wollstonecraft, 113

Walsingham (Robinson), 214

The Wanderer (Burney), 12, 14, 20, 63–78, 66, 67, 79n3, 81n27, 84n50, 222, 223, 321, 372; as politically neutral, 17; women outside male institutions in, 14

Wandering, 15, 79n3, 82n33; alienation and, 14; as escape, 71; gaining liberty and, 71; nature and, 71–72; vulnerability and, 71

Wang, Orrin, 47

Warning to the World (Southcott), 140

War Not Inconsistent with Christianity (Evans), 147

War of the Second Coalition, 165

Weinstone, Anne, 298

Wellington, Jan, 13, 19, 33–57, 371

Wells, Roger, 136

Werterism, 230n58

Wilberforce, William, 118, 130

Wilks, Mark, 137

Williams, Helen Maria, 3, 9, 132n3, 185, 186, 194, 289n26, 327, 369; on Corday, 205–209; credibility of, 328; criticisms of, 322, 324; A Farewell to England for Two Years, 321; feminine ethos of works, 319; as interpreter of Revolution, 4; Letters from France, 205–209, 206, 317, 322, 328–330; political nature of writing, 4; political views, 317; response of readers, 317–330; support for French Revolution, 11, 205, 318, 320; use of letters by, 18

Williams, Raymond, 235

Wilson, John, 151

Wollstonecraft, Mary, 110, 132*n3*, 162, 236, 263, 327, 372; affection for France, 41–42; on character, 33–57, 43–49; characterizations of women, 42–43; criticisms of, 234; critiques of national character, 13; death of, 6, 25*n9*; on education, 123–124; feminism of, 13; on French character, 39–43, 48; *French Revolution*, 34, 40, 44, 46, 47, 50; influence on Smith, 6; *Letters Written during a Short Residence*, 34, 49, 51, 53, 60*n21*; *Maria, or the Wrongs of Woman*, 213; moral issues, 42; nationalism and, 13, 22, 34; relations with Godwin, 52, 60*n23*; revaluation of French character by, 49–57; support for Revolution, 11; use of letters by, 18, 19, 60n21; *Vindication of the Rights of Woman*, 34, 42, 45, 46, 112, 370

Women: affectivity of, 301; behavior of in Britain, 70; boundedness of, 57; character of, 45, 47, 51, 59*n16*; confinement of, 69; conflicting demands on, 233; critiques of behavior of, 79*n3*, 81*n24*; cultural roles of, 21; denial of liberty to, 70; disenfranchisement of, 195; dismissal of opinions of, 274; dispossession of, 79*n3*; dissent by, 163, 268, 269; domestic safety for, 72; economic regulation and, 120; education for, 76; exclusion from benefits of British institutions, 14; exclusion from category of "man," 92; exposure of defects of, 43; feminist civic vs. domestic, 162; immanence and, 85; influence in civil society, 123; intellectual limitations of, 7; lack of opportunity for, 46; legal autonomy for, 237; marginalization of, 87, 93; moral responsibilities of, 115; natural vulnerability of, 7; "new Cordays," 193–223; oppression of, 57; as "other," 34; outsider status of, 29*n28*; pacifism of, 22; passions attributed to, 47; patriotism and, 135, 136, 163; potential for economic power, 99–100; private sphere and, 6; privatization of, 172; promiscuity and, 124; protection of, 69, 81*n20*; public action and, 74–75; relationships between, 84*n50*; relationships to Romanticism, 15; religious opinion and, 21; response to images of militancy by women, 201; sensibility and, 21–22, 269, 270, 276; sexual predation and, 14, 68–69, 198–199; stereotypes of, 89; stoicism of, 273; subordination of, 69, 308; threatened by Revolution, 326; working class, 202

Women's International League for Peace and Freedom, 99

Women's writings: assertion of apolitical nature of, 17; conservative, 7, 8, 43; constraints on, 366; differential responses to Revolution, 10; as dissent, 268, 269; diversity in, 4; double dissent in, 268, 269; effect of Revolution on, 366–374; "feminine" refusal of politics in, 18; gender issues in, 9; heterogenity of, 7; ideological contradictions in, 17; impropriety of political writing, 320; oppositional, 101; political perspectives in, 11; political range of, 9; protection of modern images on, 13; public sphere and, 6; representation of "double bind" in, 201, 202; restrictions on, 7; set in France, 195; on significance of participation in politics, 215; universalizing messages in, 279; on working class, 105*n28*

Woolf, Virginia, 99, 100, 105*n28*
Wordsworth, William, 9, 90, 94,
    103*n13*, 270, 271; abandonment
    of French Revolution, 27*n15*;
    assumption of legitimacy of
    response, 274; displacement and,
    87; *The Excursion*, 14; "I Wan-
    dered Lonely as a Cloud," 277;
    Lyrical Ballads, 296; *The Prelude*,
    10, 89, 90, 94, 271; "Tintern
    Abbey," 277, 286*n7*; transcendence
    and, 14, 87; use of memory, 286*n7*

Wu, Duncan, 263, 276, 286*n7*,
    300

Yearsley, Ann, 109, 132*n3*
Yeazell, Ruth, 343, 353
The Young Philosopher (Smith), 4,
    214, 338, 355–360
Yuval-Davis, Nira, 36

Zaret, David, 21
Zaw, Susan Khin, 47
Zimmerman, Sarah, 339